THE ORIGINAL MEANING OF THE *YIJING*

TRANSLATIONS FROM THE ASIAN CLASSICS

TRANSLATIONS FROM THE ASIAN CLASSICS

Editorial Board:

Paul Anderer

Allison Busch

David Lurie

Rachel McDermott

Wei Shang

Haruo Shirane

THE ORIGINAL MEANING OF THE *YIJING*

Commentary on
the *Scripture of Change*

Zhu Xi

TRANSLATED AND EDITED BY
JOSEPH A. ADLER

Columbia University Press
New York

Columbia University Press wishes to express its appreciation for assistance given
by the Wm. Theodore de Bary Fund in the publication of this book.

Columbia University Press
Publishers Since 1893
New York   Chichester, West Sussex
cup.columbia.edu
Copyright © 2020 Columbia University Press
Paperback edition, 2024
All rights reserved

Library of Congress Cataloging-in-Publication Data
Names: Zhu, Xi, 1130–1200, author. | Adler, Joseph Alan, translator, editor.
Title: The original meaning of the Yijing : commentary on the scripture of change /
Zhu Xi ; translated and edited by Joseph A. Adler.
Other titles: Zhou yi ben yi.
English Description: New York : Columbia University Press, [2019] | Series: Translations
from the Asian Classics | Translation of: Zhou yi ben yi. | Includes bibliographical
references and index.
Identifiers: LCCN 2019008054 (print) | LCCN 2019011858 (ebook)
| ISBN 9780231191241 (cloth) | ISBN 9780231216609 (pbk.) |
ISBN 9780231549301 (electronic)
Subjects: LCSH: Yi jing.
Classification: LCC PL2464.Z6 (ebook) | LCC PL2464.Z6 Z5814613 2019 (print) |
DDC 299.5/1282—dc23
LC record available at https://lccn.loc.gov/2019008054

COVER IMAGE
Fuxi, the reputed creator of the *Yijing* (hanging scroll by Ma Lin 馬麟,
13th century). According to one version of the myth, the Eight Trigrams (lower left)
were inspired by the markings on the shell of a tortoise. Fuxi's invention of the *Yi*
was central to Zhu Xi's theory of its "original meaning."

COVER DESIGN
Lisa Hamm

CONTENTS

Acknowledgments vii

Introduction: The "Original Meaning" of the *Zhou Changes* (*Zhouyi benyi* 周易本義) 1

Zhouyi Benyi 周易本義

1 Part A: Hexagrams 1–30 41

2 Part B: Hexagrams 31–64 161

3 Treatise on the Appended Remarks (*Xici zhuan* 繫辭傳) 261

4 Treatise Discussing the Trigrams (*Shuogua zhuan* 說卦傳) 303

5 Commentary on Assorted Hexagrams (*Zagua zhuan* 雜卦傳) 313

Appendix: Divination Ritual (*Shiyi* 筮儀) 317

Notes 323

Bibliography 375

Index 381

ACKNOWLEDGMENTS

This project had one beginning in the winter of 1971, when I was "retooling" from biology to religious studies and taking a night school course in "Theories of Personality" at Boston University. One day I was reading my homework in the employee lunchroom of the Harvard Coop and came across a discussion of the psychologist Carl Jung's theory of synchronicity, which he had described in his foreword to Richard Wilhelm's translation of the *I Ching* (now written *Yijing*). Shortly after that a friend asked what I'd like for my upcoming birthday; I mentioned that book, and she gave it to me.

Fast-forward eight years, and I'm in Berkeley studying Neo-Confucianism with Tu Weiming, who encouraged me to drop Shao Yong as a research topic and focus on Zhu Xi. My resulting dissertation, completed in 1984 at the University of California, Santa Barbara, was titled "Divination and Philosophy: Chu Hsi's Understanding of the *I Ching*." Most of my subsequent writing focused on Zhu Xi, although not specifically on the *Yijing* except for my translation of his shorter book on the *Yi*, the *Yixue qimeng* (Introduction to the study of the *Classic of Change*) in 2002. Writing a chapter on the *Yijing* for *Religion and Ecological Sustainability in China* (2014), edited by James Miller, also helped to rekindle my interest in the *Yi*.

After retiring from teaching at Kenyon College in 2014 I decided that returning to Zhu Xi's full commentary, the *Zhouyi benyi* (The original meaning of the *Yijing*), might be a good long-term project that could, possibly, occupy me for the rest of my active (scholarly) life. Completing the circle, as it were. Although it didn't take quite that long, I am pleased now that a new circle can begin.

I am grateful to Tze-ki Hon (SUNY Geneseo), Kirill Ole Thompson (National Taiwan University), and my Kenyon colleagues Yang Xiao and Chengjuan Sun for their help on some problems in the translation. I also thank Provost Joe Klesner of Kenyon College for publication financial assistance; my editors at Columbia University Press, Christine Dunbar and Leslie Kriesel; and the sharp-eyed copyeditor Mike Ashby. My greatest debt is to my wife, Ruth Woehr, for enthusiastically supporting my interest in Chinese thought and religion for lo these many years.

INTRODUCTION

The "Original Meaning" of the *Zhou Changes*
(*Zhouyi benyi* 周易本義)

The *Yijing* 易經, or *Scripture of Change*, is one of the best-known of the Chinese or "Confucian Classics."[1] Its graphic core, the sixty-four hexagrams, dates back probably to the eleventh century BCE, during the early Zhou dynasty (ca. 1045-256 BCE), while its earliest written material to the ninth century BCE.[2] The premise of the *Yijing* is that the hexagrams represent all possible configurations of change in nature and in human life, and that by understanding those patterns obtaining at the present moment one can enhance one's ability to successfully adapt to changing circumstances. It is considered, therefore, both a handbook for living a flourishing life and a guide to the "laws of nature."[3]

The *Yijing*'s association with the Zhou dynasty gives the text its original name, the *Zhouyi* 周易 (Zhou changes). However, most contemporary scholars differentiate between the *Zhouyi* and the *Yijing*: the former is the "basic text" dating to the Zhou dynasty; the latter includes the appendixes (the "Ten Wings") that were added during the Warring States period (480-222 BCE) and the early Han dynasty (206 BCE-8 CE). Although the title of the book translated here is *Zhouyi benyi* 周易本義 (The "original meaning" of the *Zhou Changes*), it is actually Zhu Xi's commentary on the more inclusive *Yijing*, including all but one of its appendixes. Zhu Xi 朱熹 (1130-1200) was the most influential Chinese philosopher since Confucius and Mencius, and his commentary on the *Yi* has been one of the most influential in the past thousand years. To my knowledge this is its first Western-language translation.

THE *ZHOUYI* AND THE *YIJING*

The core of the *Zhouyi* or *Yijing* is a collection of sixty-four six-line figures stacked vertically, each line being either solid or broken. Solid lines represent *yang* 陽, meaning "light, rising, day, heat, positive"; broken lines represent *yin* 陰, meaning "dark, sinking, night, cold, negative." Together these six-line diagrams (*gua* 卦), or "hexagrams," constitute a manual of divination, with each hexagram being a response to a question posed by a diviner. Each hexagram is a dynamic representation of the situation of the diviner at that moment, moving through time from the bottom of the hexagram to the top. A hexagram is derived by a complex manipulation of forty-nine dried stalks of the milfoil, or yarrow, plant (see the appendix).

"Divination" can be defined as a method of obtaining answers to specific questions by nonempirical means. The nonempirical means can be either a special technique (inference by rules not ordinarily followed) or a special talent involving nonordinary epistemological processes (e.g., intuition achieved through the medium of a being or power beyond ordinary human experience).[4] In both cases, "ordinary" is to be understood in the particular cultural-historical context. The sources of the answers may be specific gods, the realm of the gods or spirits in general, or the impersonal, metaphysical reality underlying the phenomenal world. Divination is thus to be distinguished from prophecy by the fact that prophets, in the strict sense (based on the model of the prophets of the Hebrew Bible), are passive recipients of their divine messages, while diviners actively pose their questions, regardless of their specificity.[5] Divination in China and elsewhere is usually about "fortune-telling," or predicting the future, as in the ubiquitous use of bamboo sticks and printed oracles in Chinese and other East Asian temples.[6] The *Yijing*, however, was unique in becoming a "book of wisdom" as well as a manual of divination.

Methods of divination historically are extremely numerous; some of the better known are oracle priests and priestesses in Greco-Roman antiquity, the interpretation of the livers of sacrificial animals, the casting of chicken bones in such Caribbean religions as Santeria, the use of tarot cards, and the interpretation of dreams. In China, before *Yijing* divination there was the interpretation of the cracks in scorched "oracle bones" by the kings and ministers of the Shang dynasty (sixteenth–eleventh centuries BCE).[7] There were also two other texts that, together with the *Zhouyi*, were called the Three Changes: the *Lianshan* 連山 (Linked mountains) and *Guicang* 歸藏 (Return to the storehouse); all three were based on multiline diagrams.⁸

The sixty-four hexagrams of the *Zhouyi* or *Yijing* are each composed of two three-line diagrams, which in Chinese are also called *gua* 卦 and in English "trigrams." The lower one is called the inner trigram and the upper is the outer trigram. In addition to that relationship, the upper and lower trigrams roughly reflect social hierarchy—for example, the relationship between ruler and minister. Each trigram has a name, one or more "images" (*xiang* 象), and one or more "virtues" (*de* 德).⁹

The original creation of the Eight Trigrams (*bagua* 八卦)—and perhaps the sixty-four hexagrams—is attributed to a mythic sage of high antiquity, Fuxi 伏羲 ("Subduer of Animals"), the earliest mythic "culture hero" of China.¹⁰ Fuxi is traditionally dated to the twenty-ninth century BCE and is also credited with the invention of animal sacrifice and implements for hunting and fishing. There are conflicting accounts concerning whether Fuxi originally created the trigrams and later doubled them, or whether he created only the trigrams and they were later combined into hexagrams by King Wen in the eleventh century BCE; Zhu Xi opts for the former scenario.¹¹ In either case, during the Zhou period the sixty-four hexagrams each accumulated several layers of written text:

- The hexagram names (*guaming* 卦名), which may or may not originally have had a logical connection with the structure of the hexagram. Some recent scholars call them tags to underline the point that some of them seem rather arbitrary.¹² Under either mentioned scenario, the hexagram names are attributed to the founding king of the Zhou dynasty, King Wen (Wen wang 文王, mid-eleventh century BCE).
- A short, oracular text for each hexagram (*guaci* 卦辭), also attributed to King Wen.
- A similar short text for each line of each hexagram (*yaoci* 爻辭), attributed to King Wen's son, the Duke of Zhou (Zhou gong 周公).

The hexagrams and these three layers of written text constitute the basic text, usually printed in two chapters (*juan* 卷), divided as 1–30 and 31–64.¹³ This is what we are calling the *Zhouyi*. *Zhouyi* divination eventually replaced oracle bone divination in the early Zhou court, where it was used by the aristocracy to determine the advisability and potential outcomes of specific courses of action they were contemplating. This use is well attested in later texts, such as the *Zuo Commentary*

TABLE I.1 The 64 hexagrams

Hexagrams 1–32

1		Qian	乾	Creating	17		Sui	隨	Following
2		Kun	坤	Complying	18		Gu	蠱	Working on What Is Ruined
3		Zhun	屯	Difficult Beginning	19		Lin	臨	Approaching
4		Meng	蒙	Dim	20		Guan	觀	Observed/Observing
5		Xu	需	Waiting	21		Shihe	噬嗑	Biting Together
6		Song	訟	Disputing	22		Bi	賁	Adorning
7		Shi	師	Army	23		Bo	剝	Declining/Breaking Down
8		Bi	比	Being Close	24		Fu	復	Returning
9		Xiaochu	小畜	Restrained/Limited by the Lesser	25		Wuwang	無妄	No Error
10		Lü	履	Treading	26		Daxu	大畜	Restrained by the Great
11		Tai	泰	Penetrating	27		Yi	頤	Jaws, Nourishing
12		Pi	否	Obstructing	28		Daguo	大過	Surpassing by the Great
13		Tongren	同人	Fellowship	29		(Xi)kan	(習)坎	(Doubly) Abysmal
14		Dayou	大有	Great Possession	30		Li	離	Clinging
15		Qian	謙	Being Modest	31		Xian	咸	Mutually Influencing
16		Yu	豫	Being Happy	32		Heng	恆	Everlasting

TABLE I.1 The 64 hexagrams *(continued)*

Hexagrams 33–64

33	䷠	Dun	遯	Withdrawing	49	䷰	Ge	革	Changing/Overturning
34	䷡	Dazhuang	大壯	Flourishing of the Great	50	䷱	Ding	鼎	Cauldron
35	䷢	Jin	晉	Advancing	51	䷲	Zhen	震	Thunder/Arousing
36	䷣	Mingyi	明夷	Wounding the Light	52	䷳	Gen	艮	Stilling/Stopping
37	䷤	Jiaren	家人	Family Members	53	䷴	Jian	漸	Gradually Advancing
38	䷥	Kui	睽	Contrary	54	䷵	Guimei	歸妹	Betrothed Sister
39	䷦	Jian	蹇	Obstructed	55	䷶	Feng	豐	Abundant
40	䷧	Xie	解	Released	56	䷷	Lü	旅	The Wanderer
41	䷨	Sun	損	Diminishing	57	䷸	Sun	巽	Entering
42	䷩	Yi	益	Enhancing	58	䷹	Dui	兌	Pleasing
43	䷪	Guai	夬	Resolving	59	䷺	Huan	渙	Dispersing
44	䷫	Gou	姤	Encountering	60	䷻	Jie	節	Limiting
45	䷬	Cui	萃	Gathering	61	䷼	Zhongfu	中孚	Inwardly Honest
46	䷭	Sheng	升	Advancing Upward	62	䷽	Xiaoguo	小過	Small Surpassing
47	䷮	Kun	困	Blocked	63	䷾	Jiji	既濟	Already Complete
48	䷯	Jing	井	The Well	64	䷿	Weiji	未濟	Not Yet Complete

TABLE I.2 The Eight Trigrams (*bagua* 八卦) with their chief images and virtues

Qian 乾 ☰	Dui 兌 ☱	Li 離 ☲	Zhen 震 ☳	Kun 坤 ☷	Gen 艮 ☶	Kan 坎 ☵	Sun 巽 ☴
Heaven, Creative	Lake, Pleasing	Fire, Clinging	Thunder, Arousing	Earth, Complying	Mountain, Stable	Water, Danger	Wind/Wood, Penetrating

Note: The difference between Kan (water) and Dui (lake) is that Kan is deep, dark water, like an abyss; Dui is shallow water, like a lake (although of course some lakes are very deep), with the more positive feeling of well-watered land. The word translated as "lake" (*ze* 澤) is sometimes translated as "marsh," but I use "lake" to avoid the negative, swampy connotations of "marsh."

The pronunciation of Sun 巽 in most dictionaries is given as *xun*. The translators Richard Wilhelm (*The I Ching*) and Richard Lynn (*The Classic of Changes*) use Sun, as does the *Mathews Chinese-English Dictionary*. Richard Rutt (*The Book of Changes*), John Minford (*I Ching*), Geoffrey Redmond (*The I Ching*), and Bent Nielsen (*A Companion to Yi Jing Numerology and Cosmology*) use Xun. The *Hanyu da cidian* 漢語大詞典 gives *xun* as the main pronunciation but notes that the Northern Song dynasty rhyme dictionary *Da Song chongxiu guangyun* 大宋重修廣韻 uses *sun*. Since Zhu Xi most likely took that dictionary as authoritative, I use Sun.

(*Zuozhuan* 左傳) on the *Spring and Autumn Annals* (*Chunqiu* 春秋), another of the "Confucian Classics."[14]

The rest of what we know as the *Yijing* consists of a collection of appendixes traditionally called the Ten Wings (*shiyi* 十翼), although there are actually only seven of them (three are each divided into two parts that are counted separately). They were traditionally attributed to Confucius (Kong Qiu 孔丘 or Kongzi 孔子, 551-479 BCE), based on the Han-dynasty historian Sima Qian's statement in the *Shiji* 史記 (Historical records [ca. 100 BCE], 47.61): "Confucius late in life took pleasure in the *Yi*. He put in order the *Tuan, Xi[ci], Xiang, Shuogua,* and *Wenyan* [appendixes]. Reading the *Yi* [so much], he broke the leather thongs [holding the bamboo slips together] three times." Ouyang Xiu 歐陽修 (1007-1072) refuted Confucius's authorship of the Wings, but Zhu Xi accepted the traditional attribution, probably because the *Yi* was extremely important in his reconstruction of the Confucian tradition (the "succession of the Way," or *daotong* 道統).[15] So to strengthen his claim that the *Yi* was the first appearance of the Confucian *dao* in the world (more on this later) he rejected Ouyang Xiu's argument.[16] No modern scholars accept Confucius's authorship of the Ten Wings; one recent estimate of their dating is mid-third to early second century BCE.[17]

In the following list, the first four (the *Tuanzhuan* and the two *Xiangzhuan*) are dated by historians to shortly after the time of Confucius, but the others were probably written as late as the first century of the Han dynasty (206 BCE–220 CE).[18] The Ten Wings are

1–2. "Commentary on the 'Judgments,'" or hexagram statements (*Tuanzhuan* 彖傳), in two parts divided the same way as the basic text.

3–4. "Commentary on the Greater Images" (*Daxiang zhuan* 大象傳) and "Commentary on the Smaller Images" (*Xiaoxiang zhuan* 小象傳). The "Greater" is composed of comments on the imagery associated with each of the component trigrams (see table I.2) and its implication for the proper behavior of the "superior person" (*junzi* 君子) or ruler. As Richard Rutt points out, this is "the most Confucian part of *Yijing*."[19] The "Smaller" contains brief statements on each individual line, usually quoting all or part of the line statement (*yaoci*). In Zhu Xi's arrangement these are collated together, and the two combined are divided into two chapters like the basic text.

5. "Commentary on the Words of the Text" (*Wenyan zhuan* 文言傳), containing commentary on the first two hexagrams: Qian 乾 and Kun 坤. This may or may not be the surviving remnant of a complete commentary on all sixty-four hexagrams, although it is cobbled together from different sources.

6–7. "Treatise on the Appended Remarks" (*Xici zhuan* 繫辭傳), also called the "Great Treatise" (*Dazhuan* 大傳), in two parts (not divided according to hexagrams). This is the most philosophically rich appendix and was enormously influential in the Song-dynasty (960–1279) revival of Confucianism that Zhu Xi systematized.

8. "Discussion of the Trigrams" (*Shuogua zhuan* 說卦傳), primarily setting forth the correlative imagery of the Eight Trigrams. Its first three sections (of eleven), though, are much like the *Xici* and may even have been part of it originally.

9. "Commentary on the Sequence of Hexagrams" (*Xugua zhuan* 序卦傳), containing short rationales for the particular sequence of hexagrams in the "received" text of the *Yi* (the "King Wen" sequence). This is the only appendix for which Zhu Xi has no commentary (except for one very brief textual note), and so it is not translated here.[20]

10. "Commentary on Assorted Hexagrams" (*Zagua zhuan* 雜卦傳). Very brief statements on all the hexagrams, in groups of two or more, in random order. Zhu Xi comments very briefly on some of them.

The original *Zhouyi* was composed during the Bronze Age of China to assist the Zhou kings and court in conducting affairs of state, much of which involved war. It includes, for example, many references to military expeditions and captives (often to be sacrificed), in addition to royal marriages and alliances, feudal lords, and sacrifices to local deities and royal ancestors. This original context, however, has been recognized only since the twentieth century, because from the Han dynasty onward it was obscured by the addition of the Ten Wings, which introduced a moralized, "Confucianized" perspective that determined how later generations of scholars interpreted the text. In China, the modern "Doubting Antiquity School" (*Yigupai* 疑古派), and in particular its foremost *Yijing* scholar, Gu Jiegang (1892–1980), began this effort to uncover the original meaning of the *Zhouyi* in its own historical context, before the addition of the Ten Wings. English-language scholarship in this vein continued with an influential article by Arthur Waley in 1933 and by the dissertations of Edward Shaughnessy and Richard Kunst in the 1980s. In 1996 a new translation reflecting this approach was published by the British Catholic (formerly Anglican) priest Richard Rutt: *The Book of Changes (Zhouyi): A Bronze Age Document.*[21]

The Ten Wings, written by anonymous but Confucian-influenced literati in a distinctly different cultural-historical context, introduced what became the standard set of assumptions regarding the *Yi* for the next two thousand years. The basic hermeneutical assumption has been that the purpose of the *Yi* was to assist people in making moral decisions regarding their behavior in order to enhance the well-being and success of themselves and those around them. For example, the key Confucian term "superior person" (*junzi*)—meaning the morally "noble" person—occurs only fifteen times in the *Zhouyi* but eighty-seven times in the Ten Wings. Another example is the word *fu* 孚, which is part of the name of hexagram 61 and occurs forty-two other times in the *Zhouyi* and twenty-four times in the Ten Wings. The original meaning of the word was "captive, prisoner of war" (later that meaning became limited to the character *fu* 俘), and it is translated as such by Rutt, Minford, and Redmond. However, from the Han dynasty onward it was interpreted as "honesty, sincerity," which is how it appears in the earlier translations that do not take into account the original Bronze Age context.[22] Yet another example is the words *heng* 亨 and *zhen* 貞, which in their original context referred to the ritual dyad of sacrifice and divination but since the Han dynasty have been considered two of the "Four Virtues" of the first hexagram, Qian (see "Key Terms and Concepts" later in this chapter).

INTERPRETIVE APPROACHES TO THE *YI*

Confucianism became the "orthodox," or officially sanctioned, school of thought in the second century BCE, under the Han emperor Wudi (r. 140–87 BCE). What this meant in practice is that people seeking positions in government had to master one or more of what came to be known as the Five Classics (or Scriptures), beginning with the *Yijing*. The others were the *Shujing* 書經 (Scripture of documents), the *Shijing* 詩經 (Scripture of odes), the *Liji* 禮記 (Record of ritual), and the *Chunqiu* (Spring and autumn [annals]). An Imperial Academy was established to train officials, with a curriculum based on these texts, all of which were connected in some way (some rather loosely) to Confucius and his followers.[23]

The Han dynasty also witnessed the development of two general interpretive approaches to the *Yi*, called the *xiangshu* 象數 (image and number) and *yili* 義理 (meaning and principle) schools. The difference between them hinged on the *locus of meaning* they considered most significant. The *Yi* is a composite text, consisting of both graphic elements (trigrams and hexagrams) and textual elements (hexagram and line statements and the Ten Wings). Which of these represents the essential meaning of the *Yi*?[24] The *xiangshu* school focused primarily on the graphic level—the trigrams and hexagrams themselves, their genetic and transformational relations, their numerological values, and their symbolic correlations with a variety of cosmological categories and diagrams (*tu* 圖) associated with the *Yi*.[25] Prominent Han-dynasty names in this interpretive school include Jiao Yanshou 焦延壽, Meng Xi 孟喜, Jing Fang 京房 (all in the first century BCE), and Yu Fan 虞翻 (164–233 CE).[26] In the Song dynasty the most prominent *xiangshu* scholar was Shao Yong 邵雍 (1012–1077), who strongly influenced Zhu Xi.

The other major interpretive approach, *yili* (meaning and principle), takes the written text of the *Yi* as the locus of meaning and is more focused on its moral principles than on its cosmological associations. During the Han it was less widespread than *xiangshu*; its most prominent exponents were Fei Zhi 費直 (first century BCE) and Zheng Xuan 鄭玄 (127–200 CE), although the latter also used some *xiangshu* techniques. But shortly after the fall of the Han in 220 CE, Wang Bi 王弼 (226–249) wrote a tremendously influential commentary to the *Yi* in the *yili* vein, in fact reacting against what he thought were the excesses and irrelevancies of the popular *xiangshu* commentaries.[27] In the seventh century Wang Bi's commentary was enshrined in the official version of the Classics for the Tang dynasty

(618–906), the *Correct Meaning of the Five Classics* (*Wujing zhengyi* 五經正義), edited by Kong Yingda, a direct descendant of Confucius. This was the orthodox version of the *Yi* until the Song dynasty, by which time the Five Classics had grown to thirteen. Wang Bi's general *yili* approach was followed by Cheng Yi 程頤 (1033–1107) in the Song, whose *Commentary on the* Yi (*Yizhuan* 易傳) became equally influential in Confucian circles by Zhu Xi's time.

ZHU XI AND "NEO-CONFUCIANISM"

Cheng Yi was one of the central figures in the revival of Confucianism that first flourished in the Song dynasty—today usually called Neo-Confucianism. Between the Han and Song dynasties Confucianism had been overshadowed by Buddhism and Daoism, both of which were relatively new in China. Since Confucianism had been closely associated with the Han state, it was discredited by the fall of the Han and the disunity that followed until the late sixth century. Buddhism had entered China from India through Western Asia in the first century CE, while the Daoist religion began in China in the second century CE.[28] Many literate Chinese were attracted to Buddhism and Daoism, and consequently there were few new developments in the Confucian tradition during the period of disunity. This began to change in the late Tang dynasty, when a few intellectuals argued that Confucianism was better suited than Buddhism or Daoism to provide a theoretical basis for Chinese social ethics and government. In the Song dynasty, this movement—along with Chan (Zen) Buddhism—came to dominate intellectual life in China.[29]

One "party" of Confucian revivalists coalesced around Cheng Yi and his brother, Cheng Hao 程顥 (1032–1085). Their teachings, along with those of their contemporaries Zhou Dunyi 周敦頤, Zhang Zai 張載, and Shao Yong 邵雍, were passed down through three generations of the Cheng brothers' students to Zhu Xi 朱熹 (1130–1200), who systematized and synthesized them. Through his voluminous writings, letters, recorded conversations, and commentaries (twenty-seven thick Chinese volumes in a 2002 collection), Zhu's interpretation of Confucianism became the dominant one in China, Korea, and Japan. Today it is often called the Cheng-Zhu school of Confucianism (also the "school of principle" [*lixue* 理學], although this term is misleading). The other major strand of Confucianism is the

Lu-Wang school, named after Lu Jiuyuan 陸九淵 (a contemporary of Zhu Xi's) and Wang Yangming 王陽明 of the Ming dynasty (1368–1644). During the Song there were other strands too, but they eventually faded into obscurity. All these schools collectively have come to be known in the West as Neo-Confucianism.

The chief characteristics that distinguish this revived form of Confucianism from earlier forms are (1) the incorporation of elements from Buddhism (e.g., meditation) and Daoism (e.g., cosmology); (2) a new interest in metaphysics, centered on the concept of "principle" or "order" (*li* 理); (3) a more elaborate theory of mind and self-cultivation; and (4) a shift of emphasis from the "Five Classics" to the "Four Books." The Four Books are the *Analects* of Confucius (*Lunyu* 論語), the *Mencius* (*Mengzi* 孟子), the *Great Learning* (*Daxue* 大學), and the *Centrality and Commonality* (*Zhongyong* 中庸). The latter two were originally chapters in the *Liji*. The main reasons for the shift of emphasis were that the Four Books were more concerned than the Five Classics with personal cultivation, psychology, cosmology, and metaphysics, which were topics that were well developed in Buddhism and Daoism but somewhat lacking in early Confucianism. The Four Books were also much shorter than the Classics, with more coherent messages—in part because they were thought to have single authors—and so were easier to master.[30] Although this shift began earlier in the Song, it was Zhu Xi who first published the Four Books together, with his commentaries, and made them the core of his program of higher education.

There was, however, a major exception to the "from Five Classics to Four Books" generalization: the *Yijing* actually came to receive *more* attention by the Song Confucians than it had earlier. In fact, the *Yijing*—especially the appendixes—was one of the major sources of concepts and terminology for the Neo-Confucian revival. For example, Cheng Yi's commentary on the *Yi* was the only full-length book he ever wrote; Zhou Dunyi quoted extensively from the *Yi* in both his major writings; Shao Yong's philosophy of history was based on a passage from the *Xici* appendix; Zhu Xi wrote two books on the *Yi* (the commentary translated here and a manual of *Yijing* divination), as well as several essays; and in his *Classified Conversations* (*Zhuzi yulei* 朱子語類), approximately 11 percent of the total number of pages are devoted to the *Yi*.[31]

Zhu Xi's fundamental hermeneutic principle regarding the *Yijing* was that "the *Yi* was originally created for divination" (*Yi benwei bushi'er zuo* 易本為卜筮而作)—a claim found dozens of times in his *Classified Conversations* and *Collected Papers*

(*Hui'an xiansheng Zhu wengong wenji* 晦庵先生朱文公文集) and referring specifically to Fuxi's original creation of the hexagram divination method.[32] He announced his discovery of this principle in 1175 in a letter to his close friend, Zhang Shi 張栻 (1133–1180): "I recently had an idea about how to read the *Yi*. When the sage[s] created the *Yi* it originally was to cause people to engage in divination, in order to decide what was permissible or not in their behavior, and thereby to teach people to be good. . . . Thus the hexagram and line statements are based simply on the images."[33]

The premise of this interpretive theory is the myth, taken as a historical datum by Zhu Xi, of Fuxi's creation of the *Yi*. The myth, as told in the *Xici*, goes as follows:[34]

> In ancient times, when Baoxi [Fuxi] ruled all under Heaven, he looked up and contemplated the images [*xiang* 象] in Heaven; he looked down and contemplated the patterns [*fa* 法] on Earth; he contemplated the markings [*wen* 文] of the birds and beasts and their fitness [i.e., adaptation] to the earth. From nearby he took from his own body; from afar he took from things. In this way he first created the Eight Trigrams, to spread the power/virtue [*de* 德] of his spiritual clarity [*shenming* 神明] and to classify the dispositions of the myriad things. (*Xici* B.2.1)

From this and later accounts of the contributions of King Wen, the Duke of Zhou, and Confucius, Zhu Xi constructed his understanding of the history and purposes of the *Yi*:

> The *Yi* was originally created for divination. Thus Confucius [in *Xici* A.10.1] said, "The *Yi* contains the Way of the Sages in four respects: in speech we honor its phrases" (Master Cheng's discussions are an example of this)[35]; "in activity we honor its fluctuations" (this is divination. The *Yi*'s fluctuations are prognostications; thus it says, "The superior person at rest contemplates the images and enjoys the remarks; in activity he contemplates the fluctuations and enjoys the prognostications" [*Xici* A.2.6]); "in making implements we honor its images" (referring to thirteen hexagrams)[36]; "in divining we honor its prognostications." The remarks of King Wen and the Duke of Zhou are all about divination. (*Zhuzi yulei* 67:1658)

People reading the *Yi* today should divide it into three levels: Fuxi's *Yi*, King Wen's *Yi*, and Confucius's *Yi*. If one reads Fuxi's *Yi* as if there were no *Tuan*, *Xiang*, and *Wenyan* discussions, then one will be able to see that the original intention [*benyi* 本意] of the *Yi* was to create the practice of divination. (*Zhuzi yulei* 66:1629)

Zhu Xi insisted that people in his time needed the assistance of the ancient Sages in their efforts of moral self-cultivation, and so they should take into account the Sages' "original intention" in creating the *Yi*. Fuxi had created the hexagrams explicitly for the purpose of divination. King Wen and the Duke of Zhou had written the hexagram and line statements as aids for people to use in interpreting the hexagrams they received in divination. Confucius had written the Ten Wings (Zhu thought) as further interpretive aids and (in the case of the *Xici*) to explain the theory underlying the mechanism and purpose of divination. "The *Yi* was originally created for divination," not as a book of moral principle or moral guidance simply to be read—even though its textual layers did contain valuable moral principle and guidance. But that guidance in the process of self-cultivation was intended to be accessed *through and only through* the mechanism of divination. When done properly, said Zhu Xi, divination "enables everyone from kings and dukes to the common people to use it for self-cultivation and ordering the state."[37]

In addition to his focus on divination, Zhu Xi was particularly interested in correcting the interpretive approach to the *Yi* taken by Wang Bi—the "orthodox" commentator for the past nine hundred years—and by Zhu's honored predecessor, Cheng Yi. Wang Bi and Cheng Yi, as mentioned, both followed the *yili* 義理 (meaning and principle, or moral principle) approach to the *Yi*, focusing primarily on the textual levels to derive moral guidance for proper behavior by the superior person (*junzi*), who by implication was literate. But since "the hexagram and line statements are based simply on the images," Zhu Xi felt that the images—particularly the *yin-yang* and positional characteristics of the hexagrams and lines—required equal, if not greater, attention.

To illustrate Zhu Xi's divergence from the typical *yili* approach to the *Yi*, let us compare the comments by Wang Bi, Cheng Yi, and Zhu Xi on the name and hexagram statement of Dayou 大有, "Great Possession" (hexagram 14, ䷍), which is composed of the Qian (Heaven) trigram below and the Li (Fire) trigram above. The name and hexagram statement are "Great Possession: Supreme success."

14 INTRODUCTION

Wang Bi's comment:

Without great commonality [*tong* 通], what else could great possession come from?[38]

Note that Wang Bi, in this uncharacteristically short comment, addresses only the hexagram name.

Cheng Yi's comment:

The qualities [*cai* 才] of the hexagram can be considered "primacy and success."[39] As for the virtues of hexagrams in general, there are cases of the *name* of the hexagram itself containing the meaning, such as "Bi: Auspicious" [hexagram 8] and "Qian: Success" [15]. There are cases where one derives the meaning of the hexagram from the *counsel and admonition*,[40] such as "Shi: Correct. The strong man has good fortune" [7] and "Fellowship in the field: Success" [13]. And there are cases [such as the present] in which it is expressed in terms of the hexagram *qualities*, such as "Great possession: Supreme success." Since [the *Tuanzhuan* refers to the virtue of this hexagram as] "firm and strong, elegant and bright; responding to Heaven and acting in a timely way," it [the hexagram text] can be "supreme success."[41]

All three of the loci of meaning Cheng discusses here (italicized) are based on the hexagram statement. He does not mention the trigram/hexagram structure or *yin-yang* relationships.

Zhu Xi's comment:

"Great Possession" means the greatness of what one possesses. Li resides above Qian, fire above Heaven, so everything is illuminated. Also, the 6 in the fifth, a single *yin* occupying the place of honor, is central, while the five *yang* lines correspond with it, so this is great possession. Qian is strong and Li is bright. Abiding in respect and responding to Heaven is a Way of success. If the diviner has these virtues, then there will be great goodness and success.[42]

Zhu Xi begins his comment with an explanation of the *yin-yang* relationships of the lines and the imagery of the component trigrams. On that basis he attempts to clarify the relationship between the lines and the statements, drawing particular attention to the oracular pronouncements. This is a good example of his synthesis of the *xiangshu* and *yili* approaches and is typical of his comments on the hexagrams. He makes extensive use of the graphic and numerological elements but combines them with the textual levels to derive moral guidance. The first of the four chapters of his shorter book, the *Yixue qimeng* 易學啟蒙 (Introduction to the study of the *Yi*), is in fact entirely devoted to the *xiangshu* analysis of the lines, trigrams, hexagrams, and associated numerological diagrams. Much of this is also found in the "Nine Diagrams" that Zhu Xi (or perhaps a follower) appended to the beginning of his commentary, the *Zhouyi benyi*.[43]

Zhu Xi also differed with Wang Bi and Cheng Yi on the question of whom the *Yi* was created for: "If we regard [the *Yi*] as [a book of] divination, then all people—scholars, farmers, artisans, and merchants—will be able to make use of it in all their affairs. If this sort of person divines, he will make this sort of use of it. If another sort of person divines, he will make another sort of use of it."[44] In other words, Fuxi's original intention in creating the *Yi* was to aid all people, not only literate *junzi*, in making moral decisions by means of hexagram divination. (Zhu Xi would probably have assumed that most farmers—even in the Song, when public education had expanded significantly—were illiterate.) In Zhu Xi's view, Fuxi had first intuited the linkages between the moral order (*daoli* 道理) and the natural order (*tianli* 天理) and thereby had first brought the Confucian *dao* 道 (Way) into the world. Hence the title of Zhu's commentary, *The Original Meaning of the* Zhouyi.

Of course this hermeneutic principle applies primarily to the divinatory core of the *Yijing*: the basic text itself and the appendixes that comment specifically on it—that is, all except the *Xici* and *Shuogua* appendixes. The *Xici* appendix does contain one section (A.9) devoted to the divination method and several subsections that comment on specific hexagrams (A.8.5-11, A.12.1, and B.5.1).[45] But in general the *Xici* presents a theory explaining *how* the divination system works and *why* it is relevant to moral self-cultivation. Zhu Xi too believed that *Yijing* divination was an important method of self-cultivation but should be used only for moral guidance when one's own resources are exhausted. The specific genius of the *Yi* was its ability to detect incipient (*ji* 幾) changes in events and their potential direction of change, enabling people who use and interpret it correctly to align their own behavior with the direction and flow of the *dao* and thereby to maximize the moral flourishing of their lives and endeavors. Much of the theory and terminology underlying this set of beliefs was contained in the *Xici*, which therefore was extremely important to Zhu Xi.[46]

ARRANGEMENTS OF THE TEXT

One of the distinctive features of Wang Bi's commentary on the *Yi* was his rearrangement of the text. Originally the Ten Wings, or appendixes, had been separate works. Wang collated the commentary Wings (the *Tuan*, *Daxiang*, *Xiaoxiang*, and *Wenyan*) with the hexagrams, "using the appendixes to explain the basic text."[47] Wang's methodology and the epistemological theory it exemplified were founded on his metaphysical theory of "original substance" (*benti* 本體) or "original nonbeing" (*benwu* 本無). This, according to Wang, is the indeterminate, unfathomable *dao* that constitutes the meaning and order underlying the otherwise chaotic multiplicity of phenomena. His basic statement of this doctrine is found in his commentary on the first chapter of the *Laozi*, in which he says, "All being originates in non-being."[48] The reason or principle of a thing, he argues, cannot be found in the particularity of that thing. It must be found on a higher level of generality, and it must be dialectically distinct from it, as nonbeing is to being. In terms of an epistemological approach to the *Yijing*, this doctrine implies that the meaning of a hexagram is not given by its particular structural context or its symbolic associations. It lies instead in a single underlying idea or intention (*yi* 意), which is expressed by the one line that is the "ruler" of the hexagram (explained subsequently), and by the hexagram name and text:

> Therefore when we cite the name of a hexagram, in its meaning is found the controlling principle [ruler], and when we read the words of the Judgment, then we have got more than half the ideas involved.... Since the words are the means to explain the images, once one gets the images, he forgets the words, and since the images are the means to allow us to concentrate on the ideas, once one gets the ideas, he forgets the images. Similarly, "the rabbit snare exists for the sake of the rabbit; once one gets the rabbit, he forgets the snare. And the fish trap exists for the sake of fish; once one gets the fish, he forgets the trap."[49]

If the meaning matches that of compliance, why is it necessary that Kun [hexagram 2] be a cow? If the meaning corresponds to strength, why is it necessary that Qian [hexagram 1] be a horse? Yet some have determined that Qian is a horse. They cite the text and label the hexagram, [yet in the end] they have a horse but don't have Qian! Thus artificial theories overflow and spread, and it is difficult to keep track of them.[50]

By placing the relevant commentary passages together with the hexagram and line statements, Wang Bi enabled the reader to focus on and grasp the essential idea expressed by each hexagram. Ultimately one hopes to grasp the unified system, expressing the principle of bipolar change on the indeterminate ground of the *dao*.[51]

Cheng Yi, in the eleventh century, agreed with Wang Bi concerning the primacy of the text, so he used the same arrangement, collating the relevant appendixes with the hexagrams. He also included under each hexagram the relevant sentence from the *Xugua*, or "Sequence of Hexagrams," commenting on it to show how the hexagram fit into the overall, unified process or principle (*li* 理) of change.[52] Like Wang Bi, he was "concerned to demonstrate the unitariness underlying all phenomena, not only in general terms but in specific instances."[53]

Zhu Xi's arrangement of the text was fully consistent with his general hermeneutic theory. As a corollary to his insistence on the original intention of the *Yi*, he returned to the original structure of the text, with the appendixes separate from the basic text. This arrangement, he thought, more accurately reflected the history of the *Yi*'s compilation and therefore better represented the original intentions of its Sagely creators.[54] Unfortunately, this arrangement makes the text rather difficult to read, as it breaks up the connections between the various levels. For example, the *Tuan* appendix ("Commentary on the Judgment") refers directly to the hexagram statement, and the *Xiaoxiang* (Smaller image) appendix quotes the *Tuan*. When the *Tuan* and *Xiaoxiang* are each printed as a whole, separate from the hexagrams (as Zhu Xi would have it), seeing those connections is difficult. For that reason, most editions of Zhu's commentary, especially the many popular editions, ignore his arrangement and collate the various levels, following the model of Wang Bi and Cheng Yi—with the exception of hexagram 1 (see the following text box and note). This practice actually dates back to some of Zhu Xi's students shortly after his death.[55] Examples include the Imperial Academy (Guozijian 國子監) edition, one of the two editions in the *Complete Library of* the Four Treasuries (*Siku quanshu* 四庫全書) collection, and most popular reprints. The *Siku quanshu* also contains an "Original Version of the *Zhouyi benyi*" (*Yuanben Zhouyi benyi* 原本周易本義), in Zhu Xi's arrangement; other examples of the original arrangement are found in the *Yijing jicheng* (compiled by Yan Lingfeng, 1976) and the twenty-seven-volume *Zhu Xi's Complete Works* (2002). The two arrangements are as follows:

Arrangements of the *Zhouyi benyi*

Zhu Xi's arrangement

Examples:
- *Siku quanshu* (1): *Yuanben Zhouyi benyi* 原本周易本義
- *Zhu Xi's Complete Works* (2002)

Chapters (*juan* 卷):

1-2: hexagram & line statements
3-4: *Tuan*
5-6: *Xiang* (Larger and Smaller combined)
7-8: *Xici*
9: *Wenyan*
10: *Shuogua*
11: *Xugua*
12: *Zagua*

Collated arrangement

Examples:
- *Siku quanshu* (2): *Zhouyi benyi* 周易本義
- Imperial Academy (Taipei: Hualian, 1978)

Chapters (*juan* 卷):

1-2: Under each hexagram except Qian (1):[56]
    Hexagram statement
    Tuan
    Daxiang
    Line statements with *Xiaoxiang*
    Wenyan (hexagrams 1 and 2)
3: *Xici*
4: *Shuogua, Xugua, Zagua*

I began working on this translation following Zhu Xi's plan but soon found it cumbersome, and I thought it important for the connections between the several commentaries to be more evident. I therefore changed it to the collated arrangement as in the right column in the box. My apologies to Zhu Xi; but I think he sacrificed readability and usefulness just to make the point regarding his theory of the "original meaning" and to maintain consistency with it. I take as support for this decision the fact that most published editions ignore Zhu Xi's arrangement, and that this practice may go back as far as his own students. I fully understand and respect, though, the opinion of those who disagree.

ABOUT THE TRANSLATION

I am not aware of any complete Western-language translations of Zhu Xi's commentary, the *Zhouyi benyi*. The most noteworthy translations of the *Yijing* itself, all of which I have consulted, are those by James Legge, Richard Wilhelm and Cary F. Baynes, Richard John Lynn, Richard Rutt, and Geoffrey Redmond. Legge and Wilhelm both based their translations largely on the Qing-dynasty compilation, *Zhouyi zhezhong* 周易折中 (The *Yijing* judged evenly), which in turn was based on the commentaries of Zhu Xi and Cheng Yi, so I have taken that into account when deciding how to translate the text as Zhu Xi understood it. Lynn's translation reflects Wang Bi's interpretation, and both Rutt and Redmond attempted to capture the original Bronze Age meaning before it was "Confucianized." Edward Shaughnessy also has an important translation of the Mawangdui version of the *Yijing* (discovered in 1973), but that was not the text Zhu Xi used.[57]

Aside from the arrangement of the text, where I have departed from Zhu Xi's preference, I have tried to scrupulously follow his theory of interpretation. Implied in his approach is the rather modern view that meaning *emerges* in the relationship between the author, the text, and the reader.[58] Therefore, for the most part Zhu Xi does not spell out all the moral philosophical implications of the text. As a result, his commentary is briefer than the commentaries of Wang Bi and Cheng Yi. And that means that the scriptural text itself must remain as gnomic, or runic, as it really is. In other words, I have resisted the impulse to make sense of the text where that sense is not evident. The text is jumbled, fragmentary, cryptic, and exceedingly obscure, and for the most part I have left it that way. I therefore disagree with Geoffrey Redmond's principle that "since the *Zhouyi* was understandable to the readers of 3,000 years ago, a translation should make it understandable to readers of today."[59] I suspect that much of the basic text was probably opaque and puzzling even during the early Zhou period. Moreover, since Zhu Xi's hermeneutic principle is that the meaning of the *Yi* emerges *only* in the reader's (or user's) personal encounter with the text, mediated by the ritual of divination, I think it would be a mistake to translate the text itself into a fully coherent form for all readers. Zhu Xi's commentary, which of course is consistent with his hermeneutic principle, does not do that. Instead, he gives the reader (or user) the tools to derive the meaning most appropriate to that particular person (whatever his or her station in life) in that particular circumstance. The closer we get to the bare words of the text the clearer it becomes that much of the *Yi*'s meaning must come from the mind of the reader. Zhu's strategy is perfectly consistent with his general "methodology of reading" (*dushu fa* 讀書法), about which Curie Virág says, "Truly 'getting' a text, that is, grasping its *li*, lies not in the apprehension of the text *per se* but in the encounter between the reader and the text. It also means that there is not one meaning but infinite possibilities of meaning, and therefore infinite possibilities of discoursing about it."[60]

What is unique about reading the *Yijing*, according to Zhu, is that divination must be part of the interpretive process. This is why his commentary is rather "minimalist" compared with his commentaries on other texts, such as the Four Books. Only occasionally does he elaborate moral implications that he considers especially significant and that might not be evident to the reader; for the most part his commentary is quite brief. Compared with Wang Bi and Cheng Yi, Zhu Xi is much more concerned with the *yin-yang* symbolism and relationships of the lines (since that is the original form of the *Yi* before the written texts were added) and with helping the user to identify the various characteristics of the lines and text. These include

- the structural relations among the lines; for example, whether they are "central" or "correct" (explained subsequently);
- the function of each phrase; for example, explaining the hexagram's name or the virtues of the component trigrams;
- the "ruling" (*zhu* 主) line of the hexagram (in just a few cases);
- the admonition or warning (*jie* 戒)
- the conditionality of the prognostication (*zhan* 占); for example, "*If* the diviner has these virtues, this will happen").[61]

Zhu's commentary on the divinatory portions of the *Yi* is somewhat reminiscent of the old grammar exercise of diagramming sentences. The point is to facilitate an analysis of the text, which follows from the general principle of understanding which of the four Sages (Fuxi, King Wen, the Duke of Zhou, and Confucius) was responsible for each level of the text, and what his intentions were.

Zhu Xi's minimalist commentary did not prevent him from using the text to express his own philosophy—as every commentator inevitably does. The Chinese commentarial tradition was, in fact, one of the major modes of philosophical writing. In Zhu's case, his "editorial conservatism" served the purpose of "hermeneutic activism."[62] This is the reason for the quotation marks around "original meaning" in the title of this introduction. Zhu Xi sincerely believed that he had grasped the authorial intention of Fuxi and the other Sages who had created the *Yi*; that the key to that intention was the *use* of the *Yi* as a divination text; that this method of divination provided access to the minds of those Sages, who had first intuited and put into practice the Way of Heaven; and that this access was an invaluable tool in the process of self-cultivation by which ordinary people could approach Sagehood themselves. The "original meaning" that Zhu Xi discerned, however, is quite different from what historically oriented modern scholars understand as the original meaning of the *Yi* in the context of Bronze Age statecraft and ritual. The focus of this book, then, is really Zhu Xi more than the *Yijing* itself. Thus in my notes I attempt to elucidate how specific points in the text and commentary contribute to Zhu Xi's overall project of understanding the natural/moral order (*tianli* 天裡 / *daoli* 道理) and "learning to become a Sage" (*sheng xue* 聖學).

The *Zhouyi benyi* was completed in 1188. Zhu Xi had written an earlier commentary, called *Yizhuan* 易傳 (Commentary on the *Yi*), in 1177, but that is now lost except for its preface, which is included here.[63] In 1186 he had published a shorter work on the *Yi*, the *Yixue qimeng*, in which he re-creates the sketchy method of divination found in the *Xici* appendix, explains in detail how to go about practicing divination, and also explains the numerology and symbolism of various diagrams associated with the *Yi*—relying heavily on the *xiangshu* and divination expert Shao Yong, a friend of the Cheng brothers. Together the *Yixue qimeng* and the *Zhouyi benyi* constitute an example of Zhu Xi as "the great synthesizer" of the Confucian tradition—in this case synthesizing the two schools of *Yijing* interpretation into something new. Partly for this reason, Zhu Xi's commentary quickly overshadowed all previous ones, including that of Cheng Yi—even though both were included in the Qing-dynasty edition sponsored by the Kangxi emperor, the *Zhouyi zhezhong*, in 1716. According to Bent Nielsen, between 1265 and 1918 at least thirty editions of the *Zhouyi benyi* were published in China alone.[64]

It is difficult to overstate the historical significance of the *Yijing* in Chinese thought and religion. It was venerated and used in Confucianism, Daoism, popular religion, and even Buddhism. As Roger Ames puts it, "perhaps no single text can compete with [it] in terms of the sustained interest it has garnered from succeeding generations of China's literati, and the influence it has had on Chinese self-understanding."[65] Although in the popular imagination today it is often associated more closely with Daoism,[66] throughout East Asian history it has received at least as much if not more attention from Confucians, beginning with its classification as one of the Five Classics. In my view this has to do with its integration of what I have called the natural order and the moral order. As I have mentioned, Zhu Xi saw the primordial Sage Fuxi as the first to intuit the linkage between these realms: the idea that Confucian moral values are not merely conventional (as the early Daoists said) but are part of a larger order—the Dao—that includes what we call natural law. That is, Fuxi saw the moral implications of natural patterns of *yin-yang* change and interaction, which he symbolized in the lines, trigrams, and hexagrams. This connection, enabling a vision of a fundamental, integral, natural/moral order, functioned as legitimation (for Zhu Xi) of Confucian values vis-à-vis Daoism and Chinese Buddhism. In this sense Fuxi brought the Confucian *dao* into the world and made it experientially accessible to all people through the method of divination. Zhu Xi acknowledged the importance of this in the context of defining what it meant to follow the Confucian *dao* in the Song, as opposed to the Ways of Daoism and Buddhism. With his two books on the *Yi* he tried to facilitate the flourishing of the Confucian *dao*, and thereby (in his view) the flourishing of humanity.[67]

KEY TERMS AND CONCEPTS

Change[68]

The most general word for "change" is *yi* 易, as in the title of the book. *Bian* 變 and *hua* 化 are subsets of *yi*. *Bian* is "fluctuation," or alternating (oscillating) *yin/yang* change. For example, the *Xici* says, "alternately closing and opening is called fluctuation [A.11.4];" "when change [*yi* 易] reaches a limit there is fluctuation [B.2.5]." *Hua* is "transformation," or change from one state to another, such as the change from one of the Five Phases (*wuxing* 五行) to another. *Bian* and *hua* are often used together (fluctuation and transformation). Another word often paired with *bian* is *tong* 通, which most often means "penetrate," or "permeate," but as a pair I translate *biantong* as "fluctuation and continuity," the latter meaning continuity through time as a process, as opposed to permanence, which implies something unchanging.[69]

Related to these terms is the concept of life, growth, or generation (*sheng* 生), which is inherent in the fundamental stuff of which all things are composed, *qi*

INTRODUCTION 23

氣 ("psychophysical stuff"). This was an important principle for the Song Confucians, who related the creativity of life to the moral creativity of *ren* 仁 (humanity). The *Xici* was a major textual source of this concept:

> Generation and regeneration [or life and growth, *sheng sheng* 生生] are the meaning of change. (A.5.6)
>
> As for Qian [hexagram 1], in stillness it is focused; in activity it is direct. This is how it is greatly life-giving [*da sheng* 大生]. As for Kun [hexagram 2], in stillness it is condensed; in activity it is diffuse. This is how it is broadly life-giving [*guang sheng* 廣生]. (A.6.2)
>
> The great virtue of Heaven and Earth is life [*sheng* 生]. (B.1.10)

Cheng Yi, in a comment on hexagram 24 (Fu, Return), says, "One *yang* returning to the bottom is the mind of Heaven and Earth to generate things [*sheng wu* 生物]."[70] Elsewhere he says, "The transformations of Heaven and Earth are natural generation and regeneration without end [*sheng sheng buxiong* 生生不窮] ... The Way is natural generation and regeneration without cessation [*sheng sheng buxi* 生生不息]."[71]

The phrase *sheng sheng* is found many other times in the Cheng brothers' complete works, attributed to both brothers, and is quoted frequently by Zhu Xi and others in the Cheng-Zhu school. For example, Zhu Xi's important essay "Discussion of Humanity [*ren* 仁]" begins with Cheng's comment on Fu, quoted in the preceding. That essay contains Zhu's fullest discussion of the correlation between natural and human (moral) creativity.[72] Such a correlation was central to the meaning of the *Yijing* for Song-dynasty Confucians and, as I have suggested, to the meaning of Confucianism itself.

Time (*shi* 時)

"Time" is a crucially important concept in the *Yijing*.[73] Indeed, "change" and "time" are inherently overlapping concepts. The traditional Chinese concept of time was/is distinctly different from the Newtonian concept of time that still predominates in Western thought. Isaac Newton (1642–1727) said that both time and space are neutral, featureless backdrops against which material objects exist and move. The Chinese concept is that time itself varies qualitatively, like seasons—in fact, *shi* means both "time" and "season." So, for example, when the text refers to the "time of surpassing by the great" (hexagram 28) or the "time of letting go" (40); or when Zhu Xi refers to "the time of difficulty" (3) or "the time of restraint by the lesser" (9), they are pointing to the qualities of those moments themselves, not to events occurring in those moments. Therefore, part of the challenge of acting properly and maximizing one's success in life with the help of the *Yijing* is to understand the quality of the time and to act in such a way as to accord with its character. It is to understand what *season* it is, and the activities appropriate to that season—not just the calendar date and clock time. This is similar to what is called going with the flow, often in the context of early Daoist thought (e.g., Zhuangzi's image of a man falling into a raging river and surviving by following the currents and eddies, not fighting against them).[74] In a sense, time *is* nothing but change.

The hexagrams themselves are understood to be temporal configurations of *yin* and *yang* on two levels. First, each hexagram itself is said to describe a temporal frame, starting from the bottom of the hexagram and ending at the top. Thus each hexagram represents a process, not a static condition ("the six lines intermingling are simply temporal things" [*Xici* B.9.1]). Second, the *yin* or *yang* nature of each line is part of a temporal process of cyclical alternation. *Yin* and *yang* are not substances themselves; rather they are *modes* of the constant transformation of *qi*; they are modalities of change. *Yin* describes *qi* in its dark, cold, sinking, condensing phase; *yang* describes the light, warm, rising, expanding phase. Therefore each line is *yin* or *yang* only temporarily: when its *yin* or *yang* activity reaches a maximum, it changes direction, so to speak, and begins to act in the opposite mode (see figure I.1). The constantly changing nature of the *yin* and *yang* lines means that each hexagram too is inherently changing. A hexagram yielded by the divination method represents an inherently dynamic, changing situation as well as its direction of change, like a vector (a force with both magnitude and direction). The particular configuration of that dynamism points to another hexagram, which can be interpreted as the *potential* future state that the present state is tending toward. This is the aspect of *Yijing* divination that is popularly considered "fortune-telling."

In *xiangshu* theory—applying both to the process of divination and to cosmic symbolism and numerology—the production of one hexagram from another is called hexagram fluctuation (*guabian* 卦變), of which there are many forms. The one that Zhu Xi primarily discusses is where the original and resulting hexagrams have the same number of *yin* and *yang* lines, which have shifted positions (chap.

1, Diagram 9). He refers to this method in his comments on nineteen hexagrams (6, 11, 12, 21, 22, 25, 26, 31, 32, 35, 38, 39, 40, 41, 42, 46, 50, 53, 59).

However, as he demonstrates in his *Yixue qimeng* (chap. 4), any hexagram can change into any other, or remain the same. In the divination process this depends upon the numbers derived from the milfoil divination method. The numbers produced by each step of the method are either 2 or 3, but three operations are required for each line, so the resulting numbers are either 6, 7, 8, or 9. The numbers 6 and 9 produce changing lines because they are composed of all *yin* (2 + 2 + 2 = 6) or all *yang* (3 + 3 + 3 = 9) numbers and are therefore "mature" (*lao* 老) *yin* and *yang*, respectively. Mature lines are about to change their direction of development, as illustrated in this sine curve depicting the fluctuation of *yin* and *yang* during a day:

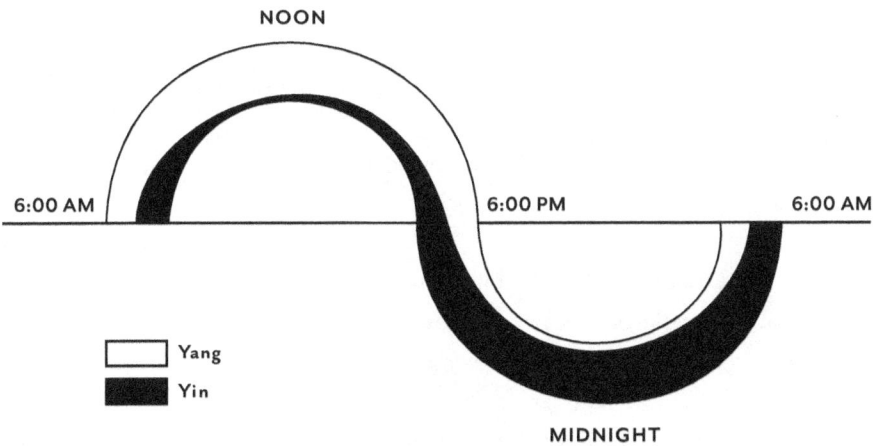

FIGURE I.1 *Yin-yang* fluctuation

The numbers 7 and 8 are *relatively* static because they are composed of mixtures of 2s and 3s; they are called young (*shao* 少) *yang* and *yin*. The two hexagrams yielded by each divination (except for the rare cases in which none of the six lines is changing) are called the original hexagram (*bengua* 本卦) and the derived hexagram (*zhigua* 之卦).[75]

Another example of hexagram fluctuation is the "waxing and waning hexagrams" (*xiaoxi gua* 消息卦), attributed to the Han-dynasty *xiangshu* master Meng Xi 孟喜 (first century CE). "Waxing" plots the growth of *yang*: Fu 復 ䷗ (24) → Lin

臨 ䷒ (19) → Tai 泰 ䷊ (11) → Dazhuang 大壯 ䷡ (34) → Guai 夬 ䷪ (43) → Qian 乾 ䷀ (1). "Waning" refers to the sequence in which *yin* grows in the hexagram: Gou 姤 ䷫ (44) → Dun 遯 ䷠ (33) → Pi 否 ䷋ (12) → Guan 觀 ䷓ (20) → Bo 剝 ䷖ (23) → Kun 坤 ䷁ (2). These twelve hexagrams are called the sovereign hexagrams (*bigua* 辟卦) and are correlated with the twelve lunar months:

TABLE I.3 Hexagrams correlated with months

Lunar month	Gregorian equivalent	Hexagram	Lunar month	Gregorian equivalent	Hexagram
1st	Feb.–March	䷊ 11 Tai 泰	7th	Aug.–Sept.	䷋ 12 Pi 否
2nd	March–Apr.	䷡ 34 Dazhuang 大壯	8th	Sept.–Oct.	䷓ 20 Guan 觀
3rd	April–May	䷪ 43 Kuai 夬	9th	Oct.–Nov.	䷖ 23 Bo 剝
4th	May–June	䷀ 1 Qian 乾	10th	Nov.–Dec.	䷁ 2 Kun 坤
5th	June–July	䷫ 44 Gou 姤	11th	Dec.–Jan.	䷗ 24 Fu 復
6th	July–Aug.	䷠ 33 Dun 遯	12th	Jan.–Feb.	䷒ 19 Lin 臨

In "Fuxi's Directional Positioning of the Sixty-Four Hexagrams" (Diagram 6) these months would be mapped as shown in figure I.2 (*top*, Arabic numbers). Note that in the inner square arrangement the hexagrams Qian, Dui, Li, Zhen, Sun, Kan, Gen, and Kun are numbered differently, not correlating with months: 1–8, starting from the lower right and moving diagonally to the upper left (Chinese numbers). This sequence is based on "Fuxi's Sequence of the Eight Trigrams" (Diagram 3 and figure I.2, *bottom*) or its expanded version, "Fuxi's Sequence of the Sixty-Four Hexagrams" (Diagram 5).

Image (xiang 象)

"Image" is another important term in the *Yijing*, especially in the *Xici* appendix, where it occurs nearly forty times. For example, *Xici* A.12.2 argues that the imagery of the *Yi* conveys concepts that cannot be expressed in words, and that this is the key to its profundity. The graphic core of the *Yi* is basically, after all, a set of images and a symbol system. The range of meanings of the term includes the

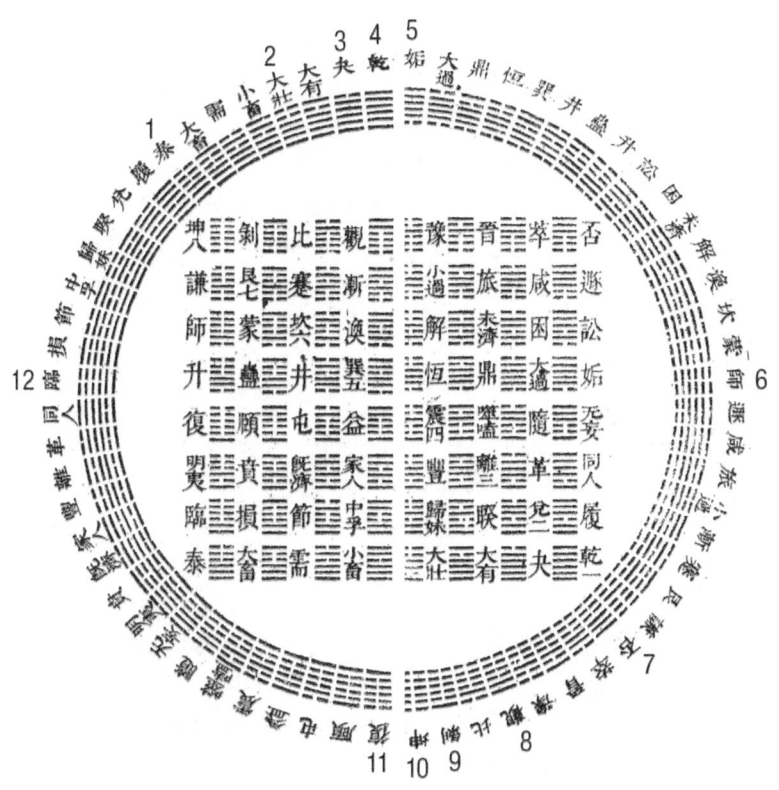

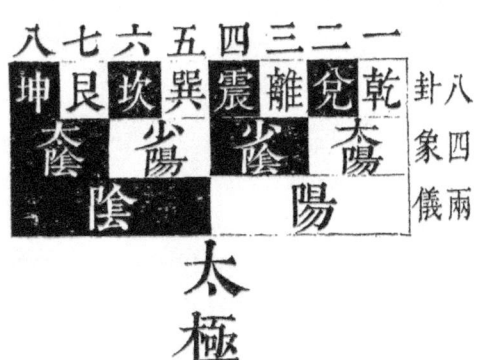

FIGURE I.2 Fuxi sequences

concrete objects after which Fuxi modeled the hexagrams, the hexagrams and trigrams themselves as line diagrams, their *yin-yang* meanings, the various symbolic correlations elaborated in the *Shuogua* and mentioned in the hexagram and line texts, and literary imagery in the texts. Zhu Xi argues that the more concrete, graphic images of the *Yi*—that is, those actually produced by Fuxi—are more important than the symbolic correlations and the metaphorical images found in the texts, such as the dragon of Qian (hexagram 1) and the mare of Kun (2).[76]

Number (*shu* 數)

The *Yi* "maximizes numbers" (*Xici* A.5.8) in the sense that it makes full use of numerical relationships and symbolism to express the truths of the natural/moral order (*li* 理). To take just one example, since odd numbers symbolize *yin* and even symbolize *yang*, the locations and relationships of odd numbers (unbroken lines) and even numbers (broken lines) in the positions of the hexagram, numbered one through six, are one of the primary determinants of the hexagram and line meanings—especially in Zhu Xi's exegesis. A modern theory, unknown to Zhu Xi, is that the broken and unbroken lines constituting the trigrams and hexagrams were originally numbers, specifically 1 (*yi* 一) and 6 (*liu* 六). In some early antecedents of the *Zhouyi* text that we have today, the broken lines are written with two angled strokes, like the bottom part of the character *liu*. Thus the connection between the *Zhouyi* and numbers might be even more direct than premodern commentators thought.[77]

Li (理)

Li, conventionally translated as "principle" but sometimes as "pattern" or "coherence," occurs only eight times in the *Yijing*, and only in the appendixes (*Wenyan*, *Xici*, and *Shuogua*), but Zhu Xi uses it extensively in his commentary. It is the most important concept in Confucian thought since the Song dynasty. Its original meaning was the veins or patterning in jade: the left side of the character is in fact the word for jade, *yu* 玉, while the right side is the phonetic component. Although it was occasionally used in a philosophical context—for example, by Wang Bi in the third century—it basically meant "pattern" until Huayan Buddhists in the Tang dynasty adopted it for the ultimate "principle" of all things—namely, "emptiness" (*kong* 空), or the nonexistence of any independent, autonomous existence. Then in the early Song dynasty the Cheng brothers began to use it in a Confucian context to mean the abstract "ordering principle" of the cosmos—both natural and moral—the most fundamental reality but *not* separable from concrete things.[78] All things that exist, including matter, energy, mind, and spirit, are constituted by *qi* 氣, or "psychophysical stuff": all *qi* is ordered by *li*, and *li* never exists apart from *qi*.[79] The *li* of things is also their "nature" (*xing* 性), and in the Mencian line of Confucian thought human nature—the "principle" of being human—is fundamentally good. The goal of self-cultivation is therefore to fully realize or actualize that nature or principle, which is the human expression of the principle, both natural and moral, that orders the universe.

If human nature, or the principle of being human, is good, why is moral self-cultivation necessary? Mencius's reply was that when he says human nature is good he means that people are "capable of becoming good" (*Mencius* 6A.6). Therefore what we are born with is moral *potential*, in the form of certain innate "dispositions" (*qing* 情) that can be cultivated into full-fledge virtues (*de* 德).[80] In his view, what keeps us from realizing that potential is either lack of positive nurturance, such as education, or active negative influence, such as indulging in selfish behavior. The Confucians of the Cheng-Zhu school in the Song dynasty reframed these ideas in terms of the "psychophysical nature" (*qizhi zhi xing* 氣質之性), or our given endowment of *qi*. Unless our *qi* is clear and free-flowing throughout the body and mind, it tends to obscure the *li* by which it is ordered, like cloudy water. The purpose of learning and other forms of self-cultivation is actually to clarify our *qi*, which constitutes the mind as well as the body, to allow its *li* to be clearly knowable and naturally put into practice. As Zhang Zai had put it, learning (*xue* 學) can "transform the psychophysical endowment" (*bianhua qizhi* 變化氣質).[81] Zhu Xi understood *Yijing* divination to be a learning tool that people can use to more fully realize the *li* in themselves and in their environment. It does this by helping people to recognize the moral meanings of natural (*yin/yang*) and social patterns and to act accordingly.

In my opinion "order/ordering" is the most accurate translation of *li*, but in most cases I use the more conventional "principle." My use of "principle," however, should *not* be construed as necessarily entailing either a linguistic proposition or a transcendent principle existing separately from things to which it gives meaning. "Pattern" seems to me a flatter, more two-dimensional term. For example, Zhu Xi sometimes (in other contexts) mentions the *li* of a boat, which is more than simply its blueprint pattern; it is what makes it a boat, its "boatness," and for this I see no problem in referring to it as the principle of a boat, or the nature of a boat. In fact, Zhu Xi said that the nature of a thing is simply its principle (*xing ji liye* 性即理也). One of the reasons I like "order/ordering" is that it connotes something like "world ordering" as the creation of order from chaos, with religious associations much like those of *taiji* 太極 (Supreme Polarity)—and Zhu Xi also equated *li* with *taiji*. "Coherence" as a translation of *li* is less apt than "order" or "principle" because it suggests an element of human understanding, while Zhu Xi's *li* is independent of human understanding.[82]

Ming (命)

Ming is conventionally translated as "decree" or "mandate," as in the "Mandate of Heaven" (*tianming* 天命). This is the political theory dating back to the early Zhou period, according to which Heaven grants the authority to rule to a family or dynasty on the basis of their moral virtue (*de* 德) and removes that mandate when their virtue declines, as it inevitably does. Thus "Heaven decrees and Heaven punishes" (*tianming tiantao* 天命天討), as an old saying goes.[83] Outside the political context, *ming* denotes the "givenness" of life: those aspects about which we have no choice, such as where, when, and to whom we are born. In this sense the saying just quoted can be translated as "Heaven gives and Heaven takes away." For Zhu Xi a crucial part of *ming* is our given endowment of *qi*, which determines how easy or difficult it will be to fully realize our moral nature (*xing* 性). This is *tianming* (天命) on the level of the individual, "what is given by Heaven" or "Heaven's endowment." Thus when the context is political I translate *ming* as "decree"; when it refers to human beings I translate it as "endowment," as in "human nature and endowment" (*xing ming* 性命). *Ming* by itself is often translated as "fate" or "destiny," but these terms are highly misleading, as they suggest an element of predestination.[84]

The "Four Virtues" of Qian

The first line of the *Yijing*, the hexagram name and text of Qian (Creating), is, in Zhu Xi's interpretation, "Qian: Supreme and penetrating, appropriate and correct" (*Qian: Yuan heng li zhen* 乾元亨利貞). *Yuan*, *heng*, *li*, and *zhen* appear frequently in the hexagram statements, individually and in various combinations (including five additional times all together: hexagrams 3, 17, 19, 25, and 49). As a group of four, since the Han dynasty they have been interpreted as four virtues (*si de* 四

德), as they are explicitly referred to in the *Wenyan* appendix under Qian. Actually this reading is found as early as the *Zuozhuan* commentary to the *Spring and Autumn Annals*, a text tentatively dated to the late fourth century BCE, in a story about the sixth century BCE woman Mu Jiang 穆姜.[85] But by the Han dynasty the "Four Virtues" reading had become standard. It presumes that the basic text, or *Zhouyi*, reflects the same set of Confucian moral concerns as the later appendixes—an assumption made by all premodern commentators, as well as the translators Legge and Wilhelm. But in their original Zhou-dynasty ritual context (sacrifice and divination), the four terms were probably two semantic units. Thus Kunst renders them as "Grand treat. A favorable determination"; Shaughnessy as "Primary receipt: beneficial to divine"; and Rutt as "Supreme offering. Favorable augury." Geoffrey Redmond suggests that the line is an "invocation," translating it, "Begin with an offering for favorable divination." Other translators, following the post-Han commentarial tradition, translate the line as the Four Virtues of Qian; for example, Legge: "great and originating, penetrating, advantageous, correct and firm"; Shchutskii: "beginning, penetration, definition, stability"; and Lynn: "fundamentality, prevalence, fitness, and constancy." Rutt translates the Four Virtues as "sublimity (*yuan*), accomplishment (*heng*), furtherance (*li*), and perseverance (*zhen*)," and Zhu Xi's interpretation as "great / all-accomplishing and / proper steadfastness." The Wilhelm translation is "Sublime success / Furthering through perseverance."[86] While Zhu was generally concerned with retrieving the "original meaning" of the *Yi*, his redefinitions of these four key terms demonstrates how in some respects he moves away from the original divinatory context and moralizes the text. This shift was characteristic of virtually all post-Han commentators.

Yuan 元 basically means "origin" or "primal" but also "supreme," as Zhu Xi says under the first line of the *Tuan* commentary to Qian: "*Yuan* means great and beginning." However, since the *Tuan* commentary contains seven instances of *da heng* 大亨 (great and penetrating), I have reserved "great" for *da*.

Heng 亨 and *zhen* 貞, in the early Zhou-dynasty context of the original *Zhouyi*, had to do with the ritual dyad of sacrifice and divination. *Heng* referred to the "receipt" of a sacrifice by an ancestor, hence "success" in the ritual (cf. the Wilhelm translation of *yuan heng*, "supreme success"); it was cognate with *xiang* 享, "receive, enjoy," as in a spirit enjoying a sacrificial offering. Therefore Zhu Xi's definition, "penetrating" (*tong* 通), partially overlaps the original meaning of the word: the offering "getting through" to the spirit. Accordingly I translate it, depending upon the context, as either "penetrating" or "success." "Penetrating" also has epistemological connotations, as in a "penetrating mind" (e.g., in the hexagram statement of *Xikan*, hexagram 29).

Zhen 貞 originally meant the act of divination itself, or "to divine."[87] Zhu Xi's definition—"correct" (*zheng* 正), which also means "upright" or "settled"—has a scriptural basis in the first line of the *Tuan* commentary under hexagram 7 (Shi). *Zhen* can also mean "steadfast" or "persistent," and I sometimes use that where "correct" would not work (e.g., the fifth line of Yu, hexagram 16).

Li 利 basically means "benefit, advantage," and Zhu Xi sometimes uses it in that sense, although in the context of the Four Virtues of Qian he defines it as "appropriate" (*yi* 宜), and I follow him in the text of the *Yi* even though the conventional meaning also works. For the frequent combination *li zhen* 利貞, which appears mostly in hexagram statements (the eminently quotable "Perseverance furthers" in the Wilhelm translation), I have used "appropriate and correct" instead of "appropriate to be correct," consistent with my principle of not imposing more meaning than the text itself requires.

In addition to his comments on the hexagram statement of Qian, Zhu Xi discusses the Four Virtues under the first line of the *Wenyan* appendix, where they are explicitly called the Four Virtues. They are closely related in his system of thought with the "Four Constant Virtues" of Mencius (humanity, rightness, ritual propriety, and wisdom)—for example, in Zhu Xi's important essay "Discussion of Humanity" (Renshuo 仁說). Nevertheless, he occasionally seems to treat them as two semantic units; for example, near the end of his commentary on the Qian hexagram statement, where he says, "King Wen considered the Way of Qian to be greatly penetrating [*datong* 大通] and perfectly correct [*zhizheng* 至正]." And in his comments on the hexagram statement and Judgment Commentary of Wuwang (hexagram 25), he inserts a preposition (*yu* 於) between *li* and *zhen*, making it "benefiting from correctness." This is probably why Wilhelm, who generally follows Zhu Xi, render the hexagram statement as "Sublime success / Furthering through perseverance." In the present translation I translate them as separate virtues when all four are given, but in cases of the first pair alone I use "supreme success."

"Central" (*zhong* 中), "Correct" (*zheng* 正), and "Corresponding" (*ying* 應)

"Central" and "correct" refer both to line positions and human virtues. In terms of line positions, "central" refers to the second and fifth positions (the centers of the component trigrams); "correct" refers to *yang* lines in odd-numbered positions and *yin* lines in even-numbered positions, because in Chinese cosmology and numerology odd numbers are *yang* and even numbers are *yin*; this is called the principle of "matching positions" (*dangwei* 當位).⁸⁸ In terms of human virtues, "central" alludes to *zhong* 中 (centrality, equilibrium, hitting the mark) in the *Zhongyong*, where it is associated with *he* 和 (harmony).⁸⁹ This passage played a crucial role in Zhu Xi's theory of mind and self-cultivation:

> Before the feelings of pleasure, anger, sorrow, and joy are expressed [*weifa* 未發] it is called centrality. When these feelings are expressed [*yifa* 已發] and each and all attain due measure and degree, it is called harmony. Centrality is the great foundation of the world, and harmony is its universal path. When centrality and harmony are realized to the highest degree, heaven and earth will attain their proper order and all things will flourish.⁹⁰

"Correctness" as a human virtue refers to "rightness," *yi* 義, or behavior that is appropriate to the circumstances, one of Mencius's Four Constant Virtues.

"Corresponding": Two lines are said to correctly correspond when they occupy matching positions in the inner and outer trigrams (i.e., 1 and 4, 2 and 5, 3 and 6) and one is *yin* and the other *yang*. This is an auspicious characteristic.

Hexagram Rulers (*zhu* 主)

Each hexagram has two kinds of "rulers," or dominant lines. The "ruler of the complete hexagram" (*cheng guazhi zhu* 成卦之主), or "constituting ruler," is the line that most clearly embodies the meaning of the hexagram—for example, the first line of Zhun (Difficult), hexagram 3: ䷂, which is a *yang* at the beginning that is pushing itself up with difficulty, like a sprout. Each hexagram also has a "governing ruler" (*zhu guazhi zhu* 主卦之主), which is usually the line in the fifth position, the center of the upper trigram. Over the centuries several schema of ruling lines have been proposed. For one prominent example, see that of Li Guangdi, editor of the official Qing-dynasty compilation of the *Yijing* commentaries of Cheng Yi and Zhu Xi.⁹¹

Xiantian 先天 ("before Heaven") *and Houtian* 後天 ("after Heaven")

I generally use "a priori" for *xiantian* because I understand the term to refer to analytic (not synthetic) or mathematical/logical relationships. For example, in the *Yixue qimeng* Zhu Xi approvingly quotes a statement by Shao Yong, "There was an

Yi before [the hexagrams] were drawn."[92] *Houtian* deals with relationships of existing things, and so I translate it as a posteriori. The two terms, which come from the *Wenyan* (Qian, 29), are roughly equivalent to "metaphysical" and "concrete/physical," although those terms have different Chinese equivalents (which also come from the *Yijing, Xici* A.12.4).

Fabrizio Pregadio translates *xiantian* and *houtian* as "precelestial" ("the domain prior to the generation of the cosmos") and "postcelestial" ("the domain in which the individual creatures, objects, and phenomena live, exist, and occur"); Anne Birdwhistell as "theoretical" and "phenomenal." Tze-ki Hon explains them as "natural and primordial (*xiantian*)" and "human-made and moral (*houtian*)."[93] Shao Yong was the first to use the two terms in reference to the trigram sequences depicted in Diagrams 4 (the Fuxi sequence) and 8 (the King Wen sequence).

Fu 復 (return)

Hexagram 24 ䷗, "Return," has extraordinary depth of meaning for the Cheng-Zhu school, so I discuss it here even though it explicitly concerns only one hexagram. The idea of the hexagram is that, after *yin* has taken over all six lines in Kun (hexagram 2), a single *yang* line has "returned" to the beginning, restarting the *yin-yang* cycle (months 10 and 11 in table I.3). The importance of the Fu hexagram to Zhu Xi is suggested by the fact that in his *Classified Conversations* there are five times more entries (49) on Fu than the average of all other hexagrams, excluding Qian (231) and Kun (51). The average of the sixty-one others is 9.9. The next largest after Fu are Gen (25) and Xian (20).

In Zhu Xi's comment on the last line of the Commentary on the Judgment ("In Fu is seen the mind of Heaven and Earth"), he says, "Below the accumulated *yin* a single *yang* is reborn. 'The mind of Heaven and Earth to give birth to things' is incipient in extinction.[94] Reaching this point [in the cyclical process], its return can be seen. In human beings it is activity at the maximum of stillness;[95] goodness at the maximum of the bad; the original mind beginning to reappear just at the point of vanishing." This represents the fundamental insight that *yin-yang* polarity and cyclical change is the most fundamental cosmic principle, which Zhu Xi called *taiji* 太極 (Supreme Polarity). Or to put it another way, *change* is fundamentally real, not permanence—directly contradicting Plato in *The Republic*. More specifically, stillness and activity have a relationship of metaphysical interpenetration: activity in stillness and stillness in activity.⁹⁶ Another canonical statement of this idea is *Xici* B.1.10: "The great virtue of Heaven and Earth is called life [or giving birth]."

Zhu's comment continues with a poem by Shao Yong that refers to Fuxi and begins with the phrase "At midnight on the winter solstice." This was the moment in the imperial ritual calendar when the emperor made his annual sacrifice to Heaven. As I have written elsewhere,

> This is the point in the year when *yin* is at its highest point and *yang* at its lowest, when the sun at noon is at its lowest point of the year. This is the turning point, when the sun begins to rise higher in the sky each day at noon, when the *yang* forces in the cosmos begin to increase again, eventually to reach their peak on the summer solstice. The function of the emperor at this moment, and at the corresponding moment on the summer solstice, was to facilitate the *yin-yang* fluctuation of cosmic forces by ritually enacting his filial role as "Son of Heaven."⁹⁷

The Fu hexagram symbolizes this moment of immanent creative potential springing forth spontaneously from the natural world—what he calls "the original mind beginning to reappear just at the point of vanishing." In Zhu Xi's "Discussion of Humanity" he develops the moral implications of natural principle. This essay, like Zhu's comment on Fu, begins with a paraphrase of Cheng Yi's comment on Fu, "The mind of Heaven and Earth is to produce things" and systematically relates the Four Virtues of Qian to the Four Constant (Universal) Virtues of Mencius: humanity (*ren* 仁), rightness (*yi* 義), propriety (*li* 禮), and wisdom (*zhi* 智).⁹⁸ Fu therefore represents the immanent natural and moral creative potential inherent in *qi*, the stuff of the universe, which is also the stuff of the human mind. In a recorded comment on Fu, Zhu Xi says,

> "In Fu is seen the mind of Heaven and Earth." The subtle and vague beginning of movement in this is most suitable for revealing the incessance of the generation of *qi*. Only by looking at it like this can we readily see that, as Heaven [Nature] has spring, summer, fall, and winter, so human beings have humanity, rightness, propriety, and wisdom.... Mind is a functioning thing that contains the principle of these four. In absolutely no other thing can this experiential verification be seen. (*Zhuzi yulei* 71:1790)

Thus creation or creativity has no need of a transcendent source, like a creator God. Creativity is inherent in the natural world and includes the uniquely human potential to bring to completion the moral potential of the universe—or, as the *Zhongyong* puts it, to "assist in the transforming and nourishing process of Heaven and Earth."[99] Similarly, Shao Yong is reported to have said, "Is not the alternation of stillness and activity the most wonderful thing in the universe? Is not the point between stillness and activity [i.e., the point of incipient creation] the most wonderful of the most wonderful things in Heaven, Earth and humanity?"[100] Shao here represents a strain in Song Confucianism that gives expression to the this-worldly, life-affirming attitude characteristic of Chinese thought. He implies that there is impenetrable mystery in each new beginning, each new rebirth. The continuous creativity inherent in the cosmos is dependent upon the continual reversal of natural processes of birth, growth, decay, and death. That new life should come from death seems to have impressed Shao Yong and others as gratuitously wonderful—much like God's *creatio ex nihilo* has struck many Westerners. We might say that, according to the Chinese concept, what is ex nihilo is not the created substance but rather the dynamic reversal (*fu* 復) of the transformative process—except that it doesn't come from nothing; it comes from the very nature of *qi*, which is inherently dynamic. The "incessance of the generation of *qi*" therefore lends to Zhu Xi's theory of mind and self-cultivation a sense of religious awe.

NOTE ON THE SEQUENCE OF HEXAGRAMS

The "received" sequence of hexagrams—the one in Wang Bi's edition of the *Yijing*, also called the King Wen sequence—is not random. It is composed of thirty-two pairs, following two rules. The general rule is that (a) each one of a pair is the *inverse* of the other (turned upside down)—for example, ☷ (3) and ☷ (4). However, for hexagrams that would be the same when inverted, the rule is that (b) *yin* lines become *yang* and vice versa—for example, ☰ (1) and ☷ (2). The hexagram pairs that follow (b) are 1/2, 27/28 (☷/☷), 29/30 (☷/☷), and 61/62 (☷/☷). Only some of the thirty-two pairs have complementary meanings as well as complementary structures; for example, 1/2 (Creating/Complying), 11/12 (Penetrating/Obstructing), 41/42 (Diminishing/Enhancing), 51/52 (Arousing/Stopping), 59/60

(Dispersing/Limiting), and 63/64 (Already Complete/Not Yet Complete). There is, however, no generally accepted principle or logic to the sequence of the hexagram pairs.[101]

CONVENTIONS

- In places where Zhu Xi stretches the evident meaning of the text to accommodate his system of thought, I have translated according to his interpretation and indicated the difference in my notes.
- At the beginning of each passage of commentary Zhu indicates the pronunciation of one or more potentially ambiguous characters in the text, and I follow his suggestions in my translation but do not translate those comments themselves.[102]
- There are roughly twenty to thirty lines of text for which Zhu Xi has no comment. Most of them are in the Commentary on the Smaller Images.
- I have tried wherever possible to avoid reification, especially in the hexagram names (e.g., Being Happy, not Happiness). This is consistent with the fact that Chinese thought is based more on process than on substance or essence.
- I do not translate the hexagram name in the hexagram statement, except in the four cases (hexagrams 10, 12, 13, 52) where it is best understood as part of a sentence.
- The numbers 6 and 9, representing *yin* and *yang* lines, respectively, are not spelled out because they are used in this context as symbols.
- I capitalize Heaven and Earth because they are the core meanings of the first two hexagrams, Qian and Kun.
- Unlike Cheng Yi, Zhu Xi does not comment on the *Xugua* appendix, so I have not translated it.

TECHNICAL TERMS

gang 剛: firm / *rou* 柔: yielding (antonyms)
guati 卦體: usually "component trigrams," but sometimes "hexagram structure"
ji 吉: auspicious, good fortune / *xiong* 凶: ominous, bad fortune (antonyms)

COMMON RELATED TERMS

di 帝: lord / *hou* 后: sovereign / *hou* 侯: marquis
fu 孚: honest / *xin* 信: trustworthy / *dun* 敦 : sincere / *cheng* 誠: authentic
hui 悔: regret / *lin* 吝: disgrace
jun 君: noble, ruler, master / *junzi* 君子: superior person / *xiaoren* 小人: petty/ inferior person
wen ming 文明: elegant and bright
zai 災 : disaster / *huan* 患: trouble / *sheng* 眚: calamity
zhan 占: prognostication / *zhanzhe* 占者: diviner

SOURCES FOR THE CONFUCIAN "FOUR BOOKS" AND DAOIST CLASSICS

Zhu Xi, *Sishu jizhu* 四書集注 (Collected comments on the Four Books)
Great Learning (*Daxue* 大學) and *Centrality and Commonality* (*Zhongyong* 中庸): Wing-tsit Chan, trans., *A Source Book in Chinese Philosophy*
Analects (*Lunyu* 論語): Annping Chin, *The Analects*
Mencius (*Mengzi* 孟子): D. C. Lau, *Mencius*
Laozi 老子: D. C. Lau, *Lao Tzu: Tao Te Ching*
Zhuangzi 莊子: Victor H. Mair, *Wandering on the Way*

Zhouyi benyi
周易本義

CHAPTER ONE

PART A: HEXAGRAMS 1–30

PRELIMINARIES[1]

As mentioned in the introduction, the *Zhouyi benyi*, completed in 1188, was Zhu Xi's second commentary on the *Yijing*. His first, in 1177, was simply called *Yizhuan* 易傳 (Commentary on the *Yi*). Until recently scholars have used that earlier date for the *Zhouyi benyi*, but Shu Jingnan has refuted that in his *Chronological Record of Zhu Xi* (2001), which should now be considered authoritative.[2] During the twenty-nine-month period between Zhu's completion of the *Yixue qimeng* 易學啟蒙 (Introduction to the study of the *Yi*, 1186) and the *Zhouyi benyi*, he also completed his commentaries on the major writings of Zhou Dunyi: the *Taijitu shuo* 太極圖說 (Discussion of the Supreme Polarity diagram) and the *Tongshu* 通書 (Penetrating the *Yi*).[3] It was in these commentaries that he developed his theory of the interpenetration of activity and stillness, which was the solution to the major "spiritual crisis" of his career and his reason for claiming that Zhou Dunyi was the first true Confucian Sage since Mencius. This concentrated period of work on Zhou Dunyi and the *Yijing* therefore witnessed the maturation of some of the fundamental elements of Zhu Xi's synthesis: *taiji* (Supreme Polarity, which he equated with *li* or principle); the theory and practice of "preserving the mind and nourishing the nature in order to serve Heaven" (*Mencius* 7A.1) by understanding one's own mind in both its active and still phases; and the "succession of the Way" (*daotong* 道統), his theory of the normative lineage of the Confucian Way that began with Fuxi's creation of the *Yi*.[4]

The preface included here, is, again according to Shu Jingnan, all that survives from Zhu Xi's first attempt at a commentary, the *Yizhuan*. It is found in the Imperial Academy edition of *Zhouyi benyi*, one of the two versions in the *Siku quanshu* collection, and many other editions. It is not included in the *Zhuzi quanshu* (2002) edition of *Zhouyi benyi*, nor in the *Zhouyi zhezhong* or *Master Zhu's Collected Papers* (*Zhuzi wenji*). The reason for this inconsistency is that in some sources it is attributed to Cheng Yi; for example, by Wang Tingzhen (fl. thirteenth century) in his *Guwen jicheng* 古文集成, and by the compiler of the *Collected Papers of the Two Chengs* (*Er Cheng wenji* 二程文集), where it is accompanied by another preface that actually was written by Cheng Yi.[5] Shu Jingnan refutes Cheng Yi's authorship and reproduces this preface from the *Xingli qunshu jujie* 性理群書句解 by Xiong Jie 熊節 (*jinshi* 1199), where it is identified as Zhu Xi's preface.[6] Since Xiong Jie was a student of Zhu Xi's and Wang Tingzhen was not; and since the *Er Cheng wenji* was not compiled by Tan Shanxin until the early 1320s, this is strong evidence that the preface is by Zhu Xi. Some editions, such as the *Yuanben Zhouyi benyi* (Original edition of the *Zhouyi benyi*) in the *Siku quanshu* collection, include a shorter preface by Wu Ge 吳革, dated 1265, in place of this one.

The Nine Diagrams appended to the beginning of the *Zhouyi benyi* have also occasioned some controversy, insofar as it is not certain when or by whom they were first included. Zhu Xi's Qing-dynasty chronicler, Wang Mouhong, said the diagrams were not added by Zhu Xi, but the editor of the version in *Zhuzi quanshu* (2002), Wang Tie 王鐵, says that they were.[7] Shu Jingnan (2001) does not address the question. Four of the nine diagrams are also found in Zhu's *Yixue qimeng*.[8] The short postscript after them definitely sounds like Zhu Xi, emphasizing the original intention of the *Yi* and the need to remain cognizant of the differences between the successive graphic and textual layers.[9] For that reason I am inclined to agree with Wang Tie that the diagrams and explanations are by Zhu Xi.

ZHU XI'S PREFACE TO THE *YIZHUAN* 易傳 (1177)

The *Yi* as a book provides the meanings of the hexagrams [*gua* 卦], lines [*yao* 爻], the judgments [*tuan* 彖], and the images [*xiang* 象], and displays the dispositions of the myriad things in Heaven and Earth.[10] The Sage's [Fuxi 伏羲] concern about later generations was extreme! Under [the category of] metaphysics [*xiantian* 先天] he "disclosed things"; under [the category of] existent things [*houtian* 後天] he "completed efforts."¹¹ For this reason he "maximized [*ji* 極] its numbers" in order to determine the images [*xiang* 象] of all under Heaven, and put forth the images in order to determine the auspicious and ominous [meanings] of all under Heaven.¹²

The sixty-four hexagrams and three hundred eight-four lines are the means by which to comply with the principle of human nature and the endowment [*ming* 命], and to complete the Way of fluctuation and transformation [*bianhua* 變化]. Dispersed among patterns, [the Way of transformation] is the myriad things. Unified as the Dao, it has no duality. Because "In Change there is Supreme Polarity, which generates the Two Modes,"¹³ the Supreme Polarity is the Dao, and the Two Modes are *yin* and *yang*. *Yin* and *yang* are the unitary Dao, and the Supreme Polarity is nonpolar.¹⁴ The generation of the myriad things "carries *yin* and embraces *yang*" [*Laozi* 42]. None lacks the Supreme Polarity, and none lacks the Two Modes. In their subtle and profound mutual stimulation, fluctuation and transformation are unlimited. Once forms receive life and once spirit expresses wisdom,¹⁵ the genuine and artificial appear therein, and the myriad beginnings arise. The *Yi* is how we determine what is auspicious and ominous [*ji xiong* 吉凶] and initiate the Great Undertaking.¹⁶ Therefore the *Yi* is the Way of *yin* and *yang*, the hexagrams are the embodiments of *yin* and *yang*, and the lines are the activity of *yin* and *yang*.

Although the hexagrams are not the same, what is common to them is their odd and even [numbers]. Although the lines are not the same, what is common to them is the 9 and 6 [by which they are derived]. In this way the sixty-four hexagrams are the substance [of the *Yi*] and the three hundred eight-four lines are its function. Externally in the world and internally within the body, as quick as the blink of an eye and as subtle as [the transition between] activity and stillness,¹⁷ everything contains the images of the hexagrams, everything contains the meanings of the lines. Perfect indeed is the *Yi*! Its Way is the greatest and most inclusive; its function is the most spiritual and immanent.

Moments [*shi* 時] certainly never have starting points, and hexagrams never have fixed images. Situations [*shi* 事] certainly are never exhausted, and lines also never have fixed positions. To use a single moment [*yishi* 一時] and connect it with a hexagram is to cling to the unchanging; it is not [the proper way to use] the *Yi*. To use a single situation [*yishi* 一事] to clarify a line is to be constrained and not penetrating [*tong* 通]; it is not the *Yi*.[18] To understand the meanings of the hexagrams, lines, judgments, and images and not to understand their function [i.e., divination] is also not the *Yi*. Therefore to get it through the movement of one's essential spirit [*jingshen* 精神] and the activity of the techniques of the mind [*xinshu* 心術], "to match one's virtue with that of Heaven and Earth, to match one's clarity with that of the sun and moon, to match one's orderliness with that of the four seasons, and to match one's good and bad fortune with that of ghosts and spirits"[19]—only then can we say that we understand the *Yi*.

However, since the *Yi* has hexagrams, the *Yi* is already formed; since the hexagrams have lines, the hexagrams are already visible. What is already formed and already visible we can understand with words, but what is not formed and not visible we cannot seek with names. So in the final analysis, what can compare with the *Yi*? This is what students must understand.[20]

THE NINE DIAGRAMS

[1] The River Chart [*Hetu*][21]

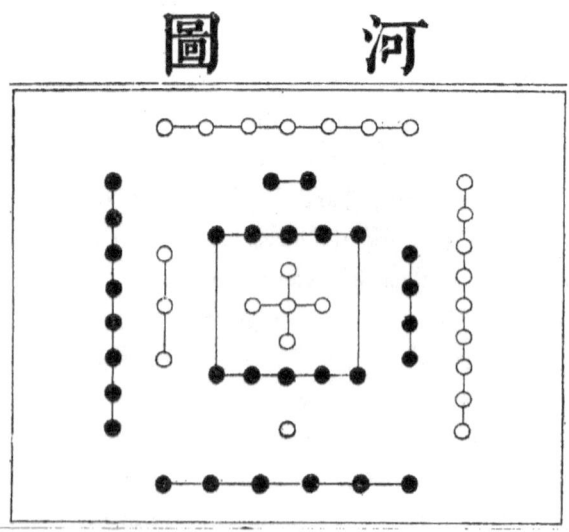

FIGURE 1.1

[2] The Luo Writing [Luoshu]

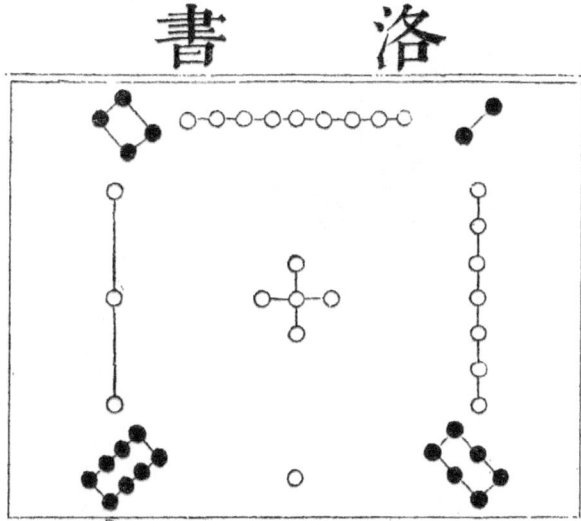

FIGURE 1.2

The "Treatise on the Appended Remarks" [*Xici* A.11.8] says, "The [Yellow] River gave forth the Chart, and the Luo [River] gave forth the Writing. The Sages [Fuxi and Yu the Great] took them as models."[22] It also says, "Heaven is 1, Earth is 2, Heaven is 3, Earth is 4, Heaven is 5, Earth is 6, Heaven is 7, Earth is 8, Heaven is 9, Earth is 10. There are five numbers of Heaven and five numbers of Earth. The five positions cooperate and each has its match. The numbers of Heaven are 25; the numbers of Earth are 30. Altogether the numbers of Heaven and Earth are 55. This is how they bring about fluctuation and transformation and activate the ghosts and spirits."[23] These are the numbers of the *Hetu*. The *Luoshu* is based on the image of the tortoise. Thus its numbers are 9 at the top and 1 at the bottom, 3 on the left and 7 on the right, 2 and 4 are the plastron, 6 and 8 are the feet.[24]

Cai Yuanding says, Kong Anguo and Liu Xin in the Han, Guan Lang (Ziming) in the Wei, and Shao Yong (Kangjie, Yaofu) in the Song all described the *Hetu* and *Luoshu* in this way. Liu Mu was the first to change [reverse] their names, and later scholars followed him. Thus I now follow the old and restore [the original names].[25]

[3] Fuxi's Sequence of the Eight Trigrams[26]

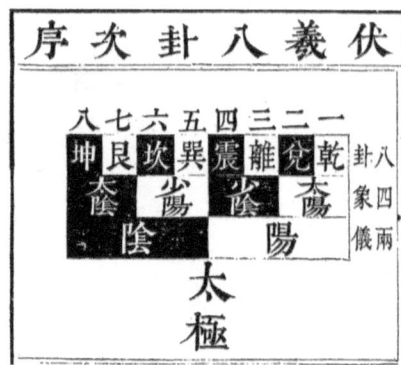

FIGURE 1.3

The "Treatise on the Appended Remarks" [*Xici* A.11.5] says, "In Change there is the Supreme Polarity, which generates the Two Modes. The Two Modes generate the Four Images, and the Four Images generate the Eight Trigrams." Master Shao said, "One divides into two, two divides into four, and four divides into eight."[27] The "Treatise Discussing the Trigrams" [*Shuogua* 3.2] says, "The *Changes* calculates in reverse." Master Shao said, "Qian is 1, Dui is 2, Li is 3, Zhen is 4, Sun is 5, Kan is 6, Gen is 7, and Kun is 8."[28] From Qian to Kun, in each case [progressing from 1 to 8] yields a not-yet-generated trigram, so it is like going through the four seasons in reverse order. "[Fuxi's] Sequence of the Sixty-Four Hexagrams" [Diagram 5] below expands on this.[29]

[4] Fuxi's Directional Positioning of the Eight Trigrams[30]

FIGURE 1.4

The "Treatise Discussing the Trigrams" [*Shuogua* 3] says, "Heaven and Earth determine the positions. Mountain and Lake interpenetrate their *qi* 氣. Thunder and Wind arouse each other. Water and Fire do not combat each other. [Thus] the Eight Trigrams intermingle. Calculating the past accords [with the movement of Heaven]. Knowing the future reverses [the movement of Heaven]." Master Shao said, "Qian is south and Kun is north, Li is east and Kan is west, Zhen is northwest and Dui is northeast, Sun is southwest and Gen is northwest. From Zhen to Qian accords with [Heaven]; from Sun to Kun reverses [Heaven]."[31] [Fuxi's] Directional Positioning of the Sixty-Four Hexagrams [Diagram 6] below expands on this.

[5] Fuxi's Sequence of the Sixty-Four Hexagrams

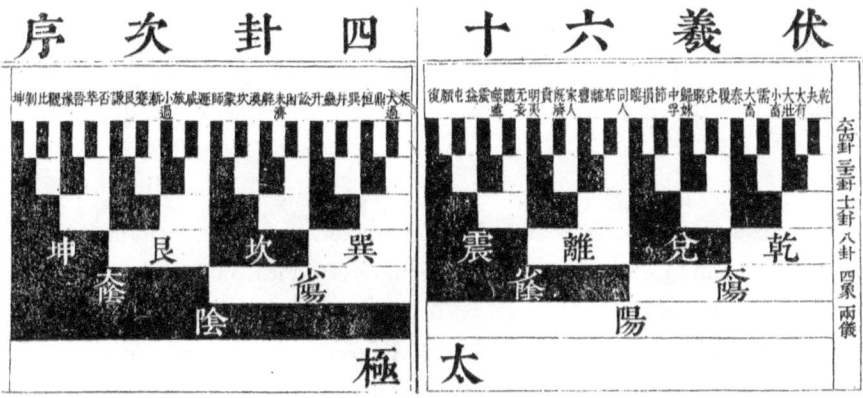

FIGURE 1.5

The [Fuxi] Sequence of the Eight Trigrams [Diagram 3] above is exactly what the *Xici zhuan* means by "the Eight Trigrams achieve their arrangement" [B.1.1]. This diagram is exactly what it means by "when they are doubled" [B.1.1]. Thus the lower three lines are the eight trigrams of the former diagram and the upper three lines are added in sequence to them, and so the lower eight trigrams are each expanded into eight. If we generate the lines one by one, which Master Shao described as 8 dividing into 16, 16 dividing into 32, and 32 dividing into 64, we will even more clearly see the natural wonder of the patterns and images.

[6] Fuxi's Directional Positioning of the Sixty-Four Hexagrams[32]

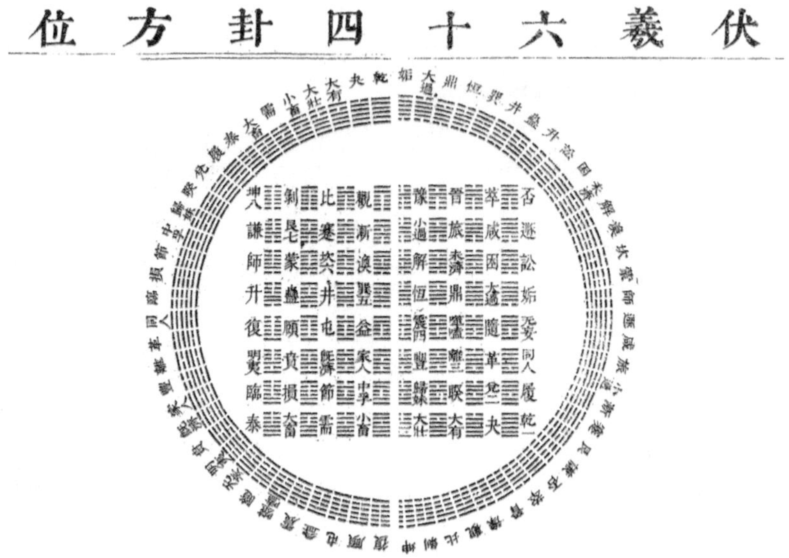

伏羲六十四卦方位

FIGURE 1.6

The explanations of Fuxi's fourth diagram all come from Mr. Shao [Yong], who received it from Li Zhicai (Tingzhi). Tingzhi received it from Mu Xiu (Bochang), who received it from Chen Tuan (Xiyi, Tunan) of Mount Hua.[33] It is what is called a priori ["before Heaven"] learning. In this diagram's circular arrangement, Qian is the peak of summer [*wu* 午, south], Kun is the peak of winter [*zi* 子, north], Li is the peak of spring [*mao* 卯, east], Kan is the peak of autumn [*you* 酉, west].[34] *Yang* is born in the north/winter and peaks [*ji* 極] in the south/summer; *yin* is born in the south/summer and peaks in the north/winter. *Yang* is located in the south; *yin* is located in the north. In the [inner] square arrangement, Qian begins it in the northwest [lower right] and Kun ends it in the southeast [upper left].[35] Here *yang* is in the north and *yin* is in the south. These two [arrangements] deal with the numbers of *yin* and *yang*. The circular one on the outside is *yang*, and the square one inside is *yin*; the activity of the circular one is Heaven and the stillness of the square one is Earth.

PART A: HEXAGRAMS 1-30   49

[7] King Wen's Sequence of the Eight Trigrams

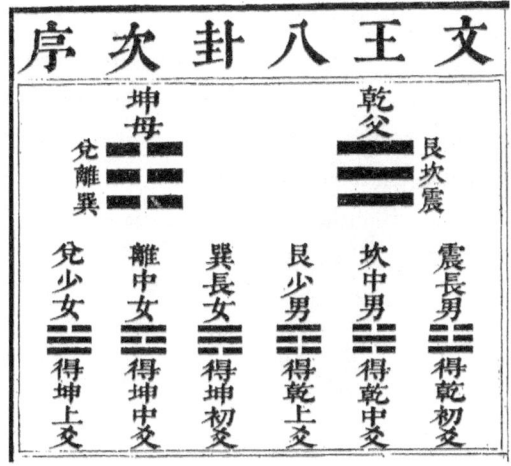

FIGURE 1.7

[8] King Wen's Directional Positioning of the Eight Trigrams[36]

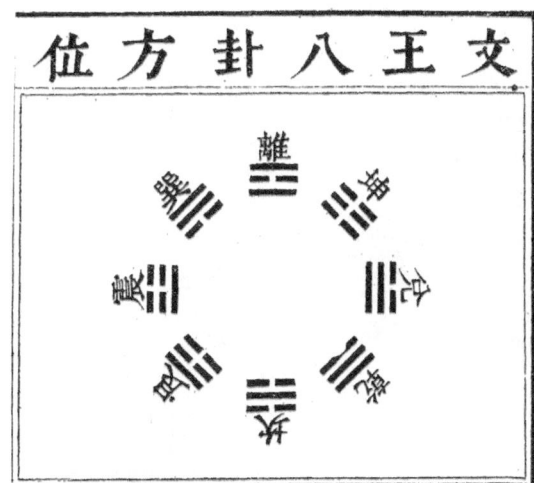

FIGURE 1.8

These [7 and 8] illustrate the *Shuogua*. Master Shao said, "These are King Wen's Eight Trigrams, in positions corresponding to human functioning; this is a posteriori [or "after Heaven"] learning."[37]

[9] Diagrams of Hexagram Fluctuation
(Guabian tu 卦變圖)[38]

The *Tuanzhuan* [Commentary on the Judgments] sometimes uses hexagram fluctuation in its discussion,[39] so here I include this diagram for clarification. However, in terms of the main idea of the *Yi*, it is not [Fuxi's] original intent in creating the *Yi* by drawing the hexagrams.[40] The hexagrams with either one *yang* or one *yin* line are six each, starting from Fu 復 and Gou 姤.

FIGURE 1.9A

The hexagrams with either two *yin* or two *yang* are fifteen each, starting from Lin 臨 and Dun 遯.

FIGURE 1.9B

The hexagrams with either three *yin* or three *yang* are twenty each, starting from Tai 泰 and Pi 否.

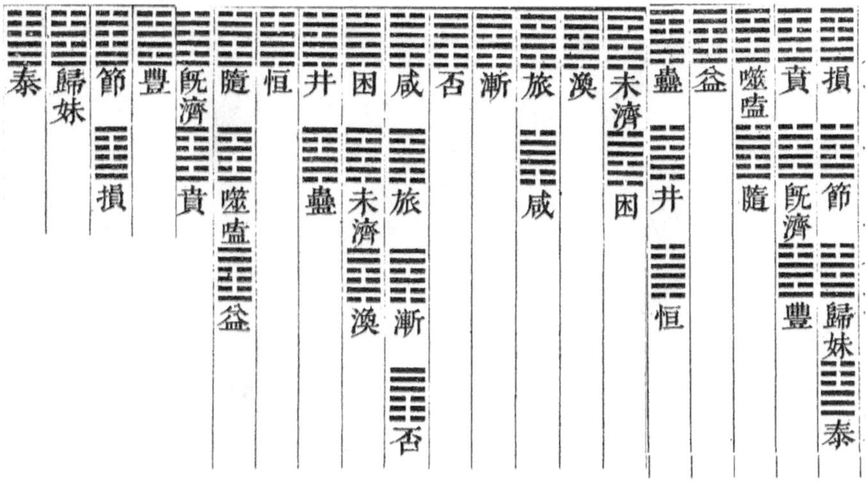

FIGURE 1.9C

The hexagrams with either four *yin* or four *yang* are fifteen each, starting from Dazhuang 大壯 and Guan 觀.

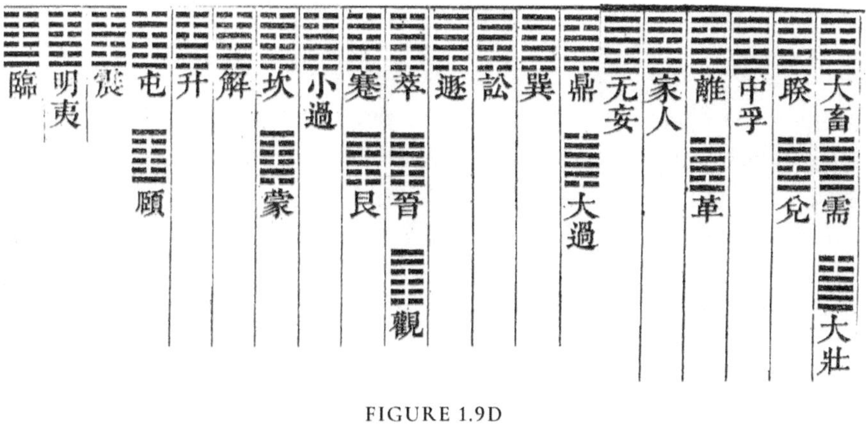

FIGURE 1.9D

The hexagrams with either five *yin* or five *yang* are six each, starting from Guai 夬 and Bo 剝.

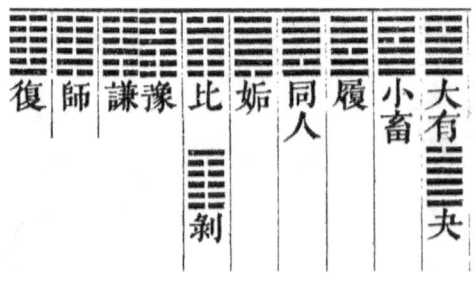

FIGURE 1.9E

These are the Nine Diagrams of the *Yi*, containing the natural *Yi* of Heaven and Earth, the *Yi* of Fuxi, the *Yi* of the Duke of Zhou, and the *Yi* of Confucius. Before Fuxi there were no texts, only diagrams and lines. With appropriately profound contemplation we can see their original subtle intention. Starting from King Wen there were texts, and this is what is today's *Zhouyi*. But readers should be informed about the text [they are reading], and not take Confucius's discussion as King Wen's discussion.[41]

PART A

Zhou is the dynasty name; *Yi* is the name of the book. Its hexagrams were originally drawn by Fuxi; they change by interacting and change by fluctuating [*jiaoyi bianyi* 交易變易], which is why it is called the *Changes*. Its texts were appended by King Wen and the Duke of Zhou, which is why we attach the name Zhou to it. Since it would be quite large if bound together, it is divided into two parts, A and B. The scripture [*jing* 經] is what was drawn by Fuxi plus the texts of King Wen and the Duke of Zhou. With the ten commentaries [*zhuan* 傳] composed by Master Kong, altogether there are twelve sections. Its contents are rather confusing to most scholars [*ru* 儒]. Mr. Chao [Yuezhi] recently began to correct its deficiencies, but was unable to completely match the old text.[42] Mr. Lü [Zuqian 呂祖謙, 1137–1181] made further corrections and published the Scripture in two chapters [*juan* 卷] with the commentaries [separately] in ten chapters, thereby returning to the old [text] of the Kong [Confucius's] clan.[43]

[1] ䷀ 乾   Qian (Creating)[44]

Qian [heaven] below, Qian [heaven] above.[45]

Qian: Supreme and penetrating, appropriate and correct [*yuan heng li zhen* 元亨利貞].[46]

    The six strokes are the hexagram drawn by Fuxi.[47] The solid lines are odd, a *yang* number. Qian means creating [*jian* 建], the nature of *yang*.[48] The word Qian in the textual comment ["Qian below, Qian above"] refers to the trigrams. The lower one is the "inner" trigram and the upper one is the "outer." The word Qian in the scripture itself [in bold in the preceding] refers to the hexagram.

    When Fuxi "looked up to contemplate" and "looked down to examine" [*Xici* B.2.1] he saw that *yin* and *yang* had odd and even numbers, so he drew a single line to symbolize [*xiang* 象] *yang* and drew a double [broken] line to symbolize *yin*. He saw that each *yin* and *yang* [line] generated the images of another *yin* and *yang*, so from bottom to top he drew a second and a third, making the Eight Trigrams. He saw that the nature of *yang* is being strong [*jian* 健], and that the greatest thing that gives form is Heaven, so he called the trigram Qian to suggest Heaven. Once the three lines were done and the Eight Trigrams thus completed, he repeated the three lines to make six, adding eight trigrams to each of the Eight Trigrams to complete the sixty-four hexagrams.

    This hexagram's six lines are all odd, with both upper and lower trigrams being Qian, so it is the purest *yang* and the most creative. Thus Qian's name and Heaven's image are both unchanging. *Yuan heng li zhen* is the remark appended by King Wen to judge [*duan* 斷] whether the hexagram is auspiciousness or ominous. This is why it is called the *tuan* 彖 statement [judgment].[49] *Yuan* [here] means "great" [*da* 大]; *heng* means "penetrating" [*tong* 通]; *li* means "appropriate" [*yi* 宜]; *zhen* means "correct" [*zheng* 正].[50] King Wen considered the Way of Qian to be greatly penetrating and perfectly correct. Thus in divination if one gets this hexagram with all six lines unchanging, we say that the prognostication [*zhan* 占] will be greatly penetrating, and it will surely be appropriate to be solidly correct; only then can [the course of action being considered] be maintained to its end. This is why the Sages created the *Yi*: their essential idea was to teach people to divine so that they can "reveal things and complete affairs."[51] The rest of the hexagrams are also like this.[52]

LINE STATEMENTS (YAOCI 爻辭)[53]

[Line 1] 9 at the beginning: Hidden dragon. Do not use.[54]

"9 at the beginning" is the term for the *yang* line at the bottom of the hexagram. When hexagrams are drawn they go from bottom to top, so the bottom line is the first. Of the *yang* numbers [obtained through the divination procedure], 9 is the mature [*lao* 老] and 7 is the young [*shao* 少]; the mature fluctuates [into *yin*] and the young does not fluctuate. Thus we refer to the *yang* line as 9.[55]

"Hidden dragon; do not use" is the statement added by the Duke of Zhou to judge the auspicious or ominous [character] of each line, so we call it the line statement [*yaoci* 爻辭]. "Hidden" means stored away, and the dragon is a *yang* creature. The first *yang* line at the bottom cannot yet be put to use, so its image is a hidden dragon, and the prognostication is "do not use." Whenever this hexagram is encountered [in divination] and this line is changing, we should contemplate this image and appreciate this prognostication; the same for the rest of the lines.

[Line 2] 9 in the second: A dragon appearing in the field. Appropriate to see the great person.

"Second" means the second line from the bottom; similarly for the other lines. The 9 in the second place is firm and creative, central and correct.[56] It is emerging from hiding and separating from the darkness. Its glow now reaches the creature, the creature that it is advantageous to see.[57] Therefore the image is "a dragon appearing in the field," and the prognostication is "appropriate to see the great person." Although 9 in the second place is not in its proper position, nevertheless it displays the virtue of the great person, and the ordinary person is not sufficient to match it. Therefore if one comes upon this line and it is changing [i.e., 9], it only means that it is appropriate to see this person, but it can also mean the great person [in the text] below [9 in the fifth]. This means that the line and the diviner are related as host and guest. Manifesting the virtue of a dragon would be the case of the "great person" whom it is "appropriate to see" in 9 in the fifth place.[58]

[Line 3] 9 in the third: The superior person is creative all day; at night he is alert. Precarious; no blame.

9 is a *yang* line and the third is a *yang* position. This doubly firm line is not central, residing at the top of the lower trigram, a precarious position. But its nature and substance are firm and strong, so its image is being able to be constantly creative and alert in danger; hence the prognostication. "Superior person" refers to the prognosticator, one who is capable of fearful concern, so although his position is precarious there is no blame.

[Line 4] 9 in the fourth: Hesitantly leaping in the deep. No blame.

"Hesitantly" is a term for doubt and uncertainty. "Leaping" is having no connection to the earth but not really flying. "The deep" is empty above and cavelike below: a deep, dark, unfathomable place. When a dragon is there it is like being down in the field, "hesitantly leaping" up, facing toward Heaven. 9 is *yang* and 4 is *yin*. It is located at the bottom of the upper [trigram], at the boundary of a shift, a moment of uncertainty as to advance or retreat; hence this image [of hesitancy]. The prognostication is that if one is able to advance or retreat at the appropriate time, there will be no blame.

[Line 5] 9 in the fifth: Flying dragon in heaven. Appropriate to see the great person.

Firm and creative, central and correct, [this line] resides in the position of honor, like the Sage's virtue residing in the Sage's position; hence this image. The prognostication is the same as that for 9 in the second place. What is especially appropriate to see is the great person above. Depending on one's position it is [also] appropriate to see the great person below in the second.

[Line 6] 9 at the top: A dragon going too far. There will be regret.[59]

"At the top" is the uppermost line. "Going too far" is the idea of rising up and being unable to come down. At the peak of *yang* above, activity must lead to regret; hence the image and the prognostication.

[Additional line][60] Using [all] 9s: Seeing a flock of dragons without heads. Auspicious.

"Using 9s" means the divination results in all *yang* lines, every one using 9, not 7. Among all the hexagrams there are 192 *yang* lines. This hexagram is pure *yang* and comes first, so it appears like this. The Sage [King Wen] accordingly appended this statement, so when one gets this hexagram and all six lines are changing, this is the prognostication. When all six *yang* lines change the firm can yield, and this is an auspicious Way. Thus the image is "a flock of dragons without heads" and the corresponding prognostication is "auspicious." The [Zuo] *Commentary* on the *Spring and Autumn Annals* says, in reference to Qian becoming Kun, "Seeing a flock of dragons without heads; auspicious."[61] It is the idea of the pure [yin] Kun hexagram statement, "The correctness of the mare . . . first lost and then found . . . losing friends in the north and east."[62]

COMMENTARY ON THE JUDGMENT
(*TUANZHUAN* 彖傳)

"Judgment" [*tuan* 彖] means the statement added by King Wen [i.e., the hexagram statement]; "commentary" [*zhuan* 傳] means the statements with which Confucius explains the scripture [*jing* 經]. Likewise all subsequent references to "commentary."[63]

Great indeed is the originating [yuan 元] [power] of Qian! The myriad things are given their beginnings by it, and so it controls [tong 統] Heaven.[64]

This focuses on the Way of Heaven to clarify the meaning of Qian. It also separates *yuan heng li zhen* into the Four Virtues to bring them to light.[65] This section begins by explaining the meaning of *yuan*. "Great indeed" is a term of admiration. "Originating" means great and beginning. The originating [power] of Qian is the great beginning of Heavenly virtue. Therefore the lives of the myriad things all depend on it for their beginnings. As the head of the Four Virtues it connects the beginnings and ends of Heavenly virtue, and so it is said to "control Heaven."

Clouds move and rain falls, and the various kinds of things assume their forms.

This explains the penetrating power [*heng*] of Qian.

Greatly clarifying the ends and beginnings, and bringing about the six [line] positions according to their times, [the Sage] mounted the six dragons and steered through Heaven according to the times.

"Beginning" means origination [*yuan*]. "End" means correctness [*zhen*]. Without an end there is no beginning, and without correctness there is no origination. This refers to the Sage's great clarification of the ends and beginnings of the Way of Qian. It reveals how the hexagram's six positions were each completed in due time, and how, by mounting [riding] these six *yang* [lines] to enact the Way of Heaven, the Sage [Fuxi] was "supreme and penetrating" [*yuan heng*].⁶⁶

The Way of Qian fluctuates and transforms, and each [thing] is correct in its nature and endowment.⁶⁷ It preserves accord with the Great Harmony; it is appropriate and correct.

"To fluctuate" [*bian* 變] is a step of transformation; "to transform" [*hua* 化] is the completion of a fluctuation. What things receive is their "nature" [*xing* 性]; what Heaven confers is their "endowment" [*ming* 命]. The "Great Harmony" is *qi* when mixed together harmoniously.⁶⁸ "Each [thing] is correct" means what they get at the very beginning of life [i.e., their nature and endowment]. "Preserving accord" is completing what follows after birth. This refers to the fluctuation and transformation of the Way of Qian, with nothing that is not appropriate, and the myriad things each getting their nature and endowment to complete themselves. This explains the meaning of "appropriate and correct."

With [the Sage's] head emerging from the multitude, all nations are at peace.

The Sage being above, emerging above all things, is like the fluctuation and transformation [wrought by] the Way of Qian. All nations achieving their place and "being at peace" is like the myriad things each being "correct in its nature and endowment" and "preserving accord with the great harmony." This refers to the Sage being "appropriate and correct."

Now let us discuss "control" [*tong* 統] [in "it controls Heaven"].⁶⁹ "Originating" [*yuan* 元] is the coming to life of things; "penetrating" [*heng* 亨] is the flourishing [*changmao* 暢茂] of things. Being appropriate it tends toward actuality [*shi* 實]; being correct its actuality is realized. Once actuality is realized, then roots and stems are free to return to seed and generate again. This is how the Four Virtues circulate [regenerate] endlessly. However, among the Four, the vital *qi* flowing out without interruption is how origination [*yuan*] encompasses the Four Virtues and "controls Heaven."

The statements about the Sage are Master Kong's idea; he considered this hexagram as the Sage having a position in Heaven and putting into effect the Way of Heaven, leading to the prognostication of great peace [*taiping* 太平]. Although his [Master Kong's] interpretation is not the original one of King Wen [in the hexagram statement], readers should each use their own intentions and act without contradiction. The Kun hexagram is also like this.⁷⁰

COMMENTARY ON THE GREATER IMAGES
(*DAXIANG ZHUAN* 大象傳)

"The images" are the two images of the upper and lower trigrams and their six lines, to which the Duke of Zhou appended [line] statements.[71]

The text beginning with "Heaven's movement" is what former scholars called the "Larger Image" [commenting on the two trigrams]. The text beginning with "hidden dragon" is what former scholars called the "Smaller Images" [commenting on the individual lines]. The same for the rest [of the hexagrams].[72]

Heaven's movement is strong; the superior person strengthens himself unceasingly.

"Heaven" is the image of the Qian hexagram. In general, [hexagrams that are] doubled trigrams have doubled meanings.[73] This alone is not so, as Heaven is simply unitary. But when speaking of Heaven's movement we see it revolve once a day and again the next day, like the image of repeated return. If it were not so strong it would be incapable of this. The superior person models himself on this, without human desires injuring the firmness of his Heavenly virtue. Thus he can strengthen himself unceasingly.

COMMENTARY ON THE SMALLER IMAGES
(*XIAOXIANG ZHUAN* 小象傳)

[Image 1] "Hidden dragon; do not use" is the *yang* below.
"Yang" means 9. "Below" means hidden.

[Image 2] "A dragon appearing in the field" is virtue spreading widely.

[Image 3] "Being creative all day" is turning back to the Way.
"Turning back" is the idea of carrying out activity repeatedly.

[Image 4] "Hesitantly leaping in the deep" is advancing without blame.
One can advance when it is not necessary to advance.

[Image 5] "Flying dragon in Heaven" is the great person creating.
"Creating" [zao 造] is like "making" [zuo 作].

[Image 6] "A dragon going too far; there will be regret" means flourishing but unable to be long-lasting.

[Additional Image] "Using [all] 9s" means Heaven's virtue cannot be at the head.
This says that the firm *yang* cannot be first among things, so when all six lines fluctuate it is auspicious.[74]

COMMENTARY ON THE WORDS OF THE TEXT (*WENYAN ZHUAN* 文言傳)[75]

This section [i.e., the *Wenyan*] illustrates the meanings of the Judgment [*Tuan*] and Image [*Xiang*] commentaries by fully [explaining] what is inherent in the Qian and Kun hexagrams. The discussions of the rest of the hexagrams can accordingly be implied.[76]

[Source 1A]

[1] "Originating" is the growth of goodness.

"Penetrating" is the gathering of excellence.
"Being appropriate" is the harmonizing of rightness.
"Being correct" is the trunk of affairs.[77]
"Originating" [yuan 元] is the beginning of living things,
    the virtue of Heaven and Earth;
    nothing is prior to this.
        Therefore in regard to seasons it is spring,
        in regard to people it is humanity [ren 仁];
        it is the chief of all things good.
    "Penetrating" [heng 亨] is the penetrating power of living things;
    the perfection of things lies in this,
    and everything is excellent and beautiful.

> Therefore in regard to seasons it is summer,
> in regard to people it is ritual propriety [*li* 禮];
> it gathers all things beautiful.
>
> "Being appropriate" [*li* 利] is the success of living things,
> each thing achieving its proper [place]
> without mutual harm.
>
> Therefore in regard to seasons it is autumn,
> in regard to people it is rightness [*yi* 義],
> the harmony of achieving one's allotted [portion].
>
> "Being correct" [*zhen* 貞] is the achievement of living things,
> embodying actualized principle,
> each step appropriate.
>
> Therefore in regard to seasons it is winter,
> in regard to people it is wisdom [*zhi* 智];
> the trunk of all affairs.[78]

[2] **The superior person embodies humanity [*ren* 仁] enough to lead others; he gathers excellence enough to accord with ritual propriety [*li* 禮]; he benefits things enough to harmonize with rightness [*yi* 義]; his correctness is strong enough to support affairs.**

With humanity as his substance, not a single thing is off the mark of what is loved; thus he is sufficient to lead others. Excellence is what he gathers, so nothing [he does] is not in accord with ritual propriety. The things he manages all get what is appropriate [to them], so their rightness is all harmonious. The strength of his correctness [*zhen* 貞] is such that he understands where correctness [*zheng* 正] lies and strongly preserves it.[79]

[3] **The superior person is one who puts into effect these Four Virtues. Therefore [the hexagram statement] says, "Qian: Supreme and penetrating, appropriate and correct."**

If not for the superior person's utmost strength, nothing would be carried out like this. Therefore it says, "Qian: Supreme and penetrating, appropriate and correct."

This first section [above] extends the meaning of the Judgment commentary. It differs [slightly] from the statement by Mu Jiang in the *Zuozhuan*. I suspect that in antiquity this dialogue spoken by Mu Jiang already existed, and Confucius [allegedly writing the *Wenyan*] quoted it. Thus the text below says, "the Master said," indicating that it was Confucius's own statement. Those who passed [this text] down used the old quote in a desire to clarify the section.

[*Source 1B*]

[4] 9 at the beginning says, "Hidden [*qian* 潛] dragon; do not use." What does this mean? The Master [Confucius] said, "It refers to one who has a dragon's virtue yet remains hidden [*yin* 隱]; he does not change for the world, does not accomplish for fame; he conceals himself from the world without being depressed; he is not recognized yet is not depressed. When pleasure arises he experiences it; when worry arises he ignores it. Surely he cannot be uprooted; he is a hidden dragon."

The "dragon's virtue" is the Sage's virtue; from below it appears hidden. "Change" means changing what he preserves [*shou* 守].[80] Basically the *Wenyan* clarifies the six lines of Qian in terms of the Sage; whether hidden or manifest he is neither shallow nor deep.

[5] 9 in the second says, "A dragon appearing in the field; appropriate to see the great person." What does this mean? The Master said, "It means one who has the virtue of a dragon and is correct and central. His ordinary speech is honest; his ordinary behavior is cautious. He defends against corruption and maintains his authenticity; he betters the world and does not attack it; his virtue is broad and transformative. Where the *Yi* says, 'A dragon appearing in the field; appropriate to see the great person,' it is referring to the virtue of the noble [person]."

"Being correct and central" refers to times when [the Sage] is not hidden but not yet fully active. Even his everyday speech is honest and his everyday behavior is cautious. This is "the perfection of flourishing virtue."[81] "He defends against corruption and maintains his authenticity" and never wearies of protecting it. This refers to the virtue of the noble [person] and explains how the "great person" is 9 in the second place.

[6] 9 in the third says, "The superior person is creative all day; at night he is alert. Precarious; no blame." What does this mean? The Master said, "The

superior person advances in virtue while carrying on his undertakings. Being loyal and honest is how he advances in virtue. Cultivating speech and establishing his authenticity are how he abides in his undertakings. Understanding goals and achieving them is how he can participate in the incipiency [of the moment].[82] Understanding [proper] ends and ending there is how he preserves rightness. For this reason when occupying a high position he is not arrogant; when in low position he is not worried. Thus he is cautious while always being creative and alertly in tune with the season. Although this is precarious, there is no blame."

"Being loyal and honest" refers to one who emphasizes his mind without a single inauthentic [*bucheng* 不誠] thought.[83] "Cultivating speech" refers to one who sees into matters without a single untrue word. Even if one has a loyal and honest heart-mind, if one does not "cultivate speech and establish one's authenticity," then there is no way to abide in [one's work].[84] "Understanding goals and achieving them" is the act of "advancing in virtue." "Understanding ends and ending there" is the act of "abiding in one's work." This is the reason he is creative all day and alert at night. Whether in high or low position, he is neither arrogant nor worried. This is what "no blame" means.

[7] 9 in the fourth says, "Hesitantly leaping in the deep. No blame." What does this mean? The Master said, "Although there is no consistency in its rising and falling, it is not corrupt. Although there is no constancy in advancing and retreating, it is not leaving one's group. The superior person advances in virtue and cultivates his undertakings, desiring to be ready for the times. Therefore there is no blame."

The inner [lower] trigram refers to moral learning; the outer [upper] trigram refers to timely position [in society]. Advancing in [inner] virtue and cultivating [outer] achievements, 9 in the third is prepared. This [line], then, is "desiring to be ready for the times" and advancing [when appropriate].[85]

[8] 9 in the fifth says, "Flying dragon in Heaven. It is appropriate to see the great person." What does this mean? The Master said, "Similar sounds respond to each other; [things of] similar *qi* seek each other. Water flows to moistness; fire goes to dryness; clouds follow dragons; wind follows tigers; the Sage creates and the myriad creatures observe. What is based in Heaven looks up; what is based in earth looks down, each following its kind."

[The Sage] "creates" means he initiates. "Creatures" are like humans. "Observe [the Sage]" explains the idea, "it is appropriate to see [the great person]." "What is based in Heaven" means animals; "what is based in earth" means plants. Things each follow their kind. The Sage is the head of humankind. Therefore he initiates above and all people observe him.[86]

[9] 9 at the top says, "A dragon going too far; there will be regret." What does this mean? The Master said, "Honored yet without position, high yet without a populace, having worthies in subordinate positions but no assistance; for this reason action will bring regret."[87]

"Having worthies in subordinate positions" means 9 in the fifth below. "No assistance" means the upper 9 has passed to the top and fulfilled its will, but there is no help forthcoming.

This second section illustrates the ideas of the *Xiang* commentary.

[Source 2]

[10] [9 at the beginning:] "Hidden dragon; do not use" is the lower [trigram].

[9 in the second:] " A dragon appearing in the field" means to abandon at the proper time.
  This refers to not yet being the right time to be useful.

[11] [9 in the third:] "Being creative all day" is carrying out affairs.

[9 in the fourth:] "Hesitantly leaping in the deep" is testing oneself.
  Not in a hurry to act, but for the time being checking whether one should.

[12] [9 in the fifth:] "Flying dragon in Heaven" is ascending to govern.
  Residing above so as to govern those below.

[13] [9 at the top:] "A dragon going too far; there will be regret" means that going to the end will result in disaster.

[Additional line:] "The originating [power] of Qian," "using [all] 9s," is the governing of all under Heaven.

The statement "the originating [power] of Qian using 9s" appears different from the rest of the hexagram. The Way of the noble is firm, yet is able to be yielding, and so all under Heaven are governed.

This third section [above] again illustrates previous ideas.

[Source 3]

[14] [9 at the beginning:] "Hidden dragon; do not use" is the hidden store of *yang qi*. [9 in the second:] " A dragon appearing in the field" means all under Heaven is elegant and bright [*wenming* 文明].[88]

Although [9 in the second is] not in the top position, all under Heaven are transformed by it.

[15] [9 in the third:] "Being creative all day" means acting together in a timely way.
"Timely way" is what ought to be.[89]

[16] [9 in the fourth:] "Hesitantly leaping in the deep" means the Way of Qian is overturning.

Moving away from the lower and rising at the time for radical change [*biange* 變革].

[17] [9 in the fifth:] "Flying dragon in Heaven" means taking a position in Heavenly virtue.

"Heavenly virtue" is the position of Heaven. Only with such virtue can one suitably occupy this position; hence its name.

[18] [9 at the top:] "A dragon going too far; there will be regret" is diametrically opposed to the times.

"The originating [power] of Qian," "using [all] 9s," displays Heaven's rules.
Being firm and yet able to yield is Heaven's governance.
This fourth section also illustrates previous ideas.

[Source 4A]

[19] "The originating [power] of Qian" is what begins and penetrates.
Having begun, it must penetrate. This is the power of order/principle.

[20] "Appropriate and correct" is the nature and dispositions.

Gathering and returning to the storehouse shows the reality of the nature and dispositions.

[21] Qian's beginning is able to use the appropriateness of beauty to benefit all under Heaven. Without speaking of what is beneficial, it is indeed great.

The "beginning" is origination and penetration [*yuan heng*]. What "benefits all under Heaven" is being appropriate [*li*]. "Without speaking of what is beneficial" is being correct. Some say that this "appropriateness" refers to the appropriateness of a mare in Kun [hexagram 2].

[22] Great indeed is Qian! It is firm and strong, central and correct, pure and unadulterated essence [*jing* 精].

"Firm" is in terms of substance; "strong" is in terms of function. "Central" is going neither too far nor not far enough. "Correct" is standing impartially. These four are virtues of Qian.[90] "Pure" means unmixed with any yielding *yin*; "unadulterated" means unmixed with any corruption or evil. This is the essence of the utmost extreme of the firm and strong, central and correct; the utmost extreme of purity. Some question whether the firmness of Qian has no yielding [or *yin*], but if that were the case we could not call it central and correct, so it is not so. Between Heaven and Earth there is fundamentally just the flowing out of the unitary *qi*, which has activity and stillness. In terms of the controlling substance of this outflow we can only call it Qian, which embraces everything. Only by distinguishing its activity and stillness can we differentiate between *yin* and *yang*, firm and yielding.

[23] As the six lines develop and expand, they penetrate dispositions to all sides.[91]

"Penetrate to all sides" is like getting to the end in a roundabout way.

[24] Mounting six dragons in season, riding to Heaven. "Clouds move and rain falls,"[92] and all under Heaven are at peace.

This refers to the Sage "mounting six dragons in season and riding to Heaven," which is like Heaven causing the "clouds to move, the rain to fall, and all under Heaven being at peace."

This fifth section again illustrates the ideas of the head verse [the hexagram statement].

[Source 4B]

[25] [9 at the beginning:] The superior person acts on the basis of achieved virtue, and his actions can be seen daily. The word "hidden," meaning not yet visible, refers to acting when [virtue is] not yet achieved. In this case the superior person should not act.

"Achieved virtue" is virtue already achieved. The first 9 has definitely achieved virtue, but its action cannot yet be seen.

[26] [9 in the second:] The superior person learns in order to accumulate it [virtue], questions in order to analyze it; he is lenient in order to abide in it, and humane in order to practice it. The *Yi* says, "A dragon appearing in the field; appropriate to see the great person." This is the superior [person's] virtue.

Follow these four to achieve the virtue of the great person. Repeating the term "superior [person's] virtue," this profoundly clarifies the "great person" of 9 in the second place.

[27] 9 in the third is doubly firm but not central; neither in Heaven above nor in the field below. Therefore be creative in a timely manner but alert. Although precarious, there is no blame.

"Doubly firm" means a *yang* line in a *yang* position.

[28] 9 in the fourth is doubly firm but not central; neither in Heaven above nor in the field below nor in the central human [realm]. Therefore it hesitates. Hesitation is questioning, so there is no blame.

9 in the fourth is *not* doubly firm, so I suspect that the word "doubly" is superfluous. "In the human" means the third place. "Hesitation" means according with the season but not yet certain.[93]

[29] [9 in the fifth:] The great person's virtue matches that of Heaven and Earth; his clarity/brightness [*ming* 明] matches that of the sun and moon; his sense of sequence matches that of the four seasons; his sensitivity to the auspicious and ominous matches that of ghosts and spirits. When he precedes Heaven, Heaven does not oppose him; when he follows Heaven he respects Heaven's timing.[94] As Heaven does not oppose him, how can humans? How can ghosts and spirits?

"The great person" is the great person whom the line statement explains it is appropriate to see. Having these virtues and properly holding his position, one may emulate him. Humans, Heaven and Earth, and ghosts and spirits have fundamentally the same order/principle [*li* 理], which is merely concealed by the selfishness of the individual. For this reason it is trapped in the physical body and cannot interpenetrate [*xiangtong* 相通].⁹⁵ [But] the great person lacks selfishness; he takes the Way as his substance. So how can we speak of him in terms of this and that, or preceding and following? "Preceding Heaven but not opposed" refers to his ideas, which quietly register the Way. "Following Heaven" and "respecting Heaven" means that he understands principle and respectfully practices it. According to the Uighurs, Guo Ziyi said, "The diviner says that [we] must see the great person or else." This prognostication is the same. [Guo] Ziyi, although he didn't reach the level of what Confucius [here] describes, was selfless in his utmost impartiality, so we can call him a great person of that time.⁹⁶

[30] [9 at the top:] "Going too far" is knowing when to advance but not knowing when to retreat; knowing when to preserve but not knowing when to lose; knowing when to acquire but not knowing when to let go.

These are why activity brings regret.

[31] Only the Sage! He knows when to advance or retreat, preserve or lose, without losing his correctness. Only the Sage!

Understanding the power of principle like this and carrying it out by means of the Way, one will have no occasion for regret, and there will certainly be no calculating self [trying] to avoid harm. As for the repetition of the words "only the Sage," the former is like posing a question and the latter is responding to it.

This sixth section again illustrates the ideas of the second, third, and fourth.

[2] ䷁ 坤 Kun (Complying)

Kun [earth] below, Kun [earth] above.

Kun: Supreme and penetrating; appropriate with the correctness of a mare. Wherever the superior person goes, leading is confusing but following is effective; strongly appropriate. Finding friends in the south and west; losing friends in the north and east. Settling in correctness [*zhen* 貞] is auspicious.

The broken line is even, a *yin* number. Kun means complying [*shun* 順], the nature of *yin*. In the textual comment ["Kun below, Kun above"] it is the name of the trigrams; in the scripture itself [in bold] it is the name of the hexagram. Of the embodiments of *yin*, nothing is greater than Earth. Since the trigram's three lines are all even, its name is Kun and its image is earth. Doubling it also yields Kun, so it is pure *yin*, the most complying. Its name and its image are both unchanging.

The mare complies, yet also acts creatively.[97] *Yang* precedes *yin*.[98] *Yang* emphasizes propriety and *yin* emphasizes being appropriate. South and west are *yin* directions; north and east are *yang* directions. "Settling" [*an* 安] is the act of complying; "correctness" is holding on to the creative. One who encounters this hexagram has the prognostication "greatly penetrating"; it is appropriate to be correct in both complying and creating. If one is going somewhere, "leading is confusing but complying is effective and is strongly appropriate." Going south and west will attract friends, but going north and east will lose friends. If one is generally able to settle in correctness [*zheng* 正] then it will be auspicious.

COMMENTARY ON THE JUDGMENT

Perfect indeed is the originating [power] of Kun! The myriad things rely on it for their birth, complying with what they receive from Heaven.

This clarifies the meaning of Kun by means of the Way of Earth, referring first to "origination." "Perfect" means "extreme," but a bit less than the common meaning. "Beginning" [*shi* 始] is the beginning of *qi*; "birth" [*sheng* 生] is the beginning of form. Compliantly receiving what Heaven bestows is the Way of Earth.[99]

The richness of Kun supports things; its virtue accords with the boundless. It contains all that is glorious, so that all kinds of things [develop with] success.

This refers to "penetrating/success" [*heng* 亨] [in the hexagram statement]. "Its virtue accords with the boundless" means it complements Qian.

The mare [*pinma* 牝馬] is in the category of Earth; it roams the earth without bound. Yielding and complying, appropriate and correct, it is the superior person wherever he goes.

This refers to "appropriate and correct." "Horse" [*ma* 馬] is an image of Qian and yet is considered to be in the category of Earth.[100] "Female" [*pin* 牝] is a *yin* creature, and yet as a horse it is a creature that roams the earth. "Roaming the earth without bound," then, is being compliant and also strong. "Yielding and complying, appropriate and correct" is the virtue of Kun. "The superior person wherever he goes" is what a person does with the virtue of Kun. When one acts like this, the prognostication will be according to what the text says below.

"Leading is confusing"; it loses the Way. "Following is compliant"; it achieves the norm. "Finding friends in the south and west" one can act with them. "Losing friends in the north and east," in the end there will be celebration.

Yang is greater and *yin* is lesser; *yang* can serve as *yin*, but *yin* cannot serve as *yang*.[101] Therefore the virtue of Kun always diminishes Qian by half. Although one loses friends in the north and east, it is the opposite in the south and west, so in the end there will be celebration.

The auspiciousness of settling in correctness is responding to the boundlessness of Earth.

Settling and yet being correct is the virtue of Earth.

COMMENTARY ON THE GREATER IMAGES

The power of Earth: Complying. The superior person with abundant virtue supports things.

Earth is the image of Kun. It too [like Heaven] is simply unitary, so we cannot speak of doubling.[102] Yet we do speak of the compliance of its power: we see its inexhaustibility throughout, harmonizing high and low. With its utmost compliance and extreme abundance, everything is supported.

LINE STATEMENTS WITH COMMENTARY ON THE SMALLER IMAGES

[Line 1] 6 at the beginning: Treading on frost. Hard ice will arrive.

"6" is the name of the *yin* line. Of the *yin* numbers, 6 is mature and 8 is young, so we call the *yin* line 6. "Frost" is congealed *yin qi*. When fully [congealed], water freezes into ice. When this line's *yin* is first generated at the bottom, its beginning [*duan* 端] is extremely subtle. Its tendency is necessarily to fully [congeal], so the image is "treading on frost" knowing that hard ice is about to arrive.

As for *yin* and *yang*, they are the basis of creation [*zaohua* 造化] and cannot negate each other. Growth and decline are constant and humans cannot diminish or enhance them. But *yang* emphasizes life and *yin* emphasizes death, so they are morally distinct [*shu te* 淑慝] categories. Therefore when the Sages created the *Yi* they [*yin* and *yang*] could not negate each other, and this clarified the categories of creating and complying, humanity and rightness, with no one-sided emphasis. Thus the boundary between growth and decline and the distinction between good and evil always involve the idea of supporting *yang* and suppressing *yin*. This is the profound meaning of "assisting in the transforming and nourishing" [processes] and "forming a triad with Heaven and Earth" [*Zhongyong* 22]. Regardless of the diviner, this subtle idea can be seen in the image.[103]

[Image 1] "Treading on frost, hard ice" is *yin* beginning to congeal. When it gradually attains its Way it becomes hard ice.

"Gradually" means with following and repeating.

[Line 2] 6 in the second: Direct, square, and great. Without repetition everything is appropriate.

The yielding line complying with the correct and strong is the directness of Kun. Bestowing form with definition is Kun's squareness. Virtues combining without separation is Kun's greatness. 6 in the second, a yielding line complying, is central and correct, the purity of the Way of Kun. Thus its virtues are directness within and squareness without, and it grows great. "Everything is appropriate" without depending on learning and repetition. If the diviner has these virtues the prognostication will be like this.

[Image 2] The activity of 6 in the second is direct and square. "Without repetition everything is appropriate"; this is the glory of the Way of Earth.

[Line 3] 6 in the third: Concealing one's excellence can be correct. If one goes into the service of a king but does not claim accomplishment, one will serve to the end.

6 is *yin* and the third [position] is *yang*. Holding inside one's excellence one can maintain one's correctness. But if one rises above one's lowly position one cannot

keep it hidden to the end; sometimes one must emerge and engage in the affairs of those above. Although at first one accomplishes nothing, eventually one must serve to the end. This is the line's image, so the diviner is admonished to have this virtue; hence the prognostication.

[Image 3] "Concealing one's excellence can be correct," but one may express it at the right time. "If one goes into the service of the king" one's wisdom is radiant and great.

[Line 4] 6 in the fourth: A tied-up sack. No blame, no praise.

The tied-up sack means a closed mouth with nothing coming out. "Praise" is a word for exaggeration [false praise]. When cautious and discreet like this, there is neither blame nor praise. 6 in the fourth is a double *yin* [*yin* line in a *yin* position] but is not central; hence the image and the prognostication. In some situations one should be cautious and discreet; at some times one should hide oneself away.

[Image 4] "A tied-up sack; no blame"; if one is cautious there is no harm.

[Line 5] 6 in the fifth: Yellow lower garment. Supremely auspicious.

Yellow is the color of the center, and the lower garment is a lower adornment.[104] 6 in the fifth is *yin* in the place of honor. The virtue of centrality and compliance is full within and visible without. Hence the image, and the prognostication is extremely good and auspicious. The diviner's virtue must be like this to get this prognostication. In the *Chunqiu* [*Zuo*] *zhuan*, when Nan Kuai was about to rebel, the diviner got this line and "took it as extremely auspicious [to attack]." Zifu Huibo said, "With loyalty and trust the affair can be successful. Otherwise you will certainly be defeated. Being outwardly strong and inwardly warm is loyalty. Being harmonious in making the [divinatory] charge is honest. Therefore it says, 'Yellow lower garment, greatly auspicious.' Yellow is the color of the center, and the lower garment is a lower adornment. 'Great' is the height of goodness. Being at the center but not loyal, one does not get [to wear] this color. Being lower but not getting along, one does not get [to wear] this garment. To be involved but not good, one does not go all the way. As for the *Yi*, one cannot take the prognostication as dangerous. If the three [virtues mentioned above] are deficient, even if the divination is correct, don't go."[105] In the end, Kuai was defeated. From this we can see the pattern of the prognostication.

[Image 5] "A yellow lower garment; supremely auspicious." Refinement [*wen* 文] is within.

Refinement is within but is visible without.

[Line 6] 6 at the top: Dragons fighting in the wilds; their blood is dark and yellow.

Yin grows to its peak until it contends with *yang*. They both attack and are injured; this is the image. If the diviner is like this, his bad fortune will be understandable.

[Image 6] "Dragons fighting in the wilds"; the Way [of Kun] has been exhausted.

[Additional Line] Using [all] 6s: Appropriate to be constantly correct.

"Using 6s" means that all the lines are *yin* and all used [were derived with] 6, none used 8; this is the general rule. This hexagram is pure *yin* and comes first, so it appears like this. When one gets this hexagram and all six lines are changing, the prognostication follows this statement. When the yielding *yin* cannot strongly hold on, it fluctuates into *yang* and is able to be constantly correct. Thus the admonition to the diviner is "appropriate to be constantly correct." It is the same as Qian's "appropriate and correct." This is changing from Kun [into Qian], so it is not as good as "greatly penetrating" [as Qian is described].

[Additional Image] "Using [all] 6s, constantly correct"; and so a great ending.

Yin at the beginning, then *yang*. Therefore "a great ending."

COMMENTARY ON THE WORDS OF THE TEXT

[Source 4B, continued]

[1] Kun is the utmost yielding, yet its activity is firm. It is the utmost stillness, yet its virtue is square.[106]

"Firm" and "square" explain "the correctness of the mare." "Square" means the constancy [or norm] of living things.

[2] By following one can find a master and have constancy.

Cheng [Yi's] *Commentary* [on the *Yi*] says that after "master" [*zhu* 主] should be the word "appropriate" [*li* 利].[107]

[3] It [Kun] embraces the myriad things and its transformations are radiant.

This again clarifies the meaning of "penetrating" [*heng*].

[4] How compliant is the Way of Kun! It receives from Heaven and carries it out in due time.

This again clarifies the meaning of "complying with what is received from Heaven," illustrating the idea mentioned above in the Judgment commentary.

[5] [6 at the beginning:] The family that accumulates what is good will certainly have much to celebrate. The family that accumulates what is not good will certainly have much disaster. When a minister kills his ruler [*jun* 君] or a son kills his father, the reason is not what happened in a single day; it has come about gradually. It comes from something that should have been disputed but was not disputed early enough. When the *Yi* says, "Treading on frost, hard ice will arrive" it is referring to compliance.

The word "compliance" [*shun* 順] here is interchangeable with "caution" [*shen* 慎], so I would say that it should be written "caution," as it refers to the subtlety of proper disputation.

[6] [6 in the second:] Being "direct" means being correct [*zheng* 正]; being "square" means being right [*yi* 義]. The superior person [practices] reverent composure [*jing* 敬] to direct himself within and rightness to square himself without.[108] With reverent composure and rightness established, one is virtuous and not alone. "Direct, square, and great. Without practice everything is appropriate," so there is no doubt about what to do.

This refers to learning [to become a Sage]. "Being correct" means the original substance [*benti* 本體].[109] "Being right" means judgment. "Reverent composure" means holding on to one's original substance. "Being direct within and square without" is fully discussed in *Cheng's Commentary* [see following]. "Not alone" refers to being great. If one questions, then with practice [everything will be] appropriate. Without questioning, how can one pretend to practice?

[The collated editions quote Cheng Yi's *Commentary* here:]

"Being direct refers to being correct; being square refers to being right. The superior person emphasizes reverent composure so as to be direct internally, and holds on to rightness so as to be square externally. When reverent composure is established and one is internally direct, rightness takes form and one is externally square. When rightness takes form externally it is not [really] external.[110] Once reverent composure and rightness are established, one's virtue flourishes. When one is great in times that are not great, one's virtue is not alone. When everything that is used is complete and everything that is carried out is appropriate, how can one question it?" [*Er Cheng ji*, 712].

[7] [6 in the third:] Although there is beauty in *yin*, one should conceal it in conducting the affairs of a king and not presume to [take credit for] their completion. This is the Way of Earth, the Way of the wife, and the Way of the minister. The Way of Earth does not [take credit for] completion, but works for ends on behalf [of Heaven].

[6 in the fourth:] When Heaven and Earth fluctuate and transform, plants and trees flourish. When Heaven and Earth are obstructed, the worthy person retires. The *Yi* says, "A tied-up sack. No blame, no praise," referring to being cautious.

[8] [6 in the fifth:] The superior person, yellow and central, thoroughly understands principle.

"Yellow and central" refers to the virtue of centrality within. This explains the meaning of the word "yellow" [in the line statement].

[9] His position is correct, yet he resides in the [lower] trigram.[111]

Although this is an honored position, he [the superior person] resides in the lower trigram. This explains the meaning of the word "lower garment" [in the line statement].

[10] His beauty is within, yet it frees his four limbs and expresses itself in his affairs and undertakings: the perfection of beauty.

"His beauty is within" again explains "yellow and central." "Frees his four limbs" again explains "resides in the [lower] trigram."

[11] [6 at the top:] When *yin* suspects it is *yang*, they must battle, for it is dissatisfied that it lacks *yang*; thus [the text] speaks of the dragon [*yang*]. It has not departed from its category, so it speaks of blood [*yin*]. The "dark and yellow" is the mixing of Heaven and Earth: Heaven is dark and Earth is yellow.[112]

"Suspects" means [considering oneself to be] equal to one's foe, with no difference between great and small. Although Kun has no *yang*, *yang* is never absent.

Blood is a *yin* category; *qi* is *yang* and blood is *yin*. "Dark and yellow" are the proper colors of Heaven and Earth; this refers to *yin* and *yang* both being wounded.

This expands on the ideas of the "Image Commentary."

[3] ䷂ 屯 Zhun (Difficult Beginning)[113]

Zhen [thunder] below, Kan [water] above.

Zhun: Supreme and penetrating; appropriate and correct. Do not undertake to go anywhere. Appropriate to establish a marquis [*hou* 候].[114]

Zhen and Kan are the names of the two trigrams. Zhen has a single *yang* line moving in beneath two *yin* lines, so its virtue is activity and its image is thunder. Kan has a single *yang* trapped between two *yin* lines, so its virtue is being trapped, or danger; its image is clouds, rain, or water. Zhun is the name of the hexagram: Difficult [*nan* 難]. It means the point when something is beginning to arise but has not yet fully come through. In terms of the character, it represents a sprout beginning to break out of the earth but not yet through. The hexagram is Zhen encountering Kan, which is Qian [1] and Kun [2] beginning to interact and encountering danger; hence the name is Difficult Beginning. Zhen is active below and Kan is danger above; this is the ability to act in the midst of danger. Although the ability to act can be penetrating/successful [*heng* 亨], when in danger it is better to hold on to correctness and not to advance suddenly. Therefore when a divination yields this [hexagram], the prognostication is greatly successful, appropriate and correct, but one cannot suddenly have somewhere to go. Also 9 at the beginning, the *yang* residing below the *yin*, is the "constituting ruler."[115] This is the image of the worthy subordinate who is able to gain [the support of] the people to become a ruler. Therefore if a diviner who establishes a noble receives this [hexagram], it will be auspicious.

COMMENTARY ON THE JUDGMENT

Zhun: As the firm and yielding are beginning to interact, birth is troublesome.[116]

Explaining the meaning of the hexagram name in terms of the two component trigrams. "Begin to interact" means Zhen [the inner trigram]. "Birth is troublesome" means Kan [the outer trigram].

Acting in the midst of danger; great success and correctness.

Explaining the hexagram statement in terms of the virtues of the two component trigrams. "Acting" is what Zhen does; "danger" is the basis of Kan. From here on explains "Supreme and penetrating, appropriate and correct," using King Wen's original ideas.

The activity of thunder and rain [makes things] replete. In the chaotic darkness [*caomei* 草昧] of Heaven's creation, it is fitting to establish a marquis and not be complacent.

Explaining the hexagram statement by means of the images of the two component trigrams. Thunder is the image of Zhen; rain is the image of Kan. "Heaven's creation" is an expression for the turning of Heaven. *Cao* 草 [grass, weeds] means mixed and confused; *mei* 昧 means dark. *Yin* and *yang* interact and thunder and rain are produced; chaos and darkness fill the space between them. The world is not yet defined and the distinctions of names are not yet clear. [Thus] it is fitting to set up a ruler to take charge; one cannot yet call it a time of peace. If one does not grasp the meaning of 9 at the beginning there are many clues to choose from, and I provisionally recommend this one.

COMMENTARY ON THE GREATER IMAGES

Clouds and thunder: Difficult Beginning. The superior person administers accordingly.

When Kan refers not to water but to clouds, it means it is not yet complete. *Jinglun* 經綸 means the act of organizing threads [hence "administer"], guiding and ordering them. Times of difficulty are times for the activity of the superior person.

LINE STATEMENTS WITH COMMENTARY ON THE SMALLER IMAGES

[Line 1] 9 at the beginning: Hesitant. Appropriate to abide in correctness, appropriate to establish a marquis.

"Hesitant" means appearing to have difficulty advancing. The beginning of Zhun's difficulty, the *yang* at the bottom, resides in the active trigram and corresponds above to the yielding *yin* [in the fourth place]. It is a dangerous line; hence the image of hesitancy. But it occupies a correct [*zheng* 正] position, so the prognostication is "appropriate to abide in correctness [*zhen* 貞]." The ruler of this hexagram, the *yang* beneath *yin*, is what the people return to, the image of the marquis; hence this image. If the diviner is like this, then the one he establishes will be considered a marquis.

[Image 1] Although hesitant, be intent on acting correctly. If the honorable lowers himself to the humble he will gain [the loyalty of] the people in great measure.

[Line 2] 6 in the second: Difficult, back and forth, like a chariot and horse pulling apart [*ban* 班]. He is not a bandit; he wants to marry. The woman is correct and not betrothed ["named" *zi* 字]; in ten years she will be betrothed.

Ban means spreading apart, as if unable to advance. *Zi* means betrothed [because] the *Li*[*ji*] says, "When a girl is promised in marriage, she is pinned and named."[117] 6 in the second place is yielding *yin* that is central and correct. It corresponds to what is above, yet it "rides" the firm line at the beginning.[118] Therefore it is "difficult, [going] back and forth," and not advancing. But the bottom line is not a bandit; he simply seeks to marry [the *yin* line]. She only holds on to her correctness, so she does not promise him. After ten years, when she has completely fulfilled this principle [correctness] and the foolish seeker has gone, she will join in correct correspondence [with the *yang* line in the fifth place] and can be promised. Since the line has this image, it is accordingly a warning to the diviner.[119]

[Image 2] The trouble with 6 in the second place is that it rides on a firm line [9 in the first]. "In ten years she will be betrothed" means returning to the constant [Way].

[Line 3] 6 in the third: Going after deer without a gamekeeper one would only enter the midst of the forest. The superior person [sees] subtle signs that it is better to refrain. To go forward would be disgraceful.

This yielding *yin* line residing in the lower [trigram] is not central, not correct, and does not correctly correspond [with the *yin* line at the top].[120] Reckless action invites difficulty. This is the image of following a deer into the midst of a forest without a gamekeeper. The superior person sees the subtle signs [*ji* 幾] that it is better to refrain. If one were to go forward and not refrain it would definitely lead to shame and disgrace. The warning to the diviner is therefore fitting.

[Image 3] "Going after a deer without a gamekeeper" means tracking and capturing [by oneself]. The superior person refrains from it. "To go forward would be disgraceful" and a failure.

[Line 4] 6 in the fourth: Like a chariot and horse pulling apart, seeking marriage. Going forward is auspicious; all will be appropriate.

The yielding *yin* line resides in difficulty, unable to advance upward; hence the image of the chariot and horse pulling apart. But 9 at the beginning maintains correctness residing below, corresponding with this line. Therefore the prognostication is if one seeks below for marriage it will be auspicious.

[Image 4] "Seeking" [marriage] and "going forward" are clear.

[Line 5] 9 in the fifth: Difficulty in blessings. Correctness in minor [affairs] is auspicious; correctness in major [affairs] is ominous.

Although 9 in the fifth is a firm *yang* line, central and correct, occupying the position of honor, it is a time of difficulty. One has fallen into danger. Although there is correct correspondence with 6 in the second place, the yielding *yin* is weak and insufficient to overcome [the danger]. 9 at the beginning "gains [the loyalty of] the people" below, and they all return to him. 9 in the fifth is in the Kan trigram, and blessings cannot be bestowed. This is the image of "difficulty in blessings." If the diviner conducts minor affairs then he will maintain correctness and may still obtain good fortune. If he conducts major affairs, then even though he is correct he will not avoid bad fortune.

[Image 5] "Difficulty in blessings"; bestowing them is not illuminating.

[Line 6] 6 at the top: Chariot and horse pulling apart. Weeping blood in streams.

The yielding *yin* line does not correspond [with the *yin* line in the third]. The end of a period of difficulty. As there is no place to advance there is worry and fear; hence the image.

[Image 6] "Weeping blood in streams." How long can this last?

[4] ䷃ 蒙　Meng (Dim, Ignorant)

Kan [water] below, Gen [mountain] above.

Meng: Success [*heng* 亨]. It is not I who seeks out the young fool; the young fool seeks out me. With the first divination he is informed; a second or third one is bothersome; being bothersome, he is not informed. Appropriate and correct.

Gen is the name of a trigram. A single *yang* rests above two *yin* lines, so its virtue is stability/stopping [*zhi* 止] and its image is a mountain.[121] *Meng* means dim [*mei* 昧]. When something is first generated it is dim and dark. This hexagram is Kan encountering Gen. Below the mountain there is danger, a place of dimness. Inner danger and outer stability is the idea of being "dim, ignorant," so its name is Meng.[122] From "success" to the end is the prognostication remarks.

9 in the second place is the ruler of the inner trigram, a firm line residing in the center. It is able to dispel [*fa* 發] the ignorance of others, and corresponds in terms of *yin* and *yang* with 6 in the fifth. Therefore one who encounters this hexagram will have a path of success. The "I" [in the text] is the second position. The "young fool," the youngster or ignorant youth, is the fifth position. If the diviner is bright, then people should seek "me" [the diviner] out so as to have success. If the diviner is ignorant, then I should seek out others so as to have success. The person who seeks me should look at the pros and cons and respond to them. When I seek another, I should emulate his single-mindedness and control myself. The bright one will nourish the dim one, and along with the dim one nourishing himself, both will be "appropriate and correct."

COMMENTARY ON THE JUDGMENT

Meng: Danger below the mountain; stopping when in danger is ignorant.

Explaining the hexagram name by means of the trigram images and the trigram virtues, yielding two meanings.

Meng: success. Hitting the timely mean by acting successfully. "It is not I who seeks out the young fool; the young fool seeks out me." Our purposes correspond. "With the first divination he is informed," as the firm [line] is central. "A second or third one is bothersome; being bothersome, he is not informed," as being

bothersome is ignorant. To nourish correctness in the ignorant is the achievement of the Sage.

Explaining the hexagram statement in terms of the component trigrams. 9 in the second place, since it allows for a path of success, dispels the ignorance of others and achieves the centrality of the moment. It is like the situation referred to in the following text, always "acting successfully" and properly. "Our purposes correspond" means that the firm line in the second place is bright and the yielding line in the fifth place is dim, so the second does not seek out the fifth, but the fifth does seek out the second; their purposes naturally correspond with each other.[123] The firm, central line, being firm and central, is able to inform with moderation. "Bothersome" means the questioner who divines two or three times is very bothersome, so the one who informs him is bothered. "To nourish correctness in the ignorant," which constitutes "the meritorious achievement of the Sage," explains the meaning of "appropriate and correct."

COMMENTARY ON THE GREATER IMAGES

Below the mountain emerges a spring: Dim. The superior person nurtures his virtue by improving his behavior.

A spring is where water begins to emerge. Where it must move there will be moistening [influence].

LINE STATEMENTS WITH COMMENTARY ON THE SMALLER IMAGES

[Line 1] 6 at the beginning: To dispel ignorance it is appropriate to apply punishment but to remove manacles and shackles.[124] To go on would be disgraceful.

With *yin* residing at the bottom, dimness/ignorance is extreme. If the diviner encounters this, he should dispel ignorance. But the way to dispel it is to abandon punishment after a while and see what follows. If it continues and is not abandoned, then it is certainly a disgrace. The diviner must be warned like this.

[Image 1] "Appropriate to apply punishment" in order to rectify the law.

At the beginning of dispelling ignorance it is necessary that the law be correct. Discipline is how to "rectify the law."

[Line 2] 9 in the second: Taking charge of the ignorant: auspicious. Taking a wife: auspicious. The son can carry on the family.

9 in the second is the firm *yang* as the ruler of the inner trigram. It controls the group of [two] *yins* and has the responsibility to dispel ignorance. But once good order is extensive [in the state], if the nature of things [in the family] is not regulated, one cannot consider it completely certain.[125] The virtue of the line is firm but not excessive, making it an image of the ability to forgive. Also, the *yang* accepting the *yin* is also an image of taking a wife, and residing in the lower position [of the hexagram] and being able to take responsibility for affairs above is an image of the son carrying on the family. Therefore, if the diviner has these virtues and undertakes these affairs, [the result] will be accordingly auspicious.

[Image 2] "The son can carry on the family" means the firm and yielding join together.

Referring to the correspondence of the second and fifth lines.

[Line 3] 6 in the third: Do not select a woman [for a wife] who sees a man of substance [literally, "gold"] and has no self-control. Nothing is appropriate.

The 6 in the third place is a yielding *yin*, so it is not central and not correct. The image is a woman who sees a man of substance and is unable to control herself. If the diviner encounters this line, then the woman selected will certainly be like this one, and nothing will be appropriate. "A man of substance" is probably one who displays his own wealth, like Qiu Hu of Lu did.[126]

[Image 3] "Do not select a woman [for a wife]" means to proceed would not be cautious.

Shun 順 [compliant] should be written *shen* 慎 [cautious]. *Shun* and *shen* in ancient writing were used interchangeably. In the *Xunzi* [for example], *shun mo* 順墨 [to follow dark (ways)] is written *shen mo* 慎墨 [cautious and dark].[127] Moreover, "to proceed would not be cautious" is very close to the meaning of the text, so we should follow it here.

[Line 4] 6 in the fourth: Distress and ignorance; disgrace.

Being far from the *yang*, and not correctly corresponding [with another line]: the image of ignorance in distress.¹²⁸ If the diviner is like this, there can be shame and disgrace. If he is able to seek the bright virtue of the firm and draw near to it, this can be avoided.

[Image 4] The disgrace of "distress and ignorance" comes from being alone and far from the solid [*yang* lines].

[Line 5] 6 in the fifth: Youthful ignorance; auspicious.

The yielding line is central, residing in the place of honor, and corresponds below with 9 in the second place. It is purely unified and does not express itself, but listens to others. Hence the image of youthful ignorance, yet the prognostication, accordingly, is auspicious.

[Image 5] The auspiciousness of "youthful ignorance" comes from being compliant and gentle.

[Line 6] 9 at the top: Strike at the ignorant, but it is not appropriate to act like an enemy. Appropriate to guard against enemies.

The firm line residing at the top controls the ignorant who might transgress against the firm; thus the image of striking at the ignorant. But in the case of an extreme transgression, applying the rules with extreme thoroughness will certainly backfire. If one only defends against external [enemies], with guidance that is completely true and pure, then even if the transgression is private, [the correction] can be appropriate. Therefore the warning to the diviner. In all matters like this, do not stop at teaching others.

[Image 6] "Appropriate to guard against enemies." The one above and the one below are in accord.¹²⁹

Guarding against enemies with the firm [line], the one above and the one below both attain the Way.

[5] ䷄ 需 Xu (Waiting)

Qian [heaven] below, Kan [water] above.

Xu: With honesty [*fu* 孚], radiant success. Being correct is auspicious; appropriate to cross a great river.[130]

Xu is waiting [*dai* 待]. Qian encounters Kan, Qian being strong and Kan being dangerous. Firmness encounters danger, and doesn't hastily advance to be trapped in danger. This is the meaning of waiting. *Fu* 孚 is the inner core of trust [*xin* 信]: the hexagram's 9 in the fifth position, the heart of the Kan trigram. This firm *yang* is central and correct and resides in the honored position: the image of honesty yielding correctness. Kan's water is ahead, and Qian's strength approaches it: the image of being about to cross the water but not easily advancing. Therefore if the diviner is one who waits, and can be trusted, there will be "bright success." If he can also be correct, it will be "auspicious" and "appropriate to cross a great river." Being correct there is definitely nothing that is not appropriate, and in crossing a river it is especially valuable to be able to wait, so do not desire to hurry and run into obstacles.

COMMENTARY ON THE JUDGMENT

Xu is waiting: danger is ahead. Firm, strong, and not trapped; this means one is not in dire straits.

This uses the trigram virtues to explain the meaning of the hexagram name.

"Waiting. With honesty, radiant success. Being correct is auspicious." Taking the position of Heaven, it is central and correct.[131] "Appropriate to cross a great river": going forward is meritorious.

Using the component trigrams and the two images to explain the hexagram statement.

COMMENTARY ON THE GREATER IMAGES

Clouds rising to Heaven: Waiting. The superior person drinks and eats in enjoyment of a feast.

"Clouds rising to Heaven"; there is no way to make them return; one must wait for *yin* and *yang* to harmonize and produce rain. If one waits properly for things it is unnecessary to do any more. Just "drink and eat in enjoyment of a feast," anticipating its arrival. As soon as it does there is no waiting.

LINE STATEMENTS WITH COMMENTARY ON THE SMALLER IMAGES

[Line 1] 9 at the beginning: Waiting outside the city; appropriate to be persistent. No blame.

"Outside the city"[132] means a place far away; the image of not being close to danger. The first 9 is a firm *yang* line, the image of being able to persist in its place. Hence the advice to the diviner can be like this, with no blame.

[Image 1] "Waiting outside the city," not to risk moving into trouble. "Appropriate to be persistent, no blame" is not losing touch with the constant [norm].

[Line 2] 9 in the second: Waiting in sand. A few may have words [of criticism], but in the end, auspicious.

"Sand" is close to danger, a colloquial word for injury, less serious than disastrous harm.[133] Hastily advancing close to Kan, hence this image. Firm and central, it is able to wait; therefore "in the end, auspicious." Hence this warning to the diviner.

[Image 2] "Waiting in sand," tolerantly occupying the center. Although "a few may have words [of criticism]," it will end auspiciously.

Yan 衍 [abundant, spread out] means "tolerant" [*kuan* 寬]. Tolerantly residing in the center, one does not hasten to advance.

[Line 3] 9 in the third: Waiting in mud, causing thieves to approach.

"Mud" means one is about to sink into danger. "Thieves" means the harm will be great. 9 in the third escapes as danger comes even closer, yet it is excessively firm and not central; hence this image.

[Image 3] "Waiting in mud"; disaster is outside. I myself cause thieves [to approach], but if I am respectful and cautious I will not be defeated.

"Outside" means the outer trigram. "If I am respectful and cautious I will not be defeated" reveals a prognostication by someone other than the diviner. The idea shown people by the Sage is incisive.

[Line 4] 6 in the fourth: Waiting in blood, getting oneself out of the hole.

"Blood" means a place of murder and injury. "Hole" means a place of danger. The fourth place interacts with the Kan [upper] trigram, entering into danger; hence the image of "waiting in blood." But this yielding line is correct, waiting and not advancing; hence the image of "getting oneself out of the hole." If the diviner is like this, even though in a place of injury, he will in the end get out.

[Image 4] "Waiting in blood"; complying and listening.

[Line 5] 9 in the fifth: Waiting with wine and food; being correct is auspicious.

"Wine and food" are provisions of a banquet, referring to resting while waiting. 9 in the fifth is a firm *yang* line that is central and correct, waiting in the honored position; hence this image. If the diviner is accordingly correct and strong, then he will have good fortune.

[Image 5] "With wine and food; being correct is auspicious," because it is central and correct.

[Line 6] 6 at the top: Going into a hole, three uninvited guests have come. Respect them, and the end will be auspicious.

Yin resides at the peak of danger and can no longer wait: the image of falling into a hole. [This line] corresponds below with 9 in the third, which, along with the two *yang* lines beneath it, are waiting urgently to advance together. This is the image of three uninvited guests. The yielding line cannot resist but can comply; the image of respecting them. If the diviner is in the midst of danger and something unexpected comes, if he respectfully waits, then "the end will be auspicious."

[Image 6] "Uninvited guests arrive. Respect them, and the end will be auspicious." Although it is not properly positioned, there is no great loss.

The *yin* residing at the top is properly positioned; the statement, "not properly positioned" is unclear.[134]

[6] ䷅ 訟 Song (Disputing)

Kan [water] below, Qian [heaven] above.

Song: With honesty obstructed, cautiously holding to the center is auspicious; going to the end is ominous. Appropriate to see the great person; not appropriate to cross a great river.

Song is disputing [*zhengbian* 爭辯]. Qian above and Kan below; Qian is firm and Kan is danger. The firm above controls what is below; the one in danger below keeps an eye on the one above. This is also inner danger and outer strength, one's own danger and another's strength, both [following] the path of disputation. The 9 in the second place is central and full, but does not correspond with the one above; this adds concern. Moreover, by hexagram fluctuation it comes from Dun 遯 [hexagram 33 ䷠], with the firm line coming to reside in the second place, right in the middle of the lower trigram.[135] Here there is the image of one who is honest yet sees obstruction, and who is anxious about attaining the center. The upper [three] 9s are already firm, occupying the peak of Song: the image of the ultimate end of disputation. The 9 in the fifth is firm and strong, central and correct, occupying the position of honor: the image of the "great person." With the firm riding on danger, truly stepping into a trap, we have the image of "not appropriate to cross a great river." Hence the warning that the diviner must engage in disputation, and will meet good fortune or misfortune according to his place.

COMMENTARY ON THE JUDGMENT

Song: Firm above, danger below. Danger and strength: disputation.

Explaining the meaning of the hexagram name by means of the trigram virtues.

"Disputing. With honesty obstructed, cautiously holding to the center is auspicious": the firm comes and attains the center. "Going to the end is ominous": disputation cannot be completed [resolved]. "Appropriate to see the great

person": the esteemed [9 in the fifth] is central and correct. "Not appropriate to cross a great river:: entering into an abyss.

Explaining the remarks on the hexagram by means of hexagram fluctuation, the component trigrams, and the trigram images.[136]

COMMENTARY ON THE GREATER IMAGES

Heaven and water moving apart: Disputing. The superior person, in carrying out affairs, considers their inceptions.

Heaven rises and water sinks, their movements opposed to each other. "In carrying out affairs [he] considers their inceptions" because disputes have beginnings and ends.

LINE STATEMENTS WITH COMMENTARY ON THE SMALLER IMAGES

[Line 1] 6 in the first: Without perpetuating the affair a few may have words [of criticism], but in the end, auspicious.

The yielding *yin* line residing below cannot dispute to the end; hence this image and prognostication.

[Image 1] "Without perpetuating the affair" disputes cannot be extended. Although "a few may have words [of criticism]," the argument can be clarified.

[Line 2] 9 in the second: Cannot overcome disputation; go back and avoid it. One's neighbors are [only] three hundred households. No calamity.

9 in the second is a firm *yang* line, the ruler of danger [the Kan trigram], basically desiring to dispute. But since it is a firm line residing in a yielding position in the middle of the lower trigram, and it corresponds above with 9 in the fifth, which is a firm *yang* line occupying the honored position, its power cannot be comparable; hence the image and the prognostication. "[One's] neighbors are [only] three hundred households," a minority of the village.[137] This means one's own position is tenuous but one can avoid disaster and trouble. Hence the prognostication, "no calamity."

[Image 2] "Cannot overcome disputation; go back to avoid it"; escape. To dispute from below with one above would be to invite trouble.

"To invite" means to personally choose.

[Line 3] 6 in the third: To imbibe the virtue of the past is correct. Danger, but ultimately auspicious. One may follow the affairs of a king, but do not claim accomplishment.[138]

To "imbibe" refers to what is received. 6 in the third is a weak *yin* line, and is not capable of disputation. Therefore it keeps to the correctness of its ancient residence. Then, although there is danger, [the situation is] "finally auspicious." Although one may go out and follow the affairs of one's superior, there will certainly be no meritorious accomplishment. If the diviner holds to constancy and does not go out, it will be good.

[Image 3] "To imbibe the virtue of the past" and to follow the one above is auspicious.

"To follow the one above" means that if one accords with another it will be auspicious. If one displays affairs that one has led oneself, there will be no meritorious accomplishment.

[Line 4] 9 in the fourth: Cannot overcome disputation, so return at once to the decree. To change and to rest in correctness is auspicious.

Ji 即 [is precisely] means *jiu* 就 [then, at once]. "The decree" [*ming* 命] [of Heaven] is the correct principle [*zheng li* 正理]. "To change" [*yu* 渝] is to fluctuate. 9 in the fourth is firm but not central, and so is the image of disputation. It resides in a yielding position, so it does not overcome and returns to the correct principle. Changing one's mind-heart is the image of relaxing in the correctness of one's place. If the diviner does this there will be good fortune.

[Image 4] "Return at once to the decree; change and rest in correctness"; one will not lose.

[Line 5] 9 in the fifth: Disputing: supremely auspicious.

The firm *yang* line is central and correct, and resides in the position of honor. It hears the dispute and obtains fairness. If the diviner encounters this line, disputing will be principled, and what is obtained will certainly last.

[Image 5] "Disputing: supremely auspicious." It is central and correct.

Being central, one listens but is not partial. Being correct, one's judgment accords with principle.

[Line 6] 9 at the top: One may be bestowed a leather belt. By the end of the morning it will be stripped off three times.

The leather belt is a decoration of the official costume. As the firm line resides at the peak of Song, in the end disputation will be able to prevail; hence the image of the officially bestowed costume. Although one receives it by disputing, how can one relax for a long time? Thus the image of having it "stripped off three times by the end of the morning." The prognostication is that disputing to the end is not principled. Although one may seize dominance, one must eventually lose what one has gained. The meaning of the Sage's warning is profound indeed.

[Image 6] One may receive a costume by disputing, but it is not sufficiently respectful.

[7] ䷆ 師 Shi (Army)

Kan [water] below, Kun [earth] above.

Shi: Correct. The strong man has good fortune; no blame.

Shi means army [*bingzhong* 兵眾, military troops]: Kan below, Kun above. Kan is danger, Kun is complying; Kan is water, Kun is earth. The ancients drew their armies from the peasantry, submitting them to extreme danger [Kan] and great obedience/compliance [Kun]. They concealed the hazards [Kan] in the midst of extreme stillness [Kun].[139] The hexagram has only one *yang* line, residing in the middle of the lower trigram: the image of the general. The five *yin* lines above and below comply with and follow it: the image of the troops. The 9 in the second is a firm line residing below, functioning in service [to the ruler in the fifth]. The 6 in the fifth is a yielding line residing above, in charge of the former: the image of the people's ruler issuing commands to the army. Therefore the name of the hexagram is Army. "Strong man" is a term for the experienced chief [the general]. Following the Way of the army is appropriate in obtaining correctness, and is the responsibility of a mature man who will obtain "good fortune with no blame." Hence the necessary admonition to the diviner.

COMMENTARY ON THE JUDGMENT

Shi: The troops. *Zhen* 貞 means "correct" [*zheng* 正].[140] **Enabling correctness by means of the troops, one can thereby rule.**

This explains the meanings of "army" and "correct" in terms of the component trigrams. "By means of" refers to one's advisers. The single *yang* line is at the center of the lower trigram, and the five *yin* lines are there for it. "Enabling correctness by means of the troops" refers to the army of the ruler.

The firm line is central and corresponds [to the yielding line in the fifth]. To proceed is dangerous yet compliant [obedient]. In this way [even if] everyone is injured, the people will follow. Auspicious; how can there be any blame?

This explains the meaning of "The strong man has good fortune; no blame" by means of the component trigrams and their virtues. "The firm line is central" refers to 9 in the second. "Corresponds" means 6 in the fifth corresponds with it. "To proceed is dangerous" means proceeding is the path of danger. "Obedient" means compliant with the human mind-heart. This is not something that the virtue of a mature adult is incapable of. "Injured" means harmed. When an army arises to travel, it cannot be without harm to everyone. But when it has this talent and virtue, the people happily follow it.

COMMENTARY ON THE GREATER IMAGES

Water within earth: Army. The superior person gathers troops by being tolerant of people.

Water is not separate from earth; an army is not separate from the people. Therefore being able to nourish the people one can gain troops.

LINE STATEMENTS WITH COMMENTARY ON THE SMALLER IMAGES

[Line 1] 6 at the beginning: The army goes out according to rules. If they are contrary to excellence, ominous.

"Rules" are laws. "Contrary to excellence" means not good. Mr. Chao [Yuezhi] says, "The word 'contrary to' [fou 否] was often used by former scholars for 'not' [bu 不]," and this is right. The beginning of the hexagram is the starting point of the army. The way the army goes out must be cautious at the start. If it is according to the rules, auspicious, but if they are not excellent, ominous. The warning to the diviner is that one must be careful at the start and hold to the law.

[Image 1] "The army goes out according to rules." Losing sight of the rules is ominous.

[Line 2] 9 in the second: [The leader] within the army: auspicious, no blame. The king bestows three awards.

9 in the second, in the lower [trigram], is [the leader] that the *yin* troops follow, with the virtues of a firm, central line. It corresponds with the fifth line above, which is the dragon [the king] in charge; hence the image and the prognostication.

[Image 2] "Within the army, auspicious": receiving favor from Heaven. "The king bestows three awards": he cherishes all regions.

[Line 3] 6 in the third: The army may cart off corpses; ominous.

"Carting off corpses" means defeated army soldiers being returned as corpses in carts. As a *yin* line occupying a *yang* position, this is weak in ability but firm in resolve. It is not central and not correct, yet crime is not its lot; hence the image and the prognostication.

[Image 3] "The army may cart off corpses"; greatly lacking in merit.

[Line 4] 6 in the fourth: The army turns to the left; no blame.

"Turn to the left" means to retreat. This yielding *yin* line is not central, yet it occupies a *yin* position and so is correct; hence this image. With the whole army in retreat the worthy one, 6 in the third, is distant; hence the prognostication.[141]

[Image 4] "Turns to the left; no blame." It has not yet lost its [constant] norm.

Understanding difficulty and retreating is the army's norm.

[Line 5] 6 in the fifth: There are game animals in the fields; appropriate to talk about capturing them; no blame. The elder son leads the army; the younger sons cart off corpses. Correct, but ominous.

    6 in the fifth functions as the ruler of the army. It is a yielding line that is compliant and central, so it does not initiate military action. When a foe dominates, one can do nothing but respond to him; hence the image of "game animals in the field," and the prognostication that it is appropriate and blameless to capture them. "To talk" is to speak words. "The elder son" is 9 in the second; "the younger sons" are the third and fourth [lines]. The warning to the diviner focuses on taking responsibility. If the superior person acts responsibly and the inferiors emulate him, then he will have them cart off corpses and go back. Thus, although correct, he cannot avoid misfortune.

[Image 5] "The elder son leads the army" by proceeding in equilibrium. "The younger son carts off corpses": this assignment is improper.

[Line 6] 6 at the top: When a great noble has command he founds a state or enfeoffs a family. He has no use for inferior people [xiaoren 小人].

    When the army is finished and compliance [obedience] is at its peak, it is time to decide on merit-based awards. Kun is earth; hence the image of founding states and enfeoffing families. Although inferior people may have merit, one cannot allow them to become nobility, but to decorate them with gold and silk is acceptable. The warning is to the person making awards, so inferior people cannot use this prognostication. If an inferior person obtains this line [in divination] he cannot use it.[142]

[Image 6] "When a great noble has command" his merit comes from correctness. "No use for inferior people"; they will surely bring chaos to the country.

    The Sage's warning is indeed profound.

[8] ䷇ 比   Bi (Being Close)

Kun [earth] below, Kan [water] above.

Bi: Auspicious. Tracing to the source and divining is fundamental, enduring, and correct: no blame. Coming while there is no peace: [coming] late is ominous.

Bi is being close and supportive [*qinfu* 親輔].[143] The 9 in the fifth achieves its correctness as a firm *yang* residing in the center of the upper trigram. The five *yin* lines above and below are close and follow it: the image of the one man controlling the myriad states and [all within] the four seas looking up to the one man. Therefore when the diviner gets this [hexagram], he must be the one whom the people closely support. However, it is necessary to divine again for self-examination [to see if] one has the virtues of fundamental goodness, long-lasting endurance, and correct strength. Only then can one be [the person] to whom the masses turn without blame. [Then,] before being close, while things are still unsettled, they will all come and turn to him. If they are slow and arrive later, then close relations will already be strong, and those who came late will meet with misfortune. If one desires to be close to people, one must by all means observe oneself in this way.

COMMENTARY ON THE JUDGMENT

Being close is auspicious.

I suspect that these words are superfluous text.

Being close is supporting, with those below following and complying.

This explains the meaning of the hexagram name by means of the component trigrams.

"Tracing to the source and divining is fundamental, enduring, and correct: no blame": the firm central line. "Coming while there is no peace": those above and those below respond. "[Coming] late is ominous": its Way is exhausted.

Also explaining the hexagram statement by means of the component trigrams. "The firm central line" is 9 in the fifth. "Those above and those below" means the five *yin* lines.

COMMENTARY ON THE GREATER IMAGES

Above earth is water: Close. The former kings established the myriad states and had close relations with the various marquises.

"Above earth is water": water is close to the earth, allowing no gap between them. "Established states and had close relations with the marquises" is how the former kings were close to all under Heaven with no gaps. The idea of the Judgment [Commentary] is that people come close to me [the diviner], selecting me to go out and be close to people.

LINE STATEMENTS WITH COMMENTARY ON THE SMALLER IMAGES

[Line 1] 6 in the first: When there is honesty, draw close to it; no blame. Being honest is like a full jar; in the end what comes will be the good fortune of others.

The first line of Bi is honorable and trustworthy, so there can be no blame. If it is fully developed, others will also have good fortune.

[Image 1] The 6 at the beginning of Bi is "the good fortune of others."

[Line 2] 6 in the second: Drawing close from the inner [trigram]: correct and auspicious.[144]

[This line is] yielding and complying, central and correct, and corresponds above with 9 in the fifth. "Drawing close from the inner" and being correct [*zhen* 貞] is the Way of good fortune. A divination like this is correct and auspicious.

[Image 2] "Drawing close from the inner": one will not lose oneself.

If one achieves correctness, one will not lose oneself.

[Line 3] 6 in the third: Being close to criminals.

This yielding *yin* line is neither central nor correct. The lines above, below, and corresponding are all *yin*; the image of being close to those who are not human.[145] The prognostication is extremely ominous and can be understood without words.[146]

[Image 3] "Being close to criminals." Is this not injurious?

[Line 4] 6 in the fourth: Drawing close from the outer [trigram]; correct and auspicious.

This yielding line occupying a yielding position is close to 9 in the fifth in the outer, and so achieves correctness: a path of good fortune. If the diviner is like this he will be correct and have good fortune.

[Image 4] "Drawing close from the outer" to the worthy: following the one above.

[Line 5] 9 in the fifth: Manifesting closeness, the king employs beaters [in a hunt] on three sides, forgoing the game in front. The villagers do not warn him; good fortune.

The single *yang* occupies the place of honor: firm and strong, central and correct, and the various *yin* lines of the hexagram come close to it. "Manifesting closeness" unselfishly, the Son of Heaven does not encircle but opens one side of the net, so what comes in will not be kept out and what goes out will not be pursued. Hence the image of "employing beaters on three sides, forgoing the game in front" and "the villagers do not warn him." Although this can be considered selfish, it also explains the idea above: if you don't guard against each other, one's search [hunt] will certainly be successful. In general this is an auspicious path, so if the diviner is like this, it will be auspicious.

[Image 5] The good fortune of "manifesting closeness": one's position is correct and central. To abandon those who go back and select those who comply is to "forgo the game in front." "The villagers do not warn him": the one above regards them as central.

Following the virtue of the one above causes them not to deviate.

[Line 6] 6 at the top: Close with no head [leader]; ominous.

The weak *yin* line occupying the top position, not close to what is below; an ominous Way. Thus the image is having "no head" and a prognostication that is "ominous."

[Image 6] "Close with no head [leader]": there is no end.[147]

In terms of the image of those above and below, there is no head. In terms of the image of ending and beginning, there is no end. With no head there is no end.

[9] ䷈ 小畜 Xiaochu (Restrained by the Lesser)[148]

Qian [heaven] below, Sun [wind, wood] above.

Xiaochu: Success. Dense clouds; no rain from our western suburbs.

Sun 巽 is the name of the [upper] trigram. Its single *yin* lies beneath two *yang* lines, so its virtue is mildness, or entering, and its image is wind and wood.[149] "Lesser" is *yin*. "Restrained" means limited [*zhi* 止] by something. With Sun above and Qian below, the *yin* restrains the *yang*. The only *yin* in the hexagram is 6 in the fourth; five *yang* lines above and below it are restrained; hence "restrained by the lesser." With *yin* restraining *yang*, it can restrict but not strongly; hence the image of the lesser as the one that restrains.

The inner is strong and the outer is mild. The second and the fifth are both *yang*, each occupying the center of its trigram and carrying out affairs. Having firmness and ability in the center is the image of their purposes being carried out. Therefore the prognostication should be thoroughly successful. However, the restraint is not yet extreme and its conduct is not yet carried out; hence the image of "dense clouds, no rain from our western suburbs." "Dense clouds" are *yin* things; "western suburbs" is a *yin* direction. "Our" refers to King Wen himself. While King Wen was explaining the *Yi* [in prison] in Youli, he observed that the Zhou in Qi were in the west and adjusted to a time of restraint by the lesser [the Shang].[150] If the diviner gets this, the prognostication will be [cloudy] like the image.

COMMENTARY ON THE JUDGMENT

Xiaochu: The yielding achieves position and those above and below correspond with it; this is called Restrained by the Lesser.

Explaining the meaning of the hexagram name by means of the component trigrams. "The yielding achieving position" indicates 6 occupying the fourth. "Those above and below" mean the five *yang* lines.

Strong and mild, the firm is central and its purposes are carried out: success.

In terms of the component trigrams and their virtues, *yang* can still be successful.

"Dense clouds, no rain": still moving forward. "From our western suburbs": its conduct not yet carried out.[151]

"Still moving forward" says that the restraint is not yet extreme; its *qi* is advancing upward.

COMMENTARY ON THE GREATER IMAGES

Wind moving above Heaven: Restrained by the Lesser. The superior person refines his civil virtue.

Wind has *qi* but no substance [*zhi* 質], so it is able to restrain but cannot last long. Hence the image of Restrained by the Lesser. "Refines his civil [*wen* 文] virtue" means he is unable to fully accumulate [virtue] and administer from afar.[152]

LINE STATEMENTS WITH COMMENTARY ON THE SMALLER IMAGES

[Line 1] **9 at the beginning: Returning to its own Way, how can there be blame? Auspicious.**

The lower trigram is Qian, which is fundamentally a superior thing; it wants to advance upward, yet it is restrained by *yin*. Although 9 at the beginning embodies Qian, it resides below and achieves correctness, and is distant from the *yin* ahead of it. Although it corresponds correctly with the fourth and is able to hold itself in correctness, it is not what is restrained. Therefore there is the image of advancing and returning to its own Way. If the diviner is like this there will be blameless good fortune.

[Image 1] **"Returning to its own Way": the meaning is auspicious.**

[Line 2] **9 in the second: Pulling back: auspicious.**

The three *yang* lines have the same purpose. The 9 in the second, gradually approaching the *yin*, is firm and central. Therefore it is able to join with 9 at the beginning and return: an auspicious Way. If the diviner is like this there will be good fortune.

[Image 2] "Pulling back" in the center, one will also not lose oneself.

"Also" refers to the preceding line.

[Line 3] 9 in the third: The cart separates from its wheel [literally, "spokes"]; husband and wife are at odds with each other.[153]

The 9 in the third also wants to advance upward. Although it is firm, it is not central, so it comes near to the *yin* but still does not correctly correspond [with the *yang* at the top]. But since the *yin* and *yang* [third and fourth lines] have separated from each other, they are restricted and restrained, with neither one able to advance.[154] Hence the image of a "cart separating from its spokes." However, its purpose is firm, so its struggle cannot be even; hence the image of a "husband and wife at odds with each other." With a warning to the diviner like this one cannot advance, and there will be struggle.

[Image 3] "Husband and wife are at odds with each other": unable to have a correct home.

Master Cheng [Yi] says, "Separating from its spokes" and "at odds with each other" embody the third line.[155]

[Line 4] 6 in the fourth: With honesty, blood vanishes and fear departs: no blame.

With the single *yin* restraining all the *yang* lines, originally there is injury, harm, worry, and fear. [But] the yielding compliant line achieves correctness, and the empty center of the Sun trigram is assisted by the two *yang* lines. Thus the image: "with honesty, blood vanishes and fear departs." It is appropriate that there is no blame. Therefore if the diviner also has these virtues there will be no blame.

[Image 4] "With honesty, fear departs": joining purposes with the one above.

[Line 5] Being honest and well connected, one can enrich one's neighbors.

The three lines of the Sun trigram all powerfully nurture Qian: the image of neighbors.[156] The 9 in the fifth occupies the central position of honor; its influence can be exerted both above and below. Therefore its honesty and connections are strong: the image of the power to "enrich one's neighbors."

[Image 5] "Being honest and well connected": one is not rich alone.

[Line 6] Rain has come, one's place is achieved, valuing the accumulation of virtue. The wife's correctness is endangered, like the moon almost full. If the superior person goes forth, bad fortune.

When maximal restraint is accomplished, *yin* and *yang* are harmonious; hence the image, "rain has come, one's place is achieved." This is honoring and valuing the virtue of *yin*, to the point of fully accumulating it. *Yin* is added to *yang*, so although it is correct [in its position], it is also dangerous. However, although the *yin* flourishes and protects the *yang*, the superior person cannot act. A prognostication like this is a serious warning.

[Image 6] "Rain has come, one's place is achieved": virtue has been accumulated. "If the superior person goes forth, bad fortune": there is reason to doubt.

[10] 履 Lü (Treading)[157]

Dui [lake] below, Qian [heaven] above.

Treading on the tiger's tail, one is not bitten: success.

Dui is the name of the [lower] trigram, where a single *yin* appears above two *yang* lines. Thus its virtue is pleasing, and its image is lake.[158] Lü has the meaning of going forward by stepping. With Dui encountering Qian, after gladly stepping firmly and strongly, there is the image of treading on the tiger's tail without experiencing injury.[159] Therefore the hexagram is Treading, and the prognostication follows from this. If one is able to be like this, one can dwell in danger and not be injured.

COMMENTARY ON THE JUDGMENT

Lü: The yielding treads on the firm.

Explaining the meaning of the hexagram name in terms of the two trigrams.

Pleasantly responding to Qian; in this way "treading on the tiger's tail, one is not bitten": success.

Explaining the Judgment text by means of the trigram virtues.

Being firm, central, and correct, one treads on the position of the lord [*di* 帝] [ruler] without guilt: bright and clear.

Again clarifying by means of the component trigrams, and referring to 9 in the fifth [the "governing ruler" of the hexagram].¹⁶⁰

COMMENTARY ON THE GREATER IMAGES

Heaven above, water below: Treading. The superior person, by distinguishing between high and low, settles the aims of the people.
Cheng [Yi]'s *Commentary* fully covers this. The *Commentary* says,¹⁶¹

> Heaven is above, lake resides below: the correct principle of hierarchy [superior and inferior]. Where people tread should be like this, so this image is used for Lü. The superior person observes this image of Lü and distinguishes the distinction of high and low to "settle the aims of the people." Only when the distinction between high and low is clarified can the aims of the people be settled. Only when the aims of the people are settled can we speak of ruling. When the aims of the people are not settled, the Empire [all under Heaven] cannot be ruled. In ancient times, the positions of dukes, lords, and ministers on down each designated their virtues/powers, and [even] if they occupied those positions their whole lives they understood their portions [the limits of their powers and responsibilities]. If their positions did not reflect their virtues, the ruler [*jun* 君] would promote and advance them. If literati cultivated their learning the ruler would seek out their perfected learning. There was never any self-seeking. Farmers, artisans, and merchants respectfully valued their affairs, and success was limited.¹⁶² Therefore all aims were settled and the minds/hearts of all under Heaven could be unified. In later generations, minor officials, dukes, and lords spend their days seeking dignity and honor; farmers, artisans, and merchants aim all day for wealth and excess. The minds/hearts of the multitudes all indulge in profit and all are in confusion; how then can they be unified? Desiring an end to disorder is difficult; this comes from the lack of settled aims of those above and below. The superior person observes the image of Lü and distinguishes between high and low, causing each to live up to his portion [in life] by settling the minds and aims of the people.¹⁶³

LINE STATEMENTS WITH COMMENTARY ON THE SMALLER IMAGES

[Line 1] 9 at the beginning: Treading simply, going forward without blame.

The *yang* below, occupying the beginning of Lü, is not yet shifting, but it goes along with "treading simply." If the diviner is like this he can go forward and have no blame.

[Image 1] Going forward by "treading simply," one carries out one's wishes alone.

[Line 2] 9 in the second: The way that is trod is flat and level. The secluded person is correct: auspicious.

Firm and central below, not corresponding above. Therefore the way that is trod is even and flat; the image of a secluded loner who holds to correctness. The secluded person who treads the way and meets with this prognostication will be correct and have good fortune.

[Image 2] "The secluded person is correct: auspicious." Being central, not confusing oneself.

[Line 3] 6 in the third: One eye yet able to see; lame yet able to tread. Treading on the tiger's tail, it bites the person: ominous. Military men make great rulers [*jun* 君].

6 in the third is neither central nor correct, a yielding line aiming to be firm, and thus treading on Qian: it must experience injury and harm. Hence the image is like this, and the prognostication is ominous. It is also the image of a firm military man who pursues his aims and is selfish and wild, like the Qin regime and Xiang Ji. How can it be long-lasting?[164]

[Image 3] "One eye yet able to see," but not well enough to have clarity. "Lame yet able to tread," but not well enough to keep up. The misfortune of being bitten; one's position is not proper. "Military men make great rulers"; their purposes are firm.

[Line 4] 9 in the fourth: Treading on the tiger's tail: fear and trepidation, but ultimately auspicious.

9 in the fourth is neither central nor correct: it treads on the firm 9 in the fifth. But it is a firm line occupying a yielding position, so it is able to be watchful and fearful and ultimately auspicious.

[Image 4] "Fear and trepidation, but ultimately auspicious": purposes are carried out.

[Line 5] 9 in the fifth: Treading resolutely, correct when in danger.

9 in the fifth, firm, central, and correct, is in the lord's [ruler's] position of Lü. It responds to the pleasure of Dui below. All affairs should be undertaken without questioning or obstruction. Therefore its image is resolutely deciding to tread. Although carrying out [affairs] can be correct, it is a path of danger. Therefore the prognostication is danger although correct: a serious warning.

[Image 5] "Treading resolutely, correct when in danger": one's position is correct and proper.

Injuring what one depends upon.

[Line 6] 9 at the top: Watch where you tread and examine the signs. The cycle is supremely auspicious.

At the conclusion of "watching where you tread and examining the signs," going all around thoroughly can be "supremely auspicious." The diviner's adversity and happiness [depend upon] watching where you tread before it is decided.[165]

[Image 6] "Supremely auspicious" at the top: rejoicing in great measure.

If one gets "fundamentally auspicious" one will have great happiness.

[11] ䷊ 泰 Tai (Penetrating)[166]

Qian [heaven] below, Kun [earth] above.

Tai. The petty depart, the great arrive: auspicious success.

Tai means penetrating [*tong* 通]. As a hexagram it is Heaven and Earth interacting and their two *qi* [inter]penetrating; hence Tai. It is the hexagram of the New Year.[167] "The petty" is *yin*, "the great" is *yang*. This says that Kun departs and resides outside, while Qian approaches and resides inside.[168] It comes from

Guimei 歸妹 [54 ䷵], with a 6 departing to reside in the fourth and a 9 arriving to approach in the third.[169]

COMMENTARY ON THE JUDGMENT

"Tai: The petty depart and the great arrive; auspicious success." This is Heaven and Earth interacting and the myriad things [inter]penetrating; the upper and lower interacting and their purposes coinciding. It is inner *yang* and outer *yin*, inner strength and outer compliance, inner superior person and outer petty person, the Way of the superior person growing and the Way of the petty person declining.

COMMENTARY ON THE GREATER IMAGES

Heaven and Earth interact: Penetrating. The sovereign [*hou* 后] trims and completes the Way of Heaven and Earth and assists in the harmonization of Heaven and Earth for all the people.

He "trims and completes" in order to correct excess; he "assists" in order to supplement [cases of] not going far enough.[170]

LINE STATEMENTS WITH COMMENTARY ON THE SMALLER IMAGES

[Line 1] 9 at the beginning: Pulling out thatch grass in clumps; going forth is auspicious.

The three *yang* lines at the bottom advance by being interconnected: the image of pulling out thatch grass" in interconnected clumps; the good fortune of going forth.

[Image 1] "Pulling out thatch grass . . . going forth is auspicious": one's purposes are directed externally.

[Line 2] 9 in the second: Embracing the undisciplined, using them to ford a river. Not neglecting the distant, forgetting one's friends, gaining honor in moderate actions.[171]

9 in the second is a firm line occupying the position of the yielding, in the center of the lower trigram, corresponding above with 6 in the fifth. It is the ruler of Tai and achieves the Middle Way.[172] If the diviner is able to be broad-minded in regard to the undisciplined and defiled, to be decisive and firm in one's decisions, to not neglect the distant and not stick with friends and colleagues [to the exclusion of others], then one can join with this line in the Way of moderate action.

[Image 2] "Embracing the undisciplined . . . gaining honor in moderate actions": by making one's radiance great.

[Line 3] 9 in the third: There is no plain without a slope, no departing without returning. Being correct when in difficulty, there is no blame. Do not worry if you are honest; there is happiness in eating.[173]

About to go beyond the Mean, Tai is about to peak when Pi desires to approach. Being "honest" is trusting one's expectation. "To worry" is to be anxious. The warning to the diviner is to hold on to correctness when in difficulty; then there will be "happiness" and "no blame."

[Image 3] "No departing without returning": the boundaries of Heaven and Earth.

[Line 4] 6 in the fourth: Fluttering, not using wealth in dealing with neighbors, being honest and not admonishing them.

Having already gone beyond the Mean, Tai has already peaked. Therefore the three *yin* lines float [flutter] back below without depending on wealth to get their associates to follow them, trusting without depending on warnings or commands. The prognostication [in the hexagram statement] is that there are petty people conspiring to harm the correct Way, which the superior person properly admonishes. *Yin* is empty and *yang* is full, so in general the words about not being wealthy refer to all the *yin* lines.

[Image 4] "Fluttering, not using wealth": all have lost their solid [positions]. "Being honest and not admonishing": the desire of the inmost heart.

The *yin* originally resides below; when above it loses its solidity.

[Line 5] 6 in the fifth: Sovereign Yi [of Shang] married off his younger sister [to King Wen of Zhou] for blessings and supreme good fortune.[174]

The *yin* occupying the place of honor is the [other] ruler of Tai. As a yielding line in the empty center, corresponding below with 9 in the second, it is the Way of good fortune. When Di Yi married off his younger sister he also received this line. With a prognostication like this there will be blessings and supreme good fortune. Throughout the Scripture, all references to men of old, such as the Exalted Ancestor or Jizi, are like this.[175]

[Image 5] "For blessings and supreme good fortune": being central to carry out one's desires.

[Line 6] 6 at the top: The city walls fall back into the moat. Do not use the army; issue commands only in your own city. Correctness, disgrace.

When Tai peaks it becomes Pi [12]: the image of the city walls falling back into the moat. The diviner, warned, cannot forcefully struggle, but can preserve himself. Although he can achieve correctness, he cannot avoid shame and disgrace.

[Image 6] "The city walls fall back into the moat": his decrees are in ruins.

"His decrees are in ruins," thus it returns to Pi [Obstruction]. Announcing decrees is how one puts things in order.

[12] ䷋ 否 Pi (Obstructing)

Kun [earth] below, Qian [heaven] above.

Criminals who obstruct are not appropriate to the correctness of the superior person. The great depart and the petty approach.

Pi is obstructing [*bisai* 閉塞], the hexagram of the seventh month.[176] In terms of correctness it is the opposite of Tai, thus it says "criminals," meaning it is not the human Way. The prognostication is "not appropriate to the correct Way of the superior person." Qian, departing, occupies the outer, and Kun, arriving, occupies the inner. It comes [by "hexagram fluctuation"] from Jian 漸 [53 ䷴], with 9 departing [the third place] to reside in the fourth and 6 arriving [from the fourth] to reside in the third. Some suspect that the word "criminals" is superfluous text, wrongly taken from 6 in the third line of Bi [8]. It is evident that the appendixes do not specifically explain its meaning.

COMMENTARY ON THE JUDGMENT

"Criminals who obstruct are not appropriate to the correctness of the superior person. The great depart and the petty approach." Heaven and Earth do not interact, and the myriad things do not [inter]penetrate; above and below do not interact, under Heaven there are no states. The inner is *yin* and the outer is *yang*, the inner is yielding and the outer firm, the inner is petty and the outer the superior, the Way of the petty person grows and the Way of the superior person declines.[177]

COMMENTARY ON THE GREATER IMAGES

"Heaven and Earth do not interact": Obstructing. The superior person conceals his virtue to ward off difficulty, and cannot be honored with salary.

He conceals his virtue, not showing it externally, in order to ward off the difficulty of the petty person. People cannot use salary and rank to honor themselves.

LINE STATEMENTS WITH COMMENTARY ON THE SMALLER IMAGES

[Line 1] 6 at the beginning: Pulling out thatch grass in clumps; being correct is auspicious and successful.

The three *yin* lines at the bottom are in a time of obstruction: the image of the petty person with similar associates advancing. At the beginning the evil is not yet formed, so the warning is that if one is correct then it will be auspicious and successful. If one can be like this, then one can change [*bian* 變] into a superior person.

[Image 1] "Pulling out thatch grass," "being correct is auspicious." Be devoted to the ruler [*jun* 君].

When the petty person changes into a superior person, he is able to love his ruler in his thoughts and not calculate selfish concerns.

[Line 2] 6 in the second: Undertaking what comes from above; auspicious for the petty person, obstruction for the great person; success.

The yielding *yin* line is central and correct: the image of the petty person being able to open-mindedly receive and comply with the superior person; the auspicious Way of the petty person. Therefore if the diviner is a petty person there will accordingly be good fortune. If he is a great person then he must calmly accept the obstruction; his Way will be successful later. If one cannot undertake what comes to oneself from another, one will lose what one has preserved in oneself.[178]

[Image 2] The great person, though obstructed, is successful. He is not confused by the crowd.
This says that he is not confused by the crowd of petty people.

[Line 3] 6 in the third: Embracing shame.
The *yin* line occupying a *yang* position is neither central nor correct. The petty person intends to subdue the good but is unable: hence the image of "embracing shame." Although he has not expressed [his intention], there is no warning of bad fortune or blame.

[Image 3] "Embracing shame." His position is improper.

[Line 4] 9 in the fourth: With the Decree, there is no blame. Companions who stick together will have blessings.
While the obstruction is passing through is the moment when it is about to end. 9 in the fourth is a *yang* line occupying a *yin* position, not maximally firm. Therefore the prognostication is "there is a decree, no blame," and the three similar *yang* lines will all obtain happiness. "Decree" means the Decree [Mandate] of Heaven.

[Image 4] "With the Decree, there is no blame." One's purposes will be carried out.

[Line 5] 9 in the fifth: Ceasing the obstruction, good fortune for the great person. Death! Death! Fasten to a thick mulberry.
The firm *yang* line is central and correct, occupying the position of respect. It is able to cease the time of obstruction; the business of a great person. Therefore the prognostication for this line, when the great person encounters it, is auspicious. However, there is also the proper warning to be apprehensive, as the *Xici zhuan* says.[179]

[Image 5] The great person's good fortune: his position is correct and proper.

[Line 6] 9 at the top: Overturning the obstruction. First obstruction, then happiness.

The firm *yang* line occupying the peak of Pi is what is able to overturn the time of obstruction. The prognostication is "first obstruction, then happiness."

[Image 6] The obstruction has ended and is overturned; how could it be long-lasting?

[13]   ䷌   同人   Tongren (Fellowship)

Li [fire] below, Qian [heaven] above.

Fellowship in the field: success. Appropriate to cross a great river, appropriate for the superior person to be correct.

Li is the name of the [lower] trigram. The single *yin* line is balanced between the two *yang* lines, so its virtue is balanced, elegant, and bright. Its image is fire, the sun, lightning. Fellowship is being joined with others. Li encountering Qian is fire rising to join with Heaven. The 6 in the second place is well positioned and central, corresponding above with 9 in the fifth. The hexagram's sole *yin* line is joined together with five *yang* lines; therefore it is Fellowship. "In the field" means vast and broad, with nothing selfish: a Way of success.[180] Acting with strength, one is able to cross the river. Internally the hexagram is elegant and bright, externally it is firm and strong. The 6 in the second is central, correct, and responsive [to 9 in the fifth], so it is the Way of the superior person. If the diviner is able to be like this there will be success, and he can pass through danger. But it is necessary that he join together with the Way of the superior person in order to be appropriate.

COMMENTARY ON THE JUDGMENT

Tongren: Yielding obtains position and centrality, and corresponds with Qian; it is called Fellowship.

Explaining the meaning of the hexagram name by means of the component trigrams. "Yielding" is 6 in the second; "Qian" is 9 in the fifth.

Tongren says . . .
   Superfluous text.

"Fellowship in the field: success; appropriate to cross a great river" is Qian acting. Elegant and bright in strength, central, correct, and responsive, is the correctness of the superior person. Only the superior person is able to penetrate the purposes of all under Heaven.

Explaining the hexagram statement by means of the hexagram virtues and the component trigrams. "Penetrating the purposes of all under Heaven" is the "Great Commonality";[181] otherwise one is simply bound by selfish feelings. How could one achieve success and appropriately cross?

COMMENTARY ON THE GREATER IMAGES

Heaven and fire: Fellowship. The superior person distinguishes among things according to their kinds and affiliations.

Heaven is above and fire burns upward; their natures are the same. "Distinguishing among things according to their kinds and affiliations" is how to examine differences and reach commonality.

LINE STATEMENTS WITH COMMENTARY ON THE SMALLER IMAGES

[Line 1] 9 at the beginning: Fellowship at one's gate; no blame.
   At the beginning of Fellowship there is not yet an individual ruler. As a firm line below, with no connection or correspondence above, there can be no blame. Hence this image and prognostication.

[Image 1] Leaving one's gate with fellows, who can be at blame?

[Line 2] 6 in the second: Fellowship with the clan: disgrace.
   The "clan" [zong 宗] is a faction [dang 黨]. Although 6 in the second is both central and correct, it corresponds [with the fifth] above. One cannot make a Great

Commonality by linking with one's own; this is a Way of disgrace. Hence the image and prognostiction.[182]

[Image 2] "Fellowship with the clan": the Way of disgrace.

[Line 3] 9 in the third: Conceal weapons in the bush; climb the high hill. For three years do not rise up.

Firm but not central, without correct correspondence above, wanting to join with the second but not being correct, fearful of 9 in the fifth seeing one's attack; hence this image.

[Image 3] "Conceal weapons in the bush": one's opponent is firm. "For three years do not rise up": how could you proceed?

This says one is unable to proceed.

[Line 4] 9 in the fourth: Climbing the city wall but unable to attack; auspicious.

[This line is] firm but not central or correct. Nothing corresponds with it, and it desires to join with 6 in the second, but is separated from it by the third. Therefore it climbs the city wall in order to attack it. But it is a firm line occupying a yielding position, hence the image of turning back on itself, unable to attack. If the diviner is like this, then he is able to correct his transgressions and achieve good fortune.

[Image 4] "Climbing the city wall," rightness fails. "Good fortune" is being in trouble and returning to the rules.

Climbing the city wall, but with insufficient power. In particular, "rightness fails" and one does not attack. But one is able to judge what is right, and return to the rule of law when in trouble; thus good fortune.

[Line 5] 9 in the fifth: Fellows first cry and wail, but then laugh. The great army overcomes, and they come together.

The fifth line is firm, central, and correct, and corresponds below with the second, which is yielding, central, and correct: they are like-minded. Yet they are separated by the third and the fourth and cannot join. However, moral principle [*yili* 義理] is what joins them, and things cannot come between them; hence this image. But 6 in the second is yielding and weak and the third and fourth are firm and strong; therefore it must use a great army to defeat them. Only then can they come together.

[Image 5] Fellowship at first, central and straight. "The great army" and "come together" refer to their mutual victory.

"Straight" means the straightness of principle.

[Line 6] 9 at the top: Fellowship outside the city: no regret.

Residing outside, with no correspondence, there is nothing to join with. But there can also be no regret, hence this image and prognostication. "Outside the city" means in the countryside, but not very far. It is just that in uncultivated rural areas there is no one to join with.

[Image 6] "Fellowship outside the city": one's purpose is not yet achieved.

[14] ䷍ 大有   Dayou (Great Possession)

Qian [heaven] below, Li [fire] above.

Dayou: Supreme success.

"Great Possession" means the greatness of what one possesses. Li resides above Qian, fire above Heaven, so everything is illuminated. Also, 6 in the fifth is a single *yin* occupying the place of honor and is central, while the five *yang* lines correspond with it, so this is great possession.[183] Qian is strong and Li is bright. The one occupying the place of honor [6 in the fifth] corresponds with Heaven, so it is a Way of success. If the diviner has these virtues he will be very happy and successful.

COMMENTARY ON THE JUDGMENT

Dayou: The yielding line achieves the place of honor in the great center, and corresponds with those above and below. This is called Great Possession.

Explaining the meaning of the hexagram name in terms of the component trigrams. "The yielding line" is 6 in the fifth. "Above and below" means the five *yang* lines.

Its virtue is firm, strong, elegant, and bright. It corresponds with Heaven and acts in a timely way; in this way it is "supreme and penetrating."

Explaining the hexagram statement in terms of the virtues of the component trigrams. What "corresponds with Heaven" is 6 in the fifth.

COMMENTARY ON THE GREATER IMAGES

Fire above Heaven: Great Possession. The superior person prevents the bad and promotes the good, complying with Heaven and resting in its decree.

"Fire above Heaven": what is illuminated is vast, the image of great possession. If that which has become great has nothing to govern it, faults will sprout up in it. In the Decree of Heaven there is good but no bad, so preventing the bad and promoting the good is how to comply with Heaven. If one goes against it personally it will be like that.

LINE STATEMENTS WITH COMMENTARY ON THE SMALLER IMAGES

[Line 1] 9 at the beginning: No relationship with harm, no blame. In difficulty, no blame.

Although it is the proper time for great possession, this *yang* line occupies the lowest position and has no link or correspondence above.[184] At the beginning of an event, if one does not step into harm, how can there be any blame? Even if there must be difficulty in managing it, there is no blame. The warning to the diviner is thus appropriate.

[Image 1] 9 at the beginning of Great Possession: "No relationship with harm."

[Line 2] 9 in the second: A big wagon for loading; wherever you go, no blame.

The firm central line below responds [to the yielding fifth] above; the image of the "big wagon for loading." Wherever you go like this, there may be no blame. The diviner must have these virtues [being firm and centered] in order to respond to the prognostication.

[Image 2] "A big wagon for loading": pile up in the center; it won't break.

[Line 3] 9 in the third: A duke makes an offering to the Son of Heaven. A petty person cannot.

In the *Zuo Commentary on the Spring and Autumn [Annals]*, *heng* 亨 [offering] is written *xiang* 享 [receive, enjoy], meaning court tribute.[185] Anciently, the *heng* of *hengtong* 亨通 [proceeding smoothly], the *xiang* of *xiangxian* 享獻 [to present], and the *peng* of *pengren* 烹飪 [to cook] were all written with the character *heng* 亨. The 9 in the third resides at the top of the lower trigram: the image of the duke or marquis, firm and correct. Above there is the noble 6 in the fifth, with the worthy below the empty center; hence the image of "offering to the Son of Heaven." If the diviner has these virtues the prognostication will be like this. The petty person lacks the virtues of firmness and correctness, so even if he gets this line he cannot deserve it.

[Image 3] "A duke makes an offering to the Son of Heaven." For a petty person it is harmful.

[Line 4] 9 in the fourth: Restraining his abundance; no blame.

Peng 彭 [abundance] is pronounced *pang* 旁 [side]. Neither the pronunciation nor the meaning of *peng* is clear. Cheng [Yi]'s *Commentary* says "appearance of fullness," which is possibly the correct principle.[186] 6 in the fifth is the noble of the yielding center, near the firmness of 9 in the fourth, disliking aggression. But it is empty and yielding, so it is the image of not completely flourishing, and accrues no blame. Hence the appropriate warning to the diviner.

[Image 4] "Restraining his abundance; no blame." Clear, discriminating, and fair.
"Fair" means clear in appearance.

[Line 5] 6 in the fifth: His honesty is engaging and dignified; auspicious.

In an age of great possession, the yielding is compliant and central, placing itself in a position of respect. Emptying itself to respond to the worthy 9 in the second, with those above and below turning to it, is the engaging character of honesty and trust. However, the Way of the noble is honorable and firm, and by this supreme act of yielding [emptying itself] it declines, properly matching it [9 in the second] in dignity, so it is auspicious. Thus the image and prognostication like this are also words of warning.[187]

[Image 5] "His honesty is engaging": trusting and promoting [others'] purposes.

The trustworthiness of this person is sufficient to promote the purposes of those above and below.

The good fortune of being dignified: easily, without preparation.

With a supreme act of yielding a person can lead easily, without fearful preparation.

[Line 6] 9 at the top: With assistance from Heaven, good fortune; everything is appropriate.[188]

In an age of great possession, the firm resides above and can be followed below by 6 in the fifth. Thus it is able to tread honestly, think compliantly, and promote the worthy. It is full but not to excess, and so the prognostication is like this.

[Image 6] "Good fortune" at the top of Great Possession: "assisted from Heaven."

[15] ䷖ 謙 Qian (Being Modest)[189]

Gen [mountain] below, Kun [earth] above.

Qian: Success. The superior person achieves his ends.[190]

Being modest means possessing but not dwelling on it. Stilling within and complying without is the idea of being modest.[191] The mountain reaching high and the earth reaching low, submitting and stilling below, is the image of being modest. If the diviner is like this, his success will pervade and he will "achieve his ends." "Achieving ends" means first submitting and then extending.

COMMENTARY ON THE JUDGMENT

Qian: Success. The Way of Heaven extends aid below and is radiant and bright. The Way of Earth is lowly and has moved upward.[192]

This expresses how being modest must be successful.

The Way of Heaven decreases what is full and increases what is modest. The Way of Earth changes [bian 變] what is full and spreads what is modest. Ghosts and spirits injure the full and bless the modest. The Way of Humanity dislikes the full and likes the modest. Being modest when honored is radiant; when lowly it cannot be exceeded. Thus the superior person achieves his ends.

"Changes" means to diminish and destroy [what is full].[193] "Spreads" means to gather and follow. If a person can be modest, then if his station is honored his virtue will be exceedingly radiant; if his station is lowly, no one will be able to surpass him. This is how the superior person achieves his ends.

COMMENTARY ON THE GREATER IMAGES

Within the earth is a mountain: Being Modest. The superior person decreases what is too much and increases what is too little. He assesses things and evens them out.

The lowly accumulates above: the image of being modest. "Decreasing what is too much and increasing what is too little" is how he assesses the suitability of things and evens them out. Diminishing the high and augmenting the lowly in order to attain evenness is the idea of being modest.

LINE STATEMENTS WITH COMMENTARY ON THE SMALLER IMAGES

[Line 1] 6 at the beginning: Modest, modest, is the superior person. Crossing a great river is auspicious.

The yielding line residing below is the utmost of modesty. How can the movement of the superior person, in this difficult crossing, proceed without crossing? Thus if the diviner is like this, it will be appropriate to cross the river.

[Image 1] "Modest, modest, is the superior person." He stays low in order to take care of himself.

[Line 2] 6 in the second: Expressing modesty; correct and auspicious.

The yielding line is compliant, central, and correct, and so its modesty is known, correct, and even auspicious. Hence the prognostication.

[Image 2] "Expressing modesty, correct and auspicious": achieving one's inmost heart.

[Line 3] 9 in the third: Toiling modestly, the superior person achieve his ends; auspicious.

The only *yang* line of the hexagram, residing at the top of the lower trigram, is firm and correct and is followed by those above and below. With meritorious effort, despite a person's difficulty, he will achieve his ends and good fortune. If the diviner is like this then so will be the response.

[Image 3] "The superior person who strives to be modest": the myriad people obey.

[Line 4] 6 in the fourth: Everything appropriate, displaying modesty.

Yielding and correct, able to descend from above, the prognostication is "everything appropriate." But it is above 9 in the third, so the warning is the idea that it is especially necessary to develop one's modesty, and to show that one does not dare to be self-satisfied.

[Image 4] "Everything appropriate, displaying modesty": not departing from rules.

Referring to not committing transgressions.

[Line 5] 6 in the fifth: Not using wealth in dealing with neighbors; appropriate to engage in invasion and attack. Everything is appropriate.

A yielding line occupying the place of honor, above and yet able to be modest; thus the image of not using wealth, yet able to deal with neighbors. Those who follow may indeed be numerous. If it seems that they are not obedient, then it is appropriate to attack them, and other matters will also all be appropriate. If a person has these virtues he will have this prognostication.

[Image 5] "Appropriate to engage in invasion and attack": striking those who disobey.

[Line 6] 6 at the top: Expressing modesty, it is appropriate to set in motion the army to attack a city or state.

Modesty at its peak makes itself known. If others are involved, one can "set in motion the army." But the material of this line is yielding and lacks [proper] position. Therefore one can attack only one's own city or state.[194]

[Image 6] "Expressing modesty," one's purposes are not achieved. One can "set in motion the army to attack a city or state."

The *yin* yielding line lacks position, so its talent and power are insufficient; therefore "one's purposes are not achieved." When it comes to the point of "setting in motion the army," even if one has enough [power], use it only to rule one's own city.

[16] ䷏ 豫 Yu (Being Happy)[195]

Kun [earth] below, Zhen [thunder] above.

Yu: Appropriate to establish a marquis and set in motion the army.

Yu is being harmonious and happy [*he le* 和樂]. The human mind is harmonious and happy in responding to those above. The 9 in the fourth is the only *yang* line; those above and below respond to it, so his purposes can be set in motion. As it is Kun encountering Zhen, its activity is compliant; therefore the hexagram is Being Happy, and the prognostication is that it is appropriate to establish a ruler and to use the army.

COMMENTARY ON THE JUDGMENT

Yu: The firm corresponds and its purposes are set in motion. Compliantly acting; being happy.[196]

Explaining the meaning of the hexagram name in terms of the component trigrams and their virtues.

Being happy is being compliant in activity. Therefore Heaven and Earth are like this; [how can it not be appropriate to] establish a marquis and set armies in motion?

Explaining the hexagram statement in terms of the trigram virtues.

Heaven and Earth are compliant in activity; therefore the sun and moon do not transgress each other and the four seasons do not err. The Sage is compliant in activity; so his punishments are clear-cut and the people obey. The meaning of happy times is indeed great!

Fully expressing and praising the greatness [of being happy].

COMMENTARY ON THE GREATER IMAGES

Thunder emerges and the earth shakes: Being Happy. The former kings exalted virtue by creating music. They offered it in fullness to the High Lord, in the company of their ancestors.

"Thunder emerges and the earth shakes" is the perfection of harmony. "The former kings created music" to symbolize its sound and grasp its meaning. *Yin* 殷 means fullness.

LINE STATEMENTS WITH COMMENTARY ON THE SMALLER IMAGES

[Line 1] 6 at the beginning: Expressing happiness: ominous.

The yielding *yin* line is the petty person. Aided by strength from above, he seizes the time and rules the situation. Therefore he does not overcome his happiness and expresses it himself, which is an ominous Way; hence the prognostication. The hexagram originally gets its name from being harmonious and happy, but the hexagram statement means the happiness of the group, while the line statements, except for 9 in the fourth, which is the same as the hexagram [text], are all about their own happiness. This is how good fortune and bad fortune differ.

[Image 1] "6 at the beginning: Expressing happiness." Purposes fulfilled are ominous.

"Fulfilled" means completely satisfied.

[Line 2] 6 in the second: Hard as a rock, but not all day; correct and auspicious.[197]

Although happiness is chiefly joyful, a person can easily become absorbed in it, and once absorbed, it can then turn into sadness. This is the only line in the hexagram that is central and correct. Above and below this they are all absorbed in happiness, and only this one is able to preserve itself in centrality and correctness; hence it is "hard as a rock." Its virtue is peaceful and still, yet firm and solid. Therefore one's thinking and deliberation can clarify and judge, but not waiting all day to see the incipient subtleties of all events. The *Great Learning*

[*Daxue*] says, "Only after being at ease can one deliberate; only after deliberating can one achieve [one's ends]." This is exactly the idea. If the diviner is like this, then it is correct and auspicious.

[Image 2] "Not all day, correct and auspicious"; it is central and correct.

[Line 3] 6 in the third: Looking upward for happiness: regret. With delay there is [also] regret.

Xu 盱 means looking upward. This *yin* line is neither central nor correct, but it is close to the fourth, and the fourth is the ruler of the hexagram. Therefore 6 in the third looks upward to the fourth, and those below are absorbed in happiness, so it is appropriate that they have regret. Therefore the image is thus, and the prognostication is that matters should bring quick regret. If regret is delayed, there will nevertheless be regret.

[Image 3] "Looking upward for happiness," there is regret. Its position is not proper.

[Line 4] 9 in the fourth: From happiness, great possession is achieved. If you do not doubt, won't friends gather?

9 in the fourth is the reason for the hexagram being happiness; hence this image, and the prognostication is "great possession achieved." But one must also be perfectly authentic [*cheng* 誠] and without doubt. Then friends and associates will gather and follow you. Therefore this is also a warning. *Zan* 簪 means "to gather." It also means "quick."[198]

[Image 4] "From happiness, great possession is achieved." Purposes will be greatly carried out.

[Line 5] 6 in the fifth: Persistent illness, hanging on and not dying.

Just at the moment of being happy, a yielding line occupies the place of honor, infatuated with happiness and riding on the firm 9 in the fourth.[199] No more is gathered, and the strength of the position is weakened; hence the image of "persistent illness." However, it has achieved the central position; hence the image of "hanging on and not dying." Contemplating just the images, the prognostication is implicit in them.[200]

[Image 5] "6 in the fifth: Persistent illness": riding on the firm. "Hanging on but not dying": centrality not yet lost.

[Line 6] 6 at the top: Happiness darkened. If changes are made, no blame.

As a *yin* yielding line occupying the peak of Yu, it is the image of darkening happiness. It is also the trigram of activity, so even though the matter may be completed, it can be an image of change. With a warning to the diviner like this, correcting an error and having no blame is how to fully transition to the realm of the good.

[Image 6] "Happiness darkened" at the top: how can it go further?

[17] ䷐ 隨 Sui (Following)[201]

Zhen [thunder] below, Dui [lake] above.

Sui: Supreme and penetrating, appropriate and correct. No blame.

Sui means following [*cong* 從]. In terms of hexagram fluctuations, starting from Kun [47 ䷮], a 9 comes [from the second position] to reside at the beginning; from Shihe [21 ䷔], a 9 comes [from the top position] to reside in the fifth; and from Weiji [64 ䷿] we have both these fluctuations. These all mean that a firm line comes to a weak line in Sui. In terms of the two component trigrams, one [Zhen] is activity and the other [Dui] is pleasure, and this also means following; thus it is Sui. If one is able to follow things and things come to follow oneself, they follow each other with thorough [penetrating] ease; thus the prognostication is "supreme and penetrating." As it must be appropriate and correct, there is no blame. If what is followed is not correct, then even though it is greatly penetrating, it will not avoid blame. The *Spring and Autumn* [*Zuo*] *Commentary* says, Mu Jiang said, "With these Four Virtues [*yuan heng li zhen*], Sui involves no blame. If I lack all of them, how can I follow?" I would now comment that although [Mu Jiang's definitions] are not the original meanings of the Four Virtues [as defined by Zhu in his comment on the hexagram statement], her following statements profoundly capture the idea of the prognostication method.[202]

COMMENTARY ON THE JUDGMENT

Sui: The firm comes in below the yielding; pleasure in activity: following.
    Explaining the meaning of the hexagram name by means of the hexagram fluctuations and trigram virtues.

With great success and correctness with no blame, all under Heaven will follow him.
    Wang Su's edition has *zhi* 之 [it, him] for *shi* 時 [time], and I now follow it.[203] This explains the hexagram statement, saying that if one can be like this, then all under Heaven will follow him.

How great is the meaning of a time of following!
    Wang Su's edition has *shi* 時 [time] after *zhi* 之 [possessive particle], and I follow it.[204]

COMMENTARY ON THE GREATER IMAGES

Within the lake there is thunder: Following. The superior person goes in before dark for quiet rest.
    Thunder is stored in the lake. At a time of following, take a nap.

LINE STATEMENTS WITH COMMENTARY ON THE SMALLER IMAGES

[Line 1] 9 at the beginning: There is a change of officials; correct and auspicious. There is merit in going outside the gate for associations.
    The meaning of the hexagram is things following, while the meaning of the lines is following things. The 9 at the beginning is a *yang* line in a lower position; it is the ruler of Zhen, which is why the hexagram follows it.[205] Once there is something to follow there is emphasis on partiality and a change in the norm. Only by achieving correctness can there be good fortune. One must "go outside the gate" for associations, so as not to be selfish in what one follows; then there will

be merit. Therefore the image and prognostication are like this, and accordingly a warning.

[Image 1] "There is a change of officials": to follow what is correct is auspicious. "There is merit in going outside the gate for associations": one will not lose.

[Line 2] 6 in the second: Clinging to the little child, losing the mature man.

The *yang* at the beginning is below and close; the fifth *yang* correctly corresponds and is distant. The second position is a yielding *yin* line that cannot preserve itself, so it needs the correct correspondence [with the fifth]; hence the image. Bad fortune and regret is evident; it need not be said.[206]

[Image 2] "Clinging to the little child": not involved with either [the child or the man].

[Line 3] 6 in the third: Clinging to the mature man, losing the little child. In following there is seeking and finding. Appropriate to abide in correctness.

The "mature man" is 9 in the fourth. The "little child" is [9 at] the beginning. The third closely clings to the fourth and loses [contact with] the beginning. The image is exactly the opposite of 6 in the second. The fourth *yang* must be in charge, and one follows it. When you seek you will find, but [here] there is no correct correspondence, so one will be incorrect and guilty of insincere flattery. Hence the prognostication and the warning to dwell in correctness.

[Image 3] "Clinging to the mature man": intending to abandon [the child] below.

[Line 4] 9 in the fourth: By following one hits the mark; persisting is ominous. Being honest in the Way and understanding it, how can there be any blame?

9 in the fourth is a firm line residing at the bottom of the upper trigram, with the same virtue as the fifth. Thus the prognostication is "following and hitting the mark." But its strength usurps that of the fifth, so even if one is correct, it is ominous. Only if there is honesty and clarity in the Way can the one above be at ease and the one below follow it, and there be no blame. The diviner must take charge of the moment and appropriately take heed of this warning.

[Image 4] "By following one hits the mark" means bad fortune. "Trusting in one's path" is to understand one's achievement.

[Line 5] 9 in the fifth: Honest in excellence; auspicious.

The *yang* firm line is central and correct, and corresponds below with one that is central and correct; this is trusting in what is good. If the diviner is like this, good fortune is appropriate.

[Image 5] "Honest in excellence: auspicious." The position is correct and central.

[Line 6] 6 at the top: Grasp and cling to it, thus binding it. The king makes offerings to the western mountain.

Occupying the peak [*ji* 極] of Sui, following becomes firmly restrained and cannot be loosened. With the highest [peak] of authentic intention one can spread one's spiritual clarity [or connect with the gods]; thus the prognostication is "the king makes offerings to the western mountain." "Offerings" [*heng* 亨] should be understood as sacrificial offerings [*ji heng* 祭亨]. In terms of the Zhou [dynasty], Mount Qi was in the west, so the shamans who sacrificed to the mountain and rivers would achieve it. If one has authentic intentions like this, there will be good fortune.[207]

[Image 6] "Grasp and cling to it": at the top it is exhausted.

"Exhausted" [*qiong* 窮] means maximized [*ji* 極].

[18] ䷑ 蠱   Gu (Working on What Is Ruined)

Sun [wind, wood] below, Gen [mountain] above.

Gu: Supreme success; appropriate to cross a great river. Three days before the first, three days after the first.

"Gu" means there is work to be done [*shi* 事] when ruin [*huai* 壞] peaks. The firm Gen trigram resides above, the yielding Sun resides below; above and below do not interact. The lowly Sun below is improperly stopped from rising, so the hexagram is "ruined."[208] Some say that the firm above and yielding below means that via hexagram fluctuation [*guabian* 卦變] either [1] it comes from Bi [22 ䷕], whose first line rises and second line sinks; [2] it comes from Jing [48 ䷯], whose fifth line rises and top line sinks; [3] or it comes from Jiji [63 ䷾], with both of these. These are all cases of a firm line rising and a yielding line sinking, which is why they are "ruined." When ruin and destruction reach their maximum, disorder must return to order; thus the prognostication is "supreme success" and "appropriate to cross a great river." "The first" [*jia* 甲], or the first day [of the week], is when work begins. "Three days before the first" is *xin* 辛; "three days after the first" is *ding* 丁.²⁰⁹ When prior matters transgress the Mean and are heading for ruin, one can renew oneself to begin future matters so as to avoid causing them to reach a state of great ruin. Then when future matters have begun they will tend to be renewed. But the idea of bringing about ease on the *ding* day is even more important: by managing the failures of previous matters one does not cause [future matters] to be quickly ruined. The Sage's [King Wen's] admonition is profound.²¹⁰

COMMENTARY ON THE JUDGMENT

Gu: Firm above and yielding below. Gently stopped: ruined.

Explaining the meaning of the hexagram name by means of the component trigrams, hexagram transformations, and trigram virtues. According to these, gradual collapse leads to ruin.

"Gu: Supreme success": all under Heaven is ordered. "Appropriate to cross a great river": going on, there will be things to do. "Three days before the first, three days after the first": after an ending there is a beginning; this is the course of Heaven [nature].

Explaining the hexagram statement. Ordering what has been ruined leads to "supreme success" [penetrating]: the image of disorder being put back in order. The end of disorder and the beginning of order is how Heaven revolves.

COMMENTARY ON THE GREATER IMAGES

Below the mountain is wind: Working on What Is Ruined. The superior person invigorates the people and nurtures their virtue.

"Below the mountain is wind": things are ruined and there is work to do. There are no greater works than these two: the Way of ordering the self and ordering others.

LINE STATEMENTS WITH COMMENTARY ON THE SMALLER IMAGES

[Line 1] 6 at the beginning: Managing what the father has ruined. With a son, the departed father is blameless. Danger, but in the end good fortune.

"Managing/supporting" [*gan* 幹] is like the trunk [*gan* 幹] of a tree, which connects and supports the branches and leaves. What is "ruined" is the result of what forebears have ruined. Therefore several of the lines [all but the top] contain images of the father or mother. The son is able to manage, so correct order arises again. With 6 at the beginning the ruin is not profound and matters can easily be saved. Therefore the prognostication is that with a son who can order what has been ruined, the departed accrues no blame, although there is danger. In this way the diviner is appropriately warned. If he understands the danger and is capable of being admonished, then "in the end good fortune."

[Image 1] "Managing what the father has ruined": intending to succeed the deceased father.

[Line 2] 9 in the second: Managing what the mother has ruined. Cannot be correct.

9 in the second is firm and central, corresponding above to 6 in the fifth: the image of the son managing what the mother has ruined and achieving centrality. The firm supports the yielding and orders what has been ruined. Thus the warning that one cannot maintain correctness. This refers to Sun entering.[211]

[Image 2] "Managing what the mother has ruined": achieving the Way of the Mean.

[Line 3] 9 in the third: Managing what the father has ruined. Slight regret, no great blame.

The excessive firm line is not central, so there is "slight regret." The Sun trigram is correct, so there is "no great blame."[212]

[Image 3] "Managing what the father has ruined": in the end, no blame.

[Line 4] 6 in the fourth: Tolerating what the father has ruined. Going on would witness disgrace.

The *yin* line occupies a *yin* position, and is unable to act: the image of leniently tolerating what is ruined.

[Image 4] "Tolerating what the father has ruined." Going on would not achieve anything.

[Line 5] 6 in the fifth: Managing what the father has ruined, thereby to be praised.

The yielding line is central and occupies the place of honor, and 9 in the second supports it with virtue, in this way managing what is ruined. This can result in hearing praise; hence this image and prognostication.

[Image 5] "Managing the father," "thereby to be praised": supporting [him] with virtue.

[Line 6] 9 at the top: Not serving a king or marquis; looking higher for service.

The firm *yang* line resides at the top, outside of service; hence this image. The prognostication and admonition are both implicit there.

[Image 6] "Not serving a king or marquis": this aim can be a model.

[19] ䷒ 臨 Lin (Approaching)

Dui [lake] below, Kun [earth] above.

Lin: Supreme and penetrating, appropriate and correct. Reaching the eighth month there will be bad fortune.

"Lin" means to advance [*jin* 進], to confront and close in on something.[213] The two *yang* lines gradually rise to close in on the *yin*: hence "approaching." It is the hexagram of the twelfth month.²¹⁴ Also, as for the trigrams, below is the pleasure of Dui and above is the compliance of Kun. The 9 in the second, as a firm line occupying the center, corresponds with 6 in the fifth; therefore the diviner will greatly succeed and will benefit from being correct. But "reaching the eighth month" there must be bad fortune.

The "eighth month" [associated with Guan ䷓, hexagram 20] means the month differing by one *yang* line from Fu [24 ䷗], or the month leading to Dun [33 ䷠] by [hexagram fluctuation of] two *yin* lines.²¹⁵ This is the time of *yin* rising and *yang* "withdrawing" [*dun* 遯]. Or we could say that the Xia [dynasty] set the eighth month hexagram as Guan, which is the opposite of Lin.²¹⁶ Follow the prognostication as a warning.

COMMENTARY ON THE JUDGMENT

Lin: The firm gradually grows.
Explaining the hexagram name by means of the component trigrams.

Pleasure and compliance; the firm is central and corresponds.²¹⁷
Expressing the goodness of the hexagram by means of the component trigrams and their virtues.

Great success by being correct is the Way of Heaven.
When the firm grows there will be this goodness; hence this prognostication.

"Approaching the eighth month there will be bad fortune," but the decline will not be long-lasting.
This says that although the revolutions of Heaven must be like this, the superior person properly understands the warning.

COMMENTARY ON THE GREATER IMAGES

Above the lake there is earth: Approaching. The superior person expresses inexhaustible concern by teaching; his tolerance and protection of the people are limitless.²¹⁸

Earth approaches the lake, the upper approaches the lower. Both approach the affairs of the lower. The inexhaustibility of the teaching is Dui; the limitlessness of tolerance is Kun.

LINE STATEMENTS WITH COMMENTARY ON THE SMALLER IMAGES

[Line 1] 9 in the first: Approaching together; correct and auspicious.

The hexagram has only two *yang* lines, and altogether four *yin* lines; thus the image of both [*yang*] lines approaching together. The 9 at the beginning is firm and correct; thus the prognostication is correct and auspicious.

[Image 1] "Approaching together; correct and auspicious": one's purpose will be carried out correctly.

[Line 2] 9 in the second: Approaching together: auspicious. All is appropriate.

The firm line is correct and its power is advancing upward; thus the prognostication is "auspicious" and "all is appropriate."

[Image 2] "Approaching together: auspicious. All is appropriate." Not complying with commands.

Unclear.[219]

[Line 3] 6 in the third: Pleasantly approaching, nothing is appropriate. Once you have concern about it, no blame.

The yielding *yin* line is neither central nor correct, and resides at the top of the lower [trigram]. It is the image of pleasantly approaching others. The prognostication is strong: there is nothing that is appropriate. But if one is able have concern and change it, then there is no blame.

[Image 3] "Pleasantly approaching": its position is not proper. "Once you have concern about it," blame will not grow.

[Line 4] 6 in the fourth: Perfect approach: no blame.

One's location is now one's [proper] position, corresponding below with 9 at the beginning, having come to the end of their mutual approach. It is appropriate that there is no blame.[220]

[Image 4] "Perfect approach: no blame." Its position is proper.

[Line 5] 6 in the fifth: Wisely approaching is what is appropriate for the great ruler [*zhun* 君]. Auspicious.

The yielding line occupying the center, corresponding below with 9 in the second, does not operate on its own but takes responsibility for others. The matter of wisdom and what is appropriate for the great ruler is the auspicious Way.

[Image 5] "What is appropriate for the great ruler" is the meaning of practicing the Mean.

[Line 6] 6 at the top: Sincerely approaching: auspicious and blameless.

Occupying the top of the hexagram, located at the end of Approaching, honest and sincere in one's approach, this is the Way of good fortune and no blame. Hence this image and prognostication.

[Image 6] The good fortune of "sincerely approaching": one's purpose is directed toward the inner [trigram].[221]

[20] ䷓ 觀   Guan (Observed/Observing)[222]

Kun [earth] below, Sun [wind, wood] above.

Guan: The ablution is made but not the offering; honest and respectful.

"Being observed" is how we show ourselves to others and act so that others look up to us. 9 in the fifth resides above and the four *yin* lines look up to it. The inner is compliant and the outer is entering [*sun* 巽] 9 in the fifth is central and correct and displays itself to all under Heaven. This is why it is "being observed." "Ablution" is washing the hands before a sacrifice. "Offering" is the wine and food presented in the sacrifice. "Respect" is the attitude of honor and reverence. This speaks about extending the purity of the ablution without slighting one's own functioning. Then with honest trust in the Mean, one will be respected and admired; hence the admonition to the diviner. As someone said, "Honest and respectful" means that people below will trust and look up to you. The four *yin* lines of this hexagram growing and the two *yang* lines declining make it the hexagram of the eighth month.[223] Naming the hexagram and appending the text yield yet further meanings, as does the idea of supporting with *yang* and restraining with *yin*.

COMMENTARY ON THE JUDGMENT

The great observer is above, compliantly penetrating; central and correct in order to observe all under Heaven.[224]

Explaining the meaning of the hexagram name by means of the component trigrams and their virtues.

"Guan: The ablution is made but not the offering; honest and respectful." Those below observe and are transformed.

Explaining the hexagram statement.

Observing the spiritual Way of Heaven, the four seasons do not deviate. The Sage thereby provides teaching according to the spiritual Way, and all under Heaven submit.

Fully expressing the Way of observation. "The four seasons do not deviate"; this is how Heaven is observed. "Providing teaching according to the spiritual Way" is how the Sage is observed.

COMMENTARY ON THE GREATER IMAGES

Wind moving above earth: Observing. The former kings provided teachings by examining the [four] quarters and observing the people.

"Examining the [four] quarters and observing the people" and "providing teachings" are considered "observing/being observed."

LINE STATEMENTS WITH COMMENTARY ON THE SMALLER IMAGES

[Line 1] 6 at the beginning: Youthful observation: no blame for the petty person, disgrace for the superior person.

The meaning of the hexagram is showing [*guan shi* 觀示] [i.e., being observed], based on 9 in the fifth as its ruler. The meaning of the line statements is observing [*guan zhan* 觀瞻], all observing 9 in the fifth. 6 at the beginning is a yielding *yin* line below, which is not able to see far: the image of "youthful observing." This is the Way of the petty person, but shame for the superior person. Thus the prognostication for the petty person is "no blame," but if the superior person gets it, it can be shameful.²²⁵

[Image 1] 6 at the beginning is "youthful observing," the Way of the petty person.

[Line 2] 6 in the second: Observing secretly [through a crack] is appropriate to the correctness of a woman.

The yielding *yin* line resides inside and observes outside: the image of "observing secretly [through a crack]." This is correct for a woman; thus the prognostication. If the husband catches her, it is not appropriate.²²⁶

[Image 2] "Observing secretly" and "the correctness of a woman" both can be bad.

In a husband they are bad.

[Line 3] 6 in the third: Observing my life, advancing and retreating.

"My life" is my behavior. 6 in the third resides just below the upper trigram, and can both advance and retreat. Thus it does not observe 9 in the fifth; it observes only the free flow or blockage of its own behavior, which results in advance or retreat. This is the diviner properly examining himself.²²⁷

[Image 3] "Observing my life, advancing and retreating": not yet losing the Way.

[Line 4] 6 in the fourth: To observe the radiance of the state it is appropriate to function as guest of the king.

6 in the fourth is closest to the fifth; hence this image. The prognostication is that it is appropriate to the court to observe an official advancing.²²⁸

[Image 4] "To observe the radiance of the state," promote a guest.

[Line 5] 9 in the fifth: Observing my life; no blame for the superior person.

9 in the fifth is a firm *yang* line, central and correct, occupying the position of honor. The lower four *yin* lines look up and observe it; this is the image of the superior person. Therefore the warning for the occupant of this position: one who

gets this prognostication should observe his own behavior. A firm *yang* line that is central and correct must be like this, and will incur no blame.

[Image 5] "Observing my life" is observing the people.

The meaning referred to here by the Master [Confucius] clarifies that the monarch observes what he does himself, but not only his own successes and failures. He should also observe the good and bad aspects of the people's virtue as part of his own self-examination.[229]

[Line 6] 9 at the top: Observing this life, the superior person is blameless.

9 at the top is a firm *yang* line residing above the position of honor. Although it should not have the responsibility to serve, it is also what those below observe; therefore the statement of warning is basically the same as the fifth. But if we consider "my" [in the fifth] to be "this" [here], it is a little like the difference between host and guest.

[Image 6] "Observing this life," one's purposes are not yet balanced.

"One's purposes are not yet balanced" means that although one does not have the [ruling] position, one cannot forget to be apprehensive.

[21] ䷔ 噬嗑 Shihe (Biting Together)[230]

Zhen [thunder] below, Li [fire] above.

Shihe: Success. Appropriate to conduct a legal investigation.

Shi means biting [*nie* 齧]; *he* means together [*he* 合]. When there is a gap in something, biting brings it together. The two *yang* lines at the top and bottom of the hexagram have a void in the middle: the image of jaws and mouth. The *yang* line, 9 in the fourth, lies within it, so one must bite before coming together; thus "biting together." The prognostication should be for successful penetration [i.e., for things to go smoothly], but because of the gap there is no penetration. Biting and bringing together will result in successful penetration. The three *yin* and three *yang* lines are evenly divided between firm and yielding, with activity [Zhen, thunder] below and brightness [Li, fire] above; thunder below and lightning above. The yielding 6 in the fourth place of Yi [42 ䷩] moves upward to the fifth and occupies the center, resulting in a *yin* line residing in a *yang* position [by hexagram fluctuation]. "Although it is not its proper position, it is 'appropriate to conduct a legal investigation.'"[231] The Way of running a legal investigation is simply acting honorably to achieve the Mean with authority and clarity. Therefore if one who gets this in divination has these virtues, the response will be this prognostication.

COMMENTARY ON THE JUDGMENT

There is something between the jaws, so it is called "biting together."
    Explaining the meaning of the hexagram name by means of the component trigrams.

Success by biting together; firm and yielding divided; activity and brightness; thunder and lightning join in a pattern. A yielding line moves upward to achieve the center. Although it is not its proper position, it is "appropriate to conduct a legal investigation."
    Explaining the hexagram statement by means of the hexagram name, the component trigrams, the trigram virtues, the two images, and the hexagram fluctuation.

COMMENTARY ON THE GREATER IMAGES

Thunder and lightning: Biting Together. The former kings used clear punishments to administer laws.
    "Thunder and lightning" should be written "lightning and thunder."[232]

LINE STATEMENTS WITH COMMENTARY ON THE SMALLER IMAGES

[Line 1] 9 at the beginning: Feet in the stocks, toes gone. No blame.[233]
    At the beginning there is no [correctly corresponding] position above: the image of receiving punishment. The middle four lines are the image of administering punishment. The first line is the beginning of the hexagram, so the crime

is minor and the transgression small, and it is at the bottom of the hexagram. Thus the image of "feet in the stocks, toes gone." Stopping what is bad at the beginning leads to no blame. The diviner will suffer slightly but is blameless.

[Image 1] "Feet in the stocks, toes gone": no walking.

"Toes gone" is also the image of no advancing toward the bad.

[Line 2] 6 in the second: Biting skin, nose gone. No blame.

If a skin [leather] vessel is used in the sacrifice, the meat is probably soft and yielding, so it will be easy to bite through. 6 in the second is central and correct, so what is managed will be as easy as biting skin. But although it is very easy for the yielding [second line] to ride on the firm [first line],[234] one cannot avoid injuring or removing the nose. In the end, though, the diviner will have no blame.

[Image 2] "Biting skin, nose gone": riding on the firm.

[Line 3] 6 in the third: Biting dried meat, encountering poison. Small disgrace, no blame.

Furou 腊肉 means dried meat, made from the whole body; something strong but flexible. The yielding *yin* line is neither central nor correct. One manages people but they do not obey: the image of "biting dried meat and encountering poison." Although the prognostication is "small disgrace," the times call for biting together, so the meaning is "no blame."

[Image 3] "Encountering poison": the position is not proper.

[Line 4] 9 in the fourth: Biting dried gristle, finding cash or an arrow. Appropriate and correct in difficulty; auspicious.

"Gristle" is meat containing bone; cut-up meat. In the *Zhouli* [Rituals of Zhou], a legal case would be heard only when one put in a measure of cash or a sheaf of arrows.[235] As 9 in the fourth is a firm line occupying a yielding position, he gets to use the Way of punishment [as judge]: hence this image. It says that what is bitten is very hard, so he deserves the propriety of having the case heard. But he must be appropriate in firmly correcting the difficulty; then it will be auspicious. The warning to the diviner is thus proper.

[Image 4] "Appropriate and correct in difficulty; auspicious." No radiance yet.

[Line 5] 6 in the fifth: Biting dried meat, finding yellow gold: correct when [conditions are] tough, no blame.

"Biting dried meat" means difficulty with skin and ease with dried meat. "Yellow" is the color of the middle. "Gold" means a measure of gold. 6 in the fifth is a yielding line, compliant and central, occupying the position of honor. It administers punishment to people, but the people do not obey; hence this image. But it is necessary to be correct when [conditions are] tough; then there will be no blame, according to the statement of warning to the diviner.

[Image 5] "Correct when [conditions are] tough, no blame": achieving what is proper.

[Line 6] 9 at the top: Wearing the cangue, ears gone. Ominous.[236]

He 何 [usually "how"] means *fu* 負 [to carry, bear].[237] A *yang* line at the extreme of transgression, at the top of the hexagram, is a Way of bad fortune. Hence the image and prognostication.

[Image 6] "Wearing the cangue, ears gone": cannot hear clearly.

"Ears gone," so the criminal's hearing is not sharp. If he were able to hear accurately and quickly visualize things, then this would not be ominous.

[22] ䷕ 賁   Bi (Adorning)

Li [fire] below, Gen [mountain] above.

Bi: Success. In small matters it is appropriate wherever you go.

Bi means "adorning" [*shi* 飾]. The hexagram comes from Sun 損 [41 ䷨], with a yielding line coming from the third to ornament [*wen* 文] the second, and a firm line from the second rising to ornament the third. It also comes from Jiji 既濟 [63 ䷾], with a yielding line coming from above to ornament the fifth and a firm line rising from the fifth to ornament the top. The inner [trigram] is Li [fire] and the outer is Gen [mountain]: the image of each achieving its apportionment with elegance and clarity; hence it is "adorning." As for the prognostication: the yielding comes to ornament the firm, the *yang* receives the help of the *yin*, and Li illuminates within; therefore it is "success." The firm rises to ornament the yielding and Gen limits it from above; therefore "in small matters it is appropriate wherever you go."[238]

COMMENTARY ON THE JUDGMENT

Bi: "Success."

I suspect that the word "success" is superfluous.

The yielding comes and ornaments the firm; thus "success." The separated firm line at the top ornaments the yielding; therefore "in small matters it is appropriate wherever you go." It is the pattern/elegance [*wen* 文] of Heaven.[239]

Explaining the hexagram statement by means of the hexagram fluctuations, the interaction of firm and yielding, a natural image. Therefore it says "the elegance of Heaven." Former scholars say that before "the elegance of Heaven" should be the words "firm and yielding interact and combine," and their reasoning [*li* 理] may be correct.[240]

Elegance [or culture] enlightens by limiting: human elegance [*renwen* 人文].

Also referring to the trigram virtues. "Limiting" means each receives his apportionment.[241]

Observe the elegance [or patterns] of Heaven to examine the fluctuations of time. Observe human elegance to transform and complete all under Heaven.

This fully expresses the greatness of the Way of Adorning.

COMMENTARY ON THE GREATER IMAGES

Below the mountain there is fire: Adorning. The superior person accordingly understands government broadly, without daring to decide criminal cases.

"Below the mountain there is fire"; its light does not reach far, only to small matters. To "decide a criminal case" is a great matter. The fire of the inner [trigram] illuminates and the mountain of the outer one limits. Therefore we understand the image in this way.

LINE STATEMENTS WITH COMMENTARY ON THE SMALLER IMAGES

[Line 1] 9 at the beginning: Adorn the toes, abandon the carriage, and walk.

The virtue of the firm clarifies the trigram. Adorn oneself below to abandon a carriage that is not on the Way: the image of walking at ease on foot. If the diviner finds himself in this spot he should act like this.

[Image 1] "Abandon the carriage and walk": it is right not to ride.

The superior person's understanding of "abandoning" is decided solely on the basis of rightness.

[Line 2] 6 in the second: Adorn the beard.

The second is a yielding *yin* line occupying a central and correct position; the third is a firm *yang* line that is correct. Neither one corresponds [correctly with the upper trigram]. Therefore the second acts by attaching itself to the third: the image of adorning the beard. The diviner should act appropriately by following the firm *yang* above.

[Image 2] "Adorn the beard": ascend with the one above.

[Line 3] 9 in the third: Adorning and moistening: always correct and auspicious.

A single *yang* residing between two *yin* lines becomes moist and rich by adornment. However, it cannot be submerged with ease; hence the warning to be always correct.[242]

[Image 3] "Always correct and auspicious": in the end nothing will offend.

[Line 4] 6 in the fourth: Adorned and plain [white]: a white horse flying. Not a thief; a marriage relationship.

A horse is for a person to ride. If the person is plain then the horse should be white. The fourth line and the first adorn each other, but 9 in the third separates them so they cannot be fulfilled. Therefore it is plain/white and has the mind to go out and seek hurriedly, as if flying with wings. As 9 in the third is firm and correct, it is not a thief; it seeks a marriage relationship; hence the image.

[Image 4] 6 in the fourth: The proper position is doubtful. "Not a thief; a marriage relationship," so in the end no blame.

"The proper position is doubtful" means the position where it should be can be doubted. "In the end no blame" means if one can hold on to what is correct and not get involved [with distractions], nothing can worry him.

[Line 5] 6 in the fifth: Adorning hills and gardens, the bundles of silk are meager. Frugality is auspicious in the end.

6 in the fifth, yielding and central, is the ruler of Bi. Fundamentally honest and valuing the real, it achieves the Way of adornment; hence the image of "hills and gardens." But the nature of *yin* is frugal and sparing; thus the image "the bundles of silk are meager." The bundles of silk are slight things; "meager" means shallow and small. Although it is shameful for a person to be stingy like this, nevertheless simple ritual is preferable to lavish. Thus it can be "auspicious in the end."

[Image 5] The auspiciousness of 6 in the fifth is happiness.

[Line 6] 9 at the top: plain adornment, no blame.

The extreme of adornment reverts to the basic, returns to the colorless; the good compensates for excess. Hence the image.[243]

[Image 6] Plain and adorned: no blame. The superior achieves his purposes.

[23] 剝 Bo (Declining/Breaking Down)[244]

Kun [earth] below, Gen [mountain] above.

Bo: Not appropriate wherever you go.

Bo means declining/breaking down [*luo* 落]. The five *yin* lines below are just coming to life; the single *yang* line above is about to be exhausted: the hexagram of the ninth month. *Yin* flourishes and *yang* weakens; the petty person is vigorous and the superior person is ill. The inner [trigram] is Kun and the outer is Gen: the image of limiting in due time. Therefore a diviner who gets this cannot have anywhere to go.

COMMENTARY ON THE JUDGMENT

Bo is declining. The yielding changes [*bian* 變] the firm.

Explaining the meaning of the hexagram name in terms of the component trigrams, referring to the yielding advancing toward the *yang*, changing the firm into yielding.

"Not appropriate wherever you go": the petty person increases. Complying and limiting [oneself] is to observe the image. The superior person esteems waxing and waning, fullness and emptiness, which is the course of Heaven.

Explaining the hexagram statement in terms of the component trigrams and their virtues.

COMMENTARY ON THE GREATER IMAGES

Mountain attached to earth: Declining. Those above, by being generous to those below, are secure in their homes.

LINE STATEMENTS WITH COMMENTARY ON THE SMALLER IMAGES

[Line 1] 6 at the beginning: Breaking the leg of the bed, extinguishing correctness. Ominous.

Decline rises from below, extinguishing correctness, and so is ominous. Hence the prognostication. *Mie* 蔑 [disdain] means *mie* 滅 [extinguish].

[Image 1] "Breaking the leg of the bed": extinguishing what is below.

[Line 2] 6 in the second: Breaking the frame of the bed, extinguishing correctness. Ominous.

Bian 辨 [to distinguish] is pronounced like *ban* 辦 [to manage] and means the frame [*gan* 幹] [main structure] of the bed.[245] [The *yin* is] advancing and rising.

[Image 2] "Breaking the frame of the bed": not yet providing.
Not yet greatly flourishing.

[Line 3] 6 in the third: Breaking it; no blame.
All the *yin* lines are about to break the *yang* [at the top], yet only this one corresponds with it, so it departs from its associates and follows what is correct: the Way of no blame. If the diviner is like this, he will accrue no blame.

[Image 3] "Breaking it; no blame": losing above and below.
"Above and below" means the four [other] *yin* lines.

[Line 4] 6 in the fourth: Breaking the bed and the skin [of the person in it]. Ominous.
The *yin*'s harm cuts into the body. Therefore it doesn't speak again of "extinguishing correctness," but states directly, "ominous."

[Image 4] "Breaking the bed and the skin": cutting what is near is disaster.

[Line 5] 6 in the fifth: A string of fish, like the favor of the court ladies. Everything is appropriate.
Fish are *yin* objects. Court ladies are the beauty of *yin* and are managed by the *yang*. The fifth line is the chief of all the *yin* lines, and properly regulates the others, while being managed by the *yang*; hence this image. If the diviner is like this, then "everything is appropriate."[246]

[Image 5] "The favor of the court ladies": in the end, no blame.

[Line 6] 9 at the top: The large fruit is not eaten. The superior person gets a palanquin; the petty person's house falls down.[247]
The single *yang* at the top means that the decline is not complete and life is able to return [or Fu (the next hexagram) comes to life]. The superior person at the top is what supports all the *yin*. If a petty person resided here, then decline would reach the top, the subject would fail to return, and there would be no more images of "large fruit" and "getting a palanquin." When this image is clarified, then

the prognostications for the superior person and the petty person are not the same, and the dispositions of the Sages can better be seen.[248]

[Image 6] "The superior person gets a palanquin," which is carried by the people. "The petty person's house falls down": in the end it cannot be used.

[24] ䷗ 復   Fu (Returning)[249]

Zhen [thunder] below; Kun [earth] above.

Fu: Success. Going out and coming in without harm. Friends arrive; no blame. The Way reverts and returns; on the seventh day it comes back. Appropriate wherever you go.

"Return" is the *yang* reborn below. Bo [23 ䷖] is exhausted, making pure Kun [2 ䷁], the hexagram of the tenth month, and yet the *yang qi* is already coming alive below. Only when it has collected for another month does the *yang* substance begin to form and come back. Therefore the hexagram of the eleventh month is Return.[250] Since the *yang* has gone and has returned, it is a Way of "success." With Zhen as the inner [trigram] and Kun as the outer, it is the image of *yang* active below and moving compliantly upward. Therefore the prognostication is that in one's "going out and coming in" [i.e., daily affairs] there will be no harm, and when friends and associates arrive there will be no blame.

Also, from the first birth of one *yin* in the Gou 姤 hexagram [44 ䷫] in the fifth month, up to this seventh line, where the single *yang* comes back, is the natural process of Heaven's revolution.[251] Thus the prognostication is "the Way reverts and returns" until the seventh day, when it must come back. Since at this point the virtue of firmness is growing, the prognostication is "appropriate wherever you go." "The Way reverts and returns" is the idea of going and coming back, coming and going back. "Seven days" is how long it takes for the prognostication to come back.

COMMENTARY ON THE JUDGMENT

Return: Success. The firm reverts.

The firm reverting is success.

Activity and compliant movement; thus "going out and coming in without harm. Friends arrive; no blame."

Speaking of the hexagram virtue.

"The Way reverts and returns; on the seventh day it comes back" is the movement of Heaven.

Yin and yang wax and wane, like the turning of Heaven.

"Appropriate wherever you go"; the firm is growing.

Speaking of the hexagram structure: once born, [the yang] gradually grows.

In Fu is seen the mind of Heaven and Earth.

Below the accumulated yin a single yang is reborn. "The mind of Heaven and Earth to give birth to things" is incipient in extinction.[252] Reaching this point [in the cyclical process], its return can be seen. In human beings it is activity at the maximum of stillness;[253] goodness at the maximum of the bad; the original mind beginning to reappear just at the point of vanishing. Master Cheng discussed this in detail.[254] Master Shao also said in a poem,

> At midnight on the winter solstice
> The mind of Heaven is without movement.
> At the point of yang's first activity,
> When the myriad things have not yet been born,
> The taste of the Dark Wine is mild,
> And the sound of the Great Tone is very faint.[255]
> If you do not believe these words,
> Then go ask Baoxi [Fuxi].[256]

Perfectly said! Students ought to exert their minds on this.

COMMENTARY ON THE GREATER IMAGES

Thunder within the earth: Returning. The former kings closed the passes on the solstice. Merchants did not travel, and the sovereign did not inspect the realm.

Peace and quiet in order to nourish the subtle *yang*. The "Yue ling" ["Monthly Commands" chapter of the *Liji*] says, "This month is when one fasts ... and retires oneself ... in order to wait for the stabilization of *yin* and *yang*."[257]

LINE STATEMENTS WITH COMMENTARY ON THE SMALLER IMAGES

[Line 1] 9 at the beginning: Returning from not far away, no need for repentance. Supremely auspicious.[258]

The single *yang* reborn below is the ruler of Fu. If one rests at the beginning of an affair, erring but not by much, one will be able to return to goodness, without reaching the point of repentance. This is a Way of great goodness and good fortune. Hence this image and prognostication.

[Image 1] "Returning from not far away" in order to cultivate the self.

[Line 2] 6 in the second: Relaxed return. Auspicious.

Yielding, compliant, central, and correct; next to 9 at the beginning and able to submit to it. This is the relaxed beauty of Fu, an auspicious Way.

[Image 2] The auspiciousness of "relaxed return" is submitting to humaneness.

[Line 3] 6 in the third: Repeated return. Danger, no blame.

The *yin* line occupying a *yang* position is neither central nor correct, in a place of maximum activity. Returning but not resolutely: the image of frequent error and frequent return. Frequent error means danger, but return is blameless. Hence this prognostication.

[Image 3] "Repeated return" is dangerous, but rightness is blameless.[259]

[Line 4] 6 in the fourth: Proceeding centrally, returning alone.

The fourth place is in the middle of the group of *yin* lines; it alone corresponds with the beginning. It is the image of the individual who is able to follow the good while acting in a group. At this moment the *yang qi* is very subtle, as yet insufficient for action. Therefore there is no mention of good fortune. But it is the normativity of principle, so good or bad fortune is not discussed. As Dong [Zhongshu] said, "The humane person is correct and proper, and does not scheme for profit. He is clear about the Way and does not calculate rewards."[260] The 6 in the third position of Bo [23] and this line [both] illustrate this.

[Image 4] "Proceeding centrally, returning alone" is following the Way.

[Line 5] 6 in the fifth: Sincerely returning without regret.

Occupying the position of honor with centrality and compliance, at the moment of necessary return: the image of "sincerely returning"; a Way without regret.

[Image 5] "Sincerely returning without regret": being central for self-realization.

Kao 考 [examine] is to complete/realize [cheng 成].

[Line 6] 6 at the top: Confused return: ominous. There are disasters and calamities. If one were to set troops in motion it would end in great defeat, resulting in bad fortune for the country's nobles. Even in ten years one could not correct it.

A yielding yin line residing at the end of Fu: the image of ending in confusion and not returning, an ominous Way. Hence this prognostication.

[Image 6] The bad fortune of "confused return" is to oppose the noble Way.

[25] 无妄 Wuwang (No Error)

Zhen [thunder] below, Qian [heaven] above.

Wuwang: Supreme and penetrating, appropriate and correct. If one is not correct, there is calamity; inappropriate wherever you go.

Wuwang means the naturalness of actualized order/principle [shili 實理].[261] In the Shiji [史記, Historical records, ca. 100 BCE] it is written wuwang [无望, or 毋望], meaning to get something without expecting it; this meaning is also to the point.[262] The hexagram results from a fluctuation of Song (6 ䷅), with 9 in the second place coming to reside at the beginning. This is the ruler of Zhen [the inner trigram], which is active and without error: thus Wuwang. Also, the two component trigrams are Zhen, which is active, and Qian, which is strong; 9 in the fifth, firm and central, corresponds with 6 in the second. Therefore the prognostication is great and penetrating, benefiting from correctness. If one is not correct "there is calamity; inappropriate wherever you go."

COMMENTARY ON THE JUDGMENT

Wuwang: The firm [9 at the beginning] comes from without to become the ruler of the inner [trigram].[263] [Zhen is] active and [Qian is] strong. [9 in the fifth] is firm and central, and corresponds [correctly with 6 in the second]. Great and penetrating in its correctness, this is the Decree of Heaven. "If one is not correct, there is calamity; inappropriate wherever you go." How can one proceed without error? Without the aid of Heaven's Decree, can one act?

This speaks of the hexagram fluctuation, the component trigrams, and their virtues; hence the excellence of the hexagram. Thus the prognostication is precisely "great and penetrating" and benefiting from correctness, which is the necessity of the Decree of Heaven. If one is not correct, then it is "inappropriate wherever you go." How could one desire to proceed? By opposing Heaven's Decree so that Heaven doesn't help you, you cannot do anything.

COMMENTARY ON THE GREATER IMAGES

Thunder moves beneath Heaven: things take part with No Error. The former kings nourished the myriad things by stimulating them according to the time.

"Thunder moves beneath Heaven": Zhen acts to bring forth the myriad things, each correct in its nature and endowment, so the myriad things take part with no error. The former kings regulated this by "nourishing things according to the time," according with their natures without any private [agenda].

LINE STATEMENTS WITH COMMENTARY ON THE SMALLER IMAGES

[Line 1] 9 at the beginning: No error; proceeding is auspicious.

The firm line in the inner [trigram] is the ruler of authenticity. Proceeding like this, its good fortune can be understood; hence this image and prognostication.

[Image 1] Proceeding without error will achieve one's purposes.

[Line 2] 6 in the second: If you harvest without tilling, cultivate without planting, it is appropriate wherever you go.

This yielding line is compliant, central, and correct, complying with principle according to the time, with a mind free from any private thoughts or expectations. Thus the image of "harvesting without tilling, cultivating without planting." It says nothing is done at the beginning and nothing is wished for at the end. If the diviner is like this, then it is "appropriate wherever you go."

[Image 2] "Harvesting without tilling": no wealth.

"Wealth" here is like the "wealth" of "not coveting the wealth of the empire" [*Mencius* 3B.5]. It says that one acts without calculation of profit.

[Line 3] 6 in the third: Undeserved disaster. An ox that is tethered is a passerby's gain and a villager's disaster.

The six lines of the hexagram are all without error. The 6 in the third is positioned incorrectly, so it yields this prognostication: disaster for no reason. If a passerby hauls away an ox, it is the resident's trouble to retrieve it.

[Image 3] A passerby gets the ox: disaster for the villager.

[Line 4] 9 in the fourth: If one can be correct, no blame.

A firm *yang* line in the Qian trigram, not corresponding [with the first line] below. If one can strongly hold on without blame, one cannot get the prognostication for it.[264]

[Image 4] "If one can be correct, no blame": firmly possessing it.

"Possessing" [*you* 有] is like "preserving" [*shou* 守].[265]

[Line 5] 9 in the fifth: For undeserved illness, take no medicine and there will be happiness.

This firm line in Qian is central and correct, occupying the position of honor, and corresponds with the central and correct [yielding] line below [in the second]: the ultimate innocence [no error]. If one becomes ill under these circumstances, take no medicine and one will heal on one's own. Hence this image and prognostication.

[Image 5] With no error, medicine should not be attempted.

When one is not in error yet takes medicine, it is in fact an error and will make one sick. "Attempt" means to try a little.

[Line 6] 9 at the top: Innocent action brings calamity; nothing is appropriate.

9 at the top: one is not in error, but one has come to the end and cannot act: hence this image and prognostication.

[Image 6] To act, although innocent, is complete disaster.

[26] ䷙ 大畜 Daxu (Restrained by the Great)

Qian [heaven] below, Gen [mountain] above.

Daxu: Appropriate and correct. Not eating at home is auspicious. Appropriate to cross a great river.

"Greater" refers to *yang*. Gen restraining Qian is the great that restrains.[266] The inner Qian is "firm and strong," the outer Gen is "hearty and substantial, shining and luminous" [see following]. This is how it is able to "daily renew its virtue," so it is the great that restrains.[267] In terms of hexagram fluctuation, this hexagram comes from Xu [5 ䷄], with 9 in the fifth rising. In terms of the component trigrams, the 6 in the fifth honors and promotes it. In terms of the trigram virtues, [Gen] is able to limit the strong [Qian]. None of this is beyond the ability of the great and correct. Therefore the prognostication is "appropriate and correct" and "not eating at home is auspicious." Also, 6 in the fifth corresponding below with Qian is corresponding with Heaven. Therefore the prognostication is "appropriate to cross a great river." "Not eating at home" means eating richly at court, so not eating at home.

COMMENTARY ON THE JUDGMENT

Daxu: Firm and strong, hearty and substantial, shining and luminous, daily renewing one's virtue.

Explaining the meaning of the hexagram name in terms of the trigram virtues.

The firm rises and promotes the worthy, and is thus able to limit the strong: great and correct.

Explaining the hexagram statement in terms of the hexagram fluctuation, the component trigrams, and the trigram virtues.

"Not eating at home is auspicious"; nourishing the worthy.

Referring to the image of "promoting the worthy."

"Appropriate to cross a great river": responding to Heaven.

Also speaking in terms of the component trigrams.

COMMENTARY ON THE GREATER IMAGES

Heaven within a mountain: Restrained by the Great. The superior person is broadly acquainted with the words and deeds of the past, to train [literally, "restrain"] his virtue.

"Heaven within a mountain": it is not necessary to take this literally; it is only speaking in terms of the image.

LINE STATEMENTS WITH COMMENTARY ON THE SMALLER IMAGES

[Line 1] 9 at the beginning: There is danger; appropriate to stop.

The three *yang* lines of Qian are what are limited by Gen. This is how the inner and outer trigrams each get their meaning. The 9 at the beginning is limited by 6 in the fourth. This is how the prognostication proceeds into danger, and it is "appropriate to stop."

[Image 1] "There is danger; appropriate to stop," so as not to invite disaster.

[Line 2] 9 in the second: The cart separates from its axle housing.

9 in the second is also restrained by 6 in the fifth. It occupies a central position, so it is able to limit itself and not advance; hence this image.

[Image 2] "The cart separates from its axle housing." Being central, there is no fault.

[Line 3] 9 in the third: A good horse in pursuit; appropriate and correct in difficulty. Defend the obstructed cart daily. Appropriate wherever you go.

The third, being a *yang* line occupying the position of maximum strength, ascends toward the *yang* [at the top], which occupies the position of maximum restraint: a time of maximum penetration [passing through].[268] They are all *yang* lines, so they advance together without mutual restraint: the image of a good horse in pursuit. But it is exceedingly firm and advances strongly, so the prognostication necessarily warns that it is difficult to be correct when practice is obstructed, and it is "appropriate wherever one goes." *Yue* 曰 [to say] should be *ri* 日 [sun, day] as in "sun and moon."[269]

[Image 3] "Appropriate wherever you go": one's purposes are the same as those above.

[Line 4] 6 in the fourth: The horn cover of a young ox: supremely auspicious.

"Young" means not yet [fully] horned. "Horn cover" is a flat piece of wood on the horn of an ox, to prevent injury. It is what the *Shi*[*jing*] calls a *biheng* 楅衡.[270] To limit [the ox] when it is not yet horned, when its power is easeful, is very good and auspicious. Hence the image and prognostication. The "Xueji" 學記 [chapter of the *Liji*] says, "Preventing [something bad] before it is expressed is called 'precaution'"; it is just this idea.[271]

[Image 4] 6 in the fourth is "greatly auspicious": there is happiness.

[Line 5] 6 in the fifth: The tusk of a gelded boar: auspicious.

The *yang* has already advanced and limited [this line], so it is not as easeful as at the beginning. But as a yielding line residing in the center, proper and in the honored position, it can manage by seizing opportunity; hence the image. Although the prognostication is auspicious, it doesn't say "supremely [as line 4 does]."[272]

[Image 5] The good fortune of 6 in the fifth: there is blessing.

[Line 6] 9 at the top: What is the path of Heaven? Success.

"What is the path of Heaven?" asks what is the importance of penetrating and breaking through. Penetrating at the maximum of restraint, breaking through without obstruction: hence this image and prognostication.[273]

[Image 6] "What is the path of Heaven?" The great movement of the Way.

[27] ䷚ 頤 Yi (Jaws, Nourishing)

Zhen [thunder] below, Gen [mountain] above.

Yi: Correct and auspicious. Observe the jaws and how one seeks to fill one's mouth.

"Jaws" are the [upper and lower] sides of the mouth. We nourish ourselves by taking food into the mouth, so the meaning is Nourishing [yang 養]. The top and bottom of the hexagram are both yang, and the inside holds four yin. The outside being full and the inside vacant, the upper [trigram] limiting and the lower acting, are the image of the jaws and the meaning of nourishing. "Correct and auspicious" means the diviner will achieve correctness and therefore good fortune. "Observe the jaws" means the way of "observing who/what one nourishes." "How one seeks to fill the mouth" means the technique of observing how one nourishes the body. If they are both correct, there will be good fortune.

COMMENTARY ON THE JUDGMENT

"Yi: Correct and auspicious": Nourishing correctly is auspicious. **"Observe the jaws"** is observing what is nourished. **"How one seeks to fill the mouth"** is observing how one nourishes oneself.

Explaining the hexagram statement.

Heaven and Earth nourish [yang 養] the myriad things; the Sage nourishes the worthy, who extends it to the myriad people. The time of nourishing [yi 頤] is great indeed!

Fully expressing and praising the Way of nourishing.

COMMENTARY ON THE GREATER IMAGES

Below the mountain there is thunder: Nourishing. The superior person is cautious in speech and measured in food and drink.

The two virtues of nourishment, the first task in nourishing the body.

LINE STATEMENTS WITH COMMENTARY ON THE SMALLER IMAGES

[Line 1] 9 at the beginning: Setting aside your sacred tortoise, [you] observe me with drooping jaw: ominous.

"Sacred tortoise" is something not eaten. "Drooping" is hanging down. "Drooping jaw" is an expression of wanting to eat. The 9 at the beginning is a firm *yang* line at the bottom, not worthy of being eaten. It corresponds above with the *yin* of 6 in the fourth and activates desire: an ominous path. Hence the image and prognostication.

[Image 1] "Observing me with dropping jaw" is not worthy of the honorable.

[Line 2] 6 in the second: Reversing [the normal process of] nourishment, departing from the standard. [Seeking] nourishment on a hill, proceeding is ominous.

Seeking nourishment at the beginning, then turning around and departing from the normative principle, seeking nourishment from above, leads to misfortune. "Hill" is a high place in the land, the image of what is above [the Gen trigram].

[Image 2] 6 in the second: "Proceeding is ominous." Acting, one will lose associates.

Neither the first nor those above are its associates.

[Line 3] 6 in the third: Departing from nourishment: correct but ominous. Do not do this for ten years; nothing will be appropriate.

This yielding *yin* line is neither central nor correct, positioned at the peak of activity [the lower trigram, Zhen], but departing from nourishment. Since it departs from nourishment, it is ominous even though it is correct; hence this image and prognostication.[274]

[Image 3] "Do not do this for ten years"; it deviates greatly from the Way.

[Line 4] 6 in the fourth: Reversing nourishment: auspicious. The tiger gazes intently, desiring to chase and pursue: no blame.

This yielding line resides in the upper trigram and gains the correct position. Its correspondence is also correct, yet it rejects nourishment by providing it to the one below. Therefore although it reverses [the normal process], it is auspicious. "The tiger gazes intently," focusing on what is below. "Desiring to chase and pursue" is its seeking to connect. It is capable of this, so there is no blame.[275]

[Image 4] The good fortune of "reversing nourishment" is the superior providing light [nourishment].

[Line 5] 6 in the fifth: "Departing from the standard." Its position is correct and auspicious, but it cannot cross a great river.

6 in the fifth is a yielding *yin* that is not correct: it occupies the position of honor yet is unable to nourish others. It rejects the nourishment of 9 at the top; hence this image and prognostication.

[Image 5] The auspiciousness of its correct position is that it compliantly follows the one above.

[Line 6] 9 at the top: Relied on for nourishment, auspicious in danger. Appropriate to cross a great river.

6 in the fifth rejects the nourishment of 9 at the top for nourishing others. This [line] is the 9 at the top that is relied on for nourishment. Its position is high and its responsibility heavy, so even in danger it is auspicious. It is a firm *yang* line at the top, so it is appropriate to cross a river.

[Image 6] "Relying on nourishment, auspicious in danger": great will be the blessings.

[28] ䷛ 大過 Daguo (Surpassing by the Great)

Sun [wind, wood] below, Dui [lake] above.

Daguo: The ridgepole sags. Appropriate wherever you go: success.

"Great" refers to *yang*. The four *yang* lines occupying the center surpass and flourish; therefore it is "surpassing by the great." The two *yin* lines above and below do not overcome their weight; hence the image of the ridgepole sagging. Although the four *yang* lines surpass, the second and fifth are central, the inner [trigram] is gentle, and the outer is pleasure: a Way that can be trodden.[276] Therefore it is "appropriate wherever you go" and achieves success.

COMMENTARY ON THE JUDGMENT

Daguo: The great surpasses.

Explaining the meaning of the hexagram name in terms of the hexagram structure.

"The ridgepole sags": root and branch are weak.

Again explaining the hexagram statement in terms of the component trigrams. "Root" means "beginning"; "branch" means "top" [line]. "Weak" means the yielding of *yin*.

The firm [lines] surpass and are central. Gently and joyously moving; "appropriate wherever you go," and "successful."

Explaining the hexagram statement in terms of the component trigrams and the trigram virtues.

The time of surpassing by the great is great indeed!

"The time of surpassing by the great" does not refer to the human quality of surpassing by the great, which cannot equal it; [the sentence] is [merely] admiration for the great [*yang*].

COMMENTARY ON THE GREATER IMAGES

The lake drowns the tree: Surpassed by the Great. The superior person, standing alone, is not anxious; he renounces the world without worry.

"The lake drowns the tree" [wood] is the image of Daguo. "No anxiety, no worry" is the process of surpassing by the great.

LINE STATEMENTS WITH COMMENTARY ON THE SMALLER IMAGES

[Line 1] 6 at the beginning: For a mat use white rushes; no blame.[277]

At the time of surpassing by the great, the yielding *yin* line occupies the bottom of Sun, going beyond [surpassing] fear and caution with no blame. Hence this image and prognostication. "White rushes" are things of purity.

[Image 1] "For a mat use white rushes"; the yielding is below.

[Line 2] 9 in the second: A dry poplar grows roots; an old man gets a young wife: everything is appropriate.

This is the beginning of *yang*'s surpassing, near the *yin* at the beginning; hence this image and prognostication. Roots grow down and then grow up. The man, although old, gets a young wife, like the ability to meritoriously produce children.[278]

[Image 2] "An old man gets a young wife": [both] go beyond in order to share with each other.[279]

[Line 3] 9 in the third: "The ridgepole sags": ominous.

The third and the fourth lines reside in the center of the hexagram: the image of the ridgepole. 9 in the third is a firm line residing in a firm position, but does not overcome the weight [of the fourth]; hence the image of sagging and the ominous prognostication.

[Image 3] The misfortune of "the ridgepole sagging" is that there is nothing that can support it.

[Line 4] 9 in the fourth: The ridgepole is held up: auspicious. Having another is a disgrace.

This *yang* line occupying a *yin* position surpasses but not too much; thus the image of being held up, yet the prognostication is auspicious. But it corresponds below with 6 at the beginning, a yielding line that equals it, so it surpasses the yielding. Hence the warning that "having another" is a disgrace.[280]

[Image 4] The good fortune of "the ridgepole being held up" is that it doesn't sag down.

[Line 5] 9 in the fifth: A dry poplar grows flowers; an old wife gets a young husband: no blame, no praise.

9 in the fifth is the peak of *yang* surpassing [the highest *yang* line], and is next to *yin* at the peak of surpassing [6 at the top]. Therefore the image and prognostication are the opposite of the second [line].[281]

[Image 5] "A dry poplar grows flowers": how can they last long? "An old wife gets a young husband": this can be a disgrace.

[Line 6] 6 at the top: Crossing too far, submerging one's head: ominous, no blame.

Trying to go all the way across at this place, one's talent is too weak to cross, but in terms of rightness there is no blame. It is a matter of killing oneself to achieve humaneness, hence the image and prognostication.[282]

[Image 6] The misfortune of "crossing too far" cannot be blameworthy.

[29] 習坎 Xikan (Doubly Abysmal)[283]

Kan [water] below, Kan [water] above.

Xikan: With honesty, one's mind-heart will be penetrating, and one's actions will be esteemed.

Xi means "doubled." Kan is a "dangerous pit" [*xian xian* 險陷] [abyss]. Its image is water, with *yang* submerged in *yin*.[284] The outside is empty and the inside is full. The upper and lower trigrams are both Kan, so this is doubly dangerous. The full center [of each trigram] is the image of the honest mind-heart and success. Acting according to it there will definitely be merit; hence the prognostication.

COMMENTARY ON THE JUDGMENT

Xikan: Doubly dangerous.

Explaining the meaning of the hexagram name.

Water flows without filling up; it moves into danger but does not lose its honesty.

Explaining the meaning of "with honesty" according to the trigram images, referring to the [two trigrams'] inner fullness and constant movement.

"One's mind-heart will be penetrating," as the firm is central. "One's actions will be esteemed"; setting forth will bring merit.

The firm line in the center [of each trigram] is the image of the mind-heart's penetration. If one sets forth like this there will necessarily be merit.

Heaven's danger is that one cannot ascend to it. Earth's danger is its mountains and rivers, hills and high ground. Kings and dukes manage danger in order to protect their states. The usefulness of times of danger is great indeed!

Fully expressing and praising its greatness.

COMMENTARY ON THE GREATER IMAGES

Water flows on and on: Doubly Abysmal. The superior person acts according to constant virtue and keeps on the business of teaching.

Regulating the self and regulating others both must be repetitive; only then can one be mature and at ease.

LINE STATEMENTS WITH COMMENTARY ON THE SMALLER IMAGES

[Line 1] 6 at the beginning: Doubly abysmal, entering an abysmal pit: ominous.

The yielding *yin* line resides below great danger, and the pit is deep; hence this image and prognostication.

[Image 1] "Doubly abysmal, entering an abyss." Losing the Way is ominous.

[Line 2] 9 in the second: Danger in the abyss; seek [only] small attainments.

Positioned in the middle of extreme danger, unable to get oneself out; hence the image of danger. But it is firm and has attained the center; thus the prognostication is that one can "seek small attainments."

[Image 2] "Seek [only] small attainments": not yet leaving the center.

[Line 3] 6 in the third: Coming and going, abyss after abyss. In danger and stuck there, falling into the abysmal pit: don't do it.

The yielding *yin* is neither central nor correct, and treads into the midst of extreme danger; both coming and going are dangerous. Danger in front and [tied to] a stake behind. The pit is especially deep, so one cannot do anything. Hence this image and prognostication. "Stuck" suggests the idea of "discomfort."

[Image 3] "Coming and going, abyss after abyss": in the end no merit.

[Line 4] 6 in the fourth: A jug of wine and a basket of grain. In addition use earthen vessels. Take them together from the window. In the end, no blame.

Mr. Chao [Yuezhi] says, "Former scholars read 'a jug of wine, a basket of grain' as one sentence and 'in addition use earthen vessels' as another sentence, and we follow them." *Er* 貳 (two) means "in addition" [*yizhi* 益之, "also"], as in the *Zhouli* [Rites of Zhou]: "Three repetitions of the Great Sacrifice," and in "The Duties of the Student" [chapter of the *Guanzi*]: "[The student] holds an empty platter in the left hand and holds a ladle in the right, and also refills...."²⁸⁵ 9 in the fifth is the position of honor, and 6 in the fourth is close to it, so at a time of danger, with the firm and yielding lines next to each other, one can engage only in simple rituals; hence the image of presenting together from the window with an authentic heart. The window is not the proper thing to use, yet it does allow light into the room. Although in the beginning there is serious obstruction, in the end one will incur no blame; hence the prognostication.

[Image 4] "A jug of wine and a basket of grain": firm and yielding next to each other.

Mr. Chao [Yuezhi] says, "Mr. Lu's *Shiwen* 釋文 lacks the word 'in addition' [*er* 貳]," and I follow that.²⁸⁶

[Line 5] 9 in the fifth: The abyss is not filled, just reaching the rim; no blame.

Although 9 in the fifth is the center of the Kan trigram, it is a firm *yang* line that is central and correct and occupies the position of honor, and the time is ripe to get out. Hence this image and prognostication.

[Image 5] "The abyss is not filled," the center is not yet great.

[Line 6] 6 at the top: Bound with cords and ropes, kept in a thicket of thorns, can't do anything for three years: ominous.

The yielding *yin* line occupies the place of extreme danger; hence this image and prognostication.

[Image 6] 6 at the top loses the Way: misfortune for three years.

[30] ䷝ 離   Li (Clinging)[287]

Li [fire] below, Li [fire] above.

Li: Appropriate and correct; success. Rearing an ox: auspicious.

Li is clinging [*li* 麗], the *yin* clinging to the *yang*. Its image is fire, whose substance is *yin* and function is *yang*. What something clings to is valuing the achievement of correctness. The ox is a creature that is yielding and compliant. Therefore if the prognosticator is able to be correct he will be successful, and by "rearing an ox" he will have good fortune.

COMMENTARY ON THE JUDGMENT

Li is clinging. The sun and moon cling to Heaven, the hundred grains, grasses, and trees cling to Earth. By clinging to correctness, doubled brightness [the two trigrams] transforms and perfects all under Heaven.

Explaining the meaning of the hexagram name.

The yielding clings to centrality and correctness; therefore it is successful. In this way rearing an ox is auspicious.

Explaining the hexagram statement by means of the component trigrams.[288]

COMMENTARY ON THE GREATER IMAGES

Light arises twice: Clinging. The great person extends the light and shines it in four directions.

"Make" [*zuo* 作] means "arise" [*qi* 起].

LINE STATEMENTS WITH COMMENTARY ON THE SMALLER IMAGES

[Line 1] **9 at the beginning: Treading across. Being reverent, no blame.**

The firm resides below and is located at the beginning of the hexagram, but it intends and desires to advance upward; hence the image of "treading across." If one is reverent then there is no blame, and the admonition to the diviner is thus appropriate.

[Image 1] **The reverence of "treading across" is avoiding blame.**

[Line 2] **6 in the second: Clinging to the yellow; supremely auspicious.**

"Yellow" is the color of the center. The yielding clings to the center and achieves correctness; hence this image and prognostication.

[Image 2] **"Clinging to the yellow; supremely auspicious": achieving the Middle Way.**

[Line 3] **9 in the third: Clinging to the setting sun. If one does not sing to [beaten] drums and jars, then there will be the moaning of the greatly aged: ominous.**

Between the doubled Li trigrams is the formerly bright about to be exhausted; hence the image of "setting sun." If one is not content with the usual ways of amusing oneself, one will not be able to hold one's position: ominous. The admonition to the diviner is thus appropriate.

[Image 3] **"Clinging to the setting sun": how can it last long?**

[Line 4] **Suddenly arriving, burning, dying, lost.**

When the later light [the upper trigram] is about to follow, 9 in the fourth approaches with firmness; hence this image.

[Image 4] "Suddenly arriving": nothing is acceptable.

"Nothing is acceptable" refers to "burning, dying, lost."

[Line 5] 6 in the fifth: Shedding tears in floods, grieving and sighing: auspicious.

The *yin* occupies the position of honor, the yielding clinging to the center. But it does not achieve correctness, and it draws near to the *yang* above and below. Therefore it is anxious and fearful like this, but later will have good fortune. The warning to the diviner is thus appropriate.

[Image 5] The good fortune of 6 in the fifth is clinging to kings and dukes [the *yang* above and below].

[Line 6] 9 at the top: The king launches a punitive attack. There is praise for cutting off heads and capturing evil rebels. No blame.

The light of the firm has reached far; its power has arisen to punish, but not recklessly: a path of no blame. Hence this image and prognostication.

[Image 6] "The king launches a punitive attack" to correct the country.

CHAPTER TWO
PART B: HEXAGRAMS 31–64

PART B

[31] ䷞ 咸 Xian (Mutually Influencing)

Gen [mountain] below, Dui [lake] above.

Xian: Success; appropriate and correct. Taking a wife: auspicious.

   Xian is mutually influencing [*xiaogan* 交感]. Dui is yielding above, Gen is firm below, and they mutually "influence and respond" [*ganying* 感應].[1] Gen is limiting, so it is focused influence; Dui is pleasing, so it is the perfection of response. Gen as the youngest male [son] is below the youngest female [daughter] of Dui; the male precedes the female. This is the correct [relationship] of male and female when they marry. Therefore the hexagram is mutually influencing.[2] The prognostication is "Success; appropriate and correct. Taking a wife: auspicious." Influencing implies the principle of necessarily penetrating [to success], but if you are not correct then success will be lost, which is always ominous.[3]

COMMENTARY ON THE JUDGMENT (*TUANZHUAN* 彖傳)

Xian is influencing/stimulating [*gan* 感].
   Explaining the meaning of the hexagram name.

Yielding above and firm below, the two *qi* influence and respond to each other. Limiting and pleasing, male below female. Thus "Success; appropriate and correct. Taking a wife: auspicious."

Explaining the hexagram statement in terms of the component trigrams, their virtues, and their images. Some speak of the meaning of "yielding above and firm below" in terms of hexagram fluctuation, saying, Xian comes from Lü [hexagram 56 ䷷], with the yielding ascending to occupy the sixth and the firm descending to occupy the fifth. This also works.

Heaven and Earth influence [each other] and the myriad things transform and grow. The Sage influences the human mind and all under Heaven are in harmonious peace. Observing this influence, the dispositions of Heaven and Earth and the myriad things can be seen.

Fully expressing the principle of stimulus and penetration.[4]

COMMENTARY ON THE GREATER IMAGES (*DAXIANG ZHUAN* 大象傳)

Above the mountain is a lake [*ze* 澤]: Influence. The superior person receives others with vacuity [self-effacement].

Above the mountain is a lake, pervading it with vacuity.[5]

LINE STATEMENTS (*YAOCI* 爻辭) WITH COMMENTARY ON THE SMALLER IMAGES (*XIAOXIANG ZHUAN* 小象傳)

[Line 1] 6 at the beginning: Influencing the big toe.

Mu 拇 is the big toe. Taking the image from influencing the human body, stimulating the lowest part, this is the image of "influencing the big toe." Influence can be high or low, desiring to advance but being unable. Therefore it does not mention good fortune or misfortune. Although the ruling [principle] of this hexagram is influencing, all of the six lines are fit for stillness but not fit for activity.

[Image 1] "Influencing the big toe": its purpose is external [outward directed].

[Line 2] 6 in the second: Influencing the calf [of the leg]: ominous. But remaining is auspicious.

Fei 腓 [calf] is the middle of the leg. Desiring to move, you first activate yourself, but you are confused and unable to firmly hold on. The second has proper position, but it is a yielding *yin* line and is unable to firmly hold on; hence it has this image. Nevertheless it has the virtues of centrality and correctness and so is able to remain in place. Thus the prognostication is that activity is ominous but stillness is auspicious.

[Image 2] Although "ominous, remaining is auspicious," going along does no harm.

[Line 3] 9 in the third: Influencing the thighs. Hold on to what follows; proceeding is disgraceful.

The thigh acts by following the leg; it cannot do anything on its own. "Hold on" is the idea of emphasizing what is proper and maintaining it. The lower two lines both desire to act, and the third, unable to maintain itself, follows them, so proceeding is disgraceful. Hence this image and prognostication.

[Image 3] "Influencing the thighs," also not staying put. One's purpose is to follow others, attached to those below [the first two yin lines].

"Also" refers to the former two lines, which both desire to act. These two are changeable *yin* lines, so activity is appropriate. 9 in the third is a firm *yang*, occupying the peak of stability [the Gen trigram]. If it acts although it should be still, its disgrace can be extreme.

[Line 4] 9 in the fourth: Correct and auspicious; regret vanishes. Going back and forth in agitation, [only] friends follow your thoughts.[6]

9 in the fourth rests above the thigh and below the back. It is right in the middle of the three *yang* lines, so it is the image of the mind-heart, and is the ruler of Xian. The mind's influence on things is properly correct and strong, so it gets their principles. Now this 9 in the fourth [however] is a *yang* line in a *yin* position, so it fails to be correct and cannot be strong. Accordingly the prognostication provides an admonition: if you are able to be correct and strong, then there will be good fortune and regret vanishes. If you "go back and forth in agitation," unable

to be correct and strong and tied to private stimuli, then only your like-minded friends will follow you, and they still will be unable to take you far.

[Image 4] "Correct and auspicious; regret vanishes": not yet causing harm. "Going back and forth in agitation": not yet shining greatly.

"Causing harm" means improperly influencing, which brings harm.

[Line 5] 9 in the fifth: Influencing the back: no regret.

Wei 脢, also pronounced mei, is the flesh of the back, above and behind the heart, unable to stimulate anything and without its own connections. 9 in the fifth moves into its proper position; hence this image. This warns that if the diviner is able to be like this, even though he cannot stimulate things, he can still be without regret.

[Image 5] "Influencing the back": purpose[ful action] has ended.

"Purpose[ful action] has ended" means unable to influence things.

[Line 6] 6 at the top: Influencing the cheek, jaws, and tongue.

The cheek, jaws, and tongue are what we speak with, at the top of the body. 6 at the top is a *yin* line located at the end of the speech process, the extreme point of Xian. It influences the person to speak without real meaning. Dui is the mouth and tongue [*Shuogua* 5.9, 11]; hence this image. We can know that there will be ominous error [without it being stated].

[Image 6] "Influencing the cheek, jaws, and tongue": speaking with a gushing mouth.

"Gushing" is used in the sense of running on.

[32] ䷟ 恆 Heng (Everlasting)[7]

Sun [wind, wood] below, Zhen [thunder] above.

Heng: Success; no blame. Appropriate and correct; appropriate wherever you go.

Heng means everlasting [*changjiu* 常久]. As a hexagram it has the firm Zhen above and the yielding Sun below. When those two objects interrelate, Sun follows and Zhen acts, so it is "gentle [*sun* 巽] yet active."[8] The two component trigrams and six lines all [properly] correspond as *yin* and *yang*. The four [seasons] are all the constancy of principle, and so are "everlasting." The prognostication is that you are able to be "enduring in your Way," so "success; no blame." But if it is going to be appropriate to hold on to correctness, then you must achieve the Way that is everlasting; then it will be "appropriate wherever you go."

COMMENTARY ON THE JUDGMENT

Heng is everlasting. The firm is above and the yielding below; thunder and wind relating to each other, gentle yet active. The firm and yielding all correspond: everlasting.

Explaining the hexagram name in terms of the component trigrams, the trigram images, and the trigram virtues. Some use hexagram fluctuation to explain "firm above and yielding below," saying that Heng comes from Feng 豐 [55 ䷶], with the "firm rising" to occupy the second position and the "yielding sinking" to occupy the beginning. This also works.[9]

"Heng: Success; no blame. Appropriate and correct"; long-lasting in one's Way. The Way of Heaven and Earth is everlasting and does not change.

Being everlasting, you are definitely able to have success without blame. But it is necessary to benefit from being correct in order to endure in your Way. If you are not correct then what endures is not your [proper] Way. The Way of Heaven and Earth is how to last long in correctness.

"Appropriate wherever you go": an ending is a beginning.

"Enduring in one's Way" is an ending; "appropriate wherever you go" is a beginning. Activity and stillness giving rise to each other is the principle of circulation, but it is necessary that stillness be emphasized.[10]

The sun and moon are Heaven, and can shine forever. The four seasons change and transform, and can accomplish forever. The Sage "endures in his Way," and all under Heaven complete their transformations. Observe what is everlasting, and the dispositions of all things in Heaven and Earth can be seen.

Fully expressing the everlasting Way.

COMMENTARY ON THE GREATER IMAGES

"Thunder and wind": Everlasting. The superior person takes his stand and does not change direction.

LINE STATEMENTS WITH COMMENTARY ON THE SMALLER IMAGES

[Line 1] 9 at the beginning: Deep and everlasting; correct and [yet] ominous. Nothing is appropriate.

The first and the fourth correctly correspond; this is the constancy of principle. But the first, residing below and at the beginning, cannot search deeply. The fourth, in the Zhen trigram, is *yang* in nature; it rises and does not fall, separating from the second and third. It corresponds with the idea of the first, but differs in its norm. The first, yielding and dim, is unable to limit its power. As a *yin* line residing at the bottom of Sun, it is the ruler of Sun. By nature it strives to enter, so it deeply seeks the constant principle; the image of "deep and everlasting." If the diviner is like this, even though correct, there will be bad fortune, and "nothing appropriate."

[Image 1] The bad fortune of being "deep and everlasting" is starting one's search in the depths.

[Line 2] 9 in the second: Regret vanishes.

As a *yang* line occupying a *yin* position, there should be regret. But being long-lasting in the center, it can vanish.

[Image 2] 9 in the second: "Regret vanishes"; able to last long in the center.

[Line 3] 9 in the third: One's virtue is not everlasting; some will heap shame.[11] Correct but disgraceful.

Although its position is correct, it is excessively firm and not central; its purpose is to follow what is above, and it is unable to last long in its position. Hence the image of "virtue not everlasting; some will heap shame." "Some" means you won't know who it is; "heap" means "offer." This says that people will try to offer and present it [shame], but you will not know where they come from. "Correct but disgraceful" means correct yet not everlasting, deserving of shame and disgrace. This is a warning to the diviner.

[Image 3] "One's virtue is not everlasting": nothing is tolerated.

[Line 4] 9 in the fourth: No game in the fields.

A *yang* line occupying a *yin* place: long-lasting but not in one's position; hence this image. There is nothing to catch in the diviner's fields; affairs in general will not achieve what they seek.

[Image 4] Long-lasting, but it is not one's position: how can there be game?

[Line 5] 6 in the fifth: Everlasting in virtue: correct. Auspicious for the wife, ominous for the husband.

This yielding line is central and corresponds with a firm, central line: everlasting and unchanging, correct and strong. While it is the Way of the wife, it is not fitting for the husband; hence this image and prognostication.[12]

[Image 5] The wife's correctness is auspicious; she follows [is faithful to] him to the end. The husband controls rightness; to follow the wife is ominous.

[Line 6] 6 at the top: Restless and everlasting: ominous.

"Restless" means rapid movement. 6 at the top rests at the peak of Heng, the end of Zhen. As the peak of Heng, it is not constant; as the end of Zhen it has gone past activity.[13] As a yielding *yin* line it is unable to firmly hold on, so residing at the top is not a place of ease. Hence the image of being "restless and everlasting," and the prognostication of misfortune.

[Image 6] "Restless and everlasting" at the top: greatly lacking in merit.

[33] ䷠ 遯 Dun (Withdrawing)

Gen [mountain] below, Qian [heaven] above.

Dun: Success. Appropriate for the inferior to be correct.[14]

Dun means withdrawing and avoiding [*tuibi* 退避]. In the hexagram the two *yin* lines are gradually growing and the *yang* must withdraw and avoid them; hence "withdrawing," the hexagram of the sixth month.[15] Although the *yang* must withdraw, 9 in the fifth is properly positioned and corresponds with 6 in the second below, so it is acceptable as it is. But the two *yin* lines are gradually growing below, so it must withdraw from their power. Thus the prognostication is that the superior person can withdraw. Although withdrawing himself, his path is successful. It is appropriate that the inferior person remain correct, because he cannot gradually grow and eventually supplant the *yang*. "Inferior" means the yielding, *yin*, inferior person. This hexagram's prognostication is similar to those of the first and second lines of Pi [hexagram 12, Obstructing].[16]

COMMENTARY ON THE JUDGMENT

"Dun: Success" means withdrawing is successful. The firm is properly positioned and [properly] corresponds, acting according to the time.

Explaining the meaning of "success" in terms of 9 in the fifth.[17]

"Appropriate for the inferior to be correct": gradually growing.

Explaining "appropriate for the inferior to be correct" in terms of the lower two *yin* lines.

The meaning of the time of withdrawing is great indeed!

When *yin* is just gradually growing, its position is difficult. Therefore the meaning of that time is even greater.

COMMENTARY ON THE GREATER IMAGES

Below Heaven there is a mountain: Withdrawing. The superior person keeps his distance from the inferior person, not disliking, but austere.

The substance of Heaven is inexhaustible; the mountain's height has limits: the image of withdrawing. "Austere" is the constant self-protection [reserve] of the superior person, which the inferior person is not able to approach himself.

LINE STATEMENTS WITH COMMENTARY ON THE SMALLER IMAGES

[Line 1] 6 at the beginning: The tail of withdrawal is perilous. It will not do to have someplace to go.

Withdrawing and staying behind, the image of the tail, is a path of danger: the diviner cannot have anywhere to go. Only by waiting quietly in an obscure place can he avoid disaster.

[Image 1] The peril of "the tail of withdrawal": not going forward. What is the disaster?

[Line 2] 6 in the second: Holding it using the hide of a yellow ox, nothing will successfully come loose.

If you protect yourself by complying with the Mean, no one will be able to make you let go, as you are necessarily intent on withdrawing. If the diviner holds on strongly it should be like this.

[Image 2] "Holding, using a yellow ox": strong intent.

[Line 3] 9 in the third: Being attached to withdrawal, there is sickness and danger. Keeping male and female servants is auspicious.

Being close to the two *yin* lines below is the image of having to withdraw yet being attached [to the advancing *yin* lines], a path of sickness and danger. However, "keeping male and female servants" is auspicious. This is a relationship of superior and inferior people, but only servants, not necessarily worthies, so one can "keep" them. Hence this prognostication.[18]

[Image 3] The danger of "being attached to withdrawal" is being sick and weak. "Keeping male and female servants is auspicious": they cannot engage in important affairs.

[Line 4] 9 in the fourth: To like withdrawing is auspicious for the superior person, not so for the inferior person.

This corresponds below with 6 at the beginning, and has the firmness and strength of the Qian trigram: the image of having something to like yet being able to give it up. Only the superior person is able to subdue himself, while the inferior person is unable. So if the diviner is a superior person it will be auspicious; if an inferior person, not so.

[Image 4] The superior person "likes withdrawing; not so the inferior person."

[Line 5] 9 in the fifth: Admirable withdrawal: correct and auspicious.

The firm *yang* is central and correct, and corresponds below with 6 in the second, which is yielding and compliant and also central and correct. This is the admirable beauty of withdrawing. A diviner like this who is correct will have good fortune.

[Image 5] "Admirable withdrawal: correct and auspicious": correct purpose.

[Line 6] 9 at the top: Comfortable withdrawal; everything appropriate.

The firm *yang* occupying the outside of the hexagram is not connected by correspondence with anything below. This is one who is wealthy and located far from withdrawal [retreat]. Hence this image and prognostication. "Comfortable" means one who has gained ease and wealth for himself.

[Image 6] "Comfortable withdrawal; everything appropriate": nothing to question.

[34] 大壯 Dazhuang (Flourishing of the Great)[19]

Qian [heaven] below, Zhen [thunder] above.

Dazhuang: Appropriate and correct.

"Da" 大 [great] means *yang*. The four *yang* lines flourish and grow, so it is "flourishing of the great," the hexagram of the second month. The *yang* flourishes, so the diviner will no doubt have auspicious success, as long as he is appropriate in his firm correctness.

COMMENTARY ON THE JUDGMENT

Dazhuang: The great one flourishes; firm in activity, therefore flourishing.

Explaining the meaning of the hexagram name. In terms of the hexagram structure, the *yang* grows to surpass the center; this is "the great one flourishing." In terms of the trigram virtues, Qian is firm and Zhen is active, which is how it is "flourishing."

"Dazhuang: Appropriate and correct": the great one is correct. Being correct and great, the dispositions of Heaven and Earth can be seen.

Explaining the meaning of "appropriate and correct," and fully expressing it.

COMMENTARY ON THE GREATER IMAGES

Thunder above Heaven: Flourishing of the Great. The superior person does not tread improperly.

"Overcoming oneself is strength" [*Laozi* 33].[20]

LINE STATEMENTS WITH COMMENTARY ON THE SMALLER IMAGES

[Line 1] 9 at the beginning: Strength in the toes: Going on is ominous; this is reliable.

Toes are at the bottom, yet advance; they are active things. The firm *yang* is located below at a time of flourishing, flourishing in the direction of advancement; hence this image. Residing below yet flourishing toward advancement is certainly ominous; hence the prognostication.[21]

[Image 1] "Strength in the toes": what is reliable is being exhausted.

This says that one is certainly in dire straits.

[Line 2] 9 in the second: Correct and auspicious.

As a *yang* line occupying a *yin* position, it cannot be correct itself. But its location is central, so it might be able to rely on not losing its correctness. Therefore the warning to the diviner is to try relying on centrality to achieve correctness; only then can it be auspicious.

[Image 2] "9 in the second: Correct and auspicious" by being central.

[Line 3] 9 in the third: The inferior person uses strength; the superior person uses nothing. Correct but dangerous, like a ram butting a hedge and entangling his horns.

Exceedingly firm and not central, this is a time of flourishing/strength. Accordingly the inferior person uses strength and the superior person uses nothing [relying on himself]. Seeing that there doesn't seem to be anything [external on which to rely], the superior person is one who exceeds in courage. As such, it is dangerous although correct. The ram is a firm and strong animal that likes to butt. To "entangle" is to be hemmed in. The prognostication "correct but dangerous" is based on this image.

[Image 3] "The inferior person uses strength; the superior person, nothing."

The inferior person is defeated by strength; the superior person uses nothing when in trouble.

[Line 4] 9 in the fourth: Correct and auspicious; regret vanishes. The hedge opens; no entanglement. Strength in the axle housing of a large carriage.

"Correct and auspicious; regret vanishes" is the same prognostication as Xian [31], 9 in the fourth. "The hedge opens; no entanglement" refers to the preceding passage. Ahead of the third [yang] line is a fourth, which is like a hedge [or fence, barrier]. Ahead of the fourth are two *yin* lines, so the hedge opens. "Strength in the axle housing of a large carriage" is the image of being able to advance. As a *yang* line occupying a *yin* position this is not extremely firm; hence this image.[22]

[Image 4] "The hedge opens; no entanglement": proceeding upward.

[Line 5] 6 in the fifth: Losing a ram with ease: no regret.

The hexagram structure is like Dui 兌 [trigram], with the image of the ram: yielding outside and firm inside.[23] Only 6 in the fifth is a yielding line occupying a central position. It cannot resist becoming entangled, although it loses its strength, but there is nothing to regret. Hence this image, and the prognostication is the same as 9 in the fifth of Xian [31]. "With ease" [yi 易] means one quickly becomes unaware of the loss. Some write this as yi 埸 [boundary], which also works. In the "Food and Commerce" chapter of the *History of the [Former] Han*, yi 埸 is written yi 易.[24]

[Image 5] "Losing a ram with ease": its position is not proper.

[Line 6] 6 at the top: A ram butting a hedge cannot retreat and cannot get through. Nothing is appropriate. Difficult but auspicious.

Its strength is at an end and its activity has reached its maximum, so it cannot retreat. But its substance is fundamentally yielding, so it cannot get through and advance either. Hence this image, and the prognostication can be understood. As the ram is not firm, it is able to endure the difficulty of its position, so it may be able to have good fortune.

[Image 6] "Cannot retreat and cannot get through" is unfortunate. "Difficult but auspicious" means blame will not increase.

[35] 晉 Jin (Advancing)

Kun [earth] below, Li [fire] above.

Jin: A strong marquis is granted horses in great numbers and is received [at court] three times in one day.[25]

Jin means advancing [jin 進]. "A strong marquis" is the marquis of a peaceful state. "Granted horses in great numbers and received three times in one day" says he receives great awards many times and is clearly seen to be ritually proper. The hexagram is Li above and Kun below, the image of the sun coming up above the earth, the virtue of "compliantly depending upon the great light." In terms of [hexagram] fluctuation it comes from Guan [20], with the yielding 6 in the fourth advancing upward to reach the fifth. A diviner with three such [audiences] is certain to have this good favor.

COMMENTARY ON THE JUDGMENT

Jin is advancing.

Explaining the meaning of the hexagram name.

Light rises over the earth, compliantly depending upon the great light. The yielding advances and moves upward; this is how "a strong lord is granted horses in great numbers and is received three times in one day."

Explaining the hexagram statement by means of the trigram images, the trigram virtues, and the trigram fluctuation.[26]

COMMENTARY ON THE GREATER IMAGES

"Light rises over the earth": Advancing. The superior person illuminates his bright virtue.[27]

Zhao 昭 [illuminate] means ming 明 [make clear].

LINE STATEMENTS WITH COMMENTARY ON THE SMALLER IMAGES

[Line 1] 6 at the beginning: Advancing, retreating: correct and auspicious. There is no honesty, but there is no blame in being lenient.

This *yin* line below corresponds [with the *yang* in the fourth] but is neither central nor correct: the image of wanting to advance but seeing [the necessity of] retreat. If the diviner is like this and is able to hold on to correctness it will be auspicious. In dealing with a dishonest person you should be open-minded and there will be no blame.[28]

[Image 1] "Advancing, retreating": proceeding alone is correct. "No blame in being lenient" when one has not yet received the Mandate.

The beginning resides in the lowest position and does not yet have the mandate of an official position.

[Line 2] 6 in the second: Advancing, anxious: correct and auspicious. Receiving great blessings from one's late grandmother.

6 in the second is central and correct, but is not assisted by correspondence above, so it wants to advance but is anxious. If the diviner is like this and is able to hold on to correctness it will be auspicious, and he will receive blessings from his late grandmother. "Late grandmother" indicates 6 in the fifth: you receive an auspicious prognostication from your late grandmother.[29]

[Image 2] "Advancing, anxious": central and correct.

[Line 3] 6 in the third: All true; regret vanishes.

The third is neither central nor correct, so you should have regret. But it wants to advance upward with the two lower *yin* lines, so they are all honest and regret vanishes.

[Image 3] Intending for "all to be true," moving upward.

[Line 4] 9 in the fourth: Advancing like a squirrel or rat: correct and dangerous.

This is neither central nor correct; it is stealing the high position. It is a greedy and fearful person who is a danger to the Way; hence the image of the squirrel or rat. If the diviner is like this, he is in danger even though being correct.

[Image 4] "A squirrel or rat" is "correct and dangerous": its position is improper.

[Line 5] 6 in the fifth: Regret vanishes, do not worry about gain or loss. Going forward is auspicious, everything is appropriate.

With a *yin* line occupying a *yang* position you should have regret. But with great light above and those below all following compliantly, if the diviner receives this then regret will vanish. Also, if you completely reject the mind that calculates merit and schemes for advantage, then going forward will be auspicious and everything will be appropriate. But you must have these virtues in order to correspond with this prognostication.

[Image 5] "Do not worry about gain or loss": going forward brings blessings.

[Line 6] 9 at the top: Advancing with the horns, only to attack the city. Danger, but auspicious and no regret: correct; disgrace.

Horns are firm and occupy the top [of the head]. 9 at the top has advanced to the extreme of firmness and has this image. If the diviner receives this and attacks his own city, then although dangerous, there will be good fortune and no regret. However, while ruling a small city with extreme firmness can be correct, it can also be a disgrace.

[Image 6] "Only to attack the city": the Way is not shining.

[36] ䷣ 明夷 Mingyi (Dimming the Light)

Li [fire] below, Kun [earth] above.

Mingyi: Appropriate and correct in adversity.

Yi 夷 is to impair [*shang* 傷]. As a hexagram with Li below and Kun above, the sun entering into the earth, it is the image of light being impaired; hence "dimming the light." The 6 at the top is the ruler of the dark, and 6 in the fifth is near it. Therefore the diviner will benefit by holding on to correctness in difficulty, "dimming his own light."

COMMENTARY ON THE JUDGMENT

Light enters into the earth: Dimming the Light.
   Explaining the hexagram name by means of the trigram images.

Elegant and bright inside, yielding and compliant outside, experiencing great difficulty: thus was King Wen.
   Explaining the meaning of the hexagram in terms of the trigram virtues. "Experiencing great difficulty" means the chaotic time of Zhou 紂 [evil last king of the Shang dynasty], when [King Wen was] imprisoned.

"Appropriate and correct in adversity": dimming his light. Internal difficulty, yet able to be correct in his purpose: thus was Jizi.[30]
   Explaining the hexagram statement in terms of the meaning of 6 in the fifth. "Internal difficulty" means being a close relative of Zhou's, inside his kingdom, like 6 in the fifth is close to 6 at the top.

COMMENTARY ON THE GREATER IMAGES

"Light enters into the earth: Dimming the Light": the superior person presides over the rest, using dimness to enlighten.

LINE STATEMENTS WITH COMMENTARY ON THE SMALLER IMAGES

[Line 1] 9 at the beginning: Wounding the light in flight, folding his wings.[31] The superior person in action, not eating for three days. Having somewhere to go, the host has words [about him].

Flying with folded wings is the image of being impaired. The diviner in action does not eat. As unsuitable as this is, it is certainly the meaning of the moment; one cannot avoid it.

[Image 1] "The superior person in action" does what is right and does not eat.

As long as you observe rightness, it is permissible not to eat.

[Line 2] 6 in the second: Wounding the light, wounded in the left thigh. Saved by a horse's strength: auspicious.

Impaired but not severely, seeking a quick getaway. Hence this image and prognostication.

[Image 2] The good fortune of 6 in the second is complying with the rule.

[Line 3] 9 in the third: Wounding the light while hunting in the south, capturing the great leader; cannot be correct in haste.

A firm line occupying a firm position, at the top of the light trigram, bending under the extreme darkness, correctly corresponding with 6 at the top, which is the ruler of the dark. Hence the image of facing the light and removing harm, capturing the head bad guy. But you cannot be in a hurry; hence the warning, "cannot be correct in haste." Cheng Tang [founder of the Shang] rose up from the Xia Tower [where he had been imprisoned]; King Wen [founder of the Zhou] rose up from Youli [where he had been imprisoned]. These correctly match this line's meaning, and smaller affairs will also be so.

[Image 3] The purpose of "hunting in the south" is to make a great capture.

[Line 4] 6 in the fourth: Entering into the left side of the belly, capturing the mind [intention] of dimming the light by leaving gate and courtyard.

The meaning of this line is unclear. I suspect that "left side of the belly" is a place of darkness. "Capturing the mind of dimming the light by leaving gate and courtyard" suggests the idea of going far away. This says that one who gets this in divination should be in this position. The Li [lower] trigram is the virtue of extreme light, and the Kun trigram is the extreme darkness of the earth. The lower three lines brighten the outer darkness, so depending on whether one is far or near, high or low, the positions are not the same.

6 in the fourth is yielding and correct, residing in the dark earth but still shallow. Therefore it may suggest the idea of going far away. The fifth is a yielding line at the center, residing in the dark earth and already stuck; hence the image of "internal difficulty, correct in purpose," and darkening the light.[32] The top line is extreme darkness, so by itself it impairs the light and approaches darkness enough to injure human light [clarity, intelligence]. So the lower five lines are all the superior person, and only the top line is the master of the dark.

[Image 4] "Entering into the left side of the belly," capturing the mind's intention.

[Line 5] 6 in the fifth: Jizi dimming [his] light: appropriate and correct.[33]

Residing in the extreme darkness of the earth, close to the master of extreme darkness, yet able to be correct in purpose: the image of Jizi 箕子, the ultimate of correctness. "Appropriate and correct" is an admonition to the diviner.

[Image 5] Jizi's correctness: his light could not be put out.

[Line 6] 6 at the top: Not light; dark. At first climbing to Heaven, then entering the Earth.

A *yin* line occupying the peak of Kun, not illuminating its virtue but approaching the dark. The first to occupy the high position and to impair human light. Finally he must reach the point of impairing himself and exhausting his mandate. Hence this image and the prognostication implied by it.

[Image 6] "At first climbing to Heaven," illuminating states in all four directions. "Then entering the Earth," losing [touch with] the rules.

"Illuminating states in all four directions" refers to his position.

[37] 家人 Jiaren (Family Members)

Li [fire] below, Sun [wind, wood] above.

Jiaren: Appropriate for the woman to be correct.

Jiaren means the people of one family [*yijiazhi ren* 一家之人]. The hexagram's 9 in the fifth and 6 in the second are each correct as outer and inner [respectively], thus family members.[34] "Appropriate for the woman to be correct" means that you should desire first to correct the inner [realm]. When the inner is correct, the outer is never incorrect.

COMMENTARY ON THE JUDGMENT

Jiaren: The woman's correct position is inside. The man's correct position is outside. The man and woman being correct is the great meaning of Heaven and Earth.

Explaining the meaning of "appropriate for the woman to be correct" in terms of 9 in the fifth and 6 in the second of the component trigrams.

There are stern masters in a family; they are called the father and mother.

They are also called the second and fifth [lines].

When the father is a father, the son a son, the elder brother an elder brother, the younger brother a younger brother, the husband a husband, the wife a wife, and the Way of the family is correct, this is a correct family and all under Heaven is settled.

The top line is the father, the first is the son, fifth and third are the husbands, fourth and second are the wives, fifth is the elder brother and third the younger brother. These images are implied by the hexagram strokes.[35]

COMMENTARY ON THE GREATER IMAGES

Wind emerges from fire: Family Members. The superior person has substance in his words, and his deeds are long-lasting.

With self-cultivation the family is well ordered.

LINE STATEMENTS WITH COMMENTARY ON THE SMALLER IMAGES

[Line 1] 9 at the beginning: With discipline there is a family: regret vanishes.

9 at the beginning, a firm *yang* line residing at the beginning of the family, is able to protect and discipline it, so regret vanishes. Hence the admonition to the diviner.

[Image 1] "With discipline there is a family": one's purposes do not fluctuate. When "purposes do not fluctuate," one protects them.

[Line 2] 6 in the second: Nothing to pursue, preparing food within. Correct and auspicious.

6 in the second is yielding and compliant, central and correct. It is the correct position of the woman inside; hence the image and prognostication.

[Image 2] The good fortune of 6 in the second is being compliant and gentle.

[Line 3] 9 in the third: The family members are very strict, but regret the severity: good fortune. The wife and child are very happy, but in the end, disgrace.³⁶

The firm line occupies a firm position, but is not central. It is excessively firm; hence the image of being extremely strict and severely stern. Accordingly, although regretting the severity, there is good fortune. Being very happy [xixi 嘻嘻] the opposite of being very strict [hehe 嗃嗃], is a path of disgrace. The diviner in each case responds to these virtues, hence the doubled words.

[Image 3] When "family members are very strict," they are not yet lost. When "wife and child are very happy," they have lost the family's restraint.

[Line 4] 6 in the fourth: Wealthy family: greatly auspicious.

Yang emphasizes being right; yin emphasizes being appropriate. A yin line occupying a yin place in the upper position [trigram] is able to enrich the family.

[Image 4] "Wealthy family: greatly auspicious." Compliant in one's position.

[Line 5] 9 in the fifth: The king approaches the family. Do not worry; auspicious.

Ge 假 is to approach [zhi 至], as in "approaching the royal ancestral temple."³⁷ "The family" is like saying "the state." 9 in the fifth is firm and strong, central and correct. Below it corresponds with 6 in the second, which is yielding and compliant, central and correct. The king accordingly approaches the family, so there is no reason to be anxious, and you can be certain of good fortune.

[Image 5] "The king approaches the family," interacting with love.

Master Cheng [Yi] says, "The husband loves to aid those within; the wife loves to set rules for the family."³⁸

[Line 6] 9 at the top: With honesty and majesty, good fortune in the end.

9 at the top is a firm line occupying the top, at the end of the hexagram. Therefore it refers to the Way of the correct family, lost-lasting, far and wide. The diviner will certainly be authentic and trustworthy, stern and majestic, so in the end, good fortune.

[Image 6] The good fortune of "majesty" means reflection on the self.

It is not creating majesty [out of nothing]. If you reflect on yourself and order the self, then others will treat you with awe and deference.

[38] ䷥ 睽   Kui (Contrary)³⁹

Dui [lake] below, Li [fire] above.

Kui: Good fortune in small matters.

Kui is being contrary [*guaiyi* 乖異]. The hexagram is fire above and water [lake] below, whose natures are opposite; the middle daughter [above] and the youngest daughter [below], whose aims do not agree; therefore "being contrary." However, in terms of the trigram virtues, the inner is pleasing and the outer is light. In terms of hexagram fluctuation it comes from Li 離 [30 ䷝], with the yielding [second] line advancing to occupy the third position; or from Zhongfu 中孚 [61 ䷼], with the yielding [fourth] line advancing to occupy the fifth position; or from Jiaren 家人 [37 ䷤], with both together. In terms of the component trigrams, 6 in the fifth is central and corresponds below with the firm 9 in the second. Accordingly, the prognostication is not to engage in great matters, but small matters tend toward a path of good fortune.

COMMENTARY ON THE JUDGMENT

Kui: Fire is active and rising, lake is active and sinking. Two women live together, but their aims do not go together.

Explaining the hexagram name by means of the trigram images.

Pleasing and depending upon light, the yielding advances and moves upward, becoming central and corresponding with the firm. In this way, good fortune in small matters.

Explaining the hexagram statement by means of the trigram images, hexagram fluctuations, and component trigrams.

Heaven and Earth are contrary, yet their affairs are in concord. Men and women are contrary, yet their aims are consistent. The myriad things are contrary, yet their doings are similar. Functioning in a time of contrariness is great indeed!

Fully expressing the principle [of being contrary] and praising it.

COMMENTARY ON THE GREATER IMAGES

Fire above, lake below: Contrary. The superior person differentiates on the basis of sameness.

The two trigrams agree in substance, yet their natures are not the same.[40]

LINE STATEMENTS WITH COMMENTARY ON THE SMALLER IMAGES

[Line 1] 9 at the beginning: Regret vanishes. Losing a horse, do not pursue; it will return on its own. Meeting a bad person, no blame.

With no correct correspondence with the [trigram] above, there is regret. Yet being in a time of contrariety, they do correspond with similar virtues, so regret vanishes. Hence the image of "losing a horse, not pursuing, returning on its own." But if you must meet a bad person, only then is it permissible to "avoid blame" [see the following Image 1], as in the case of Confucius and Yang Huo.[41]

[Image 1] "Meeting a bad person," avoiding blame.

[Line 2] 9 in the second: Coming upon one's master in a lane, no blame.

The second and fifth lines correspond correctly as *yin* and *yang*, but abide at a time of contrariety, and being so different, do not agree. If events make it necessary to seek and meet each other, there is no blame; hence this image and prognostication.

[Image 2] "Coming upon one's master in a lane," one does not lose the Way.
Since they correspond correctly, there is nothing wrong with this.

[Line 3] 6 in the third: Seeing the carriage dragged and the oxen held, the man has his hair and nose cut off. Nothing at the beginning, something at the end.[42]

6 in the third corresponds correctly with 9 at the top and lies between two *yang* lines. Behind it the second is dragged, and ahead of it the fourth obstructs [the third]. It is right at a time of contrariety, when the fierce resentment of 9 at the top is profound; hence the punishment of having hair and nose cut off. But being wrong is not contrary to being correct, so in the end there must be agreement; hence this image and prognostication.

[Image 3] "Seeing the carriage dragged": one's position is not proper. "Nothing at the beginning, something at the end": coming upon the firm [fourth line].

[Line 4] 9 in the fourth: Contrary and isolated, coming upon a great person, being honest with each other. Danger but no blame.

"Contrary and isolated" means no correspondence. "Coming upon a great person" refers to 9 at the beginning. "Being honest with each other" means mutual trust between those with the same virtue. But since it is right at a time of contrariety, there must be danger; yet it will result in no blame. This is also the case for the diviner.

[Image 4] "Being honest with each other," "no blame": their aims go along.

[Line 5] 6 in the fifth: Regret vanishes, his relative bites the skin. How could there be blame in proceeding?

A *yin* line occupying a *yang* position is regretful. But since it occupies the center and corresponds [correctly with 9 in the second], it is able to lose [the regret]. "His relative" indicates 9 in the second. "Bites the skin" means easily joining.[43] 6 in the fifth has the virtue of a yielding central line; hence this image and prognostication.

[Image 5] "His relative bites the skin": proceeding will be rewarding.

[Line 6] 9 at the top: "Contrary and isolated": seeing a pig covered in mud, and a cart carrying ghosts. First drawing the bow, then putting down the bow. Not a thief, a marriage. Proceeding, coming upon rain: auspicious.[44]

"Contrary and isolated" means 6 in the third is restrained by the two *yang* lines [above and below it], while its own position is a firm one, a place of extreme light and extreme opposition [contrariety], fiercely opposed contrary to Li [the upper trigram]. "Seeing a pig covered in mud" is seeing filth. "A cart carrying ghosts" means nothing is in it. "Drawing the bow" is wanting to shoot it. "Putting down the bow" is suspecting you should gradually let it go. "Not a thief, a marriage" is realizing that [6 in the third] is not a thief, and becoming truly close. "Proceeding, coming upon rain: auspicious" is suspecting you should completely let go of your contrariety and join [with the other]. 9 at the top's relation with 6 in the third is first contrary and then joining; hence this image and prognostication.

[Image 6] The good fortune of "coming upon rain" is losing all one's doubts.

[39] 蹇 Jian (Obstructed)[45]

Gen [mountain] below, Kan [water] above.

Jian: Appropriate [advantageous] in the southwest, not appropriate in the northeast. Appropriate to see the great person. Correct and auspicious.

Jian is difficult [*nan* 難]; feet unable to advance, moving is difficult. The hexagram is Gen below and Kan above: seeing danger [Kan] and stopping [Gen]; hence "obstructed." The southwest is peaceful and the northeast is dangerous. Also, Gen is a direction [northwest];[46] if there is difficulty in that direction, you should not walk into danger. The hexagram comes from Xiaoguo 小過 [62 ䷽], with the [fourth] *yang* advancing and coming to reside in the fifth place, becoming central. If it retreats back into Gen there is no advance. Therefore the prognostication says, "appropriate in the southwest, not appropriate in the northeast." At a time of obstruction you must see the great person; only then might you overcome the difficulty. Also, it is necessary to hold on to correctness; only then will you have good fortune. The hexagram's 9 in the fifth is firm and strong, central and correct: the image of the great person. From the second line upward, all five lines are correctly positioned; the meaning of "being correct." Therefore the prognostication also says, "appropriate to see the great person; being correct is auspicious." For one who sees danger it is important "to be able to stop," but you cannot remain stopped. For one who is situated in danger it is appropriate to advance, but you cannot lose your correctness.

COMMENTARY ON THE JUDGMENT

Jian is difficulty; danger ahead. Seeing danger and being able to stop is wise indeed!

Explaining the meaning of the hexagram name in terms of the trigram virtues, and praising its excellence.

"Jian: Appropriate in the southwest"; going forward and becoming central. "Not appropriate in the northeast"; this path is blocked. "Appropriate to see the great person"; going forward there is merit. Proper position, correct and auspicious, so one can correct the country. Functioning in a time of obstruction is great indeed![47]

Explaining the hexagram statement in terms of the hexagram fluctuation and component trigrams, and praising the great functioning of such times.

COMMENTARY ON THE GREATER IMAGES

Above the mountain there is water: Obstructed. The superior person cultivates his virtue by self-reflection.

LINE STATEMENTS WITH COMMENTARY ON THE SMALLER IMAGES

[Line 1] 6 at the beginning: Going is obstructed, coming is praiseworthy.
Going meets with danger; coming yields praise.

[Image 1] "Going is obstructed, coming is praiseworthy": one should wait.

[Line 2] 6 in the second: The king's subject has obstruction after obstruction, but not because of himself.

The yielding, compliant line is central and correct, and correctly corresponds above. Yet it is in the midst of danger, so there is obstruction and yet more obstruction. He attempts to overcome it, because it is not because of him. There is no mention of good fortune or bad fortune, so the diviner can only exert himself and use all his strength. Whether this will come to success or failure is not discussed.

[Image 2] "The king's subject has obstruction after obstruction"; in the end no error.

Although the matter is not overcome, there is no error.

[Line 3] Going is obstructed; he comes back.

Coming back so the two *yin* lines can be at ease.

[Image 3] "Going is obstructed; he comes back." Those inside are happy about it.

[Line 4] 6 in the fourth: Going is obstructed; coming is connecting.

Connecting to 9 in the third, combining strengths to overcome.

[Image 4] "Going is obstructed; coming is connecting." The proper position is solid.

[Line 5] 9 in the fifth: Greatly obstructed, friends come.

One who is "greatly obstructed" will not always be obstructed. 9 in the fifth occupies the place of honor, with the virtue of being firm and strong, central and correct. He will certainly have friends come to help him. If the diviner has these virtues, then he will have this help.

[Image 5] "Greatly obstructed, friends come," moderated by the center.

[Line 6] 6 at the top: Going is obstructed, coming is grand: auspicious. Appropriate to see the great person.

Already at the peak of the hexagram, there is no place to go, so take advantage of the obstruction. Come to 9 in the fifth and with it overcome the obstruction; then there will be huge merit. "Great person" refers to 9 in the fifth. The aware diviner should be like this.

[Image 6] "Going is obstructed, coming is grand"; one's aim is inside [the upper trigram]. "Appropriate to see the great person," to follow his excellence.

[40] ䷧ 解 Xie (Released)

Kan [water] below, Zhen [thunder] above.

Xie: Appropriate in the southwest. If there is nowhere to go, coming back is auspicious. If there is somewhere to go, early morning is auspicious.

Xie is being released [*san* 散] from difficulty. Being in danger but able to act, and so emerging from danger, is the image of being released. Once released from difficulty it is appropriate to be at ease and quiet, not wanting to be troubled for a long time. This hexagram comes from Sheng 升 [46 ䷭], with the third line going into the fourth [position], moving into the Kun trigram [of Sheng], and the second remaining in its place, being central. Therefore it is "appropriate in the southwest," a peaceful place.[48] If there is "nowhere to go," you should come back to your place and be quiet. If looking ahead there is somewhere to go, then you should go early and return early, so you may not be troubled for long.

COMMENTARY ON THE JUDGMENT

Xie: When it is dangerous to act, but one acts and avoids danger, that is being released.

Explaining the meaning of the hexagram name in terms of the trigram virtues.[49]

Released: "Appropriate in the southwest"; going [there] will win the multitude. "Coming back is auspicious"; it yields centrality. "If there is somewhere to go, early morning is auspicious"; in going there is merit.

Explaining the hexagram statement by means of the hexagram transformation. Kun [☷, the upper trigram of Sheng] is the multitude; "winning the multitude" means 9 in the fourth entering Kun and becoming central. "There is merit" always indicates 9 in the second.

Heaven and Earth releasing creates thunder and rain. When thunder and rain are created, the seeds of the hundred fruits, grasses, and trees all sprout. Great indeed is the time of release!

Fully expressing and praising its greatness.

COMMENTARY ON THE GREATER IMAGES

"Thunder and rain are created": Released. The superior person pardons the crimes of those who have gone too far [i.e., releases them].

LINE STATEMENTS WITH COMMENTARY ON THE SMALLER IMAGES

[Line 1] 6 at the beginning: no blame.

When released from difficulty the yielding line at the bottom corresponds correctly [with 9 in the fourth]. How can there be blame? Hence this prognostication.

[Image 1] The meaning of the border between firm and yielding is no blame.

[Line 2] 9 in the second: hunting three foxes in the field, receiving a yellow arrow: correct and auspicious.

In this line, the idea of the image is unclear. Someone says, Leaving aside 6 in the fifth, the ruling position, the remaining three *yin* lines are the image of the three foxes. Most lines like this are auspicious prognostications when divining for fields. It can also be an image of expelling deceitful flattery to achieve centrality and directness. If you are able to hold on to correctness, everything will be auspicious.

[Image 2] "Correct and auspicious" in 9 in the second: achieving the Way of centrality.

[Line 3] 6 in the third: One who carries a load yet also rides in a carriage will attract bandits. Being correct: disgrace.

The *Xici* [A.8.11] fully explains this. "Being correct: disgrace" says that even if acquiring something correctly, there can be shame. Only if you shun and reject can [shame] be avoided.

[Image 3] "One who carries a load yet also rides in a carriage" should be ashamed. If I attract barbarians myself, who should be blamed?

"Barbarians" [*rong* 戎] is "bandits" [*kou* 寇] in the old text.[50]

[Line 4] 9 in the fourth: Cut off the big toe. Friends will arrive; be honest with them.[51]

The big toe signifies the beginning [first line]. The first and fourth lines are not in their [proper] position, yet they correspond with each other; they correspond but are not proper. So the fourth *yang* and first *yin* are not the same in kind. However, if you are able to cut off and get rid of it [first line], then the superior person's friends will arrive and there will be mutual trust.

[Image 4] "Cut off the big toe"; it is not in proper position.

[Line 5] 6 in the fifth: Only the superior person can release: auspicious. The proof lies in the inferior people.

The hexagram as a whole has four *yin* lines, and 6 in the fifth has the proper, superior, position. It is of the same kind as the other three *yin* lines, but it must release and get rid of them for there to be good fortune. *Fu* 孚 is "proof, confirmation" [*yan* 驗]. The superior person's releasing is confirmed by the retreat of the inferior people.

[Image 5] The superior person releases; inferior people retreat.

[Line 6] 6 at the top: The duke shoots a hawk on top of a high wall and hits it. Everything is advantageous.

The *Xici* [B.5.6] fully explains this.

[Image 6] "The duke shoots a hawk" is eliminating resistance.

[41] ䷨ 損 Sun (Diminishing)[52]

Dui [lake] below, Gen [mountain] above.

Sun: With honesty, supremely auspicious; no blame. If you can be correct, appropriate wherever you go.

Sun is diminishing [*jiansheng* 減省]. The hexagram diminishes [*sun* 損] the *yang* of the top line of the lower trigram [of Tai ䷊ (11)] and enhances [*yi* 益] the *yin* of the top line of the upper trigram [of Tai].[53] The lake of Sun's Dui [lower trigram] is deep; the mountain of Yi's Gen is high.[54] Sun is low and Yi is high; Sun is inner and Yi is outer: the image of putting down the commoner and esteeming the superior. This is why it is Diminishing. If you diminish what should be diminished, yet with honesty and trust, the prognostication should correspond with the four lower lines [below the ruler].

How to do this? Two grain baskets can be used for the offering.

This says at a time of diminishing there is no harm in being frugal.

COMMENTARY ON THE JUDGMENT

Sun: Diminishing what is below and increasing what is above, its Way moves upward.

Explaining the meaning of the hexagram name in terms of the component trigrams.

Diminishing, yet "with honesty": supremely auspicious; no blame. "If you can be correct, appropriate wherever you go. How to do this? Two grain baskets can be used for the offering." Two grain baskets correspond with the time: the time of diminishing the firm and enhancing the yielding. Diminishing and enhancing, filling and emptying, is going along with the time.

This explains the hexagram statement. "Time" means the proper time for diminishing.

COMMENTARY ON THE GREATER IMAGES

Below the mountain there is a lake: Diminishing. The superior person limits his anger and restrains his lust.

The superior person cultivates himself, which requires diminishing. Nothing is more urgent than this.

LINE STATEMENTS WITH COMMENTARY ON THE SMALLER IMAGES

[Line 1] 9 at the beginning: When your work is finished, go quickly; no blame. But think carefully about diminishing others.

9 at the beginning is when you should diminish those below and enhance those above. Above it corresponds with the *yin* of 6 in the fourth. To stop the work you have done and hurriedly go to enhance it [6 in the fourth] is a path of no blame; thus the image and prognostication. However, abiding below and enhancing what is above, you must fully and carefully think about what is important and not important.

[Image 1] "When your work is finished, go quickly": join purposes with those above.

[Line 2] 9 in the second: Appropriate and correct; setting forth is ominous. Enhance others without diminishing [oneself].

9 in the second is firm and central; its purpose is to hold on to the self, and it is unwilling to forget advancement. Thus it is appropriate for the diviner to be correct, and setting forth is ominous. "Enhance others without diminishing [oneself]" says not to alter what you are holding on to so that you can enhance the other.

[Image 2] "9 in the second: Appropriate and correct." Make centrality one's purpose.

[Line 3] 6 in the third: When three people travel, they will diminish by one. When one person travels, he will find his friend.

The lower trigram was originally Qian [in Tai (11)], and its top line was diminished to increase Kun: this is "three people traveling" and "diminishing by one."[55] One *yang* ascending and one *yin* descending is "one person traveling" and "finding his friend." These two [lines 3 and 6] interact as one, but the three [between them] are mixed and confused, so the hexagram has this image. Therefore the warning to the diviner is that he must bring about unity.

[Image 3] "When one person travels," the three will have doubts.

[Line 4] 6 in the fourth: Diminishing one's anxiety will quickly bring happiness. No blame.

The firm *yang* of 9 at the beginning enhances itself and "diminishes the anxiety" of this yielding *yin*, quickly leading to "happiness."[56] Hence the admonition to the diviner, and no blame.

[Image 4] "Diminishing one's anxiety," one can be happy.

[Line 5] 6 in the fifth: Someone enhances you by ten pairs of tortoise shells; you will not be opposed. Supremely auspicious.[57]

Yielding, compliant, vacuous, and central: occupying the position of honor at a time of diminishing, you will be enhanced by all under Heaven. Two tortoises make a pair, so ten pairs are very precious. If someone enhances you and you are unable to decline, your good fortune can be understood. If the diviner has these virtues, he will get the corresponding [good fortune].

[Image 5] "6 in the fifth: supremely auspicious": help from [the top line] above.

[Line 6] 6 at the top: Enhancing [others] without diminishing [oneself]: no blame, correct and auspicious. Appropriate wherever you go; gaining subjects but no family.

9 at the top is a time of enhancing above and diminishing below. Residing at the top of the hexagram, it receives the maximum enhancement, yet desires to diminish itself in order to enhance others. However, residing above and enhancing those below is what is called blessing without cost. It does not depend upon diminishing oneself and only then possibly increasing others. If you are able to

be like this, there is no blame. But it is also necessary to be correct in order to have good fortune and to be "appropriate wherever you go." Blessing without cost is extensive blessing; therefore it says, "gaining subjects but no family."

[Image 6] "Enhancing [others] without diminishing [oneself]": one's purpose is greatly achieved.

[42]   ䷩   Yi (Enhancing)[58]

Zhen [thunder] below, Sun [wind, wood] above.

Yi: Appropriate wherever you go; appropriate to cross a great river.

    Yi is enhancing [*zengyi* 增益]. The hexagram diminishes the *yang* of the first line of [Pi's] upper trigram and enhances the *yin* of the first line of [Pi's] lower trigram.[59] Thus it is Enhancing. The hexagram's 9 in the fifth and 6 in the second are both central and correct. Zhen ☳ below and Sun ☴ above are both images of wood.[60] Hence the prognostications are "appropriate wherever you go" and "appropriate to cross a great river."

COMMENTARY ON THE JUDGMENT

Yi: Diminishing above and enhancing below, the people's pleasure has no bounds. Descending from above to below, its Way is greatly radiant.[61]

    Explaining the meaning of the hexagram name in terms of the component trigrams.

"Appropriate wherever you go": being central and correct is a blessing.[62] "Appropriate to cross a great river": the Way of wood is put into effect.

    Explaining the hexagram statement by means of the component trigrams and their images.

Enhancing is active yet gentle, advancing daily without bound.[63] Heaven bestows and Earth gives birth, enhancing without limit.[64] The Way of enhancing acts in accord with the time.

"Active" and "gentle" are the virtues of the two trigrams. Qian [Heaven] bestows below, and Kun [Earth] gives birth above; these are the meanings of the component trigrams in the text above. This also fully expresses praise of the greatness of Increase.

COMMENTARY ON THE GREATER IMAGES

Wind and thunder: Enhancing. When the superior person sees good he moves toward it; when he has transgressed, he reforms [himself].

The power of wind and thunder reinforce each other. Moving toward the good and reforming one's transgressions is the greatness of Enhancing; their mutual enhancement is just like this.[65]

LINE STATEMENTS WITH COMMENTARY ON THE SMALLER IMAGES

[Line 1] 9 at the beginning: Appropriate to accomplish great deeds. Supremely auspicious; no blame.

Although the beginning resides below, it is the proper time of enhancing those below. One who accepts help from above cannot vainly fail to make compensation; thus it is "appropriate to accomplish great deeds." But only if it is "supremely auspicious" can there be "no blame."

[Image 1] "Supremely auspicious; no blame." But those below should not deal with important matters.

Those below should not have responsibility for important matters. Otherwise they will not be able to avoid blame.

[Line 2] 6 in the second: Someone enhances you by ten pairs of tortoise shells; you will not be opposed. Perpetually correct and auspicious. If the king gets through to the Lord, auspicious.[66]

6 in the second is the proper time of enhancing those below. This empty central line below has the same image and prognostication as 6 in the fifth of Sun.[67] However, both line positions are *yin*, so you should take "perpetually correct" as an admonition. As it resides below and accepts enhancement from above, it is also an auspicious prognostication for the suburban divination.[68]

[Image 2] "Someone enhances you": it comes from without.

"Someone" is always a term with an uncertain focus.

[Line 3] 6 in the third: Enhancing by means of ominous business; no blame. Proceed moderately, with honesty; report to the duke with an [official] tablet.[69]

6 in the third is a yielding *yin* line, neither central nor correct, so it should not receive an enhancement. However, it is a time of enhancing those below, and this resides at the top of the lower trigram, so there is enhancement by means of some "ominous business." If the admonition rouses [the diviner] to action, there will be enhancement. Only when the diviner is like this can there be "no blame." He is also admonished to "proceed moderately, with honesty," and to "report to the duke with an official tablet." The tablet is how he conveys his honesty.

[Image 3] "Enhancing by means of ominous business": one will certainly have it.

"Enhancing by means of ominous business": if you want to take pains to carefully consider, you will "certainly have it."

[Line 4] 6 in the fourth: Proceed moderately and your report to the duke will be followed. Appropriate to use it in support of moving the state [i.e., the capital].

Neither the third nor the fourth lines are central, so "proceed moderately" is a warning to both. This says by enhancing those below wholeheartedly, and joining them in proceeding moderately, then when you report to the duke you will see him follow. The [*Zuo*]*zhuan* says, "When Zhou moved to the east, Jin and Zheng supported it." In ancient times a state was moved to benefit those below, and must have their support. Only then could [the state] be established. This line is also an auspicious prognostication for the move of a state.[70]

[Image 4] "Your report to the duke will be followed," thereby enhancing [one's] aims.[71]

[Line 5] 9 in the fifth: With honesty and a kind heart, do not ask for supreme good fortune. Being honest and kind is your personal virtue.

If the superior is honest and kind to the inferior, the inferior will likewise be honest and kind to the superior. Not asking for supreme good fortune is understandable.

[Image 5] "With honesty and a kind heart, do not ask" for anything. The personal virtue of kindness is a great achievement of one's aims.

[Line 6] 9 at the top: Nothing enhances you; someone strikes you. Your heart is not settled for long: ominous.

A *yang* line occupying the peak of Enhancing: one's quest for enhancement is not accomplished. Therefore there is no enhancement and someone strikes you. "Your heart is not settled for long" is the warning.

[Image 6] "Nothing enhances you" is a harsh statement. "Someone strikes you": it comes from without.

"Nothing enhances you" is the "harsh statement" about being one who follows and seeks enhancement. If you think more about it, it is like being struck.

[43] ䷪ 夬 Guai (Resolving)

Qian [heaven] below, Dui [lake] above.

Guai: Make it known at the king's court; honestly announce that there is danger. Notify your own city: inappropriate to immediately take up arms. Appropriate wherever you go.

Guai is resolving [*jue* 決], the *yang* resolving [the presence of] *yin*.[72] It is the hexagram of the third month [April-May]. The *yang* line in the fifth [is about to] eliminate the single *yin*, resolving it once and for all. But this resolution must correctly name the offense. With complete authenticity call out to everyone and join forces with them, while also emphasizing the danger; you cannot be complacent. Also, you should first control yourself; you cannot solely emphasize military force. Then it will be "appropriate wherever you go." These are all statements of warning.

COMMENTARY ON THE JUDGMENT

Guai is resolving, the firm resolving the yielding. Strong and pleasing, resolute and harmonious.

Explaining the meaning of the hexagram name and praising its virtues.[73]

"Making it known at the king's court" is the yielding riding on the five firm lines. "Honestly announce that there is danger"; the danger is obvious. "Notify your own city, inappropriate to immediately take up arms": what is esteemed is exhausted. "Appropriate wherever you go" is the final result of the growth of the firm.

This explains the hexagram statement. "The yielding riding on the five firm lines," speaking in terms of the hexagram structure, means a single inferior person is put over the many superior people: this is the offense. "The final result of the growth of the firm" means that with one more fluctuation it will be pure Qian.

COMMENTARY ON THE GREATER IMAGES

A lake rising to Heaven: Resolving. The superior person dispenses blessings that reach those below. He dwells in virtue and so shuns . . .

"A lake rising to Heaven" is the power of breaking through to a resolution. "Dispensing blessings that reach those below" is the idea of breaking through to a resolution. "He dwells in virtue and so shuns . . ." is not clear.[74]

LINE STATEMENTS WITH COMMENTARY ON THE SMALLER IMAGES

[Line 1] 9 at the beginning: Strength in the advancing toes. Going forward without overcoming incurs blame.

Qian 前 [ahead] is like "advancing" [jin 進]. At a time of resolution, residing below requires strength, and "not overcoming" is appropriate. Hence the image and prognostication.

[Image 1] "Not overcoming and yet advancing" is blameworthy.

[Line 2] Cries of alarm; weapons in the evening and night. Do not worry.

9 in the second is the time of resolution: it is a firm line occupying a yielding position, and "attains the Way of centrality."[75] Thus you are able to be anxious about cries of alarm, and to take precautions yourself. Even as there are "weapons in the evening and night," you can avoid trouble.

[Image 2] There are weapons, but do not worry. Attain the Way of centrality.

[Line 3] 9 in the third: Strength in the cheekbone: ominous. The superior person is doubly resolved. Walking alone and encountering rain, getting wet. Anger, but no blame.

    Qiu 頄 is the cheekbone. 9 in the third is the proper time for resolution: a firm line that has gone past the middle, desiring to resolve [the presence of] the inferior person. The firm strength is seen in the face and eyes; thus it is an ominous path.[76] Among all the *yang* lines, this alone corresponds with 6 at the top.[77] If it is able to finally effect this resolution, unconnected with private affections, then even though it is joined with 6 at the top, if it "walks alone it will encounter rain." Reaching the point of "getting wet" is what makes the superior person angry. However, at long last one will certainly be able to get rid of the inferior person, and there will be no reason for blame. The Wen Jiao / Wang Dun affair was like this.[78]

[Image 3] "The superior person is doubly resolved": in the end, no blame.

[Line 4] 9 in the fourth: With no skin on his buttocks, his walking is halting. Led like a sheep, regret vanishes.[79] Hearing the words but not believing.

    [The first sentence is] the same as in the Gou 姤 hexagram [line 3].

[Image 4] "His walking is halting": his position is not proper. "Hearing the words but not believing": not hearing/understanding clearly.

[Line 5] Pokeweed [requires] doubled resolve [to eliminate]. If you proceed centrally, no blame.[80]

    Pokeweed [*xianlu* 莧陸] is now [called] purslane [*machixian* 馬齒莧], which stimulates a great deal of *yin qi*. 9 in the fifth, at the proper time for resolution, is the master of resolution. It is the closest to the *yin* of 6 at the top, which is like pokeweed. If it effects resolution and is not excessively rough, along with walking centrally, then there will be no blame. This is an admonition to the diviner to be like this.

[Image 5] "If you proceed centrally, no blame," but the center is not yet luminous.

    Cheng's Commentary is comprehensive. It says, "The hexagram statement speaks of doubled resolution; proceeding centrally will incur no blame. The Image

[Commentary] reemphasizes this idea by saying that the center is not yet luminous. When a person's mind is rectified and his intentions are authentic, he is able to fully realize the Way of centrality and correctness and can fully develop his illustrious [mind].[81] In the fifth line, the mind is close to [the *yin* line at the top], and the meaning is that it is unable to attain resolution. Although you proceed externally, without losing one's centrality and correctness and incurring no blame, nevertheless the Way of centrality is not yet luminous and great. Once the human mind has desires, it departs from the Way. The Master [Confucius] here demonstrates the importance of intentions."[82]

[Line 6] 6 at the top: No cries, but ominous in the end.

The yielding *yin* line is the inferior person at the time of complete exhaustion, his colleagues already finished, nothing to cry out about. The end must be ominous. If the diviner has the virtue of a superior person he will match his opponent. If not, it will go against him.

[Image 6] What is ominous about "no cries" is that in the end one cannot persist.

[44] 姤 Gou (Encountering)

Sun [wind, wood] below, Qian [heaven] above.

Gou: The woman is strong. Do not choose the woman.

Gou is encountering [*yu* 遇].[83] Resolution is done, making pure *yang*, the hexagram of the fourth month. Now it comes to Gou, when a single *yin* line appears, making the hexagram of the fifth month.[84] It is not what is hoped for, yet it suddenly comes, like meeting accidentally; therefore it is encountering. The encounter is completely incorrect; the single *yin* encounters the five *yang* lines and the woman's virtue is not correct, yet she is very strong. Choosing her as a mate for oneself will surely harm the *yang*; hence this image and prognostication.

COMMENTARY ON THE JUDGMENT

Gou is encountering: the yielding encounters the firm.

Explaining the hexagram name.

"Do not choose the woman": one could not last long with her.
    Explaining the hexagram statement.

Heaven and earth encounter each other; all types of things are manifested.
    Speaking in terms of the component trigrams.[85]

The firm encounters centrality and correctness; all under Heaven proceed greatly.
    Referring to 9 in the fifth.

The meaning of the time of Encountering is great indeed!
    The Sage's [Confucius's] respect for the moment of incipient subtlety.

COMMENTARY ON THE GREATER IMAGES

Under Heaven there is wind: Encountering. The sovereign issues his commands and informs the four quarters [of the world].

LINE STATEMENTS WITH COMMENTARY ON THE SMALLER IMAGES

[Line 1] 6 at the beginning: Attached to a metal brake: correct and auspicious. Having somewhere to go will meet with bad fortune. A scrawny pig helpfully stomps its hooves.
    A brake is a means to stop a cart. When made of metal we know it is strong. A single *yin* line begins to appear. If it is still and correct then there will be good fortune; if it goes forward to advance there will be misfortune. These two ideas are therefore warnings to the inferior person not to harm the superior person; then there will be good fortune and no misfortune. But [the *yin*'s] power cannot be limited, so a scrawny pig stomping its hooves alerts the superior person, making a strong statement that he should be prepared.

[Image 1] "Attached to a metal brake": the yielding Way advances.
    It is advancing, so it should be stopped.

[Line 2] 9 in the second: Fish in a wrapper: no blame. Inappropriate for a guest.

A fish is a *yin* object. The second [line] encountering the first is the image of "fish in a wrapper." However, if you control it [the *yin* tendency] in yourself there can be no blame. If you do not control it and allow it to encounter the masses, then it will cause harm and danger; hence this image and prognostication.

[Image 2] "Fish in a wrapper": it is right not to let it reach the guest.

[Line 3] 9 in the third: With no skin on his buttocks, his walking is halting. Danger, but no great blame.[86]

9 in the third is too firm and not central. It does not encounter the beginning line below, and it does not correspond with the top line above. Its place, then, is uneasy, and it moves but does not advance; hence this image and prognostication. But since it does not encounter anything it is not injured by the unlucky *yin*. Therefore although it is in danger, there is no great blame.

[Image 3] "His walking is halting"; he walks but does not lead.

[Line 4] 9 in the fourth: No fish in the wrapper, giving rise to misfortune.

Correctly corresponding with 6 at the beginning; having already encountered the second but not reaching the self [line 5]; hence this image and prognostication.[87]

[Image 4] The bad fortune of "no fish" is being far from the people.

The people have rejected you, which is like being far from them.

[Line 5] 9 in the fifth: A willow covering a melon: holding a seal [of authority], which has fallen from Heaven.[88]

A melon is a *yin* object below [on the ground], which is sweet, beautiful, and good to break open. A willow is a tall, large, hard, and solid tree. The fifth is a firm *yang* line, central and correct, ruling the hexagram from above. It protects against the *yin* below, which is beginning to appear and will necessarily be defeated; hence this image. *Yin* and *yang* alternately predominating is the constant revolution of time. If you are able to restrain the dark and display the beauty, controlling them with stillness, then you can return to creating and transforming. "Fallen from Heaven" is the image of starting with nothing and suddenly having [this power].

[Image 5] "9 in the fifth: holding a seal [of authority]" is central and correct. "Fallen from Heaven" is being determined not to forsake the Decree [of Heaven].

[Line 6] 9 at the top: Encountering with his horns: disgrace, but no blame.

Horns are firmness above. 9 at the top is firm and occupies the top, lacking [proper] position. It cannot encounter anything, so its image and prognostication are similar to 9 in the third.

[Image 6] "Encountering with his horns": finished at the top; disgrace.

[45] 萃 Cui (Gathering)

Kun [earth] below, Dui [lake] above.

Cui: Success. The king arrives at the temple. Appropriate to see the great person; success. Appropriate and correct. Using a large sacrificial animal is auspicious. Appropriate wherever you go.

Cui is gathering [*ju* 聚]. Kun is complying and Dui is pleasing. The 9 in the fifth is firm and central, and the second corresponds with it. It is lake [or marsh] rising to [the surface of] the earth, the image of the myriad things gathering together, so it is Cui. The [first] word "success" is superfluous. "The king arrives at the temple" says that the king goes inside the ancestral temple and divines and sacrifices for an auspicious prognostication, as in the "Meaning of Sacrifice" [Jiyi 祭義] [chapter of the *Liji*], which says, "The duke arrives at the great temple."[89] The temple is where the spirits of the ancestors gather; people must be able to gather [concentrate] their own spirits so they can approach the temple and support their deceased ancestors. When they are gathered, they can surely see the great person and then have success. But it is necessary to be appropriately correct. If the place you gather is not correct, you are unable to have success.[90]

COMMENTARY ON THE JUDGMENT

Cui is gathering. Complying with pleasure; the firm [in the fifth] is central and corresponds [with the second]; thus it is "gathering."

Explaining the meaning of the hexagram name in terms of the component trigrams and their virtues.

"The king arrives at the temple," causing filial respect to penetrate [spread]. "Appropriate to see the great person; success": gathering correctly. "Using a large sacrificial animal is auspicious" and "appropriate wherever you go" are complying with the decree of Heaven.

Explaining the hexagram statement.

Observing what is gathered, the dispositions of Heaven and Earth and the myriad things can be seen.

Fully expressing and praising the principle [of gathering].

COMMENTARY ON THE GREATER IMAGES

Lake [marsh] rises to earth: Gathering. The superior person prepares instruments of war to be on guard for emergencies.

"Prepares" means to repair and gather them.

LINE STATEMENTS WITH COMMENTARY ON THE SMALLER IMAGES

[Line 1] 6 at the beginning: With honesty, but not to the end, there will now be confusion, now gathering. If one calls out, one hand clasp will bring a smile. Do not worry; no blame in proceeding.

6 at the beginning corresponds above with 9 in the fourth and is different from the two *yin* lines [above it]. At an appropriate time of gathering, if you are unable to preserve yourself and "there is honesty but not to the end," one's purpose will be confused and it would be wrong to gather. If you call out for a correct response, then the rest will take it with a smile. Just don't worry; go out and follow the correct response, and there will be no blame. The warning to the diviner must be like this.

[Image 1] "Now confusion, now gathering": one's purpose is confused.

[Line 2] 6 in the second: Drawn to good fortune, no blame. With honesty, appropriate to perform the royal ancestral sacrifice.

The second corresponds with the fifth and is in the midst of two *yin* lines, so it must be pulled and drawn into gathering: "good fortune, no blame." Also, the second is central and correct, yielding and complying: the empty center, corresponding above with 9 in the fifth, which is firm, strong, central, and correct, genuinely engaged below.[91] Therefore if one who divines and sacrifices is honest and authentic, then even a small object can be sacrificed.

[Image 2] "Drawn to good fortune; no blame": the center does not fluctuate.

[Line 3] 6 in the third: Gathering and sighing: nothing is appropriate. No blame in proceeding; small disgrace.

6 in the third is a yielding *yin* line, neither central nor correct; nothing above corresponds with it. It wants to seek out a gathering nearby, but cannot. Therefore there is sighing, and nowhere to go. Only by going out to follow what is above can it avoid blame, but it cannot find a gathering. If it goes out in distress, it will return as the peak of *yin*, an improperly positioned line: this can be a small disgrace. The warning to the diviner is that he should reject strong assistance from nearby that is incorrect, and connect with correctly responsive full engagement from far away. Then there will be no blame.

[Image 3] "No blame in proceeding": what is above is gentle.

[Line 4] 9 in the fourth: Great good fortune, no blame.

This finds gathering by being next to 9 in the fifth above and the bunch of *yin* lines below. But as a *yang* line occupying a *yin* position it is incorrect, so the warning to the diviner is that he must have "great good fortune"; only then will there be "no blame."

[Image 4] "Great good fortune, no blame," but its position is improper.

[Line 5] 9 in the fifth: Gathering in [proper] position, no blame. Without honesty, but with supreme and long-lasting correctness, regret vanishes.

9 in the fifth is a firm *yang* line, central and correct, occupying the position of honor at a time of gathering: definitely without blame. If there is no honesty, then by cultivating the virtue of "supreme and long-lasting correctness," "regret vanishes." Hence the warning to the diviner.

[Image 5] "Gathering in [proper] position": one's will does not yet shine forth.

"Not yet shine forth" means there is no honesty.

[Line 6] 6 at the top: Weeping and wailing; no blame.

At the end of the gathering place, this yielding *yin* line is out of position. It unsuccessfully seeks a gathering, so the warning to the diviner must be like this. Only then can there be no blame.

[Image 6] "Weeping and wailing": unease at the top.

[46] ䷭ 升 Sheng (Advancing Upward)

Sun [wind, wood] below, Kun [earth] above.

Sheng: Supreme success: Useful to see the great person; do not worry. Going south is auspicious.

Sheng is advancing upward [*jin'er shang* 進而上]. The hexagram comes from Xie 解 [40 ䷧], with a weak line rising to occupy the fourth position. Sun [Entering] is the inner and Complying [Kun] is the outer [trigram]. 9 in the second is firm and central, and the fifth corresponds with it; hence the prognostication.[92]

COMMENTARY ON THE JUDGMENT

The yielding line advances upward in accord with the time.

Explaining the hexagram name by means of the hexagram fluctuation [from Xie ䷧ to Sheng ䷭].

Gentle and compliant; correspondence with the firm, central line; thereby great and penetrating.

Explaining the hexagram statement by means of the component trigrams and their virtues [Sun: gentle, Kun: compliant].

"Useful to see the great person; do not worry"; there will be blessing. "Going south is auspicious"; one's purpose is carried out.

COMMENTARY ON THE GREATER IMAGES

In the midst of the earth grows a tree: Advancing Upward. The superior person, by means of the virtue of complying, accumulates the small in order to reach great heights.

In Wang Su's book, "complying" [*shun* 順] is "being cautious" [*shen* 慎]. Contemporary commentators draw from this and often write "being cautious," which is a much clearer idea. In older writing they were used interchangeably, as discussed above under Meng 蒙 [hexagram 4, Image Commentary on line 3].[93]

LINE STATEMENTS WITH COMMENTARY ON THE SMALLER IMAGES

[Line 1] 6 at the beginning: Appropriately advancing upward; greatly auspicious.

The beginning is a yielding, compliant line occupying the bottom, and is the ruler of [the trigram] Sun. At the proper time to advance upward it enters into [*sun* 巽] the two *yang*. If the diviner is like this, he can truly advance upward with great good fortune.

[Image 1] "Appropriately advancing upward; greatly auspicious": joining with the aims of the superior.

[Line 2] 9 in the second: Being honest, it is appropriate to perform the royal ancestral sacrifice; no blame.

For this idea see [the same sentence in] Cui [hexagram 45, second line].

[Image 2] The honesty of 9 in the second is being happy.

[Line 3] Advancing upward into an empty city.

Yang is full and *yin* is empty; in Kun is the image of a capital city.[94] 9 in the third is a firm *yang* line at the proper time to advance upward, and it is approaching Kun; hence this image and prognostication,

[Image 3] "Advancing upward into an empty city"; no doubt about it.

[Line 4] 6 in the fourth: The king makes offerings to Mount Qi. Auspicious, no blame.[95]

For this idea see also Sui [17].

[Image 4] "The king makes an offering to Mount Qi" in compliance with the situation.

Advancing upward in compliance [with the situation]: the image of ascending and sacrificing to the mountain.

[Line 5] 6 in the fifth: Correct and auspicious; promotion in rank.

A *yin* line occupying a *yang* position, properly advancing upward to occupy the position of honor. It must be able to be correct and strong so it can achieve good fortune and be promoted in rank. The new rank is the change resulting from advancing upward.

[Image 5] "Correct and auspicious" and "promotion in rank" are the great achievement of one's purpose.

[Line 6] 6 at the top: Advancing upward in the dark; appropriate to be unceasingly correct.

A *yin* line residing at the maximum of upward advance, it is endless darkness. If the diviner encounters this, there is nowhere appropriate to go. Only if you can reverse your endless attention to the external can you adopt unceasing correctness.

[Image 6] "Advancing upward in the dark" at the top: loss, not wealth.

[47] 困 Kun (Blocked)[96]

Kan [water] below, Dui [lake] above.

Kun: Success. Being correct, the great person has good fortune; no blame. What you have to say is not believed.

Kun means exhausting yet being unable to rouse oneself. The firmness of Kan is blocked [*yan* 揜] by the yielding of Dui.[97] The 9 in the second is blocked by the two *yin* lines [around it], and the fourth and fifth [*yang*] lines are blocked by 6 at the top; this is why it is Blocked. Kan is danger and Dui is pleasure. Being in a dangerous position yet having pleasure is [for example] when a person's Way is successful despite being blocked. The second and fifth lines are firm and central: the image of the great person. If the diviner is in a blocked position and is able to succeed, he will become correct. Were he not a great person how would he be able to do so? Therefore it says, "being correct." It also says that the great person understands that the petty person, who is not correct, is unable to match him. "What you have to say is not believed" is a warning that you should strive to be silent; you cannot "esteem speech" [see the following] and beneficially exhaust the blockage.

COMMENTARY ON THE JUDGMENT

Kun: The firm is blocked.
 Explaining the hexagram name by means of the component trigrams.

Danger and pleasure; blocked and yet not losing what is successful: who could this be but the superior person? "Being correct, the great person has good fortune," as he is firm and central. "What you have to say is not believed": esteeming speech leads to exhaustion.
 Explaining the hexagram statement by means of the component trigrams and their virtues.

COMMENTARY ON THE GREATER IMAGES

Lake without water: Blocked. The superior person sacrifices his life in pursuit of his aims.
 The water has drained downward, so the lake above is dry: thus "lake without water." "Sacrifices his life" is like giving one's life; this says that he holds on to it for others and not for the sake of existing. If you are able to be like this, then you will be successful despite being blocked.

LINE STATEMENTS WITH COMMENTARY ON THE SMALLER IMAGES

[Line 1] 6 at the beginning: Buttocks confined to a tree stump. Entering a dark valley, one will not see for three years.

"Buttocks" are a thing's bottom. "Confined to a tree stump" means injured and unable to be comfortable. The 6 at the beginning, a yielding *yin* line at the bottom of Kun, occupies an extremely dark place; hence the image and prognostication.

[Image 1] "Entering a dark valley": dark, no light.

[Line 2] 9 in the second: Blocked while eating and drinking. The crimson sash is about to arrive; appropriate to offer sacrifice.[98] Proceeding is ominous, but no blame.

"Blocked while eating and drinking" is the idea of being sick from overeating. Wine and food are what people desire, but getting drunk and overeating go beyond the appropriate, and this is contrary [to one's desire] and causes blockage. "The crimson sash is about to arrive" is responding to the one above. 9 in the second has the virtues of being firm and central. At a moment of blockage, although there is no ominous injury, it is held back by getting more than was desired; hence this image, and the prognostication of "appropriate to offer sacrifice." Proceeding with one's activity it would not be the [proper] time; hence "ominous," yet the meaning is "no blame."[99]

[Image 2] "Blocked while eating and drinking": blessings at the center.

[Line 3] 6 in the third: Blocked by stone, leaning on a star thistle. Entering the house, not seeing one's wife: ominous.

A yielding *yin* line that is neither central nor correct: hence this image and ominous prognostication. "Stone" indicates the fourth line, "star thistle" indicates the second, "house" means the third, and "wife" is the sixth. The meaning is given fully in the *Xici* [B.5.5].

[Image 3] "Leaning on a star thistle" to take advantage of firmness. "Entering the house, not seeing one's wife" is unfortunate.

[Line 4] 9 in the fourth: Coming gradually, blocked by a metal carriage. Disgrace, but achieving one's ends.

6 at the beginning and 9 in the fourth correctly correspond, but 9 in the fourth's position is not proper, so it is unable to help things. The 6 at the beginning is blocked below, covered by 9 in the second; hence this image. But the crooked cannot vanquish the correct, so although the prognostication is disgraceful,

one's ends will necessarily be achieved. "Metal carriage" is the image of 9 in the second, and is unfortunate; it is the image of a cart obstructing Kan [water].

[Image 4] "Coming gradually," one's purpose is directed below. Although not properly positioned, one will have others [as support].

[Line 5] 9 in the fifth: Nose and feet cut off, blocked by [one with] the red sash. Pleasure comes slowly; appropriate to offer sacrifice.[100]

"Nose and feet cut off" is injury above and below. When you are injured above and below, the red sash is of no use; on the contrary it will block you. 9 in the fifth is the proper time to be blocked, as it is blocked by *yin* above and rests on the firm below; hence this image. However, this line is firm and central in the trigram of pleasure, so eventually there can be long-lasting pleasure. The prognostication is contained in the image: "appropriate to offer sacrifice," and the future will certainly bring happiness.

[Image 5] "Nose and feet cut off": one's purpose is not achieved. "Pleasure comes slowly" by being central and direct. "Appropriate to offer sacrifice": one will receive blessings.

[Line 6] 6 at the top: Blocked by creeping vines and anxiety, saying, "Act regretfully." With regret, going forth is auspicious.

A yielding *yin* line positioned at the peak of Kun; hence the image of "being blocked by creeping vines and anxiety, saying, 'Act regretfully.'" However, when something reaches its end it alternates. Thus the prognostication says that if you are able to be "with regret," you can go forth auspiciously.

[Image 6] "Blocked by creeping vines": not proper. "Acting regretfully" and "with regret": good fortune will ensue.

[48] ䷯ 井 Jing (The Well)[101]

Sun [wind, wood] below, Kan [water] above.

Jing: A city can be changed but a well does not change; it neither decreases nor increases.[102] Whether going or coming, a well is [always] a well. If the rope doesn't quite reach the well [water], or the jug breaks, ominous.

A well is an opening in the earth for drawing out water. The wood of Sun enters the water of Kan below and raises up the water; hence it is Well.[103] "A city can be changed but a well does not change," so without decreasing or increasing, whether going or coming, a well is a well. When you have almost succeeded in drawing water from the well and the jug breaks before the well rope reaches the bottom, that is misfortune. The prognostication is that in one's affairs you should rely on the past and not reject it; you should respect and work on it. If you cannot come close to achieving it, you will fail.[104]

COMMENTARY ON THE JUDGMENT

Sun goes into water and raises water: The Well. The well nourishes without being exhausted.

Explaining the meaning of the hexagram name in terms of the trigram images.

"A city can be changed but a well does not change"; it is firm and central. "If the rope doesn't quite reach the well [water]," there is no accomplishment. "If the jug is broken," it is ominous.

Explaining the hexagram statement by means of the component trigrams. The two sentences "It neither decreases nor increases" and "Whether going or coming, a well is always a well" means the same as the unchanging well [itself], so they are not repeated. "Firm and central" refers to the second and fifth lines. "There is no accomplishment" and "the jug is broken" are why it is ominous.

COMMENTARY ON THE GREATER IMAGES

Above wood there is water: The Well. The superior person exhorts the people to work and encourages them [to help] each other.

"Above wood there is water" as the moisture rises upward: the image of the well. "Exhorts the people to work" is the superior nourishing the people; "encourages them [to help] each other" is causing the people to nourish each other. Both [the latter two phrases] have the meaning of the well nourishing [things and people].

LINE STATEMENTS WITH COMMENTARY ON THE SMALLER IMAGES

[Line 1] 6 at the beginning: A well's mud is not drunk; there are no animals at an old well.

A well uses a firm *yang* as its source, which rises to become effective.[105] The 6 at the beginning is a *yin* line occupying the bottom; hence this image. If the well has no source and is muddy, then there is nothing for people to drink; animals and birds also have no use for it.

[Image 1] "A well's mud is not drunk"; it is at the bottom. "There are no animals at an old well"; its time has run out.

Its time has gone.

[Line 2] Shooting carp in the well hole; the jar is broken and leaks.

The second line of Dui is firm and central, the image of a source. But it has no correspondence above, and below it is related to 6 at the beginning, so it doesn't successfully move upward; hence this image.

[Image 2] "Shooting carp in the well hole"; no one involved.

[Line 3] 9 in the third: The well is dredged but not drunk from. This gives me heartache, as it could be drawn from. If the king were clear [about this], all would receive blessings.

"Dredged" means it is no longer muddy. "The well is dredged but not drunk from," causing heartache in people, "as it could be drawn from." "If the king were clear [i.e., understood]," then water drawn from the well could be used for [people and] things; he who bestows [i.e., the king] and those who receive would all receive blessings. 9 in the third is a *yang* line in a *yang* position, at the top of the lower [trigram], yet it is not yet time for it to be used; hence this image and prognostication.

[Image 3] "The well is dredged but not drunk from," causing sorrow. Seek out a bright king to receive blessings.

Those who are "caused sorrow" are people who practice the Way, all of whom feel sorrow.[106]

[Line 4] 6 in the fourth: The well is relined [with bricks]; no blame.

Although 6 occupying the fourth position is correct, a yielding *yin* line is not a source, so it can only be repaired; it cannot extend benefit to things. Thus the image is "the well relined," and the prognostication is "no blame." If the diviner is able to repair/improve [himself through self-cultivation], then although he cannot extend benefit to things, he can still be without blame.

[Image 4] "The well is relined; no blame" is repairing the well.

[Line 5] 9 in the fifth: The well is clear; drink from a cold spring.

The firm *yang* line is central and correct: benefit extends to things; hence this image. A diviner with these virtues will match this image.

[Image 5] "Drink from a cold spring": it is central and correct.

[Line 6] 6 at the top: Collecting from the well: do not cover it. With honesty there will be supreme good fortune.

"Collecting" is drawing and taking water. Mr. Chao [Yuezhi]'s statement, "Collecting is using a pulley to collect the rope," also works. "Cover" means to conceal. "With honesty" means what comes out has an inexhaustible source. The well's excellence is [water] rising and emerging, so the opening of Kan cannot be shut. Thus although 6 at the top is not a firm *yang*, its image is like this. If the diviner corresponds with it, then certainly "with honesty there will be supreme good fortune."

[Image 6] "Supreme good fortune" at the top; great achievement.

[49] 革 Ge (Changing/Overturning)

Li [fire] below, Dui [lake] above.

Ge: At the end of the day there is honesty. Supreme and penetrating, appropriate and correct. Regret vanishes.

Ge is changing/overturning [*biange* 變革].[107] Dui or lake is above, Li or fire is below. In fire water dries up; in water fire is extinguished. The hexagram is composed of the middle and younger daughters together, with the younger above and the middle below. Their aims do not agree; hence the hexagram is Changing/Overturning. At the beginning of change people are not yet trusting; only at the end of the day do they trust. The inner trigram has the virtue of being elegant and bright [*wenming* 文明]; the outer has the air [*qi* 氣] of harmony and pleasure. Thus the prognostication, instead of changing, is both "great and penetrating" and "correct." If the one [effecting the] change is always proper, regret for change vanishes. Once there is anything incorrect, the one [effecting the] change will not be believed and won't prevail, so again there will be regret.

COMMENTARY ON THE JUDGMENT

Ge: Water and fire stop each other. When two sisters live together their aims will not agree. This is called changing/overturning.

Explaining the meaning of the hexagram name in terms of the trigram images. This is basically similar to Kui 睽 [hexagram 38, Contrary]. But differing with each other is Being Contrary, while stopping [*xi* 息] each other is changing/overturning. *Xi* can mean both "to extinguish" [*miexi* 滅息] and "to proliferate" [*shengxi* 生息]. Proliferating comes only after being extinguished.[108]

"At the end of the day there is honesty": changing yet being honest. Elegant and clear with pleasure, great and penetrating with correctness. Changing yet proper, regret vanishes.

Explaining the hexagram statement by means of the hexagram virtues.

Heaven and Earth oppose [each other] and the Four Seasons are completed. [Kings] Tang and Wu changed the Mandate [*ge ming* 革命], complying with Heaven and responding to their people. The time of change is great indeed![109]

Fully expressing and praising its greatness.

COMMENTARY ON THE GREATER IMAGES

Fire in the lake: Opposing.[110] **The superior person clarifies the seasons by ordering the calendar.**

The fluctuation of the four seasons is the greatness of Changing.[111]

LINE STATEMENTS WITH COMMENTARY ON THE SMALLER IMAGES

[Line 1] 9 at the beginning: Bound in the hide of a yellow-brown cow.[112]

Although it is properly a time of change, the line located at the beginning has no correspondence and cannot do anything; hence this image. "Bound" means strongly. "Yellow-brown" is the color of the center.[113] "Cow" is a compliant animal. "Hide" is a strong thing; its meaning here is not the same as the hexagram name. The prognostication should be to firmly and strongly maintain [oneself], and "not do anything" [see subsequently]. The Sage's changes are thus respectful.

[Image 1] "Bound in [the hide of] a yellow-brown cow"; one cannot do anything.

[Line 2] 6 in the second: Changing at the end of the day: going forth is auspicious; no blame.

The yielding, compliant line is central and correct, and is the ruler of elegance and brightness [i.e., the Li trigram]. It has correspondence above [with 9 in the fifth], and so can be considered opposing. But only after the day is over should you oppose; then "going forth is auspicious; no blame." The warning to the diviner is not to change suddenly.[114]

[Image 2] "Changing at the end of the day": acting will be excellent.

[Line 3] 9 in the third: Going forth is ominous, being correct is dangerous. When change has been discussed three times, there will be honesty.

Excessively firm and not central, the line at the peak of Li impatiently acts to bring about change. Therefore the prognostication is a warning that going forth is ominous and being correct is dangerous. But the time is right for change, so "when change has been discussed three times" then there will be honesty and change is acceptable.

[Image 3] "When change has been discussed three times," what to do?
There has been enough discussion.

[Line 4] 9 in the fourth: Regret vanishes; there is honesty. Changing the Mandate is auspicious.

This is a *yang* line occupying a *yin* position, so there is regret. But it is already past the center of the hexagram, the boundary of water and fire, so it is time for change. The firm and yielding lines are balanced and change is occurring, so "regret vanishes." But there must be honesty; only then will change become auspicious. This clarifies to the diviner that if he has this virtue and accords with the time, he will be believed, regret will vanish, and good fortune will ensue.

[Line 4] The good fortune of "changing the Mandate" is belief [by others] in one's purpose.

[Line 5] 9 in the fifth: The great person changes [*bian* 變] like a tiger. Before divining there is honesty.

"Tiger" is the image of the great person. "Changes" means molting and regrowing [fur]. In reference to the great person it is the epitome of continually renewing the people, complying with Heaven and responding to humanity's situation.[115] If others already believe he is like this, that will be enough for him to match it.

[Image 5] "The great person changes like a tiger": his designs are conspicuous.

[Line 6] 6 at the top: The superior person changes like a leopard; the petty person turns to face [him]. Going forth is ominous; abiding in correctness is auspicious.[116]

The Way of change is complete. The superior person changes like a leopard; the petty person turns to face him, listen, and follow. One cannot proceed; "abiding in correctness" is auspicious. The matter of change is not over. One cannot go too far, and the talent of 6 at the top cannot be acted upon; hence the prognostication.[117]

[Image 6] "The superior person changes like a leopard"; his designs are impressive. "The petty person turns to face [him]," compliantly following the superior.

PART B: HEXAGRAMS 31–64

[50] ䷱ 鼎 Ding (Cauldron)[118]

Sun [wind, wood] below, Li [fire] above.

Ding: Supreme success.[119]

    A *ding* is a vessel for cooked food [*pengrenzhi qi* 烹飪之器]. The bottom *yin* of the hexagram is the feet; the *yang* in the second, third, and fourth places are the bowl, the *yin* in the fifth is the "ears" [handle rings], and the *yang* at the top is the bar [inserted into the handles to carry it]: the image of a cauldron. The wood of Sun entering the fire of Li, cooking the food, is the functioning of the cauldron. Hence the hexagram is Cauldron. The Sun below is gentle, the Li above is the eyes, and the fifth is the ears: the image of gently complying within [below] and seeing and hearing without [above]. The hexagram comes from Sun 巽 [57 ䷸], with a *yin* line advancing to occupy the fifth place, corresponding below with the *yang* of 9 in the second; hence the prognostication says, "supreme and penetrating." "Auspicious" is a superfluous word.

COMMENTARY ON THE JUDGMENT

Ding is an image. Wood enters the fire and cooks the food.[120] The Sage cooks and offers sacrifice to the High Lord [Shangdi 上帝]; he cooks a great [feast] to nourish other sages and worthies.

    Explaining the meaning of the hexagram name in terms of the component trigrams and their two images, discussing them by following their greatness to the end.[121]

Gently, the ear and eye become acute and clear. The yielding advances and goes upward, attaining the center and corresponding with the firm. This is how it is "supreme and penetrating."

    Explaining the hexagram statement by means of trigram images, the hexagram fluctuation, and the hexagram structure.

COMMENTARY ON THE GREATER IMAGES

Above wood there is fire: Cauldron. The superior person rectifies [social] positions and consolidates the Mandate.

A cauldron is a heavy vessel, so it contains the idea of "rectifying positions and consolidating the Mandate." "Consolidating" is like "materializing" in "the perfect Way is not materialized" [*Zhongyong* 27]. It is also like what the [*Zuo*] *Commentary* [to the *Spring and Autumn Annals*] says, "[They were able to] harmonize with those above and below them, and to receive Heaven's blessings."[122]

LINE STATEMENTS WITH COMMENTARY ON THE SMALLER IMAGES

[Line 1] 6 at the beginning: A cauldron with upturned feet [upside down], appropriate to remove an obstruction. Acquiring a concubine for the son [she will produce]; no blame.

Residing at the bottom of Cauldron, this is the image of the cauldron's feet. It corresponds above with 9 in the fourth, and so is "upturned." Here at the beginning of the hexagram the cauldron is not yet filled, and there is a nasty accumulation of old stuff in it. Accordingly, it is appropriate to overturn it to dump it out. "Acquiring a concubine" to obtain a son is also like this; hence the image of this line, and the prognostication of "no blame." Taking what is spoiled as meritorious is taking the humble and making it honored.[123]

[Image 1] "A cauldron with upturned feet" is not offensive. "Appropriate to remove an obstruction" is to accord with what is valuable.

A cauldron with upturned feet is offensive to the Way. Yet because it enables one "to remove an obstruction" in order "to accord with what is valuable," it is not offensive.

[Line 2] 9 in the second: The cauldron is full. My companion has ill feelings but cannot reach me: auspicious.

A firm line occupying the center is the image of a full cauldron. "My companion" means the beginning [line]. The *yin* and *yang* seek each other but are not correct, so they fall into evil, yet become companions. The second is firm and central, so is able to protect itself. Thus although the beginning line is nearby, it is unable to approach; hence this image. The prognostication is also like this, so it is auspicious.

[Image 2] "The cauldron is full": be cautious where you go. "My companion has ill feelings"; in the end no error.

If you are full but not cautious where you go, then companions joining you will fall into evil.

[Line 3] 9 in the third: The cauldron's ears have fallen off: its use is blocked. The fat of the pheasant is not eaten; as soon as it rains, regret wanes. In the end, auspicious.

This *yang* line resides at the center of the cauldron's bowl, so it originally was full of fine things. But it is excessively firm and has lost its central [position], and gone past corresponding with the fifth above [like 9 in the second]. It resides at the end [top] of the lower [trigram], at a time of radical change. Therefore the cauldron's ears have fallen off, and it cannot be lifted or moved. Although it receives abundance from the elegance and brightness of the upper trigram, the beauty of pheasant fat, it cannot be eaten by people. However, being a *yang* line in a *yang* position, it achieves correctness. If it is able to protect itself, then *yin* and *yang* will be in harmony, eliminating regret. If the diviner is like this, then although the beginning will not be advantageous, the end will be auspicious.

[Image 3] "The cauldron's ears fall off": it loses its meaning.[124]

[Line 4] 9 in the fourth: the cauldron's feet break, spilling the duke's food. He is severely punished. Ominous.

Mr. Chao [Yuezhi] says, "*Xing wo* 形渥 [getting him wet] should be written *xing wu* 刑剭 [punished and condemned]," meaning severe punishment, and I follow him.[125] 9 in the fourth is in the upper [trigram], so its responsibilities are heavy. It corresponds below with *yin* of 6 at the beginning, which does not have similar responsibility; hence this image, and the ominous prognostication.

[Image 4] "Spilling the duke's food": how can he be believed?
Speaking of the loss of trust.

[Line 5] 6 in the fifth: The cauldron has yellow ears and a metal lifting bar: appropriate and correct.

The fifth symbolizes the ears [handle rings] and has the virtue of centrality; thus it says, "yellow ears."[126] "Metal" is a hard and firm object. The "lifting bar" goes through the "ears" to lift the cauldron. The fifth is the empty center that corresponds with the hard firmness of 9 in the second; hence this image. The prognostication is simply that it is appropriate to be strong in one's correctness. Some say that the metal lifting bar refers to 9 at the top, making it even better.

[Image 5] "The cauldron has yellow ears": its centrality makes it solid.

[Line 6] 9 at the top: The cauldron has a jade lifting bar: greatly auspicious, everything is appropriate.

The top symbolizes the lifting bar. It is a *yang* line in a *yin* position, firm and able to be heated. Hence the image of the jade lifting bar and the greatly auspicious prognostication: everything appropriate. One who has these virtues will get this prognostication.

[Image 6] "A jade lifting bar" at the top: firm and yielding are suitable.[127]

[51] 震 Zhen (Thunder/Arousing)[128]

Zhen [thunder] below, Zhen [thunder] above.

Zhen: Penetrating. With thunder comes fright and alarm, then laughter—ha ha! Thunder scares for a hundred *li* around, but [he] does not let go of the ladle and sacrificial wine.

Zhen is acting [*dong* 動]. A single *yang* line first arises below two *yin* lines, arousing into action. Its image is thunder [*lei* 雷], and it is associated with the eldest brother. Zhen is a penetrating [successful] Way. "With thunder comes" is the moment that thunder comes. "Fright and alarm" is the facial expression of fear and dread. "Thunder scares for a hundred *li* around" through the sound of thunder [*lei*]. "The ladle" is how one lifts the contents of a cauldron. "Sacrificial wine" is millet wine with ginger, the libation that calls down the spirits. "[He] does not let go of the ladle and sacrificial wine" refers to the eldest son. The prognostication for this hexagram is "fear and dread leading to blessings" [see subsequently] if one does not lose [sight of] what is most important.

COMMENTARY ON THE JUDGMENT

Zhen: Penetrating.

Zhen is a penetrating Way, needless to say.

"With thunder comes fright and alarm," but fear leads to blessings. "Then laughter—ha ha!" Back to normal.

"Fear leads to blessings": fear and dread leading to blessings. "Normal" is standard.

"Thunder scares for a hundred *li* around": scaring those far away and causing concern for those nearby. Coming forth, one can maintain the ancestral temple and altars of the earth and grains, acting as chief of the sacrifice.

Master Cheng [Yi] says that "those nearby" stands for "not letting go of the ladle and sacrificial wine," and I agree with him.[129] "Coming forth" refers to the chief of the sacrifice in succeeding generations. Some say that "coming forth" is a mistake for "[with] sacrificial wine."

COMMENTARY ON THE GREATER IMAGES

Repeated thunder [*lei*]: Arousing. The superior person cultivates and examines [himself] with fear and dread.

LINE STATEMENTS WITH COMMENTARY ON THE SMALLER IMAGES

[Line 1] 9 at the beginning: "With thunder comes fright and alarm, then laughter—ha ha!" Auspicious.

This is the ruler of Zhen as a whole and the beginning position of Zhen; hence this prognostication.

[Image 1] "With thunder comes fright and alarm, but fear leads to blessings. Laughter—ha ha! Back to normal."[130]

[Line 2] 6 in the second: With thunder comes danger. Alas, you lose your valuables. Climb nine hills, but do not pursue. In seven days you will get them.

6 in the second rides on the firm 9 at the beginning, so with the arrival of thunder it is dangerous.[131] The word "alas" is unclear.[132] You lose your valuables and climb up nine hills [searching], but this yielding line is compliant, central, and correct, so it is enough to preserve oneself; therefore you will get it back yourself without seeking. This line's prognostication contains imagery, but the meanings of the nine hills and seven days are unclear.

[Image 2] "With thunder comes danger": riding on the firm.

[Line 3] 6 in the third: Thunder is upsetting; if one moves when there is thunder, there is no error.

"Upsetting" is the appearance of being scattered and losing one's composure. This is a *yin* line in a *yang* position. At the moment of thunder one's position is incorrect, so it is like this [upsetting]. If the diviner is able to move in response to his fear, he will rid himself of incorrectness and can be without error.

[Image 3] "Thunder is upsetting": one's position is improper.

[Line 4] 9 in the fourth: Aroused, consequently stuck.

A firm line in a yielding position, neither central nor correct, trapped between two *yin* lines, unable to arouse itself. "Consequently" means no going back. "Stuck" means obstructed and sunk.

[Image 4] "Aroused, consequently stuck": not yet radiant.

[Line 5] 6 in the fifth: Aroused; danger coming and going. Alas, no loss; there are things to do.

As a 6 in the fifth position, at the moment of arousal, there is no time that is not dangerous. Being central, nothing is lost and one is able to do things. If the diviner does not lose this centrality, nothing will be lost despite the danger.

[Image 5] "Aroused; danger coming and going": dangerous to move. If one's affairs are central [moderate], most will not be lost.

[Line 6] 6 at the top: Thunder is startling; one's gaze is anxious, going forth is ominous. If the arousal [thunder] does not reach you or your neighbor, no blame, but your spouse and relatives will talk.

This is a yielding *yin* line in the peak position of Zhen; hence the image of being "startled" and "anxious." To move in these circumstances is certainly ominous. But if you are able to work on and examine your fears when the arousal has not yet reached you, there can be no blame. Still, you cannot avoid there being talk among your spouse and relatives; hence the warning to the diviner.

[Image 6] "Thunder is startling," but doesn't yet reach one's heart. Although ominous, "no blame." Fear for one's neighbor is a warning.

"Center" means "inmost heart."

[52] ䷳ 艮 Gen (Stilling/Stopping)[133]

Gen [mountain] below, Gen [mountain] above.

Stilling the back, not feeling the body. Going into the courtyard, not seeing anyone; no blame.

Gen is stilling/stopping [*zhi* 止]. The single *yang* stops [comes to rest] above the two *yin* lines. The *yang* has risen from below and stopped after reaching the very top [of each trigram]. Its image is a mountain, and it has the character of having grown up from the earth of Kun. It also conveys the idea of stopping at the peak and not advancing. The prognostication is that you must be able to still the back as if there were no body, to "go into the courtyard and not see anyone"; then there will be "no blame." The body is active, while only the back is stilled. "Stilling the back" is stopping where you should stop. Stopping where you should stop, you do not move with the body; this is "as if there were no body." In this way, although going into the courtyard, or anyplace with people, you will not see anyone. So, "stilling the back and not feeling the body" is being still while still; "going into the courtyard and not seeing anyone" is being still while moving. Activity and stillness [*dong-jing* 動靜] each come to rest in their place, yet both are ruled by stillness [*zhufu jing* 主夫靜]. This is how they incur no blame.[134]

COMMENTARY ON THE JUDGMENT

Gen is stilling/stopping. When it is time to be still [*zhi* 止], then be still; when it is time to move, then move. Activity and stillness do not miss their [appropriate] times; this Way is bright and luminous.

This explains the hexagram name: the meaning of Gen is stilling/stopping. But moving and being still each have their times, so being still when it is time to be still is being still. Moving when it is time to move is also being still.[135] The substance of Gen is "hearty and substantial"; thus it has the meaning of "bright and luminous." Daxu [26] also refers to Gen as "shining and luminous."[136]

"Stilling [*gen* 艮] what is still [*zhi* 止]" is stopping in one's place. Above and below respond as rivals; they do not cooperate. This is why [it says], "Going into the courtyard, not seeing anyone; no blame."

This explains the hexagram statement. The *Yi*'s word "back" is "what is still," to clarify that the back is indeed still. The back is where you are still. In terms of the component trigrams, the inner and outer trigrams, the *yin* and *yang* "respond as rivals and do not cooperate." "Do not cooperate" means that the inner does not see itself and the outer does not see others; yet there is "no blame." Mr. Chao [Yuezhi] says, "Stilling what is still" should be written "[stilling] the back," like the hexagram statement.

COMMENTARY ON THE GREATER IMAGES

Connected mountains: Stilling. The superior person, upon reflection, does not leave his position.

LINE STATEMENTS WITH COMMENTARY ON THE SMALLER IMAGES

[Line 1] 6 at the beginning: Stilling the toes; no blame. Appropriate to be constantly correct.

A yielding *yin* line occupying the beginning of Gen is the image of stilling the toes. If the diviner can be like this, there will be no blame. As a yielding *yin* line, it also warns that "it is appropriate to be constantly correct."

[Image 1] "Stilling the toes": not losing one's correctness.

[Line 2] 6 in the second: Stilling the calves, not rescuing what one follows. One's heart is not pleased.

6 in the second occupies the center and is correct; the calves have been stilled. The third [line] is the end [of the trigram], what the calf follows; it is more firm and not central, and comes to rest [*zhi* 止] at the top. The second is central and correct, but in substance it is yielding and weak so it is unable to go out and "rescue" anything. For this reason "one's heart is not pleased." This line's prognostication is inherent in the image, which also determines the line below.

[Image 2] "Not rescuing one's followers": not turning to listen.

The third comes to rest at the top, and is not willing to turn and listen to the second.[137]

[Line 3] 9 in the third: Stilling the hips, arranging the spine. Danger, clouding the heart.

Xian 限 is the boundary between the upper and lower body: the hips. *Yin* 夤 [climb, respect] is the spine. The "calves are stilled," so there is no advancing. 9 in the third is very firm but not central, at a boundary location. The "hips are stilled," so you cannot bend or stretch. Above and below are divided, like "arranging the spine." "Danger, clouding the heart" is being extremely uncomfortable.

[Image 3] "Stilling the hips: danger, clouding the heart."

[Line 4] 6 in the fourth: Stilling the body; no blame.

A *yin* line in a *yin* position, being still when it is time to be still. Thus it is the image of "stilling the body," and the prognostication is "no blame."

[Image 4] "Stilling the body": bringing the body to rest.

[Line 5] 6 in the fifth: Stilling the cheeks; speech is orderly. Regret vanishes.

6 in the fifth is the proper location of the cheeks; hence this image, and the prognostication that "regret vanishes." "Regret" means a *yin* line in a *yang* position.[138]

[Image 5] "Stilling the cheeks": central and correct.

The word "correct" is superfluous text, making it rhyme.[139]

[Line 6] 9 at the top: Sincere and still: auspicious.

A firm *yang* line occupying the peak of stilling: one who is sincere and generous in his stillness.

[Image 6] The good fortune of being "sincere and still" is being generous to the end.

[53] 漸 Jian (Gradually Advancing)

Gen [mountain] below, Sun [wind] above.

Jian: The woman marries: auspicious. Appropriate and correct.[140]

Jian is gradually advancing [*jianjin* 漸進]. The hexagram has stilling below and being gentle above, meaning advancing without haste: the image of a woman marrying. The second through fifth lines are all correctly positioned, so the prognostication is "the woman marries: auspicious," and the admonition is "appropriate and correct."

COMMENTARY ON THE JUDGMENT

Jian: [Gradually] advancing. "The woman marries: auspicious."

I suspect that the word *zhi* 之 is superfluous; it probably should be "Jian."[141]

Advancing into position; there is merit in proceeding. Advancing correctly can rectify the country.

Explaining the idea of "appropriate and correct" in terms of hexagram fluctuation. The fluctuations of this hexagram are that it comes from Huan 渙 [59 ䷺], with a 9 advancing into the third position; or that it comes from Lü 旅 [56 ䷷], with a 9 advancing into the fifth position. In both cases they acquire correct positions.[142]

As for its position, the firm attains centrality.

Speaking in terms of the component trigrams, this means 9 in the fifth.

Still and gentle; activity is not exhausted.

Speaking in terms of the trigram virtues, the meaning of gradual advance.

COMMENTARY ON THE GREATER IMAGES

On the mountain is a tree [wood]: Gradually Advancing. The superior person abides in worthiness and virtue, and improves customs.

The two [trigrams] together are Gradually Advancing. I suspect that the word "worthiness" is superfluous; it probably came after "improves."[143]

LINE STATEMENTS WITH COMMENTARY ON THE SMALLER IMAGES

[Line 1] 6 at the beginning: The wild goose gradually approaches the riverbank. The youngest son is in danger: he says things, but no blame.[144]

The wild goose's movement is orderly and its advance is gradual. *Gan* 干 is the bank of a river. It first advances at the bottom and has not yet reached a comfortable place. It does not correspond with what is above, hence this image, and the prognostication "the youngest son is in danger." Although he "says things," in regard to what is right there is no blame.

[Image 1] The danger for the youngest son incurs no moral blame.

[Line 2] 6 in the second: The wild goose gradually advances toward the cliff. Carefree eating and drinking; auspicious.

"Cliff" is a large rock. Gradually moving away from the river, advancing to the cliff and increasing comfort. "Carefree" means harmonious and happy. 6 in the second is yielding and compliant, central and correct. It is advancing gradually, and corresponds above with 9 in the fifth. Hence this image, and the auspicious prognostication.

[Image 2] "Carefree eating and drinking": not idly eating one's fill.

"Idly eating one's fill" is like "eating undeservedly" in the *Shi*[*jing*] [Scripture of odes].[145] Getting there by means of the Way, he does not merely eat his fill but resides in comfort.

[Line 3] 9 in the third: The wild goose gradually advances toward high ground. The husband goes out and does not return; the wife is pregnant but does not give birth: ominous. Appropriate to guard against enemies.

The wild goose is a water bird, so high ground is not where it is comfortable. 9 in the third is very firm but not central, and lacks correspondence; hence this image. As for the prognostication, "The husband goes out and does not return; the wife is pregnant but does not give birth": nothing could be more ominous. As it is very firm, "it is appropriate to guard against enemies."

[Image 3] "The husband goes out and does not return": he has separated from his companions. "The wife is pregnant but does not give birth": she has lost her Way. "It is appropriate to guard against enemies": being compliant for mutual protection.

[Line 4] 6 in the fourth: The wild goose gradually advances toward the tree. It may find a perch: no blame.

Wild geese do not roost in trees. "A perch" is a level branch; if it finds a level branch it could be comfortable. 6 in the fourth rides on the firm [mountain] and "complies with the gentle" [wind]; hence this image. If the diviner is like this there will be no blame.

[Image 4] "It may find a perch": complying with the gentle.

[Line 5] 9 in the fifth: The wild goose gradually advances toward a hillock. The wife does not give birth for three years, but in the end no one will surpass her: auspicious.

A hillock is a high mound. 9 in the fifth occupies the place of honor and corresponds correctly with 6 in the second below. It is separated from the third and fourth, but in the end its correctness cannot be surpassed. Hence this image. If the diviner is like this, it will be auspicious.

[Image 5] "In the end no one will surpass her: auspicious." Getting what one wishes.

[Line 6] 9 at the top: The wild goose gradually advances toward the sky; its feathers can be used for a ritual: auspicious.

Mr. Hu [Yuan] and Mr. Cheng [Yi] both say, "*Lu* 陸 [high ground] should be written *kui* 逵 [main road], meaning 'cloud road' [i.e., sky]." This is an elegant reading, and I prefer it.[146] "Ritual" refers to the use of feathered banners and streamers as adornments. 9 at the top is the highest; it has transcended human status, so the feathers can be used as ritual adornments. Its position is very high, and the image includes its use. Hence the prognostication is accordingly auspicious.[147]

[Image 6] "Its feathers can be used for a ritual: auspicious": there can be no confusion.

It has gradually advanced to surpassing heights, and it does not lack use. Its aims are dignified; how could there be confusion?

[54] ䷵ 歸妹 Guimei (Betrothed Sister)

Dui [lake] below, Zhen [thunder] above.

Guimei: Going forth is ominous; nothing is appropriate.

A wife or daughter-in-law is called *gui*. *Mei* is a young woman.[148] Dui is the youngest daughter and follows Zhen, the eldest son.[149] [Dui's] disposition is to take pleasure in activity, which is always incorrect [for a woman]; hence the hexagram is "Betrothed Sister."[150] Of the various lines of the hexagram, the second through the fifth are all incorrect [in their positions], and the third and fifth are yielding lines riding on [i.e., dominating] firm ones. Therefore the prognostication is "going forth is ominous," and nothing is appropriate.

COMMENTARY ON THE JUDGMENT

Guimei is the great meaning of Heaven and Earth. If Heaven and Earth do not interact, the myriad things will not arise. The betrothed sister is the beginning and end of humanity.

Explaining the meaning of the hexagram name. Marrying is the end [purpose] of being a woman. Birth and development are the beginning of a human.

Acting with pleasure: the one who marries is a young woman.

Speaking in terms of the trigram virtues.

"Going forth is ominous"; one's position is not proper. "Nothing is appropriate" with the yielding riding on the firm.

Explaining the hexagram statement by means of the component trigrams. The interaction of man and woman is fundamentally always correct in principle. It is just that in this hexagram they are not correct.[151]

COMMENTARY ON THE GREATER IMAGES

Above the lake is thunder: Betrothed Sister. The superior person understands that the inevitable end is ruin.

Thunder acts and Lake follows: the image of the betrothed sister. The superior person observes the incorrectness of their union and understands that in the end it will be ruined. Extending this to things and events, everything is like this.

LINE STATEMENTS WITH COMMENTARY ON THE SMALLER IMAGES

[Line 1] 9 at the beginning: The betrothed sister as a secondary wife [is like] a lame person who is able to walk. Going forth is auspicious.

9 at the beginning occupies the bottom and lacks correct correspondence; thus the image of a secondary wife. But as a firm *yang* line, the woman has the virtues of worthiness and correctness. With just the low station of a secondary wife she is just able to offer help to her master; thus the image of the lame person who is able to walk, and the prognostication, "going forth is auspicious."

[Image 1] "The betrothed sister as a secondary wife" perseveres. "A lame person who is able to walk": good fortune supporting each other.

"Persevering" [*heng* 恆] is the virtue of being everlasting.

[Line 2] 9 in the second: A one-eyed person who is able to see. Appropriate to have the correctness of a solitary person.

"A one-eyed person who is able to see" refers to assistance from the line above. 9 in the second is a firm *yang* line that is central: the worthiness of a woman. Above it corresponds correctly, opposing the incorrectness of the yielding *yin* line [in the fifth place]. It is the worthiness of a woman, but its mate [the fifth] is not good; he is unable to have the merit of completing his helpmeet. Thus the image of the "one-eyed person who is able to see," and the prognostication, "Appropriate to have the correctness of a solitary person." "A solitary person" can embrace the Way and hold on to correctness and yet not be married.

[Image 2] "Appropriate to have the correctness of a solitary person" is an unchanging norm.

[Line 3] 6 in the third: The betrothed sister waits and comes back as a secondary wife.

6 in the third is a yielding *yin* line that is neither central nor correct, and is the ruler of pleasure [the Dui trigram]. If a woman is incorrect, no one will select her; thus the image of her having nowhere to go [to be married], and coming back as a secondary wife. Some say that *xu* 須 [wait] is the woman's lowly status.[152]

[Image 3] "The betrothed sister waits": she is not proper.

[Line 4] 9 in the fourth: The betrothed sister delays; there is time to marry later.

9 in the fourth is a *yang* line in the upper trigram and lacks correct correspondence. The worthy woman does not frivolously follow others: the image of delaying and waiting to marry. It correctly opposes 6 in the third.

[Image 4] The purpose of delaying is waiting to move.

[Line 5] 6 in the fifth: When Sovereign Yi betrothed his younger sister, the princess's sleeves were not as fine as those of the secondary wife. A moon almost full is auspicious.[153]

6 in the fifth is a yielding, central line in the place of honor, and corresponds below with 9 in the second. It honors virtue but does not value adornment; thus the image of the lord's daughter marrying beneath [her station] with clothes not so rich. However, the richness of her virtue was unequaled; hence the image of the "moon almost full." If the diviner is like her, then good fortune.

[Image 5] "When Sovereign Yi betrothed his younger sister, the princess's sleeves were not as fine as those of the secondary wife": its position is central; it values action.

[Line 6] 6 at the top: The woman presents a basket with nothing in it; the man slaughters a sheep with no blood. Nothing is appropriate.

6 at the top is a yielding *yin* line at the end of Guimei, and lacks correspondence: the marriage agreement is not finalized. Hence this image, and the prognostication that nothing is appropriate.

[Image 6] 6 at the top: Nothing in it; presenting an empty basket.

[55] ䷶ 豐 Feng (Abundant)

Li [fire] below, Zhen [thunder] above.

Feng: Success. The king attains it. Do not be anxious; be like the sun at midday.

Being abundant is being great [*da* 大]. As light [fire] and activity [thunder], it is the power of becoming great. Therefore the prognostication is a path of success. However, when the king reaches this point, at the peak of growth there must be concern [lest it decline], so it is also a path of anxiety. The Sage considers this anxiety pointless; only he is able to hold on to the norm and not reach the point of excessive growth, so things will be all right. Hence the warning, "Do not be anxious; be like the sun at midday."

COMMENTARY ON THE JUDGMENT

Being abundant is being great. Acting through light: thus Abundant.
 Explaining the meaning of the hexagram name in terms of the trigram virtues.

"The king attains it," promoting greatness. "Do not be anxious; be like the sun at midday": illuminate all under Heaven.
 Explaining the hexagram statement.

"The sun [is] at midday," then it begins to set; the moon is full, then it wanes. Heaven and Earth are full and empty in accord with the circulation of time. Is this not also so for people? Is this not also so for ghosts and spirits?
 This sheds light on ideas beyond the hexagram statement, saying that one cannot go beyond centrality.

COMMENTARY ON THE GREATER IMAGES

Thunder and lightning come together: Abundant. The superior person decides lawsuits and metes out punishment.
 Drawing on the image of power [thunder] and light [fire] occurring together.

LINE STATEMENTS WITH COMMENTARY ON THE SMALLER IMAGES

[Line 1] 9 at the beginning: Encountering one's match, the ruler. Although similar, there is no blame. Proceeding, there will be honor.
 "One's match, the ruler" means the fourth line. *Xun* 旬 means "similar," referring to their both being *yang*.[154] At a time of abundance, light and activity support each other. Therefore when 9 at the beginning encounters 9 in the fourth, although they are both firm *yang* lines, the prognostication is like this.

[Image 1] "Although similar, there is no blame." Exceeding one's similar would be disaster.

Warning the diviner that he cannot seek to overcome his match. This too is an idea beyond the line statement.

[Line 2] Abundance is screened; the [Northern] Dipper is seen at midday. Proceeding brings doubt and hate. Developing with honesty, auspicious.[155]

6 in the second occupies a time of abundance and is the ruler of Li; maximum light. It corresponds above with the yielding darkness of 6 in the fifth; hence the image, "Abundance is screened; the Dipper is seen at midday." "Screened" is "obstructed." The obstruction is maximized, so it is dark even at midday. Going out to follow it, the ruler of the dark [6 in the fifth] must look within in [self-]doubt. Only by accumulating authenticity of will, feeling and expressing it, can there be good fortune. The diviner is warned that he should be like this. The empty center [yin in the second] is the image of having honesty.

[Image 2] "Developing with honesty" is developing the will with trust.

[Line 3] 9 in the third: Abundance is marshy; dim ones are seen at midday. Breaking one's right arm: no blame.

One version has "pennants" [*pei* 斾] for "marshy" [*pei* 沛], meaning various flags and curtains, hiding all like a screen.[156] "Dimness" means minor stars. The third position is the peak of light, and corresponds with 6 above. Although [the right arm] "cannot be used" [see the following], it is not blameworthy; hence the image and prognostication.

[Image 3] Abundance is concealed; cannot engage in great affairs. "Breaking one's right arm": in the end it cannot be used.

[Line 4] 9 in the fourth: "Abundance is screened; the Dipper is seen at midday"; encountering one's equal, the ruler: auspicious.

Same imagery as 6 in the second. "One's equal" means 9 at the beginning. The prognostication is meeting the ruler of the dark at a time of abundance. The one below has the same virtue, so "auspicious."

[Image 4] "Abundance is screened": its position is not proper. "The Dipper is seen at midday": dark, not light. "Encountering one's equal, the ruler": going is auspicious.

[Line 5] 6 in the fifth: Arriving and displaying, there will be blessing and praise: auspicious.

Although its substance is yielding and dim, if it is able to arrive and extend light to all under Heaven, then there will be "blessing and praise: auspicious." It can arrange this by initiating it in accordance with its yielding, dim [substance]. If the diviner can be like this then it will be like the prognostication.

[Image 5] The good fortune of 6 in the fifth: there will be blessing.

[Line 6] 6 at the top: Abundance in the house, screening the family. Looking out the door it is desolate; no one there. Seeing nothing for three years: ominous.

A yielding *yin* line occupying the peak of Feng, the position at the end of activity, has reached the peak of light and reverted to being dim. Hence the image of great abundance in the house yet reverting to hiding itself. "No one there," "seeing nothing" also refer to brightness completely hidden; extremely ominous.

[Image 6] "Abundance in the house," soaring to the border of Heaven. Peeking out the door, "it is desolate; no one there"; hiding oneself.

"Hiding" means the brightness is hidden.

[56] 旅 Lü (Traveling)

Gen [mountain] below, Li [fire] above.

Lü: Small success. When traveling, being correct is auspicious.

Lü is traveling [*jilü* 羇旅]. The mountain rests below and the fire burns above: the image of leaving what is still, not remaining; hence Traveling. 6 in the fifth is central in the outer [trigram], and complies with the two *yang* lines above and below. Gen rests and Li clings to the bright; thus the prognostication is that there can be "small success."[157] Being able to hold on to the correctness of the traveler is auspicious. The traveler is never stationary, like a transient. But his Way is present everywhere, so he can be correct himself, and cannot depart from it for an instant.[158]

COMMENTARY ON THE JUDGMENT

"Lü: Small success." The yielding [line] is central in the outer [trigram] and complies with the firm. Resting and clinging to the bright is how it is "small success; when traveling, being correct is auspicious."

Explaining the hexagram statement by means of the component trigrams and their virtues.

The meaning of the time for traveling is great indeed!

The time of traveling is a difficult situation.

COMMENTARY ON THE GREATER IMAGES

Above the mountain there is fire: Traveling. The superior person uses brightness and caution in meting out punishment and does not protract legal cases.[159]

Caution in punishment is like a mountain; not protracting is like fire.

LINE STATEMENTS WITH COMMENTARY ON THE SMALLER IMAGES

[Line 1] 6 at the beginning: When traveling involves pettiness and trifles it brings on disaster.

At the time of traveling the yielding *yin* occupies the lowest position; hence this image and prognostication.

[Image 1] "When traveling involves pettiness and trifles" one's will is exhausted: disaster.

[Line 2] The traveler arrives at a stopping place and yearns for provisions. He receives correct behavior from a young servant.

"Arriving at a stopping place," he is comfortable, and "yearns for provisions," as they are plentiful. "He receives correct behavior" and honesty from a young servant; there is no deceit and he is helpful. These are extreme good fortune for the traveler. The second line is yielding and compliant, with the virtues of centrality and correctness; hence this image and prognostication.[160]

[Image 2] "He receives correct behavior from a young servant"; in the end, no mistake.

[Line 3] The traveler's stopping place burns; he loses his young servant. Correct, but dangerous.

Excessively firm and not central, residing at the top of the lower trigram; hence this image and prognostication. "He loses his young servant": not only losing his heart. Therefore the word "correct" takes its meaning from the next sentence [line 4].

[Image 3] "The traveler's stopping place burns," causing injury. [Because of] how he dealt with his subordinate, his rightness is lost.

At a time of traveling, if one's way of dealing with subordinates is like this, then rightness must be lost.

[Line 4] 9 in the fourth: The traveler in his lodging finds provisions and an ax; my heart is not happy.

A *yang* line in a *yin* position, residing at the bottom of the upper [trigram], uses the yielding [line above it] to enable it to stay at the bottom; hence this image and prognostication. Also, it does not relate to a firm *yang* line above it, and below it only corresponds with a yielding *yin* line. Therefore there is reason for the heart to be unhappy.

[Image 4] "The traveler in his lodging" has not achieved his position. He "finds provisions and an ax," but his "heart is not happy."

[Line 5] 6 in the fifth: Shooting a pheasant; one arrow gone. In the end he is recommended for office.

A pheasant is an elegant and bright animal; an image of Li [fire]. 6 in the fifth is yielding and compliant, elegant and bright, and it achieves the Way of the center. It is the ruler of Li, so one who gets this line is the image of "shooting a pheasant." Although there is the cost of an arrow gone, what is lost is not much, and "in the end he is recommended for office."

[Image 5] "In the end he is recommended for office": he comes to the attention of those above.

"He comes to the attention of those above" says that his recommendation for office is heard above.

[Line 6] 9 at the top: The bird's nest burns; the traveler laughs at first but then cries aloud. He loses his ox through laxity: ominous.

9 at the top is excessively firm, located at the top of Lü and the peak of Li. It is arrogant and noncompliant, an ominous path. Hence this image and prognostication.

[Image 6] By traveling to the top, his rightness is burned [consumed]. "He loses his ox through laxity"; in the end he hears nothing.

[57] ☴ 巽   Sun (Entering)¹⁶¹

Sun [wind] below, Sun [wind] above.

Sun: Minor success; appropriate wherever you go. Appropriate to see the great person.

Sun is entering [ru 入]. A single *yin* line submits below the two *yang* lines. By nature it is capable of gently entering. Its image is wind and its meaning is entering. A *yin* line [at the beginning] is the ruler, so the prognostication is [only] "minor success."¹⁶² The *yin* [properly] follows along with the *yang*, so it is also "appropriate wherever you go." However, one must understand whom to follow in order to be correct, so it also says, "Appropriate to see the great person."

COMMENTARY ON THE JUDGMENT

Sun is doubled in order to reiterate the decree.

Explaining the meaning of the hexagram. Sun compliantly enters and must go down to the bottom: the image of decrees and commands. "Sun is doubled," so "the decree is reiterated."¹⁶³

The firm enters into the central and correct [position], and its purpose is carried out. The yielding always complies with the firm. Thus "minor success; appropriate wherever you go; appropriate to see the great person."

Explaining the hexagram statement by means of the component trigrams. "The firm enters into the central and correct [position], and its purpose is carried out" refers to 9 in the fifth. "The yielding" means the first and fourth.

COMMENTARY ON THE GREATER IMAGES

Winds following [each other]: Entering. The superior person carries out his affairs by reiterating commands.

"Following" means following each other.

LINE STATEMENTS WITH COMMENTARY ON THE SMALLER IMAGES

[Line 1] 6 at the beginning: Advancing and retreating; appropriate to have the correctness of a military man.

The beginning is a *yin* line at the bottom and is the ruler of Sun. It goes beyond the lowliness of Sun, so it is the image of "advancing and retreating" without result. If one manages with the correctness of a military man, then whether one succeeds or not one will achieve what is fitting.

[Image 1] "Advancing and retreating": one's aim is in doubt. "Appropriate to have the correctness of a military man": one's aim is controlled.

[Line 2] 9 in the second: Entering under the bed. Using numerous astrologers and shamanesses: good fortune, no blame.

The second is a *yang* line in a *yin* position below: the idea of discomfort. But it is the proper time for entering; it is not satisfied with being lowly, and the second occupies the center but has not reached the extreme. Therefore the prognostication is that one is able to go beyond entering. If one is polite and very cautious in one's words, by advancing one's own way one can have "good fortune and no blame." One can also makes one's intentions completely authentic in sacrificing for an auspicious prognostication.[164]

[Image 2] The good fortune of being "numerous" is that they achieve centrality [consensus].

[Line 3] 9 in the third: Repeatedly entering: disgrace.

Excessively firm and not central, at the top of the lower trigram, unable to enter. One's efforts repeatedly fail: a path of disgrace. Hence this image and prognostication.

[Image 3] The disgrace of "repeated entering" is that one's purpose is exhausted.

[Line 4] 6 in the fourth: Regret vanishes; catching three species in the hunt.

The *yin* line is yielding and lacks correspondence; those it carries and those it rides on are all firm, so it is appropriate that there be regret. Yet it is a *yin* line in a *yin* position, residing at the bottom of the upper trigram, so the regret vanishes, and the divination for the hunt yields an auspicious prognostication.

[Image 4] "Catching three species in the hunt" is meritorious.

[Line 5] 9 in the fifth: Correct and auspicious; regret vanishes; everything is appropriate. There is no beginning but there is an end. Three days before a change; three days after a change: auspicious.

9 in the fifth is firm, strong, central, and correct; it occupies the substance of Sun. Therefore when there is regret, and one has the good fortune of being correct, one will lose the regret and "everything will be appropriate." When there is regret there is "no beginning." When regret vanishes, "there is an end." *Geng* 庚 [the seventh "Heavenly Stem" or day][165] is *geng* 更 [change], a fluctuation of events. "Three days before the change" is *ding* 丁 [the fourth day]; "three days after the change" is *gui* 癸 [the tenth day]. *Ding* is how one makes a strong request before a change. *Geng* is how one reckons [the results] after a change. One who has experienced change and gets this prognostication will have good fortune like this.[166]

[Image 5] The good fortune of 9 in the fifth is that its position is central and correct.

[Line 6] Entering under the bed, losing possessions and ax. Being correct is ominous.

"Entering under the bed" is one who goes beyond entering. "Losing possessions and ax" is losing the means of deciding.[167] In this case, even though one is correct it is still ominous. Occupying the peak of Sun, it loses the virtue of being *yang* and firm; hence this image and prognostication.

[Image 6] "Entering under the bed," its rise is exhausted. "Losing possessions and ax" is correctly considered ominous.

"Correctly considered ominous" means it is certainly ominous.[168]

[58] 兌 Dui (Pleasing)

Dui [lake] below, Dui [lake] above.

Dui: Success; appropriate and correct.

Dui is pleasing [*yue* 說]. A single *yin* line advances above two *yang* lines, and its happiness is visible outwardly. Its image is a lake, which pleases the myriad things. It is also the image of blocking the downward flow of the water of Kan [hexagram 29].[169] The component trigrams are firm within and yielding without; firm within and thus pleasing and successful; yielding without and thus appropriate in being correct.[170] Being pleasing is a path of success, yet one must be on guard against being falsely pleasing; thus this prognostication. Also, being yielding without and therefore pleasing and successful, and firm within and therefore appropriate being correct, has the same meaning.

COMMENTARY ON THE JUDGMENT

Dui is pleasing.

Explaining the meaning of the hexagram name.

Firm within and yielding without, "pleasing" and "appropriate and correct." In this way, one complies with Heaven and responds to humanity. By pleasantly leading the people, the people forget their toil. By pleasantly risking difficulty, the people forget death. The greatness of being pleasing is that it encourages the people.

Explaining the hexagram statement by means of the component trigrams, fully expressing it.

COMMENTARY ON THE GREATER IMAGES

Connected lakes: Dui. The superior person discusses and practices with friends.

Two lakes connected to each other, nourishing and increasing each other. This is the image of "discussing and practicing with friends."

LINE STATEMENTS WITH COMMENTARY ON THE SMALLER IMAGES

[Line 1] 9 at the beginning: Harmonious and pleasing: auspicious.

A *yang* line occupying the trigram of pleasing, located at the very bottom, without connection [to another line] or correspondence: hence this image and prognostication.[171]

[Image 1] The good fortune of being "harmonious and pleasing" is acting without doubt.

Located at the beginning of the hexagram, this pleasure is correct. There is nothing to doubt.

[Line 2] Honest and pleasing: auspicious. Regret vanishes.

The firm central line is honest, but it resides in a *yin* position, so there is regret. If the diviner is honest and pleasing, then it will be auspicious and regret will vanish.

[Image 2] The good fortune of being "honest and pleasing" is believing [trusting] in one's purpose.

[Line 3] 6 in the third: Coming to pleasure: ominous.

The yielding *yin* line is neither central nor correct, but it is the ruler of Dui. It lacks correspondence above, and comes to seek pleasure in the two *yang* lines [below it]: an ominous path.

[Image 3] The misfortune of "coming to pleasure" is that its position is not proper.

[Line 4] 9 in the fourth: Deliberating pleasure will not be peaceful. Protecting against harm will bring happiness.

The fourth supports the central and correct 9 in the fifth above, yet it is next to the yielding and improper 6 in the third below, so it is unable to decide. It deliberates and measures, and is unable to settle. However, its substance is fundamentally *yang* and firm, so it is able to firmly hold on to what is correct

[Image 4] The "happiness" of 9 in the fourth is having blessings.

[Line 5] 9 in the fifth: Being honest in decline brings danger.

"Decline" means the *yin*'s ability to make *yang* decline. 9 in the fifth is a firm *yang* line, central and correct. But at the proper time for pleasure, and residing in the honored position, it secretly approaches 6 at the top. 6 at the top is a yielding *yin* line, the ruler of Dui at its peak, and is able to spoil pleasure by making the *yang* decline.[172] Therefore this prognostication is just a warning that trusting 6 at the top is dangerous.

[Image 5] "Being honest in decline" [although] the position is correct and proper.
Same as 9 in the fifth of Lü [10].

[Line 6] 6 at the top: Leading to pleasure.

6 at the top is the ruler of Dui, a *yin* line at the peak of pleasure. It leads the two *yang* lines below to have pleasure with it, but is unable to compel them to follow it. Therefore 9 in the fifth is properly warned, and this line doesn't say "auspicious" or "ominous."

[Image 6] 6 at the top "leads to pleasure" but is not radiant.

[59] ䷺ 渙   Huan (Dispersing)

Kan [water] below, Sun [wind] above.

Huan: Success. The king arrives at the temple. Appropriate to cross a great river. Appropriate and correct.

Huan is dispersing [*san* 散]. The hexagram has Kan at the bottom and Sun at the top: "wind moving over water" [Greater Image Commentary], the image of scattering and dissolving; hence Dispersing. By fluctuation it originates from Jian [53 ䷴]: 9 comes into the second place and becomes central; 6 goes to the third, which was 9's position; [this 6 is] the same as the fourth, so the prognostication can be "success." The ancestors' spirits have scattered, so the king must go to the temple to assemble them. The wood of Sun and the water of Kan suggest the image of a boat, so it is "appropriate to cross a great river." "Appropriate and correct" is a profound admonition to the diviner.

COMMENTARY ON THE JUDGMENT

Huan: Success. The firm arrives and is not exhausted. The yielding achieves a position on the outside, just like the one above it.

Explaining the hexagram statement by means of the hexagram fluctuation.

"The king arrives at the temple": the king is at the center.

"Center" means center of the temple.

"Appropriate to cross a great river": riding on wood has merit.

COMMENTARY ON THE GREATER IMAGES

Wind moving over water: Dispersing. The former kings sacrificed to the Lord [*di* 帝] and established [ancestral] temples.

This is how they both agree with "dispersing" [*san* 散].[173]

LINE STATEMENTS WITH COMMENTARY ON THE SMALLER IMAGES

[Line 1] 6 at the beginning: Rescued by the strength of a horse: auspicious.[174]

Occupying the beginning of the hexagram, the start of dispersion. Rescued as dispersion starts is easy with force, with the strength of a horse, so good fortune is obvious. 6 at the beginning does not have the ability to successfully disperse, but it is able to comply with 9 in the second; hence this image and prognostication.[175]

[Image 1] The good fortune of 6 at the beginning is complying.

[Line 2] 9 in the second: Dispersing: fleeing toward support. Regret vanishes.

9 occupies the second place, so it is fitting to have regret. But it is a time of dispersion, and it arrives without being exhausted, so it is able to be rid of regret. Hence this image and prognostication. 9 is what "flees," and the second position is its "support."[176]

[Image 2] "Dispersing: fleeing toward support": achieving one's wish.

[Line 3] 6 in the third: Dispersing oneself: no regret.

The yielding *yin* is neither central nor correct: the image of private focus on the self. However, it occupies a *yang* position and aims to save the moment, so it is able to "disperse" itself and achieve a state of no regret; hence this prognostication.[177]

[Image 3] "Dispersing oneself": one's purpose is directed outward.

[Line 4] 6 in the fourth: Dispersing one's group: supremely auspicious. Dispersion piles up; not what the ordinary person thinks about.

Correctly occupying a *yin* position, supporting 9 in the fifth; this has the responsibility to successfully disperse. Below there is nothing corresponding with it: the image of being able to disperse one's friends and colleagues. If the diviner is like this, there will be great happiness and good fortune. It also says one is able to disperse the small group to create a large group. Causing those who are dispersed to gather together like a hill is not something that the common person considers.[178]

[Image 4] "Dispersing one's group: greatly auspicious." Shining greatly.

[Line 5] 9 in the fifth: Dispersing great announcements like sweat: dispersing. When a [true] king occupies [the throne], no blame.

A firm *yang* line, central and correct, residing in the position of honor. At a time of dispersion, one is able to scatter one's announcements and commands and what one has accumulated at home. Then one can successfully disperse with no blame; hence this image and prognostication. 9 in the fifth is the substance of Sun; the image of announcements and commands. "Like sweat" means freely issuing, like sweat. It's like Lu Zhi's idea, "Disperse a small amount, make a large amount."[179]

[Image 5] "When a [true] king occupies [the throne], no blame": his position is correct.

[Line 6] 6 at the top: Dispersing blood so that it vanishes: fear departs, no blame.

9 at the top is a *yang* line at the peak of Huan. It is able to depart and disperse, hence this image and prognostication. "Blood" means injury and harm. *Ti* 逖 [distant] should be written *ti* 惕 [to fear], the same as 6 in the fourth line of Xiaochu [hexagram 9].[180] It says that dispersing one's blood so that it vanishes is to disperse one's fear so that it departs.

[Image 6] "Dispersing one's blood" is staying away from injury.

[60] ䷻ 節 Jie (Limiting)

Dui [lake] below, Kan [water] above.

Jie: Success. Bitter limits cannot be correct.

Jie is bounding and limiting [*xian'er zhi* 限而止]. The hexagram is Dui below and Kan above, water over lake; its appearance is bounded, so it is Limited.[181] Firm limits themselves are a path of success. Also, the hexagram's *yin* and *yang* are equally balanced, and the second and fifth [central] lines are both *yang*, so the prognostication yields success. But if one goes to extremes there is bitterness; thus the warning that one cannot hold on to [limitation] to be correct.

COMMENTARY ON THE JUDGMENT

Jie: Success. The firm and yielding are [equally] divided and the firm is central.
Explaining the hexagram statement by means of the component trigrams.

"Bitter limits cannot be correct": the path will be exhausted.
    Referring to the [moral] principle.[182]

Passing through danger with pleasure; being limited in one's proper position; penetrating with centrality and correctness.
    Referring to the component trigrams and their virtues. "Proper position" and "centrality and correctness" refer to the fifth position. Also, Kan is "penetrating" [*Shuogua* 11.4].

Heaven and Earth are limited [bounded] and the Four Seasons ensue. Making regulations with limitations does not injure property and does not harm the people.
    Fully expressing the Way of limitation.

COMMENTARY ON THE GREATER IMAGES

"Water above the lake": Limited. The superior person establishes number and measure to clarify virtuous conduct.

LINE STATEMENTS WITH COMMENTARY ON THE SMALLER IMAGES

[Line 1] 9 at the beginning: Not going out the door into the courtyard: no blame.
    [Referring to] the courtyard outside the door. The firm *yang* line is correct, occupying the beginning of Jie. It cannot yet move, so it is able to limit and restrict itself. Hence this image and prognostication.

[Image 1] "Not going out the door into the courtyard": understanding [the difference between] getting through [penetrating] and being blocked.

[Line 2] 9 in the second: Not going out the gate and courtyard: ominous.[183]
    "Gate and courtyard" refers to the courtyard inside the gate. 9 in the second should be a time when one can act, yet it is deficient in firmness and is not correct, and nothing corresponds with it above. It understands being limited but doesn't understand getting through; hence this image and prognostication.

[Image 2] "Not going out the gate and courtyard: ominous." An extreme case of missing the moment.

[Line 3] 6 in the third: No limitation; despair. No blame.
　　The yielding *yin* line is neither central nor correct. At a time of limitation it is unable to limit [itself]; hence this image and prognostication.

[Image 3] The despair of having "no limitation": who can be blamed?
　　This "no blame" is different from other lines; it means there is no one to blame.

[Line 4] 6 in the fourth: Comfortably limited: success.
　　The yielding, compliant line is correct; it supports 9 in the fifth above, and is naturally limited. Hence this image and prognostication.

[Image 4] 9 in the fifth: The success of being "comfortably limited" is the path of supporting the one above.

[Line 5] Sweet limits: auspicious. Going forward will bring esteem.
　　What this means is being limited in one's proper position, penetrating by being central and correct; hence this image and prognostication.

[Image 5] The good fortune of "sweet limits" is occupying the central position.

[Line 6] 6 at the top: Bitter limits: being correct is ominous, but regret vanishes.
　　This occupies the peak of Limiting, so it is "bitter limits." Having reached the position of maximum excess, it does not avoid bad fortune even though it is correct. However, in terms of ritual, being extravagant is better than being frugal, so although there is regret, in the end it will vanish.

[Image 6] "Bitter limits: being correct is ominous." This path is exhausted.

[61] 中孚 Zhongfu (Inwardly Honest)

Dui [lake] below, Sun [wind] above.

Zhongfu: Pigs and fish: auspicious. Appropriate to cross a great river; appropriate and correct.

Fu 孚 is being honest [*xin* 信].[184] The hexagram has two *yin* lines within and four *yang* lines without. The second and fifth *yang* lines are both central. In terms of the hexagram as a whole, it is empty inside; in terms of the two trigrams, they are full inside, and both are images of being honest and trustworthy. Also, pleasing [i.e., Dui 兌] below responds [to Sun] above, and Sun 巽 above complies [*shun* 順] [with Dui] below, and this too means being honest. "Pigs and fish" are things without understanding. Also, wood above a lake, full outside and empty inside, is the image of a boat. Perfect trust can stimulate pigs and fish to cross danger and hardship without losing their correctness. Therefore, if the diviner is able to extend the responsiveness of pigs and fish, then it will be "auspicious" and "appropriate to cross a great river," and certainly "appropriate and correct."[185]

COMMENTARY ON THE JUDGMENT

Zhongfu: Yielding within; the firm is central. Pleasing and gentle, honesty transforms the country.

Explaining the meaning of the hexagram name in terms of the component trigrams and their virtues.

"Pigs and fish: auspicious": honesty extended to pigs and fish. "Appropriate to cross a great river": riding the emptiness of a wooden boat.

Referring to the trigram images.

Inwardly honest and thereby "appropriately correct" is responding to Heaven.

Being honest and correct is "responding to Heaven."[186]

COMMENTARY ON THE GREATER IMAGES

Above the lake there is wind: Inwardly Honest. The superior person debates legal cases and is lenient with the death penalty.

Wind stimulates and water receives: the image of inner honesty. "Debating legal cases and being lenient with the death penalty" is the idea of inner honesty [moral sensitivity].[187]

LINE STATEMENTS WITH COMMENTARY ON THE SMALLER IMAGES

[Line 1] 9 at the beginning: Planning is auspicious. With others, uneasy.

This is right at the beginning of Zhongfu, corresponding with 6 in the fourth above. Being able to calculate whom one can believe, and believing them, is auspicious. With others, though, lacking the means to calculate correctness, one cannot be comfortable. The statement is a warning to the diviner.

[Image 1] "9 at the beginning: Planning is auspicious." One's purpose does not fluctuate.

[Line 2] 9 in the second: Calling crane in the shade [*yin* 陰]; its young answers it. I have a fine goblet; I will share it with you.[188]

9 in the second, the core [meaning] of Zhongfu, corresponds with 9 in the fifth, which is also the core of Zhongfu; therefore the image of the calling crane's young answering, and sharing my goblet with you. The "crane in the shade" means 9 in the second position. "Fine goblet" means attaining the center. "Share" [*mi* 靡] is the same as "attach" [*mi* 縻], referring to what the person of elegant virtue likes. Thus, although the fine goblet is mine alone, another can also be attached to and love it.

[Image 2] "Its young answers it": the wishes of its inner heart.

[Line 3] 6 in the third: Acquiring an enemy; now drumming, now stopping; now crying, now singing.

The "enemy" is 9 at the top, whose trustworthiness is exhausted. 6 in the third, a yielding *yin* line, is neither central nor correct. It resides at the peak of pleasure [Dui] and corresponds with it [the enemy]; thus it is unable to rule itself. Hence this image.[189]

[Image 3] "Now drumming, now stopping": its position is improper.

[Line 4] 6 in the fourth: The moon is almost full; the horse's mate is lost; no blame.

6 in the fourth is a *yin* line in the correct location, a position near the master: the image of the "moon almost full." "The horse's mate" refers to the beginning

line and this one being mates, and the fourth ending it. It trusts the fifth above; hence this image of "the horse's mate being lost." If the diviner is like this, there will be "no blame."

[Image 4] "The horse's mate is lost": it cuts off its own kind and goes upward.

[Line 5] 9 in the fifth: Being honest and well connected, no blame.[190]

9 in the fifth is firm, strong, central, and correct: the core of Zhongfu. It occupies the honored position and is the ruler of honesty. It corresponds below with 9 in the second and has the same virtue; hence this image and prognostication.

[Image 5] "Being honest and well connected," its position is correct and proper.

[Line 6] 9 at the top: The sound of the pheasant rises to Heaven. Being correct is ominous.

Occupying the peak of honesty, and not understanding fluctuation, it is an ominous path even though it may be correct; hence this image and prognostication. The fowl, called the "sound of the pheasant," is the image of Sun.[191] Occupying the peak of Sun, it "rises to Heaven." The fowl is not something that rises to Heaven, yet it desires to rise to Heaven. Its trust is not to be trusted, and it does not understand fluctuation; these also follow from this.

[Image 6] "The sound of the pheasant rises to Heaven"; how can it last long?

[62] 小過 Xiaoguo (Small Surpassing)[192]

Gen [mountain] below, Zhen [thunder] above.

Xiaoguo: Success; appropriate and correct. One can engage in small matters, but cannot engage in great matters. The flying bird lets go his cry. Not fitting to ascend; fitting to descend: greatly auspicious.

"Small" refers to *yin*. The hexagram has four *yin* lines on the outside and two *yang* lines within: more *yin* than *yang*, so the small surpasses [*xiaozhe guo* 小者過]. Once it surpasses the *yang*, it can be successful. But it is necessary to appropriately hold on to correctness, so it must be warned. The hexagram's second and fifth lines are both yielding and central; thus "one can engage in small matters." The third and fourth are both firm, but their positions are not central; thus "one cannot engage in great matters." The structure of the hexagram is full within and empty without, like a bird flying; its sound goes down but not up. Thus if one is able to cause a response to the "flying bird letting go its cry," it will be "fitting to descend and greatly auspicious," but one will not be able to engage in things like "great affairs."

COMMENTARY ON THE JUDGMENT

Xiaoguo: Small ones surpass and are successful.
Explaining the meaning of the hexagram name and text in terms of the hexagram structure.

Surpassing by being appropriate and correct, moving in accord with the time. The yielding achieves the center, and thereby has good fortune in small matters.
Referring to the second and fifth lines.

The firm lacks [proper] position and is not central; it thereby cannot engage in great affairs.
Referring to the third and fourth lines.

There is the image of a flying bird in it. "The flying bird lets go his cry. Not fitting to ascend; fitting to descend: greatly auspicious." Ascending is contrary; descending is compliant.
Referring to the hexagram structure.[193]

COMMENTARY ON THE GREATER IMAGES

Above the mountain there is thunder: Small Surpassing. The superior person in his behavior is surpassing in respect; in mourning is surpassing in sympathy; in consumption is surpassing in thrift.

"Above the mountain there is thunder"; its sound is the small passing through.[194] The three examples of "surpassing" are all the small surpassing. They can surpass the small and cannot surpass the great, so they can be considered "small surpassing"; they cannot be considered extreme surpassing. It is what the Judgment Commentary means by "small matters" and "fitting to descend."

LINE STATEMENTS WITH COMMENTARY ON THE SMALLER IMAGES

[Line 1] 6 at the beginning: The flying bird is ominous.

6 at the beginning is a yielding *yin* line, corresponding above with 9 in the fourth, occupying a time of surpassing; it ascends but does not descend. "The flying bird lets go his cry. Not fitting to ascend; fitting to descend"; hence this image and prognostication. In Guo Pu's *Donglin* 洞林: "If one gets this in divination, one may cause a plague of winged insects."[195]

[Image 1] "The flying bird is ominous": it cannot be any other way.

[Line 2] 6 in the second: Surpassing one's grandfather, encountering one's grandmother; not reaching the master, encountering the minister. No blame.

6 in the second is yielding and compliant, central and correct. It approaches and surpasses the third and fourth and encounters 6 in the fifth, thus surpassing the *yang* and reencountering the *yin*. In this way it does not reach 6 in the fifth but receives its own allotment; it does not reach the master but proceeds to encounter his minister. Both surpassing and not surpassing are the idea of holding on to correctness and achieving centrality, a path of no blame; hence this image and prognostication.

[Image 2] "Not reaching the master": the minister cannot surpass [him].

[Line 3] 9 in the third: If you do not strongly [surpassingly] defend yourself, someone following may injure you: ominous.

At a time of "small surpassing," all matters should be surpassing; only then can they attain the Mean. 9 in the third is a firm line occupying the correct position, and the group [pair] of *yin* lines desire to harm it. They themselves depend on its firmness and are not willing to surpass what it furnishes; hence this image and prognostication. If the diviner is able to "strongly defend himself," he may avoid this.

[Image 3] "Someone following may injure you": such bad fortune!

[Line 4] 9 in the fourth: No blame; encountering without surpassing. Proceeding is dangerous; one must be warned. Do not act; always be correct.

At a time when one should surpass, a firm line occupying a yielding position surpasses in respect: a path of no blame. "Encountering without surpassing" says that it is fitting to go along with the firm without surpassing it. "Proceeding" is to surpass, so there is danger and a proper warning. The nature of *yang* is hard and firm; thus the warning, "Do not act; always be correct."

[Image 4] "Encountering without surpassing": one's position is not proper. "Proceeding is dangerous; one must be warned": in the end one cannot grow.

The meaning of this line is unclear; it should be removed.

[Line 5] 6 in the fifth: Dense clouds, no rain from our western suburbs.[196] The duke shoots and captures that one in a cave.

A *yin* line in the place of honor, at a time when the *yin* should surpass but cannot act.[197] [The duke] "shoots and captures" 6 in the second to be an assistant; hence this image. "In a cave" is a *yin* thing [situation]. The two *yins* [second and fifth] find each other, but we know that they cannot succeed in the great matter.

[Image 5] "Dense clouds, no rain": already at the top.

"Already at the top" means extremely high [for *yin*].[198]

[Line 6] 6 at the top: Surpassing without encountering; the flying bird departs: ominous. This means disaster and calamity.

6 is a *yin* line occupying the top of the trigram of activity [Zhen]; it is located at the peak of *yin* surpassing [going too far]. It has already surpassed high and very far; hence this image and prognostication. Some suspect that "surpassing [without]

encountering" should be written "encountering [without] surpassing," with the same meaning as 9 in the fourth. Whether this is true or false cannot be known.

[Image 6] "Surpassing without encountering": already arrogant.

[63] ䷾ 既濟 Jiji (Already Complete)

Li [fire] below, Kan [water] above.

Jiji: Success is small; appropriate and correct. Auspicious at the beginning, chaotic at the end.

Jiji means matters are already complete [*jicheng* 既成]. As a hexagram, water and fire interact, each achieving their function. The positions of all six lines are correct; hence it is "Already Complete." "Success is small" should be "small success." In general this hexagram and the prognostication texts of the six lines are all ideas of admonition and warning, and the times are just right.

COMMENTARY ON THE JUDGMENT

Jiji: Success. Small matters are successful.
After "[Ji]ji" I suspect the word "small" has been removed.[199]

"Appropriate and correct": firm and yielding are correct; their positions are proper.
Referring to the hexagram structure.

"Auspicious at the beginning": the yielding is central.
Referring to 6 in the second.

Stopped at the end, so "chaotic." Its Way is exhausted.

COMMENTARY ON THE GREATER IMAGES

Above the fire there is water: Already Complete. The superior person thinks about trouble and prepares to ward it off.

LINE STATEMENTS WITH COMMENTARY ON THE SMALLER IMAGES

[Line 1] 9 at the beginning: Dragging his wheels, wetting his tail: no blame.

The wheels are below and the tail is behind: an image of the beginning. "Dragging his wheels," so the carriage doesn't advance. "Wetting his tail," so the fox doesn't cross over. At the beginning of "Already Complete" this is the respectful admonition; a path of "no blame." If the diviner is like this there will be no blame.

[Image 1] "Dragging his wheels": the meaning is "no blame."[200]

[Line 2] 6 in the second: The wife loses her [carriage] screen. Don't go after it; in seven days you will get it.

The second has the virtues of being elegant, bright, central, and correct. It corresponds with 9 in the fifth above, which is the firm, *yang*, central, and correct master. It appropriately achieves its aims being put into practice. 9 in the fifth occurs at the moment of being already complete, but it is unable to make its subordinate worthy to put into practice its Way. Hence the image of the second [the subordinate worthy] as the "wife who loses her screen." The screen is to conceal the lady in her carriage, so this says that she has lost the means to do that. However, this is a central and correct path, so it cannot decline in the end; as time passes it will take place. Hence the admonition, "Don't go after it"; you will get it yourself.

[Image 2] "In seven days you will get it" by means of the Middle Way.

[Line 3] 9 in the third: The High Ancestor attacks the Ghost Region; in three years he conquers it. Inferior people must not be used.[201]

In a situation [time] "already completed," a firm line in a firm position is the image of "the High Ancestor attacking the Ghost Region." "In three years he conquers it" says that he conquers after a long time: the idea warning the diviner that he cannot act recklessly. The prognostication, "Inferior people must not be used" is the same as 6 at the top of Shi [Army, hexagram 7].

[Image 3] "In three years he conquers it": exhausting.

[Line 4] 6 in the fourth: For dampness there are rags. Be on guard all day.

When things are already completed, a yielding line in a yielding position is able to prepare and be apprehensive; hence this image. Master Cheng says, "*Xu* 繻 [fine silk] should be *ru* 濡 [wet, damp]. *Yiru* 衣袽 [rags] are used to stop up cracks in a boat."[202]

[Image 4] "Be on guard all day"; there is something questionable.

[Line 5] 9 in the fifth: The eastern neighbor slaughters an ox. It is not as good as the western neighbor's royal ancestral sacrifice, for which substantial blessings are received.

East is *yang*, west is *yin*. This refers to 9 in the fifth in the position of honor, when the moment has already passed; it is not as good as 6 in the second, which begins to achieve the moment while below. This corresponds to the affair of King Wen and Zhou 紂 [last king of the Shang]; hence this image and prognostication. The *Tuan's* statement, "Auspicious at the beginning, chaotic at the end" is also this idea.[203]

[Image 5] "The eastern neighbor slaughters an ox. It is not as good as the western neighbor's" timing. "Substantial blessings are received": good fortune will come in great measure.

[Line 6] 6 at the top: Wetting his head: danger.

The peak of Jiji, at the top of the trigram of danger [Kan], with a yielding *yin* line occupying it, is the image of a fox crossing water and wetting his head. If the diviner is not admonished, it will be a path of danger.

[Image 6] "Wetting his head: danger." How can he last long?

[64] 未濟 Weiji (Not Yet Complete)

Kan [water] below, Li [fire] above.

Weiji: Success. The little fox has nearly crossed and wets its tail. Nothing is appropriate.

Weiji is when matters are not yet complete [*weicheng* 未成]. Water and fire do not interact and do not function together. All six lines of the hexagram lack [proper] position; hence Not Yet Complete. "Nearly crossed and wets its tail" is similar to "not yet complete." If the diviner is like this, how can anything be appropriate?

COMMENTARY ON THE JUDGMENT

Weiji: Success. The yielding achieves centrality.
  Referring to 6 in the fifth.

"The little fox has nearly crossed": it has not yet left the center. "It wets its tail; nothing is appropriate": it doesn't continue to the end. Although they are not properly positioned, the firm and yielding correspond.[204]

COMMENTARY ON THE GREATER IMAGES

Fire is above water: Not Yet Complete. The superior person cautiously separates things and puts them in their places.
  Water and fire are different things and each occupies its place. Therefore the superior person contemplates the images and judiciously separates them.

LINE STATEMENTS WITH COMMENTARY ON THE SMALLER IMAGES

[Line 1] 6 at the beginning: "It wets its tail": disgrace.
  A *yin* line positioned below is right at the beginning of Weiji. It is unable to advance itself; hence this image and prognostication.

[Image 1] "It wets its tail" and does not understand limits.
  The word "limits" is unclear, and doesn't fit with anything above or below. Some suspect it is the word "reverence." I would just ignore it.

[Line 2] 9 in the second: Dragging his wheels: correct and auspicious.
  9 in the second corresponds with 6 in the fifth; it occupies a yielding position and is central. It is able to limit itself and not advance, and is correct in the lower [trigram; see the following]. Hence this image and prognostication.

[Image 2] 9 in the second is "correct and auspicious." It is central and practices correctness.

This 9 occupies the second position, which is basically not correct, but it is central so it [acts] correctly.

[Line 3] 6 in the third: Not Yet Complete; going forth is ominous. Appropriate to cross a great river.

As a yielding *yin* line that is neither central nor correct, occurring at a time of incompleteness, if it goes forth it is ominous. But as a yielding line riding on a firm one it is about to leave the water [Kan], the image of being "appropriate to cross a great river"; hence this prognostication.

[Image 3] "Not Yet Complete; going forth is ominous." Its position is not proper.

[Line 4] 9 in the fourth: Correct [*zhen* 貞] and auspicious; regret vanishes. Thunderously [*zhen* 震] mounting an attack on the Ghost Region, in three years he will be rewarded with a great country.[205]

9 in the fourth position is not correctly [*zheng* 正] [positioned] and there is regret. If it is able to struggle to be correct, the regret will vanish. However, when property is gained incorrectly, even if one struggles to be correct, one is unable to maximize the firm *yang* and use one's strength for a long time. Hence the image of attacking the Ghost Region and receiving reward after three years.

[Image 4] "Correct and auspicious; regret vanishes": its aim is carried out.

[Line 5] 6 in the fifth: Correct and auspicious; no regret. With the radiance of the superior person there is honesty; auspicious.

6 occupying the fifth position is also not correctly [positioned]. But it is the ruler of elegance and brightness [the Li trigram, fire]; it resides in the center and corresponds with the firm [in the second]. Its impartial mind seeks assistance below; thus it is correct [*zhen* 貞] and auspicious, without regret. It has the vigor of radiant light; it is honest and true, without error: exceedingly auspicious.

[Image 5] "The radiance of the superior person": his light is auspicious.

"Light" means the spread of his radiance.

[Line 6] 9 at the top: Drinking wine with honesty: no blame. Wetting one's head: even with honesty one will lose touch with what is the case.

Firm brightness occupying the peak of Weiji: it may almost be time for action. Trusting oneself and nourishing oneself by waiting for the decree [of Heaven] is a path of "no blame." If one is indulgent and permissive, like the fox crossing the water and wetting his head, then one trusts oneself too much and loses touch with what is right.

[Image 6] "Drinking wine" and "wetting one's head" is not understanding moderation.

CHAPTER THREE

TREATISE ON THE APPENDED REMARKS (*XICI ZHUAN* 繫辭傳)

PRELIMINARIES

The *Xici zhuan*—also called the *Dazhuan* 大傳 (Great treatise)[1]—comprises two of the "Ten Wings" (*shiyi* 十翼), or appendixes, of the *Yijing*. As is well known, it was one of the chief sources of ideas and terminology for the Song-dynasty revival of Confucianism. It is a composite work by unknown authors, probably written primarily in the third century BCE; that is, shortly before the Qin conquest in 221 BCE, judging from its similarities to other texts of that period, especially the "Syncretist" chapters of the *Zhuangzi*.[2] The two references to the *Xici* in the *Shiji* 史記 (Historical records, ca. 100 BCE), by Sima Tan 司馬談 and Sima Qian 司馬遷, are the earliest known references to the text.

Considering how heavily the Song revivalists of Confucianism relied upon the *Xici*, it may strike some readers as surprising how little of it is identifiably Confucian in content. Except for a few sections that are formal commentary on passages from the *Yi*,[3] which are undoubtedly later interpolations, the terminology for the most part is that of late Zhou, early Han syncretic cosmological thought. We must bear in mind, however, that one of the hallmarks of the Song Confucian revival was precisely its syncretism, and that cosmology is the area in which "Daoist" thought was most used. Also, except for those few commentary passages, the *Xici* is not a commentary on the *Yi*; it is a collection of statements about the

Yi and how it functions, as both an oracle and a book containing the most fundamental natural and moral principles. The *Xici* explains the *Yi*'s function primarily in terms of the linkage, parallelism, or harmony of Heaven, Earth, and humanity, and how the *Yi*, by means of its inherent spiritual (*shen* 神) power, allows humanity to maintain that harmony.[4]

PART A

"Appended remarks" originally meant the remarks made by King Wen and the Duke of Zhou and appended below the hexagrams and lines; in other words, what today is the text of the scripture [*jing wen* 經文].[5] This piece is the "Treatise on the Appended Remarks" written by Confucius. It thoroughly discusses the overall substance and general outline of the entire scripture. Therefore it cannot be attached specifically to [particular parts of] the scripture, but is itself divided into two parts [A and B].

Section 1

[1] Heaven is honorable [*zun* 尊], Earth is lowly [*bei* 卑]; thus are Qian and Kun determined. The lowly and high [*gao* 高] being set out, the honored [*gui* 貴] and humble [*jian* 賤] are positioned. Activity and stillness are constant, determining the firm and yielding [lines]. Tendencies [*fang* 方] cluster in categories and things are distinguished in groups, giving rise to auspicious and ominous [prognostications]. Images come about in Heaven and forms come about on Earth, and fluctuation and transformation [*bianhua* 變化] appear.

"Heaven and Earth" are the concrete substances of the *yin* and *yang* forms of *qi*. "Qian and Kun" are the names of the pure *yin* and pure *yang* hexagrams of the *Yi*. "Lowly and high" are the higher and lower positions of the myriad things in Heaven and Earth. "Honored and humble" are the higher and lower positions of hexagram lines in the *Yi*.[6] "Activity" is the norm of *yang*; "stillness" is the norm of *yin*. "Firm and yielding" are what we call the *yin* and *yang* hexagram lines of the *Yi*. "Tendencies" are the inclinations [*xiang* 向] of events, referring to the categorical distinction of good and bad aspects of things and events. "Auspicious and ominous" refers to the prognostications of the hexagram lines in the *Yi*. "Images" are things like the sun, moon, and stars; "forms" are things like mountains, rivers, animals, and plants. "Fluctuation and transformation" refer to *yin* changing into *yang* and *yang* transforming into *yin* by means of the divination stalks and hexagram lines of the *Yi*.

This all refers to the Sage's [Fuxi's] creation of the *Yi*, making the patterns and images of the hexagrams and lines on the basis of the actual substances of *yin* and *yang*. Zhuang Zhou's statement, "The *Yi* speaks of [*dao* 道] *yin* and *yang*," is what it means.[7]

[2] **For this reason the firm and yielding mingle with each other, and the Eight Trigrams activate each other.**

This speaks of the fluctuation and transformation of the *Yi*'s hexagrams. At the beginning, the sixty-four hexagrams were simply a pair of firm and yielding lines. The two interacted, making four, the four interacted, making eight, and the eight activated each other, making sixty-four.

[3] **It [the Way of fluctuation and transformation] arouses things with claps of thunder and moistens things with wind and rain. The sun and moon revolve, now cold, now warm.**

These are images created by fluctuation and transformation.

[4] **The Way of Qian brings about the male; the way of Kun brings about the female.**[8]

These are forms brought about by fluctuation and transformation; the two divisions [male and female] also clarify how the *Yi* is seen in actual bodies. This and the text above shed light on each other.[9]

[5] **Qian understands great beginnings; Kun makes things complete.**

"Understands" [*zhi* 知] is like "masters" [*zhu* 主]: Qian masters the beginnings of things; Kun makes them complete. This continues the "male" and "female" in the previous line, speaking of the principles of Qian and Kun. All things without exception are classified *yin* and *yang*. In general, *yang* precedes and *yin* follows, *yang* bestows and *yin* receives. *Yang*'s lightness and clarity are unformed; *yin*'s weight and turbidity are discernible.

[6] **Qian understands with ease; Kun is capable with simplicity.**

Qian creates and is active; this is what it "understands," so it is able to begin things without any difficulty. Thus it easily understands the Great Beginning. Kun complies and is still; everything it is capable of follows the *yang* and does not create on its own. Therefore it is "capable" of completing things simply.

[7] What is easy is easy to know; what is simple is easy to follow. One who is easily known has intimates. One who is easy to follow has achievements. With intimates one can live long; with achievements one can be great. Being able to live long is the virtue of the Worthy; being able to be great is the undertaking of the Worthy.

If what a person does is like the ease of Qian, his mind is clear and the person is easy to know. If it is like the simplicity of Kun, then his deeds are agreeable and the person is easy to follow. Being easy to know there will be many like-minded, so he will have intimates. Being easy to follow there will be a crowd cooperating with him, so he will have achievements. Having intimates he will be unified internally, so he can live long. Having merit he will be connected externally [with others], so he can be great. "Virtue" means what one has gained oneself. "Undertaking" means what one has achieved in affairs. Above it says that the virtues of Qian and Kun are different. This says that if people modeling themselves after the Way of Qian and Kun reach this point they can be considered worthies.

[8] It is through ease and simplicity that one grasps the order/principle of all under Heaven. Having grasped the principles of all under Heaven one has achieved one's position within it.

"Achieved one's position" means the position of an adult. "Within it" means within Heaven and Earth. Reaching this point is the ultimate success of embodying the Way. The Sage is able to do this, and "can thereby form a triad with Heaven and Earth" [*Zhongyong* 22].

This first section uses the facts of creative transformation to clarify the principle of the creation of the Scripture. It also speaks of the principles of Qian and Kun, seen respectively in Heaven and Earth, which humans universally embody.

Section 2

[1] The Sages established the hexagrams by contemplating images, and appended remarks [*xici*] to them to clarify the auspicious and ominous.

"The images" are the likenesses of things. This speaks of the Sages' creation of the *Yi*. They contemplated the imagery of the hexagrams and lines and appended them with texts.

[2] The firm and yielding [lines] displace each other, giving rise to fluctuation and transformation.

This speaks of the *yin* and *yang* hexagram lines alternately displacing each other: *yin* may fluctuate into *yang*, *yang* may transform into *yin*. This is how the Sages contemplated the images and appended the texts, and how everyone can follow the milfoil and select hexagrams.

[3] For this reason the auspicious and ominous are images of success and failure; regret and disgrace are images of worry and sorrow.

"Auspicious and ominous," "regret and disgrace" are [standard] terms in the *Yi*. "Success and failure" [literally, "gain and loss"], "worry and sorrow" result from changing events. Success is auspicious; failure is ominous. Although worry and sorrow aren't quite ominous, they are enough to cause regret and shame. Auspicious and ominous are opposites, but regret and disgrace fall between them. Regret can move from being ominous to being auspicious, and disgrace can shift from being auspicious to being ominous. Therefore the Sages observed which among the hexagrams and lines contained these images and appended these remarks to them.

[4] Fluctuation and transformation are images of advance and withdrawal. The firm and yielding [lines] are images of day and night. The movements of the six lines are the Way of the Three Ultimates [*san ji* 三極].

The yielding [line] fluctuates and moves toward the firm; withdrawal reaches its ultimate and advances. The firm transforms and moves toward the yielding; advance reaches its ultimate and withdraws. After fluctuating into the firm it is day and *yang*; after transforming into the yielding it is night and *yin*. Of the six lines, the first two are Earth, the third and fourth are Humanity, and the fifth and top are Heaven. "Activity" is fluctuation and transformation. "Ultimate" is the utmost. The "Three Ultimates" are the utmost principles of Heaven, Earth, and Humanity. These "Three Powers" [*san cai* 三才] each are the unitary Supreme Polarity [*taiji* 太極].[10] This clarifies how the firm and yielding displace each other in producing fluctuation and transformation, and how the extremes of fluctuation and transformation again become firm and yielding. This [process] flows forth throughout the six lines of each hexagram. What the diviner receives according to what [hexagram] he comes upon determines the auspicious or ominous [prognostication].

[5] For this reason what the superior person rests contentedly in is the sequences of the *Yi*. What he takes pleasure in and enjoys is the line statements.

The "sequences of the *Yi*" are the necessary sequences in which the hexagrams and lines put forth the principles of affairs. What [the superior person] "enjoys" is the details of what he observes.

[6] For this reason the superior person at rest contemplates the images and enjoys the remarks; in activity he contemplates the fluctuations and enjoys the prognostications. And so he is blessed by Heaven; all is auspicious and everything is advantageous.

"Images," "remarks," and "fluctuations" have already been seen above. Every mention of "fluctuation" implies "transformation." "Prognostications" are the decisions about the auspiciousness or ominousness of whatever [hexagram] he comes upon.

This second section speaks of the Sages creating the *Yi* and the superior person studying it.

Section 3

[1] The judgments [*tuan* 彖] speak about the images. The lines [*yao* 爻] speak about the fluctuations.

The "judgments" are the hexagram statements, which were written by King Wen. The "lines" are the line statements, which were written by the Duke of Zhou. "Images" refers to the overall structures [hexagrams]. "Fluctuations" refers to the individual parts [lines].[11]

[2] "Auspicious and ominous" refer to loss and gain; "disgrace and regret" refer to minor faults; "no blame" means that one is good at correcting one's transgressions.

These are common examples of hexagram and line statements.

[3] For this reason the ranking of the honored and the humble is inherent in the [line] positions; the ordering of small and great is inherent in the hexagrams; the distinction between auspicious and ominous is inherent in the texts.

"Positions" means the positions of the six lines; "ordering" means something like defining. "Small" means *yin*; "great" means *yang*.

[4] Worrying about "regret and disgrace" lies in the transitions; what causes one to be "without blame" lies in disgrace.

"Transitions" are the beginnings of distinctions, such as the moment when a good or bad [event] has been activated but has not yet taken form.[12] To worry about this is not quite "regret and disgrace." "Causes" means activates. When one understands regret one has the mind [intention] to act to correct one's transgression, and so can be "without blame."

[5] For this reason among hexagrams there are small and great; among texts there are [indications of] danger and ease. Each of the texts indicates where to go.

"Small" is danger and "great" is ease, each according to its tendency.[13]

This third section discusses common examples of hexagrams, lines, and texts.

Section 4

[1] The *Yi* is a model of Heaven and Earth. Therefore it can stitch together threads [*milun*] of the Way of Heaven and Earth.

The hexagrams and lines of the *Yi* contain the Way of Heaven and Earth and model it exactly. *Mi* 彌 means "stitch together" [*mifeng* 彌縫]. "Threads" [*lun* 綸] conveys the idea of particular principles.

[2] Looking up [Fuxi] contemplated the Heavenly patterns [*tianwen* 天文]; looking down he examined the Earthly order [*dili* 地理].[14] In this way he understood the reasons for [the alternation of] dark and light [i.e., *yin* and *yang*]. Tracing things to their beginnings and going back to their ends, he understood the explanations of death and life. Essence [*jing* 精] and *qi* 氣 make things; the *hun* 魂 [*yang* soul] floating away causes fluctuation [*bian* 變] [death]; in this way he understood the dispositions and circumstances of ghosts and spirits.

This is about fully investigating principle/order [*li* 理]; this is how the Sage [Fuxi] created the *Yi* as a book. The *Yi* is nothing more than *yin* and *yang*. "Dark and light," "death and life," "ghosts and spirits" are all fluctuations of *yin* and *yang*, the Way of Heaven and Earth.[15] Among the "Heavenly patterns" are day and night, above and below. In the "Earthly order" are south and north, lofty and deep. "Tracing" means inferring [what came] before; "going back" means seeking [what comes] after. The *yin* essence and *yang qi* combine to make things, extending spirit.[16] The *hun* floats up and the *po* 魄 [yin soul] sinks and dissipates, resulting in a fluctuation; this is the ghost returning [to earth].[17]

[3] [The Sage] is just like Heaven and Earth; therefore he does not oppose them. His wisdom comprehends the myriad things and his Way relieves all under Heaven; therefore he does not transgress. He acts according to present circumstances and is not carried away. He rejoices in Heaven and understands its decree; therefore he does not worry. He is content in his land and sincere about being humane; therefore he is able to love.

This is about the Sage "fulfilling the natures" [of people and things].[18] The Way of Heaven and Earth is simply wisdom and humanity. "His wisdom comprehends the myriad things" is [how he is just like] Heaven. "His Way relieves all under Heaven" is [how he is just like] Earth. Since he is wise and humane, he understands without transgressing. "Acting according to present circumstances" is understanding how to weigh one's action. "Not being carried away" is the humaneness of holding on to what is correct. Since he "rejoices in the Heavenly" [natural] order and "understands the decree" of Heaven, he is able to be without worry and his understanding is beneficial and deep. Since he is always "content" wherever he goes and is never inhumane, he is able to always be mindful of his intention to relieve [people and] things and to humanely benefit them. Being humane is the principle of love and loving is the function of humaneness. Therefore they are complementary like this.

[4] He encompasses the transformations of Heaven and Earth and does not transgress. He completes all things without omission; he penetrates the Way of day and night and understands it. Therefore spirit has no location and change [yi] has no [fixed] structure.

This is about the Sage "attaining [Heaven's] decree." "Encompasses" is like the container of a mold [in metal casting]. "The transformations of Heaven and Earth" are inexhaustible, and the Sage treats them as his own boundaries. He permits nothing to transgress the Way of the Mean, and so is called one who judges and "completes." To "penetrate" [*tong* 通] is like combining [*jian* 兼]. "Day and night" refers to "dark and light, life and death, ghosts and spirits" [A.4.2]. Accordingly, although afterward we can see the mystery of perfect spirit, it "has no location." The fluctuations and transformations of change have no form or structure.

This section speaks of the greatness of the Way of change and how the Sage puts it into practice.

Section 5

[1] **The alternation of *yin* and *yang* is called the Way.**

Yin and yang constantly revolving is *qi*; its principle [*li*] is what is called the Way.

[2] **Carrying it out is good. Completing it is the nature [*xing* 性].**[19]

The Way is contained in *yin* and acts in *yang*. "Carrying it out" refers to its expression. "Good" means the accomplishment of "transforming and nourishing" [*huayu* 化育],[20] a matter of *yang*. "Completing it" refers to what is contained. "Nature" means what things receive [from Heaven]. This says that when things arise they have a nature, and each contains this Way, a matter of *yin*. The writings of Masters Zhou [Dunyi] and Cheng [Hao and Yi] speak of this thoroughly.[21]

[3] **The humane person sees it and calls it humanity; the wise person sees it and calls it wisdom. Common people practice it daily but do not understand; therefore the Way of the superior person is rare.**

Humaneness is *yang* and wisdom is *yin*; each gets "one corner" [*Analects* 7.8] of this Way, so following what one sees leads to the whole thing. They "practice it daily but do not understand"; everyone eats and drinks but they are rarely able to understand the taste. Everyone denigrates it, but there are none who lack this Way.

Someone said, The previous section says that wisdom is classified under Heaven [*yang*] and humaneness is classified under Earth [*yin*]; isn't that different from this section [where you say that humaneness is *yang* and wisdom is *yin*]? Reply: The other section is in terms of clear and turbid [*qi*], while this one is in terms of activity and stillness.[22]

[4] **[The Way] manifests itself in being humane and is concealed in its functioning. It arouses the myriad things but does not share the worries of the Sage. Its flourishing virtue and Great Undertaking are indeed perfect!**[23]

"Manifesting" is from inner to outer; "being humane" means the achievement of creating and transforming, the expression of virtue.[24] "Concealed" means from outer to inner. "Functioning" means the mystery of its operation, the basis of the [Great] Undertaking. Master Cheng [Yi] said, "Heaven and Earth have no mind, yet bring about transformation. The Sage has a mind yet does not [deliberately] act [*wuwei* 无為]."[25]

[5] **Embracing all things, it is called the Great Undertaking. Renewing itself daily, it is called flourishing virtue.**

Master Zhang [Zai] said, "'Embracing all things,' it is great and all-inclusive. 'Renewing itself daily,' it is long-lasting and inexhaustible."[26]

[6] **Life and growth [*sheng sheng* 生生] are the meaning of change.**[27]

Yin generates *yang* and *yang* generates *yin*; their fluctuations are inexhaustible. The principle [of change] and the book [the *Yi*] are both thus.

[7] **Bringing about images is called Qian; following patterns [*fa* 法] is called Kun.**

"Patterns" means the visible details of creation.

[8] **Maximizing numbers to know the future is called prognostication. Penetrating [understanding] the fluctuations is called affairs.**[28]

"Prognostication" is divining [with milfoil]. Affairs that are uncertain are categorized as *yang*. "Affairs" means daily affairs. Prognostications that are already decided are categorized as *yin*. "Maximizing numbers to know the future" is how to penetrate the changes of affairs. I think this is like what Zhang Zhongding said about official affairs having *yin* and *yang* [aspects].[29]

[9] **When *yin* and *yang* are unfathomable we call it spirit.**

Master Zhang said, "Being in two places at once is called being unfathomable."[30]

Section 6

[1] **As for the *Yi*, it is vast; it is great. In terms of being far-reaching, nothing can resist it. In terms of being near, it is still and correct. In terms of filling Heaven and Earth, it is complete.**

"Nothing can resist it" means it is inexhaustible. "Still and correct" refers to it as a thing in which principle inheres. "Complete" says that it exists everywhere.

[2] **As for Qian, its stillness is focused; its activity is direct. This is how it is greatly productive. As for Kun, its stillness is condensed; its activity is expansive. This is how it is vastly productive.**

Qian and Kun each have active and still phases; we see this in the Four Virtues.[31] Stillness is substance and activity is function; stillness differentiates and activity interacts. Qian is singular and solid; therefore in terms of its material it is great. Kun is double and empty [broken]; therefore in terms of its capacity it is vast. Although Heaven's forms comprise what is outside Earth, their *qi* always operates within Earth. This is why the *Yi* is vast and great.[32]

[3] Being vast and great [the *Yi*] matches Heaven and Earth; its flux and continuity [*biantong* 變通] match the Four Seasons; the meanings of its *yin* and *yang* [lines] match the sun and moon; the goodness of its ease and simplicity matches the utmost virtue.

The *Yi*'s vastness and greatness, its flux and continuity, and what it says about *yin* and *yang* and its virtues of ease and simplicity, all match the Way of Heaven and human affairs.

Section 7

[1] The Master [Confucius] said, "How perfect is the *Yi*! The *Yi* is how the Sages honored virtue and broadened the [Great] Undertaking. Wisdom made them exalted; ritual propriety made them humble. Being exalted, they imitated Heaven. Being humble, they modeled themselves on Earth."

The Ten Wings were all written by Confucius. Since this is inconsistent with his writing "The Master said" himself, these words were probably added by later men. When one fully investigates principle, one's wisdom is exalted like Heaven, and one's virtue is exalted. When one follows principle, ritual propriety makes one humble like Earth, and one's accomplishments are broadened.

[2] Heaven and Earth establish their positions and change [*yi*] proceeds through them. The complete nature [*cheng xing* 成性] [of people and things] is ever present, and thus is the gateway of the Way and rightness.

Heaven and Earth establish their positions and fluctuation and transformation proceed. This is like understanding ritual propriety and preserving the nature so that the Way and rightness can appear. "The complete nature" refers to the nature that is originally complete [in people and things]. "Ever present" is simply the idea of existing and still existing.[33]

Section 8

[1] The Sages had the means to see the world's mysteries, so they compared them to forms and appearances to appropriately represent things. This is why we call them images.

"Mysteries" are mixed and confused. "Images" refers to the imagery of the trigrams, as listed in the *Shuogua* [Treatise discussing the trigrams].

[2] The Sages had the means to see the activities of all under Heaven and to observe how they come together and penetrate, in order to enact the canonical rituals. They appended remarks [to the hexagram lines] in order to judge whether they were auspicious or ominous. This is why they are called line [texts].

"Come together" means how principles assemble with nothing left out. "Penetrate" means how principle can proceed without obstruction. It is like Cook Ding carving the ox: when [his knife] met a hard spot it penetrated as if it were empty.[34]

[3] [The line statements] speak of the most mysterious things under Heaven, yet we cannot consider them bad. They speak of the most active things under Heaven, yet we cannot consider them chaotic.

"Bad" means dislikable.

[4] [The Sages] compared before they spoke, and consulted before they acted. By comparing and consulting they brought about the fluctuations and transformations.

By observing the images and appreciating the statements, observing the fluctuations and appreciating the prognostications, they lawfully enacted them. The following seven passages give examples.[35]

[5] "A calling crane in the shade; its young answers it. I have a fine goblet; I will share it with you." The Master said, "The noble man might stay in his room, but if the words he speaks are good, even those from more than a thousand *li* away will respond to him. How much more so will those near to him? If he stays in his room and the words he speaks are not good, then those from more than a thousand *li* away will oppose him. How much more so will those near him? Words emerge from one's own person and benefit the people; deeds are expressed nearby but are evident far away. Words and deeds are the superior person's hinge and spring; the operation of the hinge and spring control honor and disgrace. Words and deeds are how the superior person activates Heaven and Earth. How can one fail to be cautious about them?"

This explains the 9 in the second line of Zhongfu [hexagram 61].

[6] "Fellows first cry and wail, but then laugh." The Master said,

> The Way of the superior person
> may go forth, may stay still;
> may be silent, may speak.
> The comradeship of two people
> is sharp enough to cut metal;
> the words of comradeship
> have an aroma like orchids.

This explains the 9 in the fifth line of Tongren [13]. It says that the Way of the superior person at first is not united [with others], but then it is full with no gap. "Cut metal" and "like orchids" refer to something that cannot be separated and the flavor of words [respectively].

[7] "6 at the beginning [of Daguo (28)]: For a mat use white rushes; no blame." The Master said, "Even putting it on the ground would be acceptable. How could there be any blame in using rushes for the mat? This is an extreme of caution. Although rushes are slender things, their functioning is important. If one proceeds on the basis of this kind of caution, nothing will be lost.

This explains the 6 in the first line of Daguo.

[8] "Toiling modestly, the superior person achieves his ends; auspicious." The Master said, "Toiling without boasting, having merit but not considering it a virtue, is the perfection of genuineness. This speaks of someone who uses his merit to subordinate [himself] to others. His virtue expresses fullness; his ritual propriety expresses respect. The modest person extends respect in order to preserve his position."[36]

This explains the 9 in the third line of Qian [15]. "His virtue expresses fullness; his ritual propriety expresses respect" says that virtue seeks to be full and ritual propriety seeks to be respectful.

[9] "A dragon going too far; there will be regret." The Master said, "Honored yet without position, high yet without a populace, having worthies in subordinate positions but no assistance; for this reason action will bring regret."

This explains the meaning of 9 in the top line of Qian. Since it is also in the *Wenyan* [under Qian, 9], it can be considered important.

[10] "Not going out the door into the courtyard; no blame." The Master said, "The origination of chaos begins with speech. If the superior person is not discreet he will lose his ministers; if the minister is not discreet he will lose his life; if an incipient affair is not kept quiet harm will result. For this reason the superior person is cautious and discreet, and does not go out."

This explains the 9 in the first line of Jie [60].

[11] The Master said, "Did the creators of the *Yi* understand thieves? The *Yi* says, 'One who carries a load yet also rides in a carriage will attract bandits.' Thievery is the business of a petty person; a carriage is a device for a superior person. If a petty person rides in the device of a superior person, thieves will think about stealing from him. If one is careless to those above and violent toward those below, thieves will think about attacking him. To be careless about one's treasure invites thieves, and to make up one's face is to invite licentiousness. Thus when the *Yi* says, 'One who carries a load yet also rides in a carriage will attract bandits,' it means that this is to beckon thieves."

This explains the 6 in the third line of Xie [40].

This eighth section addresses the functions of the hexagrams and lines.

Section 9[37]

[1] Heaven is 1, Earth is 2; Heaven is 3, Earth is 4; Heaven is 5, Earth is 6; Heaven is 7, Earth is 8; Heaven is 9, Earth is 10.

This section was originally at the beginning of section 10, but Master Cheng [Yi] said that it belongs here, and I now follow him.[38] It speaks of the numbers of Heaven and Earth, *yang* being odd and *yin* being even, just as they are described in the River Chart [*Hetu* 河圖].[39] Their positions [in the River Chart] are 1 and 6 residing at the bottom, 2 and 7 residing at the top, 3 and 8 residing on the left, 4 and 9 residing on the right, and 5 and 10 residing in the center. As this section discusses it, the 5 in the center is the mother of the expansion [*yan* 衍]; 10 is the child of the expansion; 1, 2, 3, and 4 are the positions of the Four Images; 6, 7, 8, and 9 are the numbers of the Four Images. The positions of the two mature ones [9 and 6] are west and north; the positions of the two young ones [8 and 7] are east and south.⁴⁰ The numbers are all interconnected with other kinds of categories.

[2] The numbers of Heaven are five; the numbers of Earth are five. The five positions [left, right, top, bottom, center] are complementary and each has its match. The numbers of Heaven [equal] 25 and the numbers of Earth [equal] 30. Together the numbers of Heaven and Earth are 55. This is how they bring about fluctuation and transformation and move ghosts and spirits.

This section originally came after the "Great Expansion" section [following this], but I think it belongs here. The five numbers of Heaven are 1, 3, 5, 7, and 9, which are all *yang*. The five numbers of Earth are 2, 4, 6, 8, and 10, which are all *yin*. "Complementary" means that 1 and 2, 3 and 4, 5 and 6, 7 and 8, 9 and 10 each take odd and even as complementary categories. "Has its match" means 1 and 6, 2 and 7, 3 and 8, 4 and 9, 5 and 10 are all matching pairs. "25" is the sum of the five odd numbers and "30" is the sum of the five even numbers. "Fluctuation and transformation" means 1 fluctuates to generate water and 6 transforms to complete it; 2 transforms to generate fire and 7 fluctuates to complete it; 3 fluctuates to produce wood and 8 transforms to complete it; 4 transforms to produce metal and 9 fluctuates to complete it; 5 fluctuates to produce earth and 10 transforms to complete it. "Ghosts and spirits" means the bending and stretching, going and coming, of the production and completion of the odd and even [numbers].⁴¹

[3] The number of the Great Expansion is 50; those that are used are 49. Divide them in two, to symbolize the Two [Modes]. Place one [between the fingers] to symbolize the Three [Powers]. Count off by fours to symbolize the Four Seasons. Put the remainder between the fingers to represent the intercalary month. In five years there are two intercalary months; therefore place again in the next space between the fingers.⁴²

"The number of the Great Expansion [*dayan* 大衍] is 50," so in the central palace of the River Chart the Heavenly 5 rides the Earthly 10 and complements it. But when it comes to using the [milfoil] stalks one only uses 49. This all comes from the naturalness of [inherently] ordered tendencies [*lishi* 理勢]; the power of human understanding can neither detract from nor add to it. "Two" refers to Heaven and Earth. "Place" means to keep the one between the small fingers of the left hand. "Three" refers to the Three Powers [Heaven, Earth, and Humanity]. "Count off" means to divide and count [the stalks]. The "remainder" means what is leftover after counting off by fours. "Between the fingers" means to hold in the two spaces between the three middle fingers of the left hand. "Intercalary months" are the extra days that accumulate each month to make another month. In five years, there are enough accumulated days to make another month, so every five years there is an intercalary month. So then, separate and raise the two divisions of the whole bunch [after one has been set aside], and take each [remainder] from those counted off in the left- and right-hand piles and place it between the fingers.[43]

[4] The stalks required for Qian are 216. The stalks required for Kun are 144, making a total of 360. This matches the days in the year.[44]

The numbers of all these stalks come from the Four Images. The four sides of the River Chart are mature *yang* [⚌] resides in 1 and connects with 9 [north → west]; young *yin* [⚏] resides in 2 and connects with 8 [south → east]; young *yang* [⚎] resides in 3 and connects with 7 [east → south]; mature *yin* [⚏] resides in 4 and connects with 6 [west → north]. In the method of casting milfoil stalks, we add the remainders of the three changes, discard the first and set it aside, take 4 as odd and 8 as even. Odd is round and encloses 3; even is square and encloses 4. For 3 we use the whole [number], and for 4 we use half [i.e., 2]. Combining and counting them yields 6, 7, 8, or 9. The number counted off in the third change and the number of [remaining] stalks should tally. So when the remainders are three odds, the number counted off is also 9, and the [number of] stalks is 4 x 9, or 36. This is the mature *yang* that resides in 1. When the remainders are two odds and one even, making 8, the number counted off is also 8, and the number of stalks is 4 x 8, or 32. This is the young *yin* residing in 2. With two evens and one odd, making 7, the number counted off is also 7, and the number of stalks is 4 x 7, or 28. This is the young *yang* residing in 3. With three evens, making 6, the number counted off is also 6, and the number of stalks is 4 x 6, or 24. This is the mature *yin* residing in 4.

This mystery of fluctuation and transformation, going and coming, advancing and retreating, separating and combining, always arises naturally; it is not what humans are able to do. The young *yin* retreats but is not yet at its peak of emptiness. The young *yang* advances but is not yet at its peak of fullness. Thus only mature *yang* and mature *yin* yield the numbers of stalks for Qian and Kun. The rest can be understood by extension. The whole period of the year, totaling 365¼ days, is only approximated here using round numbers.

[5] The number of stalks in the two parts [of the text] total 11,520, which matches the number of the myriad [10,000] things.

The two parts are the first and second parts of the Scripture. The total of *yang* lines is 192, yielding 6,912 [36 stalks x 192 lines]. The total of *yin* lines is 192, yielding 4,608 [24 x 192]. Together they yield this number [11,520].

[6] For this reason four operations make a change [*bian* 變], and eighteen changes make a hexagram.

The "four operations" are dividing [the stalks] into two, placing one [between the fingers], counting off by fours, and putting back the remainder [between the fingers]. Three changes make a line, so eighteen changes make six lines.

[7] The Eight Trigrams constitute the "small completion."

Nine changes make three lines, yielding the inner trigram.

[8] By stretching and extending them, and expanding them with analogies, everything under Heaven can be completed.

Once the six lines are completed we view how the lines fluctuate or don't fluctuate in activity and stillness. Then each hexagram can fluctuate into any of the sixty-four hexagrams, determining what is auspicious or ominous, for a total of 4,096 hexagrams [64 x 64].

[9] [The *Yi*] clarifies the Way and spiritualizes virtuous action. For this reason one can receive responses from it and can give assistance to spirits.

The Way is clarified through [the *Yi*'s] remarks, and action is spiritualized by means of its numbers. "Receive responses" means responding to questions. "Give assistance to spirits" means the meritorious action of helping spiritual transformation.[45]

[10] The Master said, "Doesn't one who understands the Way of fluctuation and transformation understand what spirits do?"

"The Way of fluctuation and transformation" is the various patterns in the preceding passages. They are beyond the human ability to create, and so Confucius praised them. His disciples added "The Master said" to distinguish this from the text above.

This section speaks of the numbers of the Great Expansion of Heaven and Earth, the method of sorting stalks to find a hexagram, but only in outline. The details of their ideas were embodied in the office of the Grand Diviner, and today cannot be examined. The *Qimeng* [chapter 3] contains an attempt to infer them.

Section 10

[1] The *Yi* contains the Way of the Sages in four respects: in speech we honor its phrases; in activity we honor its fluctuations; in making implements we honor its images; in divining we honor its prognostications.

These four are all the Way of fluctuation and transformation, the actions of the spirit.

[2] This is why the superior person, when about to make something or do something, consults it in speech, and it receives his charge [*ming* 命] like an echo. It is neither distant nor near, dark nor deep, and so he follows it to understand things to come. If it were not the finest thing under Heaven, how would we be able to participate in this?

This is "honoring its phrases" and "honoring its prognostications." It refers to people using milfoil stalks to consult the *Yi*, finding the hexagram and line statements to express [the judgment] in words. So the *Yi* receives the person's charge and announces [the judgment] like the responsive sound of an echo, deciding the auspicious and ominous aspects of what is to come. The meanings of "in speech" here and in the preceding line are the same. The "charge" is the statement addressed to the milfoil stalks when one is about to divine. It is the same as in the capping ritual [for an ordinary officer's son], where in divining for the day, "The steward, standing on the Master of Ceremonies' right, assists with the charge."[46]

[3] Threes and fives, fluctuating, mix and combine their numbers. Connecting these fluctuations makes the patterns of Heaven and Earth. Maximizing these numbers determines the images of all under Heaven. If [the *Yi*] were not the perfection of all fluctuations under Heaven, how would we be able to participate in this?[47]

This is "honoring its images." A fluctuation is before an image is determined.[48] *San* 參 is the number 3, and *wu* 伍 is the number 5.[49] When 3 fluctuates and 5 fluctuates, one after another, they check each other to ascertain their actual amounts. "Mix" means interact and alternate, left and right [hands]. "Combine" means to gather and hold, putting down and picking up. This all refers to sorting the stalks to find a hexagram. It includes placing stalks between two fingers three times to make the mature and young *yin* and *yang* lines, yielding the numbers 7, 8, 9, or 6, to determine the images of the active and still hexagrams and lines.

"Threes and fives" [*san wu* 參伍] and "mixing and combining" [*cuo zong* 錯綜] are old expressions; "threes and fives" is particularly difficult to understand.[50] For example, Xunzi says, "In scrutinizing the enemy and observing changes in his movements, desire to compare reports, so as to verify them."[51] Han Fei says, "He examines the agreements and disagreements in debate in order to determine how the various factions in the government shape up. He compares proposals and results to make certain that words are backed up by facts."[52] He also says, "Compare with concrete results; check in order to compare.[53] The *Shiji* says, "One must know the threes and fives"[54] and "study logical order so that there will be no error."[55] The *Han shu* says, "compare their values by using their category as a standard."[56] These are sufficient to clarify each other.

[4] The *Yi* is without thought and without action; silent and unmoving, when stimulated it penetrates [connects] all circumstances under Heaven.[57] If it were not the most spiritual thing under Heaven, how could we participate in this?

These four [phrases] are how the substance of the *Yi* is established and how its function works. "*Yi*" refers to the milfoil and the hexagrams. "Without thought and without action" speaks of it having no mind. "Silence" is the substance of stimulation. "Stimulating" and "penetrating" are the function of silence. The mystery of the human mind, in its activity and stillness, is also like this.

[5] The *Yi* is how the Sages plumbed the depths and researched incipiencies [*ji* 幾].

"Research" is like investigating. "Incipiencies" are subtleties. What enabled them to plumb the depths was their utmost purity [of mind]. What enabled them to research incipiencies was their utmost [sensitivity to] fluctuation.[58]

[6] Only its depths enable it to penetrate all purposes under Heaven. Only its incipiencies enable it to bring about [or complete] all efforts under Heaven. Only its spirit allows it to hurry without haste and arrive without going.

That by which it penetrates purposes and brings about efforts is the action of spirit.

[7] The Master said, "The *Yi* contains the Way of the Sages in four respects" [A.10.1]. This is what he meant.

This section continues the idea of the previous one, speaking of the *Yi*'s four-fold functioning.

Section 11

[1] The Master said, "What does the *Yi* do? The *Yi* discloses things, completes efforts, and encompasses the Ways of all under Heaven; this and nothing more. For this reason the Sages used it to penetrate all purposes under Heaven, to determine the undertakings of all under Heaven, and to resolve the doubts of all under Heaven."

"Discloses things and completes efforts" means enabling people to use divination to understand what is auspicious and ominous, and so to accomplish their affairs. "Encompasses the Ways of all under Heaven" means that once the hexagram lines are arrayed, the Ways of all under Heaven are present in them.

[2] For this reason the virtue of the milfoil stalks is round and spiritual, the virtue of the hexagrams is square to enable wisdom, and the meanings of the six lines are conveyed through changes. The Sages in this way purified their mind-hearts and retired to store their secrets. They suffered good fortune and bad fortune in common with [ordinary] people. Being spiritual they understood what was to come; being wise they stored up what had passed. [Otherwise] how could we participate in this? [It is because of] the expansive intelligence and astute wisdom of the ancients, who were spiritually martial yet nonviolent.

"Round and spiritual" means the unboundedness of fluctuation and transformation. "Square and wise" means that events have definite principles. "Conveyed through changes" means that the fluctuating changes are announced to us [by the hexagrams]. The Sages concretely embodied the virtues of the three [milfoil, hexagrams, and lines] without the slightest worldly tie. When there was nothing happening their minds were silent [*jiran* 寂然] and no one could detect them; when there was something happening, the operation of their spiritual understanding "responded when stimulated" [A.10.4]. This means they understood what was auspicious and ominous without divination. "Spiritually martial and yet nonviolent" means they apprehended principle without recourse to things.[59]

[3] Thus by clarifying the Way of Heaven and examining people's circumstances they produced these spiritual things to place before the people for their use. In doing this the Sages fasted and disciplined themselves to spiritually clarify their virtue.

The "spiritual things" are the milfoil and tortoise. Quietly purifying and unifying [oneself] is what is meant by "fasting." Solemnly admonishing and respecting is what is meant by "disciplined." Because they "clarified the Way of Heaven" they understood that the spiritual things could be produced. Because they "examined the people's circumstances" they understood that their use could only be to disclose things in advance. They therefore created milfoil divination to instruct people, and "fasted and disciplined themselves" to examine their prognostications. This made their minds spiritually clear and unfathomable, like the ability of ghosts and spirits to understand what is to come.[60]

[4] For this reason closing the door is called Kun; opening the door is called Qian; alternately closing and opening is called fluctuation [bian 變]; going and coming without end is called continuity [tong 通]. What is seen is called an image; what has shape is called an implement; what is used systematically is called a pattern [fa 法]. Putting it to good use in all situations, so that all people use it, is called spirit.

"Closing and opening" are the mechanism of activity and stillness. The former is called Kun, which acts from stillness.[61] The fluctuation and continuity of Qian and Kun are the achievement of "transforming and nourishing."[62] Seeing images and shaping implements are the order of how things are generated. A "pattern" [or model] is what is made when a Sage cultivates the Way, and "spirit" is the common people's natural daily use of it.

[5] For this reason in change there is Supreme Polarity [taiji 太極], which generates the Two Modes. The Two Modes generate the Four Images, and the Four Images generate the Eight Trigrams.[63]

Every one generates two; this is the natural order/principle. "Change" [yi 易] is the fluctuation [bian 變] of yin and yang, and taiji is its principle. The Two Modes begin with one stroke dividing into yin and yang. The Four Images are each two-stroke figure subsequently divided into mature and young. The Eight Trigrams are the subsequent three-stroke figures, completing the image of the Three Powers [san cai 三才] [Heaven, Humanity, and Earth]. These statements are truly the sequence by which the Sage [Fuxi] created the *Yi*. In completing it he did not avail himself the slightest bit of the power of wisdom; drawing the hexagrams and sorting the milfoil stalks both followed naturally. For a more detailed illustration of the sequence, see the *Qimeng* [chapter 2].

[6] The Eight Trigrams determine the auspicious and ominous; the auspicious and ominous generate the Great Undertaking.

The existence of auspicious and ominous [tendencies] generates the Great Undertaking.[64]

[7] For this reason among patterns and images nothing is greater than Heaven and Earth; in fluctuation and continuity [*biantong* 變通] nothing is greater than the Four Seasons; among images suspended above emitting light nothing is greater than the sun and moon. Among respected and eminent things nothing is greater than wealth and honor; among those who established and made implements for the benefit of all under Heaven, none is greater than the Sages. Of things that delve into profundity and seek what is hidden, bringing them up from the depths and extending them afar to determine what is auspicious and ominous under Heaven and to complete the untiring efforts of all under Heaven, nothing is greater than the milfoil and tortoise.

"Wealth and honor" means, for all under Heaven, acting in the position of the lord [emperor]. I suspect that there is some missing text after "established." "Untiring efforts" means constant work. If one becomes lazy in one's questioning, one should resolve to work.

[8] For this reason Heaven generated the spiritual things and the Sage used them as models. Heaven and Earth fluctuate and transform and the Sage [Fuxi] imitated them. Heaven suspended images [heavenly bodies] revealing auspicious and ominous [signs] and the Sage symbolized them [as trigrams and hexagrams]. The [Yellow] River gave forth the Chart and the Luo [River] gave forth the Writing, and the Sages used them as models.

These four are what the Sage followed in creating the *Yi*. For details of the River Chart and Luo Writing see the *Qimeng* [chapter 1].[65]

[9] There are Four Images in the *Yi*, which is how it reveals itself. There are phrases appended to them, which is how it announces itself. They determine the auspicious and ominous, which is how it makes judgments.[66]

The Four Images are *yin* and *yang*, [each divided into] mature and young. "Reveals" means revealing to people how to evaluate the hexagrams and lines.

Section 12

[1] The *Yi* says, "He is blessed by Heaven. Auspicious; everything is advantageous." The Master said, "Blessing is help. One whom Heaven helps is in compliance [with it]; one whom people help is trustworthy. One who acts trustworthy thinks about being compliant and respects the worthy. That is why 'He is blessed by Heaven. Auspicious; everything is advantageous.'"

This quotes the 9 at the top of Dayou [14]. But here it is out of place, so I fear there was an errant bamboo slip. It seems more appropriate at the end of section 8.[67]

[2] The Master said, "Writing does not fully express speech, and speech does not fully express ideas." So then, can the ideas of the Sages not be perceived? The Master said, "The Sages established images to fully express their ideas, laid out the hexagrams to fully express what is true and false, appended remarks to them to fully express their words, [brought about] fluctuation and continuity to fully express what is advantageous, and drummed and danced to fully express [their] spirit."[68]

What words transmit is shallow; what images reveal is deep. We can see this by observing that the two [types of] lines, odd [solid] and even [broken], contain the inexhaustible extent of fluctuation and transformation. "Fluctuation and continuity" and "drummed and danced" refer to events. The two phrases, "The Master said," would be better combined into one. But all the phrases, "The Master said," were added by later people, so this is an error. Similarly, more recently the *Tongshu* 通書 [Penetrating the *Yi*] was written by Master Zhou [Dunyi] himself, yet later people added "Master Zhou said" to each section, making it into a conversation. This is just the same.[69]

[3] Do Qian and Kun contain the [whole] *Yi*?[70] Once Qian and Kun are arranged, the *Yi* is established in them. If Qian and Kun were eliminated, there would be no way to perceive the *Yi*. If the *Yi* could not be perceived, then Qian and Kun would be about to cease.

To "contain" is to hold and store, like a garment. What the *Yi* contains is simply *yin* and *yang*. Every *yang* is Qian and every *yin* is Kun, so when the hexagrams are drawn and their positions determined, the two are arranged and the substance of the *Yi* is established. "If Qian and Kun were eliminated" means the hexagrams would be drawn but not set up. "Qian and Kun would cease" means change and transformation would not proceed.

[4] Therefore what is above form [*xing'er shang* 形而上] is called the Way; what is within form [*xing'er xia* 形而下] is called implements.[71] Transforming and regulating is called fluctuation [*bian* 變]; extending and proceeding is called continuity [*tong* 通]; raising and placing things before all people under Heaven is called affairs and undertakings.

Hexagrams and lines, *yin* and *yang*, are all "within form." Their principle is the Way. Following their natural transformation and regulation is the meaning of fluctuation. The words "fluctuation" and "continuity" in the previous section [A.11.4, 7] refer to Heaven [or *tianli* 天理, "natural principle"]; in this section they refer to humans.

[5] Therefore as for the images, the Sages had the means to see what is mixed and confused in the world, so they compared them to forms and appearances to appropriately represent things. This is why we call them images. The Sages had the means to see the activity of all under Heaven and to observe how they come together and penetrate, in order to enact the canonical rituals. They appended remarks [to the hexagram lines] in order to judge whether they were auspicious or ominous. This is why they are called line [texts].

This is a repetition [of A.8.1–2].

[6] The most extreme of all profundities under Heaven are inherent in the hexagrams. The instigation of all activities under Heaven is inherent in the statements.

"Hexagrams" here means the images; "statements" are the line statements.

[7] Transformation and regulation are inherent in fluctuation; extension and procession are inherent in continuity; spirit and clarity are inherent in the person. Accomplishing things silently and being trustworthy without speaking are inherent in virtuous action.

That by which the hexagrams and lines fluctuate and continue is inherent in the person; that by which people are able to be spiritual and clear is inherent in virtue.[72]

PART B

Section 1

[1] With the Eight Trigrams arranged, the images are present in them. When they are doubled, the lines are present in them.

"Arranged" means the classification of Qian as 1, Dui as 2, Li as 3, Zhen as 4, Sun as 5, Kan as 6, Gen as 7, and Kun as 8.[73] "Images" means the form and structure of the trigrams. "When they are doubled" means adding eight trigrams in sequence onto each trigram, making sixty-four. "Lines" are the six lines. After they are doubled each hexagram has six lines.

[2] When firm and yielding [lines] displace each other, fluctuation is present in them. When remarks are appended to them and issued as decrees, activity is present in them.[74]

When the firm and yielding displace each other and the fluctuations of the hexagram and lines go back and forth and intermingle, nothing cannot be seen [in them]. The Sages accordingly appended their remarks to decree what was auspicious and ominous. So the fact that what the diviner encounters matches the lines and images in activity does not depart from this.

[3] Auspicious and ominous, regret and disgrace, arise from activity.[75]

"Auspicious and ominous, regret and disgrace" are what the remarks decree. However, they must accord with the activity of the hexagram lines in order to be seen.

[4] The firm and yielding [lines] establish the basis. Continuous fluctuation proceeds with the time.

Each firm and yielding [line] has a definite position. From this to another they fluctuate in accord with the time.

[5] The auspicious and ominous always correctly prevail.

Zhen 貞 means correct and constant; what enables things to be correct is constant. If events under Heaven are not auspicious, they are ominous; if not ominous, then auspicious. They are constantly prevailing over each other, and nothing more.

[6] The Way of Heaven and Earth is always correctly displayed. The way of the sun and moon is always correctly bright. The activity of all under Heaven is always correctly unified.

Guan 觀 means displayed [shi 示]. The fluctuation of the activity of all under Heaven is inexhaustible, but when it complies with principle it is auspicious; when it goes against principle it is ominous. What makes it correct and constant is nothing but the unitary principle [the natural/moral order].

[7] Qian firmly displays to people what is easy; Kun deferentially displays to people what is simple.

"Firmly" means in a strong manner. "Deferentially" means in a compliant manner. This is what is meant by "always correctly displayed" [in the previous line].

[8] The lines imitate this; the images represent this.

This refers to the principle of what Qian and Kun display in the previous passage. The lines being odd or even and the waning and waxing of the hexagrams are how they imitate and represent it.[76]

[9] The lines and images are active within [i.e., inherently dynamic]; the auspicious and ominous are visible without. Meritorious undertakings are seen in the fluctuations [of the lines]; the dispositions of the Sages are seen in the remarks.

"Within" means within the stalks and hexagrams; "without" means outside the stalks and hexagrams. "Fluctuations" are the fluctuations of the activity within; "remarks" are the remarks seen without.

[10] The great virtue of Heaven and Earth is called life [sheng 生].[77] The great treasure of the Sage is called his position. How does he preserve his position? That is called humanity.[78] How does he attract people? That is called talent. Having principled talent and correct statements, forbidding his people from doing wrong, is called rightness.

Mr. Lü [Zuqian], following the ancients, says, "Without the multitude there would be none to preserve the country."[79]

This section speaks of the auspicious and ominous aspects of the hexagrams and lines, and the creation of the meritorious undertaking.

Section 2

[1] In ancient times, when Baoxi [Fuxi] ruled all under Heaven, he looked up and contemplated the images [*xiang* 象] in Heaven; he looked down and contemplated the patterns [*fa* 法] on Earth; he contemplated the markings [*wen* 文] of the birds and beasts and their fitness [i.e., adaptation] to the earth. From nearby he took from his own body; from afar he took from things. In this way he first created the Eight Trigrams, to spread the power/virtue [*de* 德] of his spiritual clarity [*shenming* 神明] and to classify the dispositions of the myriad things.[80]

Wang Zhaosu [tenth century] said, "Between the words 'to' and 'the earth' many texts have the word 'Heaven'" [i.e., "to Heaven and Earth"]. Looking up and down, near and far, what [Fuxi] took from was not just a single thing. But it did not go beyond examining the polarity [*liangduan* 兩端] of *yin* and *yang*, waning and waxing. "The power/virtue of his spiritual clarity" was, for example, the nature of creating and complying, moving and stopping. "The dispositions of the myriad things" were, for example, the images of thunder and wind, mountain and lake.

[2] He knotted cords together to make nets and snares for hunting and fishing. He probably took this from Li 離 [hexagram 30, Clinging].

These two items aid each other, and things cling [*li* 麗] to each other.

[3] When Baoxi died, Shennong arose. He carved wood to make a plow, and bent wood to make the handle. He taught all under Heaven the benefit of plowing and hoeing. He probably took this from Yi 益 [42, Enhancing].

These two structures are both made of wood, the former going into [the earth] and the latter activating it. There is nothing greater than this to benefit all under Heaven.

[4] He made markets at midday, causing all the people under Heaven to gather together all the goods under Heaven. After exchanging them and going home, each [item] achieved its place. He probably took this from Shihe 噬嗑 [21, Biting Together].

"He made markets at midday": light [Li trigram] above and activity [Zhen trigram] below. He also associated "biting" with [food] markets and "through" [*he* 嗑] with bringing together [*he* 合].

[5] When Shennong died, the Yellow Emperor, Yao, and Shun arose. They continued the [former] changes [innovations], enabling people to avoid weariness. They spiritually transformed them, enabling people to adapt to them. When change [yi 易] reaches a limit there is fluctuation [bian 變]; with fluctuation there is continuity [tong 通]; continuity is long-lasting. This is how "with assistance from Heaven, good fortune; everything is appropriate."[81] The Yellow Emperor, Yao, and Shun let their upper and lower garments hang down [informally], and all under Heaven was ordered. They probably got this from Qian and Kun [1 and 2].

Qian and Kun fluctuate and transform without [intentionally] acting [wuwei 无為].

[6] They scooped out trees to make boats and carved wood to make oars. With the benefit of boats and oars they could cross impassable [waters], going far to benefit all under Heaven. They probably took this from Huan 渙 [59, Dispersing].

Wood [Sun] atop water [Kan] [i.e., a boat]. "Going far to benefit all under Heaven" suggests expansion.

[7] They tamed oxen and harnessed horses to pull heavy loads some distance, benefiting all under Heaven. They probably took this from Sui 隨 [17, Following].

Movement [Zhen] below, pleasure [Dui] above.[82]

[8] They made double gates and set up watchmen with clappers to deal with hoodlums. They probably took this from Yu 豫 [16, Being Happy].

The idea of being prepared.

[9] They split wood to make pestles and hollowed out the ground to make mortars. The benefit of mortars and pestles helped all the people. They probably took this from Xiaoguo 小過 [62, Small Surpassing].

Stationary [Gen] below, active [Zhen] above.[83]

[10] They strung wood to make bows and sharpened wood to make arrows. The benefit of bows and arrows is to dominate all under Heaven. They probably took this from Kui 睽 [38, Contrary].

Kui deals with things by opposing and then dominating.

[11] In high antiquity people lived in caves and dwelt in open countryside. In later ages the Sages changed this to houses, with ridgepoles and roofs to deal with wind

and rain. They probably took this from Dazhuang 大壯 [34, Flourishing of the Great].

The idea of being strong and firm.

[12] In ancient times the dead were thickly wrapped in brushwood and buried in open countryside, with no grave mound or trees, and without a fixed mourning period. In later ages the Sages changed this, using coffins and vaults. They probably took this from Daguo 大過 [28, Surpassing by the Great].

The great affair of sending off the dead is surpassing in its richness.[84]

[13] In high antiquity order was kept with knotted cords. In later ages the Sages changed this to written records, which were used to order the many offices and supervise the myriad people. They probably took this from Guai 夬 [43, Resolving].

The idea of clear decision making.

This section discusses how the Sages created implements and proposed images.

Section 3

[1] For this reason the *Yi* consists of images. Images are representations.

The forms of the *Yi* hexagrams are like their ordering principles [*li* 理].

[2] The judgments [*tuan* 彖] are the material [*cai* 材].

The judgments refer to the material of each hexagram.

[3] The lines imitate the activity of all under Heaven.

To "imitate" [*xiao* 效] is to reveal [*fang* 放].

[4] For this reason the auspicious and ominous [prognostications] are generated and regret and disgrace are expressed.

"Regret and disgrace" are fundamentally subtle, so they are expressed in this way.

Section 4

[1] A *yang* trigram has more *yin* [lines], and a *yin* trigram has more *yang*.

Zhen, Kan, and Gen [☳, ☵, ☶] are the *yang* trigrams; they all have one *yang* and two *yins*. Sun, Li, and Dui [☴, ☲, ☱] are *yin* trigrams; they all have one *yin* and two *yangs*.

[2] What is the reason for this? *Yang* trigrams are odd, and *yin* trigrams are even.

In all the *yang* trigrams there are five strokes; in all the *yin* trigrams there are four strokes.[85]

[3] What are their virtues and actions? In a *yang* [trigram] the one is the noble and the two are the people. This is the way of the noble/superior person. In a *yin* [trigram] the two are the noble and the one is the people. This is the way of the petty person.

The noble is *yang* and the people are *yin*.

Section 5[86]

[1] The *Yi* says, "Going back and forth in agitation, [only] friends follow your thoughts." The Master said, "Under Heaven, what thinking and deliberation is there? All under Heaven return to the same point, but by various paths; one goal for a hundred plans. Under Heaven, what thinking and deliberation is there?"

This quotes and explains 9 in the fourth line statement of Xian [31]. It says that order/principle [*li* 理] is fundamentally nondual. The various paths and hundred deliberations are all natural, so what could thinking and deliberation do? If one must think and follow [a plan], then those who follow it will be narrow-minded.

[2] When the sun goes, the moon comes; when the moon goes, the sun comes. The sun and moon displace each other and light is generated by them. The cold goes and heat comes; heat goes and cold comes. The cold and heat displace each other and the year is thus completed. What has gone contracts and what is to come extends. The mutual stimulation of contraction and extension generates benefit.

This says that the contraction and expansion of past and future are always stimulating and responding: the constant order of nature. To be increasingly anxious about it is to be self-absorbed. That is why one must think before following [a plan].

[3] The inchworm contracts when it wants to extend. Dragons and snakes hibernate in order to preserve themselves. Essential ideas become spiritual and thereby extend their utility. Beneficial application [of these ideas] eases life and thereby ennobles virtue.

Following upon the discussion of the principle of contraction and extension, past and future, this extends to a discussion of learning and the mechanisms of nature. To deeply explore ideas, to the point of becoming spiritual, is the utmost contraction [into the self]. But what enables one to go out and reach the basis of utility, to benefit by carrying out utility without encountering anything uneasy, is the ultimate of extension. The reason for entering and ennobling one's store of virtue is to mutually nourish the inner and outer as they express each other.

[4] Beyond this no one may know. To fully investigate the spiritual and understand transformation is the flourishing of virtue.

In the matter of mundane learning one can do no more than to exert oneself fully on pure ideas, and beneficially make use of the mechanism of mutual nourishment and expression. Above this [i.e., in higher learning], there is no use for this exertion. If one has reached the point of fully investigating the spiritual and understanding transformation, one achieves on one's own the flourishing of virtue and maturation of humanity. For one who does not understand, the past contracts. For one who has reached the goal on one's own, the future extends. This is simply the natural principle of stimulus and response. Master Zhang [Zai] said, "*Qi* has [the two modes] *yin* and *yang*. When it extends into action slowly, it undergoes transformation. When it is unified and unfathomable, it is spirit."[87] The above four passages all explain the meaning of 9 in the fourth line of Xian.

[5] The *Yi* says, "Blocked by stone, holding on to a star thistle. Entering the house, not seeing one's wife. Ominous." The Master said, "If one is blocked by something that should not block him, it is certainly a disgrace to his name. If one holds on to something that one shouldn't hold on to, one's life is certainly in danger. Being disgraced and in danger, the time of one's death is nigh; how could one see his wife?"

This explains the meaning of 6 in the third line of Kun [47].

[6] The *Yi* says, "The duke shoots a hawk on top of a high wall and hits it. Everything is appropriate." The Master said, "The hawk is a bird; the bow and arrow are implements. The archer is a person. The superior person keeps implements on his person, waits for the right time, and acts. How could there be anything inappropriate? To act without hindrance is how to go out and capture [one's prey]. This speaks of one who makes implements and acts."

"Hindrance" is an obstruction. This explains the meaning of 6 in the top line of Xie [40].

[7] The Master said, "The petty person is not ashamed not to be humane, is not fearful of being in the wrong. If he sees no advantage he doesn't strive, if he is not forced he doesn't correct himself. If he is corrected in small matters and commanded in great ones, this is the petty person's blessing." The *Yi* says, "Feet in the stocks, toes vanish. No blame." This is what it means.

This explains the meaning of 9 at the beginning of Shihe [21].

[8] If goodness is not accumulated there will not be enough to make a reputation. If badness is not accumulated there will not be enough to extinguish one's life. The petty person considers small goodness unprofitable, and doesn't do it. He considers small badness unharmful and doesn't avoid it. Thus badness accumulates and cannot be concealed, and crimes become great and cannot be undone. The *Yi* says, "Wearing the cangue, ears gone. Ominous."

This explains the meaning of 9 at the top of Shihe [21].

[9] The Master said, "Danger comes from being at ease in one's position. Death comes from preserving one's existence. Disorder comes from one who rules. Therefore the superior person is at ease yet doesn't forget danger; survives yet doesn't forget death; rules yet doesn't forget disorder. This is how his life can be easeful and his country can be preserved." The *Yi* says, "Death! Death! Fasten to a thick mulberry."[88]

This explains the meaning of 9 in the fifth line of Pi [12].

[10] The Master said, "With slight virtue but honorable position, small wisdom but great plans, small power but heavy responsibility, rarely will one be unequaled." The *Yi* says, "The cauldron's feet break, spilling the duke's food, its form getting wet. Ominous." This refers to being inadequate to one's responsibilities.

This explains the meaning of 9 in the fourth line of Ding [50].[89]

[11] The Master said, "Isn't understanding incipience spirituality? The superior person, interacting with those above, does not flatter. Interacting with those

below, he does not demean. Isn't that understanding incipience? Incipience is the subtle sign of activity, when the auspicious is first visible. The superior person sees incipience and acts, without waiting all day." The *Yi* says, "Hard as a rock, but not all day. Correct and auspicious." Hard like a rock, so why wait all day? The decision can be known. The superior person understands the subtle, understands the clear, understands the yielding, understands the firm. The myriad people look to him.

This explains the meaning of 6 in the second line of Yu [16]. In the *Han shu* [History of the Han dynasty], "auspicious" is "auspicious and ominous."[90]

[12] The Master said, "Didn't the son of the Yan clan [Yan Hui] take pains to come close [to the Way]? When he did something wrong he always knew it; knowing it, he never returned to it." The *Yi* says, "Returning from not far away; nothing to regret. Greatly auspicious."

"Come close" refers to coming close to the Way. This explains the meaning of 9 at the beginning of Fu [24].[91]

[13] Heaven and earth intermingle and the myriad things transform and mature. Male and female blend their essences and the myriad things transform and grow. The *Yi* says, "With three men walking, one will be lost. With one man walking, he will find a friend." The outcome is the same [either way].

"Intermingling" is the condition of intimately interacting. To "mature" is to thicken and coalesce, referring to the transformations of *qi*. To "transform and grow" is the transformation of form. This explains the meaning of 6 in the third line of Sun [41].

[14] The Master said, "The superior person pacifies his body and only then acts; eases his mind and only then speaks; determines his interactions and only then makes requests. The superior person cultivates these three things and thus is complete. If he is fearful in his activity the people will not be with him. If he is anxious in his speech the people will not respond to him. If he makes requests without interacting the people will not be with him. When no one is with him, those who would injure him will approach." The *Yi* says, "Nothing enhances you; someone strikes you. Your heart is not settled for long: ominous."

This explains the meaning of 9 at the top of Yi [42].

Section 6

[1] The Master said, "Are not Qian and Kun the gates of the *Yi*?" Qian is a *yang* thing and Kun is a *yin* thing. When *yin* and *yang* combine their virtues, the firm and yielding [lines] become tangible. By embodying the events of Heaven and Earth, they spread the virtue of spiritual clarity [*tong shenmingzhi de* 通神明之德].[92]

The firm and yielding substance of every hexagram is formed by the joined virtues of Qian and Kun. Therefore it says, "Qian and Kun are the gates of the *Yi*." *Zhuan* 撰 [normally meaning "calculations"] here is like "events" [*shi* 事].

[2] The names [of the hexagrams] are varied but not excessive. In examining their categories, do we not see the thinking of an era in decline?

Although the myriad things are numerous, they all come from the fluctuations of *yin* and *yang*. Therefore, although the meanings of the hexagrams and lines are expressed variously, they are not in error. However, they do not come up to the thinking and deliberation of high antiquity, a time of rustic simplicity. Thus we consider them to be the thinking of an era in decline, probably the time of King Wen and Zhou 紂 [last king of the Shang dynasty].[93]

[3] The *Yi* reveals the past and examines the future, makes clear the subtle and explains the mysterious. It differentiates things and reveals their proper names, completing them with correct words and decisive phrases.

[Zhu suggests that two appearances of the word "and" [*er* 而] in the passage are probably misplaced.]

[4] The [hexagram] names are brief, but the categories they represent are great. Their meanings are far-reaching and their phrasing elegant. Their words are indirect yet on the mark. The events [they refer to] are clear yet hidden. When in doubt they can assist the people in their behavior and clarify the rewards of failure and success.

"Clear" [*si* 肆] means "set forth" [*chen* 陳]. *Er* 貳 [two, double] means "doubt" [*yi* 疑].[94]

This section contains numerous textual errors and doubtful words, so it cannot be thoroughly comprehended. Likewise the following ones.

Section 7

[1] Did the *Yi* flourish in middle antiquity? Did those who created the *Yi* have anxiety and distress?[95]

At the end of the Xia and Shang periods the Way of the *Yi* was partly imperceptible. When King Wen was imprisoned in Youli he appended the *tuan* [hexagram] statements, and the Way of the *Yi* flourished again.

[2] For this reason Lü [10, Treading] is the basis of virtue; Qian [15, Being Modest] is the handle of virtue; Fu [24, Returning] is the root of virtue; Heng [32, Everlasting] is the strength of virtue; Sun [41, Diminishing] is the cultivation of virtue; Yi [42, Enhancing] is the abundance of virtue; Kun [47, Blocked] is the discernment of virtue; Jing [48, The Well] is the ground of virtue; Sun [57, Entering] is the controller of virtue.[96]

Lü (Treading) is ritual propriety [*li* 禮].[97] When Heaven above sends down moisture, making differentiations is not easy, so it is necessary to be careful in this regard. Only later can virtue be considered to have a basis and to be established. As for Qian (Being Modest), everyone from the humble to the honored person considers ritual to be what must be grasped and not lost. All nine hexagrams refer back to personal cultivation of virtue, to manage occasions of anxiety and distress so that they occur in an orderly fashion. Its basis is how it is established, and its handle is how it is grasped. Fu (Returning) means the beginnings of goodness do not exist outside the mind.[98] Heng (Everlasting) means if one holds on to it without fluctuation, it will be constant and long-lasting. To guard against anger and suppress [diminish] desire so as to cultivate oneself is to move toward the good and reform one's transgressions, thereby enhancing one's goodness. Only after being blocked (Kun) to verify one's strength, or being in a well (Jing) without changing one's location, is one able to comply (Sun) with principle and control the fluctuations of events.

[3] Lü (Treading) is being harmonious and reaching one's goal. "Qian (Being Modest) is being honorable and shining."[99] Fu (Returning) is distinguishing among things when they are small. Heng (Everlasting) is not being fed up with complexity. Sun (Diminishing) is being difficult at first and then easy. Yi (Enhancing) is growing abundance without artifice. Kun (Blocked) is being exhausted

yet persisting. Jing (Well) is staying in place yet moving. Sun (Entering) is assessing while being hidden.

This is like the "nine virtues" of the *Shu[jing]*.[100] Ritual propriety does not exert force on the world, but events all reach their utmost extent.[101] Being modest is humbling oneself, yet one's honor shines forth. In Returning the *yang* is subtle, yet does not disorder the group of *yin* [lines]. Persevering is abiding in complexity without ever being fed up with virtue. Diminishing is first desiring the difficult and practicing it thoroughly until it is easy. Enhancing is being full without creating. Impasse is being physically blocked yet successful in one's Way. The Well is being inactive yet reaching things. Compliance is assessing the fitness of things, yet being deeply hidden and unexposed.

[4] Lü (Treading) harmonizes behavior; Qian (Being Modest) controls ritual propriety; Fu (Returning) leads to self-knowledge; Heng (Everlasting) unifies virtue; Sun (Diminishing) keeps harm away; Yi (Enhancing) promotes benefit; Kun (Blocked) lessens resentment; Jing (Well) distinguishes rightness; Sun (Entering) is acting provisionally.

To "lessen resentment" means to have few occasions of resentment and blame. To "distinguish rightness" means being able to calmly deliberate.

This section is the "three presentations of the nine hexagrams," which clarifies the [Sages'] way of dwelling in "anxiety and distress" [B.7.1].

Section 8

[1] The *Yi* as a book cannot be kept at a distance; as a Way it is always shifting. It fluctuates and moves without rest, revolving and flowing through the six vacancies, rising and falling with no constancy, the firm and yielding [lines] changing into each other. They cannot be considered fixed essences, as they simply change along with circumstances.

"Keeping at a distance" is like forgetting. "Revolving and flowing through the six vacancies" means *yin* and *yang* flowing through the six positions of the hexagram.

[2] Going and coming in turns, it causes one to understand caution within and without.

This sentence is inaccurate; I suspect something is missing.

[3] It also clarifies anxiety and distress and their reasons. Even without a teacher or guardian, it is like having a father or mother nearby.

Although one has no teacher or guardian, it is always as if one's father or mother has come near, the utmost of admonishment and caution.

[4] At first one follows the remarks and considers their prescriptions, until apprehending a constant standard. But if one is not the [right] person, the Way will not proceed.

"Prescriptions" are the Way. By first following the remarks and determining their principle one sees their constant standard. But [the ability] to spiritually clarify it exists within the person.

Section 9

[1] The material of the *Yi* as a book has its origins in beginnings and its essentials in endings. The six lines intermingling are simply temporal things.

"Material" means the structure of the hexagram. The hexagram must rise up from its beginning to its end to achieve its structure. The lines, then, are simply temporal things.

[2] The beginning lines are difficult to understand; the top lines are easy to understand. They are root and branch. The text of the first line suggests; by the end it has achieved a conclusion.

This speaks of the beginning and top lines.

[3] But to grasp the virtues of complicated things and distinguish between true and false, one cannot do without the central lines.

This means the four central lines of the hexagram.

[4] Yes, even if one seeks [answers to] life and death or what is auspicious or ominous, if one stays with it one can certainly understand. The wise person who contemplates the Judgment statements can deduce more than half.

Tuan 彖 [Judgment] refers to the overall discussion of the six-line structure of a hexagram [i.e., the hexagram statement].

[5] The second and fourth lines have the same merit yet different positions; they are good in different ways. The second is often respected; the fourth is often

anxious, as it is close [to the fifth, "ruling" line]. The Way of a yielding line is that it is not beneficial to be distant. What is important is that it be without fault; its function is to be yielding and central.

This and the next passage discuss the central lines [second through fifth]. "Same merit" means they are *yin* [even-numbered] positions. "Different positions" means their distances [from the ruler] are different. The fourth is close to the ruler, and so is often anxious. It is not beneficial for a yielding [line] to be distant, yet the second is often respected, as it is yielding and central.

[6] The third and fifth [also] have the same merit yet different positions. The third is often ominous and the fifth is often meritorious, according to their grades of honor and humbleness. A yielding line [in these positions] is precarious and a firm line is surely superior.

The third and fifth are both *yang* positions, yet they differ in their honor and humbleness. Thus a yielding line residing there is precarious, and only a firm line is able to be superior.

Section 10

[1] The *Yi* as a book is broad, great, and all-inclusive. It contains the Way of Heaven, it contains the Way of Humanity, and it contains the Way of Earth. It combines these Three Powers and doubles them, resulting in six [lines]. The six are nothing other than the Ways of the Three Powers.

The three strokes [lines] embody the Three Powers; repeating them results in six. We take the upper two lines as Heaven, the middle two lines as Humanity, and the lower two lines as Earth.

[2] The Way contains fluctuation and activity, which we call [changing] lines. The lines have gradations, which we call things. Things mix together, which we call patterns [*wen* 文]. When the patterns do not match, good fortune and bad fortune arise.

"The Way contains fluctuation and activity" means the overall structure of the hexagram. "Gradations" means differences between far and near, honorable and humble. "Mix together" means the relations between the firm and yielding positions. "Do not match" means lines not matching their positions.

Section 11

[1] Did the rise of the *Yi* correspond to the latter days of the Yin [Shang] period, when the virtue of the Zhou was flourishing? Did it correspond to the affairs of King Wen [of the Zhou 周] and Zhou 紂 [of the Shang]?[102] For this reason the statements [attributed to King Wen] concern precariousness. One who is in a precarious position can bring about peace; one who is in an easy position can bring about collapse. This Way is very great; none of the hundred things is omitted. Being anxious in regard to ends and beginnings, and considering it essential to be without blame, is called the Way of the *Yi*.

Being "precarious" and "anxious" leads to peace; being lazy certainly leads to collapse. This is the Way of the *Yi*.

Section 12

[1] Qian is the strongest thing under Heaven; by practicing its virtue it is always easy to understand danger. Kun is the most compliant thing under Heaven; by practicing its virtue it is always simple to understand obstacles.

Being the strongest, [Qian's] practice is without difficulty, hence "easy." Being the most compliant, [Kun's] practice is not troublesome, hence "simple." However, in one's affairs one should always have an understanding of their difficulty and not presume to handle them with ease. In this way when there is anxiety and distress, if a strong one starts high and descends below he will understand danger; if a compliant one starts below and moves upward he will understand obstacles. So although one can easily understand danger one doesn't fall into danger, and [although] one can simply understand obstacles one isn't trapped in obstacles. This is how one can be apprehensive and cautious, but those without ease will collapse.[103]

[2] [Qian] is able to please the mind-heart; [Kun] is able to examine deliberations. [Thus they] determine what is auspicious and ominous under Heaven and complete all untiring efforts under Heaven.

The words "the feudal lords" are superfluous.[104] "To please the mind-heart" is the mind and order combining, which is the activity of Qian.[105] "To examine deliberations" is principle according with deliberation and scrutiny, which is the activity of Kun. By "pleasing the mind-heart" one can determine what is auspicious and ominous. By "examining deliberations" one can complete one's untiring efforts.

[3] For this reason fluctuation and transformation express action, and auspicious events bring blessings. Images and events [enable us to] understand implements, and the practice of divination [enables us to] know the future.

"Fluctuation and transformation express action"; therefore "images and events" enable us to "understand implements." "Auspicious events bring blessings"; therefore the "practice of divination" enables us to "know the future."

[4] Heaven and Earth establish their positions and Sages actualize their potential [cheng neng 成能]. With the counsel of men and the counsel of ghosts, ordinary people share in this potential.

"Heaven and Earth establish their positions," and the Sages created the Yi to actualize their merit. In this way, "with the counsel of men and the counsel of ghosts," even the dullest of ordinary people can share in its potential.[106]

[5] The eight trigrams are announced by images; the lines and statements are expressed according to their conditions. The firm and yielding [lines] mix their places, and the auspicious and ominous can be seen.

"Images" means the hexagram drawings. "Lines and statements" means the hexagram and line statements.[107]

[6] Fluctuation and activity are expressed according to their appropriateness; the auspicious and ominous shift according to their conditions. For this reason love and hatred work against each other, giving rise to the auspicious and ominous; the far and near take from each other, giving rise to regret and disgrace; true and false stimulate each other, giving rise to advantage and harm. The general conditions of the Yi are such that when those near to each other do not mutually gain, there is bad fortune. If harm results, there is regret and disgrace.

"Do not mutually gain" means mutual hatred. Bad fortune, harm, regret, and disgrace all arise from this.

[7] The statements of one who is about to rebel are shameful. The statements of one who has doubts in his inmost heart are indirect. The statements of a fortunate person are few. The statements of a confused person are many. The words of a person who slanders the good are superficial. The statements of one who has lost what he should preserve are wrong.[108]

The statements of the hexagrams and lines are also like this.

CHAPTER FOUR

TREATISE DISCUSSING THE TRIGRAMS (*SHUOGUA ZHUAN* 說卦傳)

PRELIMINARIES

The first three sections of the *Shuogua* are similar in form and content to the *Xici* and very different from the rest of the *Shuogua*, which is probably much later. They are in fact combined with the *Xici* in *Yizhi yi* 易之義 (Meanings of the *Yi*), one of the texts excavated at Mawangdui in 1973.[1]

Section 3.2 of this appendix contains two instances of a word that has given commentators a great deal of trouble: *ni* 逆, which means "to go against" or "reverse": "Calculating the past is going with / according (*shun* 順). Knowing the future is going against / reversing (*ni* 逆). Thus the *Yi* calculates in reverse (*ni shu* 逆數)." The problem is how exactly to interpret the last sentence, which could also be parsed as "Thus the *Yi* has reverse [or opposing] numbers." In his *Yixue qimeng* 易學啟蒙 (Introduction to the study of the *Yi*, 1186) Zhu Xi quotes Shao Yong's comment on this passage, from Shao's *Huangji jingshi shu*, referring to Diagram 4 (chapter 2).

Master Shao said,

This section explains the Eight Trigrams of Fuxi [sequence]. The fluctuations of the Eight Trigrams illuminate their interactions and complete the Sixty-Four. "Calculating the past is according" is like movement in accordance with Heaven. This is a movement to the left [counterclockwise], in each step toward

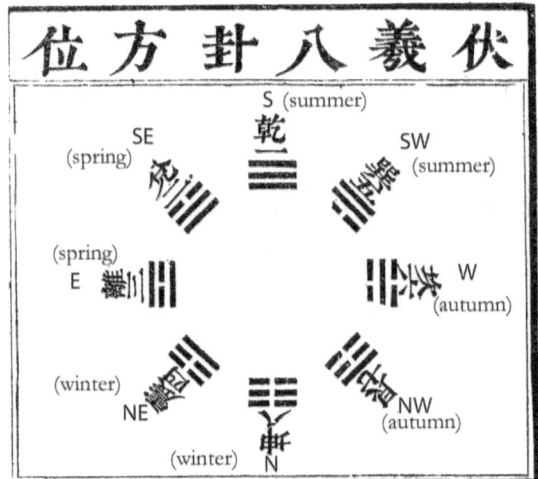

FIGURE 4.1 Fuxi's Directional Positioning of the Eight Trigrams (Diagram 4), with directions and seasons

the previously generated trigram [in terms of the seasons]. Thus it is called "calculating the past." "Knowing the future is reversing" is like movement opposite to Heaven. This is a movement to the right, in each step toward the not-yet-generated trigrams. Thus it is called "knowing the future." The calculations of the *Yi* are completed by reversing [the rotation of Heaven]. This section directly explains the ideas of [Fuxi's] chart in terms of reverse [anticipatory] knowledge of the Four Seasons.[2]

Although *ni* 逆 can also mean "anticipating" or "foreseeing," which makes obvious sense here—Legge translates it as "anticipation" and Nielsen uses "forecasting"—Richard Lynn suggests that this meaning may in fact be based on this passage.[3] However, the opposition with *shun* 順, "according," suggests that "reversing" is appropriate here.

First of all, it should be noted that the whole problem may in fact be the result of a copyist's error. In the Mawangdui manuscript of the *Yijing*, the corresponding line reads, "The *Yi* penetrates numbers." The character for "penetrates" (*da* 達) could easily have been mistaken for *ni* 逆, "reverse," by a careless copyist.[4] Nevertheless, as scholars ever since Wang Bi have had the character *ni* in their text, that is the one we must read and interpret here.

Shao Yong's phrases "movement in accordance with heaven" and "movement opposite to heaven" suggest an explanation in terms of the two common Chinese cosmological models, called *gai tian* 蓋天 (dome heaven) and *hun tian* 混天 (spherical heaven). In the former, heaven and earth are like nested hemispherical domes; in the latter they are like concentric spheres. In both models heaven rotates counterclockwise around the earth. The heavenly bodies move clockwise in relation to heaven, but more slowly than heaven's rotation, so they appear to move counterclockwise (east to west).[5] Moving from the present to the future, as in divination, one is moving clockwise, which is opposite to the rotation of heaven. To put it another way, while the seasons progress clockwise on the Fuxi chart—summer, fall, winter, spring—from the fixed human perspective the present becomes the past. Since the *Yijing* provides a method, through its numbers, of seeing from the present to the future, it is opposite to the natural flow. Hence "the *Yi* calculates in reverse." In other words, knowing the past is a natural human capacity, while the capacity to divine the future is part of the oracle's "spiritual" nature (*Xici* A.10.4).

Section 1

[1] **In ancient times, when the Sage [Fuxi] created the *Yi*, he was mysteriously assisted by [his] spiritual clarity to produce the yarrow stalks.**[6]

"Mysteriously assisted by spiritual clarity" is like the phrase "assisting in the transforming and nourishing [processes of Heaven and Earth]."[7] The "Tortoise and Yarrow Stalk" treatise [chap. 128 of the *Shiji* 史記] says, "When all under Heaven are at peace, the Kingly Way is obtained and the yarrow stalks grow long, in full clumps of a hundred stalks."[8]

[2] **He tripled Heaven and doubled Earth to give the numbers a basis.**

Heaven is round and Earth is square. A circle of one [unit diameter] has a circumference of three, and each three is one odd [number], so tripling Heaven makes three. A square of one [unit on a side] has a circumference of four, and four combines two evens, so doubling Earth makes two.[9] The numbers all arise on this basis. Therefore, after the stalks are cast for three changes [i.e., one line], if the remainders are three odds, then [the line is] 3 x 3 = 9. If the remainders are three evens, then [the line is] 3 x 2 = 6. If [the remainders are] two twos and one three it is 7; two threes and one two make 8.

[3] **He observed the fluctuations of *yin* and *yang* to establish the hexagrams. He initiated the movement of the firm and yielding to produce the lines. He harmoniously accorded with the Way and virtue to put in order [*li* 理] rightness. He fully explored the order of things [*qiong li* 窮理], fulfilled their natures [*jin xing* 盡性], and thereby attained [Heaven's] decree [*zhiyu ming* 至於命].**[10]

TABLE 4.1 Symbolism of the Eight Trigrams in the Shuogua 說卦

(Sequence of sections 7–11)	Qian 乾 ☰	Kun 坤 ☷	Zhen 震 ☳	Sun 巽 ☴	Kan 坎 ☵	Li 離 ☲	Gen 艮 ☶	Dui 兌 ☱
3.1 (text)	Heaven 天 (1)	Earth 地 (2)	Thunder 雷 (5)	Wind 風 (6)	Water 水 (7)	Fire 火 (8)	Mountain 山 (3)	Lake 澤 (4)
	Determine positions		Push against each other		Do not combat each other		Penetrate each other's qi	
3.1 (Shao Yong comm.)	S (1)	N (2)	NE (5)	SW (6)	W (7)	E (8)	NW (3)	SE (4)
4	Leads 君 (7)	Stores 藏 (8)	Thunder 雷, moves 動 (1)	Wind 風 scatters 散 (2)	Rain 雨, moistens 潤 (3)	Sun 日, dries 烜 (4)	Stops 止 (5)	Pleases 說 (6)
5.1	Battles 戰 (6)	Serves 役 (4)	Lord 帝 emerges 出 (1)	Regulates 齊 (2)	Toils 勞 (7)	Makes visible 見 (3)	Completes 成 (8)	Pleases 說 (5)
5.2	Battle 戰, NW (6)	Nourished 養 (4)	Things 物 emerge 出, E (1)	Regulated 齊, SE (2)	Toil 勞, return 歸, N (7)	Bright 明, Made visible 見 S (3)	End and begin 終始, NE (8)	Midautumn 正秋, please 說, served 役 (5)
6			Thunder 雷, activates 動 (1)	Wind 風, scatters 撓 (2)	Water 水, moistens 潤 (5)	Fire 火, dries 燥 (3)	End and begin 終始 (6)	Lake 澤, pleases 說 (4)
			Not oppose each other 不相悖		Equally matched 相逮		Penetrate each other's qi 通氣	
7	Strong 健 (1)	Compliant 順 (2)	Active 動 (3)	Entering 入 (4)	Trapped 陷 (5)	Clinging 麗 (6)	Stopping 止 (7)	Pleasing 說 (8)
8	Horse	Ox	Dragon	Fowl	Pig	Pheasant	Dog	Sheep
9	Head	Abdomen	Foot	Thigh	Ear	Eye	Hand	Mouth

(Sequence of sections 7–11)	Qian 乾 ☰	Kun 坤 ☷	Zhen 震 ☳	Sun 巽 ☴	Kan 坎 ☵	Li 離 ☲	Gen 艮 ☶	Dui 兌 ☱
10	Heaven, father	Earth, mother	1st/eldest son	1st/eldest daughter	2nd/middle son	2nd/middle daughter	3rd/youngest son	3rd/youngest daughter
11	Heaven, round, ruler, jade, father, metal, cold, ice, deep red, good horse, old horse, lean horse, tree fruit	Earth, mother, cloth, kettle, frugality, equality, calf & mother, large carriage, writing, multitude, handle, black soil	Thunder, dragon, black, yellow, courage, spreading, great road, eldest son, decisiveness, agitation, young bamboo, sedges, reeds; horses: good neigh, white rear legs, runner, white forehead; perennial crops, becomes Qian at peak	Wood, wind, eldest daughter, guideline, work, white, long, high, advance & retreat, no fruit, odor; people: balding, broad forehead, much white in eyes, good at business; becomes Zhen at peak	Water, drains & ditches, lying hidden, straightening & bending, bow, wheel; people: melancholy, sad, with earache; blood, red; horses: good back, strong heart, keep head low, thin hooves, trail behind; carriages w/ many defects; penetration, moon, thieves; trees: hard w/ strong center	Fire, sun, lightning, middle daughter, armor & helmet, sword & halberd; people: big bellied; dryness, turtle, crab, snail, clam, tortoise; trees: hollow, withered top	Mountain, back roads, small stones, gates & doors, fruit of tree & vine, guards at gate and harem, fingers, dogs, rats, black-billed birds; trees: hard w/ many joints	Marsh, youngest daughter, shaman, mouth, tongue, smashing, cutting off attachment, firm & salty soil, concubine, sheep

"Harmoniously accorded" is a summary way of speaking about following the features [of things/events] with no deviation. "[Put in] order" [*li* 理] means following along with events to apprehend their particular patterns [*tiaoli* 條理]; it is [used in two] separate ways here.[11] "Fully exploring the order" of all things under Heaven, "fulfilling the natures" of people and things, and joining with the Way of Heaven are the extreme merit of the Sage's creation of the *Yi*.

Section 2

In ancient times when the Sage created the *Yi*, he intended to accord with the principle [*li* 理] of the nature [*xing* 性] [of things] and what was decreed [*ming* 命] [by Heaven]. In this way he established the Way of Heaven, calling it *yin* and *yang*; he established the Way of Earth, calling it yielding and firm; he established the human Way, calling it humanity and rightness. He combined these Three Powers and doubled them; thus the *Yi* has six lines making each hexagram. He divided *yin* and *yang*, which function alternately as yielding and firm [lines]; thus the *Yi* has six positions making each section [*zhang* 章].

"He combined these Three Powers and doubled them" refers to the six lines as a whole. He divided them into portions, and so [the lines] mix together among the *yin* and *yang* positions to make the sections of text.[12]

Section 3

[1] Heaven and Earth determine the positions. Mountain and Lake penetrate [each other's] *qi*. Thunder and Wind arouse each other. Water and Fire do not combat each other. [Thus] the Eight Trigrams intermingle.[13]

Master Shao [Yong] said, "These are Fuxi's positions of the Eight Trigrams: Qian in the south, Kun in the north, Li in the east, Kan in the west, Dui occupying the southeast, Zhen occupying the northeast, Sun occupying the southwest, and Gen occupying the northwest. This way in which the Eight Trigrams interact, making the sixty-four hexagrams, is called a priori [*xiantian* 先天] learning."[14]

[2] Calculating the past accords [with the movement of Heaven]. Knowing the future reverses [the movement of Heaven]. Thus the *Yi* calculates in reverse [*ni shu* 逆數].

Starting from Zhen and passing through Li and Dui to Qian is calculating the already generated trigrams [from 4 to 1, clockwise in the circular Fuxi Diagram].

From Sun passing through Kan and Gen to Kun is inferring [*tui* 推] the not-yet-generated trigrams [from 5 to 8]. The sequence of the *Yi*'s generation of the trigrams is Qian, Dui, Li, Zhen, Sun, Kan, Gen, and Kun [1–8]. Thus [the *Yi*] always calculates in reverse.

Section 4

[The *Yi* uses] thunder to move [things], wind to scatter them, rain to moisten them, sun to dry them, Gen to stop them, Dui to please them, Qian to lead them, and Kun to store them.[15]

These are the positions of the trigrams facing each other, the same as in the previous section.[16]

Section 5

[1] The Lord emerges in Zhen [Thunder], regulates in Sun [Wind], makes things mutually visible in Li [Fire], causes them to be served in Kun [Earth], pleases in Dui [Lake], battles in Qian [Heaven], toils in Kan [Water], and completes in Gen [Mountain].

"The Lord" [*di* 帝] is the ruler of Heaven. Master Shao said, "These are the trigram positions that King Wen determined, which is called 'after Heaven' [a posteriori] learning."[17]

[2] The myriad things emerge in Zhen; Zhen is in the east. They are regulated in Sun; Sun is in the southeast. Regulating means purifying and regulating. Li [Fire] is bright, so the myriad things are all mutually visible; it is the trigram of the south. The Sage faces south and listens to all under Heaven; they are ruled by turning toward his brightness; it [this directional correlation] is probably taken from this. Kun is Earth; the myriad things all get nourishment from it. Thus it says [above], "it causes them to be served in Kun." Dui [Lake] is midautumn, which is what the myriad things are pleased by; thus it says, "pleases in Dui." They "battle in Qian [Heaven]" Qian is the trigram of the northwest. This says that *yin* and *yang* push against each other. Kan is water, the trigram of due north, the trigram of toil, what the myriad things return to. Thus it says they "toil in Kan." Gen [Mountain] is the trigram of the northeast, where the myriad things finally end up and where they achieve [new] beginnings. Thus it says they "are completed in Gen."

The previous passage speaks of the Lord, but this one speaks of the myriad things following the Lord in their goings and comings.

Section 6

Spirit is a word for what is mysterious in the myriad things. For activating the myriad things nothing is faster than thunder; for scattering the myriad things nothing is faster than wind; for drying the myriad things nothing burns more than fire; for delighting the myriad things nothing pleases like a lake; for moistening the myriad things nothing moistens like water; for ending and beginning the myriad things nothing succeeds like Gen. Thus water and fire are equally matched; thunder and wind do not oppose each other; mountain and lake penetrate [each other's] *qi*. Only then can there be fluctuation and transformation, which completes the myriad things.

This departs from [the discussion of] Qian and Kun and focuses on the six children, to show what spirit does. However, [as compared with] the discussions in the previous section of their positions, sequences, and functions, their meanings are not as detailed.[18]

Section 7

Qian is strong; Kun is compliant. Zhen is active; Sun is entering. Kan is sinking; Li is clinging. Gen is stopping; Dui is pleasing.

This speaks of the natures and dispositions of the Eight Trigrams.

Section 8

Qian is the horse; Kun is the ox. Zhen is the dragon; Sun is the fowl. Kan is the pig; Li is the pheasant. Gen is the dog; Dui is the sheep.

"From afar he took from things" like this.[19]

Section 9

Qian is the head; Kun is the abdomen. Zhen is the foot; Sun is the thigh. Kan is the ear; Li is the eye. Gen is the hand; Dui is the mouth.

"From nearby he took from his own body" like this.

Section 10

Qian is Heaven; therefore it is designated the father. Kun is the Earth; therefore it is designated the mother. Zhen is the first bonding [of mother and father], yielding a male; thus it is called the eldest son. Sun is the first bonding yielding a female; thus it is called the eldest daughter. Kan is the second bonding yielding a male; thus it is called the middle son. Li is the second bonding yielding a female; thus it is called the middle daughter. Gen is the third bonding yielding a male; thus it is called the youngest son. Dui is the third bonding yielding a female; thus it is called the youngest daughter.

"Bonding" is seeking, as in casting milfoil stalks to seek a line. "Male and female" refers to the alternation of *yin* and *yang* in the hexagram.

Section 11

[1] Qian is Heaven, round, the ruler, jade, the father, metal, cold, ice, deep red, a good horse, an old horse, a lean horse, and the fruit of trees.

Xun's Nine Masters has following this, "[Qian] is the dragon, directness, clothes, and speech."[20]

[2] Kun is Earth, mother, cloth, a kettle, frugality, equality, a calf and its mother, a large carriage, writing, a multitude, a handle. Among soils, it is black.

Xun's Nine Masters [also] has, "It is a female [animal], illusion, square, a bag, a skirt, yellow, silk, and sap."

[3] Zhen is thunder, the dragon, black and yellow, courage, spreading out, a great road, the eldest son, decisiveness and agitation, young green bamboo, sedges and reeds. Among horses, it is those with a good neigh, white rear legs, that use their feet [running], with white foreheads. Among crops, it is those that grow back. When it reaches its maximum strength it is luxuriant and fresh.[21]

Xun's Nine Masters has, "It is jade, the swan, the drum."

[4] Sun is wood, wind, the eldest daughter, the guideline, work, white, long, high, advancing and retreating, bearing no fruit, odor. Among people it is the balding, those with broad foreheads and much white in their eyes, those who are

familiar with profit and get threefold in the market. Reaching its maximum it becomes the trigram of agitation [Zhen].

Xun's Nine Masters has, "It is the willow, the crane."

[5] Kan is water, drains and ditches, lying hidden, straightening and bending, the bow and wheel. Among people it is the melancholy, the sick at heart, those with earache. It is the blood trigram, red. Among horses it is those with beautiful backs or strong hearts, those that keep their heads low, with thin hooves, that trail behind. Among carriages it is those with many defects. It is penetration, the moon, thieves. Among trees it is those that are hard with strong centers.

Xun's Nine Masters has, "It is the palace, the statute, permission, the ridgepole, a clump of brambles, the fox, medicinal and poisonous herbs, handcuffs and fetters."

[6] Li is fire, the sun, lightning, the middle daughter, armor and helmet, sword and battle-ax. Among people it is the big bellied. It is the trigram of dryness. It is the turtle, the crab, the snail, the clam, the tortoise. Among trees it is the hollow with withered tops.

Xun's Nine Masters has, "It is the female ox."

[7] Gen is the mountain, back roads, small stones, gates and doors, fruits of trees and vines, guards of the gate and the harem, fingers, dogs, rats, the category of black-billed [birds]. Among trees it is those that are hard with many joints.

Xun's Nine Masters has, "It is the nose, the tiger, the fox."

[8] Dui is the lake, the youngest daughter, the shaman, the mouth and tongue, smashing and breaking, cutting off an attachment. Among soils it is firm and salty. It is the concubine, the sheep.

Xun's Nine Masters has, "It is the constant, the cheeks and jaw."

This section expands upon the images of the Eight Trigrams. Much of it cannot be clearly understood, and if we check it with the Scripture it is not in full agreement.

CHAPTER FIVE

COMMENTARY ON ASSORTED HEXAGRAMS (ZAGUA ZHUAN 雜卦傳)

Qian [1, Creating] is firm, Kun [2, Complying] is yielding.

Bi [8, Being Close] is happy; Shi [7, Army] is sad.

The meaning of Lin [19, Approaching] and Guan [20, Observing] is that some provide and some seek.

To approach a thing for myself is called "providing." To observe myself from the standpoint of a thing is called "seeking." Someone said, These two hexagrams alternate the meanings of providing and seeking.

Zhun [3, Difficult Beginning] appears and does not lose its place; Meng [4, Dim] is mixed and conspicuous.

In Zhun, Zhen [Thunder] encounters Kan [Water]; Zhen acts and so is visible; Kan is dangerous and does not move. In Meng, Kan [Abyss] encounters Gen [Mountain]; Kan is dark and dim, and Gen is radiant and clear. Some say, "Zhun is spoken of first, Meng is spoken of second."

Zhen [51, Arousing] rises; Gen [52, Stilling] stops.

Sun [41, Diminishing] and Yi [42, Enhancing] are the beginning of waxing and waning.

Daxu [26, Restrained by the Greater] is timely; Wuwang [25, No Error] is disaster.

Occasionally it is time for limiting strength. Disaster can come from outside through no fault of one's own.

Cui [45, Gathering] brings together; Sheng [46, Advancing Upward] does not come.

Qian [15, Being Modest] treats lightly; Yu [16, Being Happy] is negligent.

Shihe [21, Biting Together] is eating; Bi [22, Adorning] is colorless.
White in color.

Dui [58, Pleasing] is visible; Sun [57, Entering] submits.
Dui is *yin* and is externally visible. Sun is *yin* and is internally submissive.

Sui [17, Following] has no reason; Gu [18, Working on What Is Ruined] leads to control.

Before following there is no reason. After working on what has been spoiled there should be control.

Bo [23, Declining] is breaking; Fu [24, Returning] is reversing.

Jin [35, Advancing] is midday; Mingyi [36, Wounding the Light] is eliminating.
"Eliminating" is wounding.

Jing [48, The Well] penetrating and Kun [47, Blocked] encounter each other.
The firm and yielding meet each other, and the firm's visibility is concealed.

Xian [31, Mutually Influencing] is quick; Heng [32, Everlasting] is long-lasting.
Xian is quick; constancy is long-lasting.

Huan [59, Dispersing] is separating; Jie [60, Limiting] is stopping.

Xie [40, Released] is loosening; Jian [39, Obstructed] is hard.

COMMENTARY ON ASSORTED HEXAGRAMS 315

Kui [38, Contrary] is external; Jiaren [37, Family Members] are internal.

Pi [12, Obstructing] and Tai [11, Penetrating] are opposite in kind.

Dazhuang [34, Flourishing of the Great] stops; Dun [33, Withdrawing] retreats.
  "Stops" means not retreating.

Dayou [14, Great Possession] is gathered; Tongren [13, Fellowship] is intimate.

Ge [49, Overturning] banishes the old; Ding [50, Cauldron] accepts the new.

Xiaoguo [62, Small Surpassing] is surpassing; Zhongfu [61, Inwardly Honest] is trustworthy.

Feng [55, Abundant] has many reasons; intimacy is rare when Traveling [56, Lü].
  Already bright and active, the reasons [for being plentiful] are many.

Li [30, Clinging] rises; Kan [29, Abysmal] sinks.
  Fire burns upward, water soaks downward.

Xiaochu [9, Restrained by the Lesser] is meager; Lü [10, Treading] is not stationary.
  "Not stationary" means moving forward.

Xu [5, Waiting] does not advance; Song [6, Disputing] is not close.

Daguo [28, Surpassing by the Great] is upside down; Gou [44, Encountering] is the yielding encountering the firm.

Jian [53, Gradually Advancing] is the betrothed woman waiting for the man to act; Yi [27, Jaws] nourishes correctness.

Jiji [63, Already Complete] is settled; Guimei [54, Betrothed Sister] is the end [purpose] of a woman.

Weiji [64, Not Yet Complete] is a man's fulfillment; Guai [43, Resolving] is deciding, the firm deciding [for] the yielding.

The Way of the superior person is long; the Way of the inferior person is troubling.

From Gou [44] onward the hexagrams are not in matched pairs. Some suspect that this was an errant bamboo slip. I think the style matches [what precedes], so it is probably not an error, but it is not clear what it means.

APPENDIX

DIVINATION RITUAL
(*SHIYI* 筮儀)

PRELIMINARIES

Most editions of the *Zhouyi benyi* include this set of instructions by Zhu Xi for the ritual of divination.[1] The method of manipulating the milfoil stalks in the ritual, derived from section A.9 of the *Xici*, is basically the same as that given in Zhu's *Yixue qimeng* 易學啟蒙 (Introduction to the study of the *Yi*, 1186), with two major differences in emphasis. First, the *Qimeng* contains much more discussion of the symbolism and numerology of the procedure, while the *Shiyi* mainly provides the mechanics of the setting and the formalities of the ritual. Second, only the *Qimeng* provides detailed instructions on obtaining the prognostication based on any changing lines (hexagram fluctuation).[2] Since this is an essential part of *Yijing* divination, the *Shiyi* refers the diviner to the *Qimeng* for it.

Zhu Xi re-created this procedure from the sketchy account given in *Xici* A.9.3, after making a lengthy study of methods used by previous scholars.[3] It is by no means certain that the method he settled upon actually goes back to the Zhou dynasty, but in any case it became the standard method that is still used today, although alternatives have been proposed.[4] He occasionally spoke about the simpler alternative method of tossing three coins six times, which dates to at least the Tang dynasty; but since it was not Fuxi's original method he disapproved of it.[5] Both the main text (in bold) and the comments here are by Zhu Xi.

FIGURE AP.1 *Achillea millefolium* (milfoil) From Franz Eugen Köhler (1883–1914), *Köhlers Medizinal-Pflanzen in naturgetreuen Abbildungen und kurz erläuterndem Texte*

FIGURE AP.2 Dried yarrow (milfoil) stalks Photo by Charlie Huang

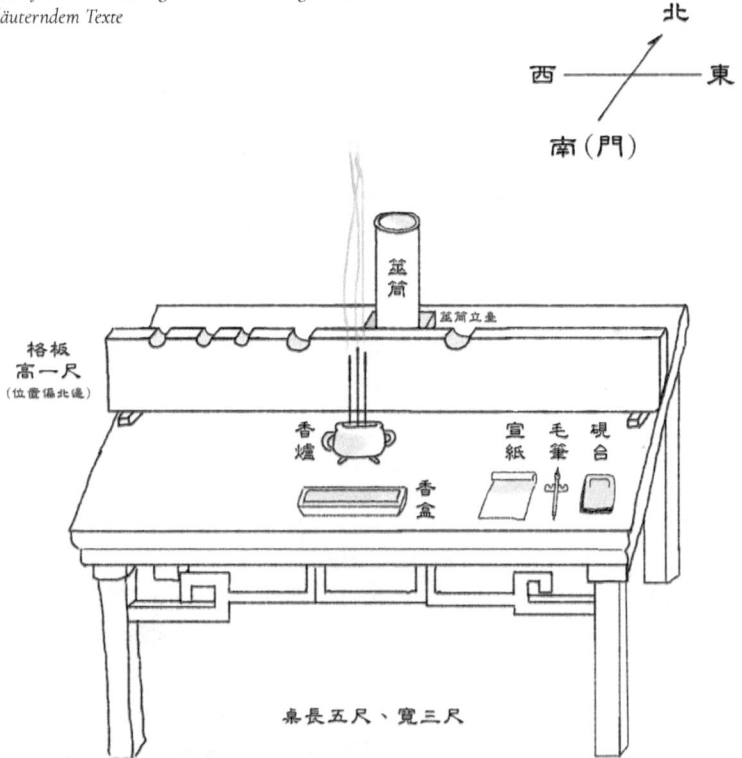

FIGURE AP.3 Drawing of the divination table described by Zhu Xi, by Amy Chang
Reprinted with permission from Kuo Ho-chieh 郭和杰, *Zhouyi guzhanfa* 周易古占筮法, 32

Select a clean place as the divination room, with a door facing south, and set out a table in the center of the room.

The table should be approximately five feet long and three feet wide, and not too close to the wall.

Take the fifty milfoil stalks, wrapped in scented silk inside a black pouch placed in a tube, and place them on the north side of the table.

Make the tube out of a bamboo cylinder, or hardwood, or lacquered cloth, three inches in diameter and as long as the milfoil. Make one end the base and one end the cover, with the lower part as the stand, supported so it won't fall down.

Set up a wooden panel to the south of the tube, sitting just north of the midline of the table.

The panel is a horizontal board, one foot high and as long as the table. Right in the center make two large notches, one foot apart. To the west of the large notches make three small notches, about five inches apart. Tilt the horizontal base downward and stand it on its edge on the table.

Place the incense burner to the south of the panel and the incense container to the south of the burner. Burn a stick of incense daily to convey reverence. When ready to divine, sprinkle and sweep [the floor] and wipe [the table]. Clean the inkstone and add water, then place a brush, ink, and a yellow lacquered board [to write on] to the east of the burner. Entering [the room] from the east, the diviner, with clean and adjusted clothes and cap, facing north, washes his hands and burns the incense to convey reverence.

For the diviner facing north, see the *Yili* 儀禮 [Etiquette and ritual].[6] If deputing someone else to divine, then after the subject has burned the incense he withdraws a little and stands facing north. The diviner advances and stands in front of the table a little to the west and faces south to receive the instructions. The subject directly states the subject of the divination, and the diviner assents. The subject moves to the right and stands facing west. The diviner moves to the right and stands facing north.

Raise the closed tube with two hands and place it to the south of the panel and the north of the burner. Remove the milfoil from the tube, remove the pouch and untie the cloth, and place them to the east of the tube. Gather the fifty stalks, and hold them in two hands in the smoke above the burner.

For a discussion of the number [symbolism] of the milfoil stalks that are used after this, see the *Qimeng* [chapter 3].

State the charge [*ming* 命]: "Prevailing upon you, supreme eternal milfoil, this official (name), now because of (the issue), does not know what is acceptable or not. I hereby question the spirits and numinous powers about what is auspicious or ominous, for success or failure, regret or disgrace, worry or concern. Only you have the spiritual power, so I beg that you clearly announce it." Then with the right hand take one stalk and put it back inside the tube. Divide the forty-nine stalks between the left and right hands, and place them into the two large notches on the left and right sides of the panel.[7]

This is the first operation; what is meant by "Divide into two to symbolize the Two [Modes]" [*Xici* A.9.3].

Next use the left hand to take and hold the stalks in the left large notch; use the right hand to take one stalk from the right large notch and insert it into the space next to the little finger.

This is the second operation; what is meant by "Insert one to symbolize the Three [Powers]."

Next, use the right hand to count off by fours the stalks in the left hand.

This is [the first] half of the third operation; what is meant by "Count off by fours to symbolize the Four Seasons" [*Xici* A.9.3].

Next, return the remaining stalks, which may be one, two, three, or four, to the space next to the unnamed finger of the left hand.[8]

This is [the first] half of the fourth operation; what is meant by "Return the remainder between the fingers to represent the intercalary month."[9]

Next, use the right hand to put back the stalks already counted off back into the left large notch.[10] Then take and hold the stalks in the right large notch, and using the left hand count them off by fours.

This is [the second] half of the third operation.[11]

Next, return the remaining stalks as before to the space next to the middle finger of the left hand.

This is [the second] half of the fourth operation; what is meant by "Place again to symbolize the second intercalary month" [*Xici* A.9.3, paraphrased]. Of the remaining stalks of the first change, if the left is one the right must be three; if the left is two the right is also two; if the left is three the right must be one; if the left is four the right is also four. Along with the one stalk inserted [second operation] there must be either five or nine. Five contains a single four and so is odd; nine contains two fours and so is even; odd is 3 and even is 2.[12]

Next, use the right hand to put back the stalks already counted off into the right large notch. Combine the single stalk inserted [second operation] in the left hand with the stalks placed in the two spaces [fourth] and place them on the divining board in the first small notch.

[First notch] from the east; same for the following.

This is the first change [*bian* 變]. Again with both hands take the stalks from the left and right large notches and combine them.

There will be either forty-four or forty stalks.

Repeat the four operations as in the procedure for the first change. Place the stalks inserted [second operation] and those placed between the fingers [fourth] into the second small notch on the divining board. This is the second change.

Of the stalks remaining from the second change [fourth operation], if the left is one then the right must be two; if the left is two then the right must be one; if the left is three then the right must be four; if the left is four then the right must be three. Together with the single stalk inserted [second], there will be either four or eight. Four contains one four and so is odd; eight contains two fours and so is even. Odd and even each have two possible arrangements of four.

Again combine the stalks in the left and right large notches.

There will be either forty or thirty-six or thirty-two.

Repeat the four operations as in the procedure for the second change. Place the stalks inserted and those placed between the fingers into the third small notch on the divining board. This is the third change.

The stalks remaining from the third change will be the same as for the second change.

When the three changes are completed, observe the stalks that were inserted and those already counted off in the spaces resulting from the three changes, and draw the line on the [writing] board.

Of the numbers inserted and placed between the fingers, 5 and 4 are odd; 9 and 8 are even. If three odds are inserted and placed, totaling thirteen stalks, then the thirty-six stalks counted off are "mature *yang*," represented as □, meaning "double." If those hanging and placed are two odds and one even, totaling seventeen stalks, then the thirty-two stalks counted off are "young *yin*," represented as --, meaning "broken." If those hanging and placed are two evens and one odd, totaling twenty-one stalks, then the twenty-eight stalks counted off are "young *yang*," represented as —, meaning "single." If those hanging and placed are three evens, totaling twenty-five stalks, then the twenty-four stalks counted off are "mature *yang*," represented as X, meaning "interacting."[13]

Thus every three changes make one line.

The first, fourth, seventh, tenth, thirteenth, and sixteenth changes [i.e., the first change of each line] are all the same. But from the third operation onward one doesn't give the charge, and only forty-nine stalks are used [i.e., the first stalk is removed from the bundle of fifty only once]. The second, fifth, eighth, eleventh, fourteenth, and seventeenth changes [second of each line] are also the same. The third, sixth, ninth, twelfth, fifteenth, and eighteenth changes are also the same.

Eighteen changes make a hexagram. Now one examines the hexagram fluctuation [i.e., any changing lines] and divines whether the matter is auspicious or ominous.

For diagrams and explanations of the hexagram fluctuations, see the *Qimeng* [chapter 4].

When the ritual is completed, wrap the milfoil in the cloth, place it back in the tube, and put on the cover. Put away the brush, inkstone, ink, and writing board. Burn incense again to convey reverence, and leave.

If someone else has been deputed to divine, then the subject burns the incense, bows to the diviner, and leaves.

NOTES

INTRODUCTION

1. They are more correctly called scriptures because they are regarded as sacred texts (see Wilfred Cantwell Smith, *What Is Scripture?*). The basic meaning of the word *jing* 經 is the "warp," or vertical, threads of a woven fabric on a loom—hence its backbone or basis, and by extension a fundamental ordering principle. The sacred connotation of *jing* is illustrated by the fact that it was chosen to translate the Sanskrit word *sūtra* (the sermons of the Buddha) when Buddhist scriptures were translated into Chinese in the first century CE, as well as "bible" for the Christian Holy Bible (*sheng jing* 聖經) much later (see Peng Guoxiang, "Spiritual and Bodily Exercise," 332-33). However, because of the familiarity of terms like "Five (or Thirteen) Classics" I use those terms.
2. Although the earliest written material is attributed to King Wen and the Duke of Zhou in the eleventh century BCE, contemporary scholarship suggests the ninth century BCE (e.g., Lisa Raphals, *Divination and Prediction in Early China and Ancient Greece*, 32). Parts of the *Shujing* 書經 (Scripture of documents) and *Shijing* 詩經 (Scripture of odes) are older than that, but the hexagrams of the *Yi* are older still, possibly dating to the time of King Wen. See Zhang Zhenglang, "An Interpretation of the Divinatory Inscriptions on Early Chou Bronzes," 92, and Richard Rutt, *The Book of Changes*, 97-100.
3. For discussions of the *Yijing*'s most important terms and concepts, see pp. 21-35.
4. The first type (inference by rules) is often called inductive divination; the second is simply called intuitive divination (see, e.g., George K. Park, "Divination"). In practice many methods of divination combine both types. I discuss these methods more fully, focusing on their epistemological dimensions, in my 1984 dissertation, "Divination and Philosophy," chap. 1. *Yijing* divination is an example of the former type.
5. Lisa Raphals points out that some scholars define divination more broadly—e.g., to include the interpretation of "spontaneous natural phenomena that are visible to all," such as eclipses. Her definition is "activities seeking to find the meaning of hidden phenomena, objects or events in the past, present, or future" (*Divination and Prediction in*

Early China and Ancient Greece, 1–2). Whether defined broadly or narrowly, divination (like prophecy) is not limited to the prediction of the future, although it may include that.

6. See, e.g., Michel Strickmann, *Chinese Poetry and Prophecy*, and Richard J. Smith, *Fortune-Tellers and Philosophers*.

7. For a concise description of Shang oracle bone divination, see Stephen L. Field, *Ancient Chinese Divination*, 25–31. For a more detailed exposition, see David N. Keightley, *Sources of Shang History*. For my earlier discussion of theories and typologies of divination, see Adler, "Divination and Philosophy," chap. 1.

8. See Field, *Ancient Chinese Divination*, 31–38. Both texts survived only in much later quoted fragments until 1993, when a partial version of the *Guicang* written on bamboo slips was excavated. For a translation of it, see Edward L. Shaughnessy, *Unearthing the Changes*, chap. 4.

9. In addition to the "inner" and "outer" trigrams, lines 2, 3, and 4 and lines 3, 4, and 5 are called the interlocking trigrams (*huti* 互體), or nuclear trigrams (Bent Nielsen, *A Companion to Yi Jing Numerology and Cosmology*, 111). Zhu Xi makes very little use of this schema in his commentary.

10. According to the *Lüshi chunqiu* 呂氏春秋 (Springs and autumns of Mister Lü), the milfoil stalks themselves were invented by Wu Xian 巫咸 (Shaman Wu) of the Shang dynasty (John Knoblock and Jeffrey Riegel, *The Annals of Lü Buwei*, 420). For a concise entry on Fuxi, see Ulrich Theobald, "Fu Xi 伏羲," http://www.chinaknowledge.de/History/Myth/personsfuxi.html.

11. See his first comment under hexagram 1, Qian. The earliest known claim that Fuxi created the sixty-four hexagrams is found in the second-century-BCE *Huainanzi* 淮南子 (Masters of Huainan), chap. 21 (*Yaolüe* 要略), 22. Sima Qian 司馬遷, in his *Historical Records* (*Shiji* 史記) a few decades later, said that King Wen "probably" (*gai* 蓋) doubled the trigrams into hexagrams (chap. 4 ["Zhou benji" 周本記], 11). Zheng Xuan 鄭玄 in the second century CE said that another mythic culture hero, Shennong 神農 ("Divine Farmer"), doubled the trigrams, and Sun Sheng 孫盛 in the fourth century said the same of Yu 禹 the Great, founder of the probably mythical Xia 夏 dynasty (Kong Yingda, *Zhouyi zhengyi*, preface, 4a).

In the seventh century, Kong Yingda 孔穎達, the editor of the orthodox Tang dynasty version of the *Yi* based on Wang Bi's commentary, said that Wang, following Sima Qian's conjecture, believed that Fuxi created the sixty-four hexagrams, and Kong Yingda agrees with him (*Zhouyi zhengyi*, 4a–5a). Kong may be right about Wang Bi, and Richard Lynn apparently agrees with him (*Classic of Changes*, 4), but there is no explicit evidence of this in Wang Bi's commentary, including his introductory essay, the *Zhouyi lüeli* 周易略例. Cheng Yi apparently believed that Fuxi created only the Eight Trigrams: "The Way of the Sages [Fuxi and Yu], for example the River Chart and Luo Writing, at the beginning was limited to deriving meaning from the drawings. When *later people* doubled the trigrams and appended texts, they sought but did not necessarily get the principle" (*Henan Chengshi yishu*, 15 [*Er Cheng ji*, 157], emphasis mine). As for the hexagram names, Zhu Xi says it is not possible to know who added them (*Zhuzi yulei* 65: 1619).

Most modern scholars think that the hexagrams probably came first and were later analyzed into two component trigrams (Rutt, *Book of Changes*, 97–98). For a detailed modern study concluding that the sixty-four hexagrams go back to the Shang dynasty (predating King Wen), see Zhang Yachu and Liu Yu, "Some Observations about Milfoil Divination." See also Bent Nielsen, "Notes on the Origins of the Hexagrams of the *Book of Change*."

12. E.g., Rutt, *Book of Changes*, 118; Redmond, *I Ching*, 44.
13. For a theory of this two-part division, see Edward A. Hacker and Steve Moore, "A Brief Note on the Two-Part Division of the Received Order of the Hexagrams of the *Zhouyi*." See also Denis Mair, "Contrasts Between the Upper and Lower Parts of the Zhouyi." For an original perspective on the received hexagram sequence, see Scott Davis, *The Classic of Changes in Cultural Context*, chap. 4. The "received" sequence is the version embedded in the commentary of Wang Bi 王弼 (226-249), which was the "orthodox" version and commentary until the time of Zhu Xi. A hitherto unknown version, with a different sequence of hexagrams, was discovered in 1973 in a Chinese tomb at Mawangdui (Hunan province). The occupant of the tomb died in 168 BCE and the text is tentatively dated to about 190 BCE, thus predating Wang Bi's version by several hundred years (see Edward L. Shaughnessy, *I Ching*, 14-15). However, according to Shaughnessy, the "received" sequence of hexagrams (sometimes called the King Wen sequence) seems to predate the Mawangdui sequence (17-18).
14. See Kidder Smith, "*Zhouyi* Interpretation from Accounts in the *Zuozhuan*." "Confucian" is the customary translation of *ru* 儒, which means something like "scholar" and originally referred to experts on the rituals and arts that were central to the followers of Confucius.
15. See Adler, *Reconstructing the Confucian Dao*, chap. 2.
16. Ouyang's main argument was that several sections of the *Xici* quote an unnamed Master who must be Confucius (*Zi yue* 子曰, "The Master said"), so Confucius could not have written it. See Zhu's comment on *Xici* A.7.1.
17. Raphals, *Divination and Prediction*, 33.
18. See Lynn, *Classic of Changes*, 3.
19. Rutt, *Book of Changes*, 384.
20. For the brief textual note, see chap. 1, n. 166.
21. Gu Jiegang 顧頡剛, *Gushibian* 古史辨; Edward Shaughnessy, "The Composition of the *Zhouyi*"; Richard Kunst, "The Original Yijing." Two more recent translations in this vein are Minford, *I Ching*, part 2, and Redmond, *I Ching*.
22. E.g., those of James Legge (*The Yi King, or Book of Changes*), Richard Wilhelm (*The I Ching, or Book of Changes*), and Lynn (*Classic of Changes*). Legge and Wilhelm based their translations on the Song-dynasty commentaries of Cheng Yi and Zhu Xi, while Lynn based his on that of Wang Bi. Needless to say, all premodern commentators, as well as the translators Legge and Wilhelm, were invested in continuing the Confucian assumptions and interpretations, and in fact were unaware of any other option.
23. See Michael Nylan, *The Five "Confucian" Classics*, 35. There may also have been a *Scripture of Music*, which was either lost or incorporated into the *Liji*. Two other ritual texts, the *Yili* 儀禮 (Etiquette and ritual) and the *Zhouli* 周禮 (Rituals of Zhou), were often grouped together with the *Liji*.
24. This question has an interesting parallel in the history of early Christianity: which is more significant, Jesus's moral teachings or his death and resurrection? For some of his earliest followers it was his moral teachings, which were essentially Jewish (with some important innovations). After Paul, however, Jesus's death and resurrection came to define what it meant to be a Christian, resulting in Christianity breaking off as a new religious movement.
25. E.g., the *Hetu* 河圖 ([Yellow] River chart) and *Luoshu* 落書 (Luo [River] writing), the first two of the "Nine Diagrams." This approach had similarities to the "New Text" (*jinwen* 近文) approach to the classics in general, which also flourished in the Han.

26. See the entries for all of them in Nielsen, *Companion*.
27. Wang Bi and Han Kangbo, *Zhouyi Wang-Han zhu*. Wang did not comment upon the *Xici*, so this edition includes Han Kangbo's 韓康伯 (332-380) commentary on that appendix. Richard Lynn has translated the entire commentary in *The Classic of Changes*.
28. Daoism as a full-fledged religion was new, but it drew in part upon older texts, such as the *Laozi* (or *Daodejing*) and the *Zhuangzi*, both of which predated the Han by a century or two. See, e.g., Adler, *Chinese Religious Traditions*, chap. 3.
29. This is obviously only a thumbnail sketch. For the Chan school of Buddhism, see Peter N. Gregory and Daniel A. Getz Jr., *Buddhism in the Sung*. The Daoist religion also flourished in the Song (see, e.g., Isabelle Robinet, *Taoism*, chap. 8).
30. Nylan, *Five "Confucian" Classics*, 56-57.
31. Cheng Yi, *Yichuan Yizhuan* 伊川易傳 (Yichuan's commentary on the *Yi*); Zhou Dunyi, *Taijitu shuo* 太極圖說 (Discussion of the Supreme Polarity diagram) and *Tongshu* 通書 (Penetrating the *Yi*); Zhu Xi, *Yixue qimeng* 易學啟蒙 (Introduction to the study of the *Yi*).
32. See especially chap. 66 of the *Zhuzi yulei*.
33. *Hui'an xiansheng Zhu wengong wenji*, 31:1350. Dated by Qian Mu, *Zhuzi xin xue'an*, 4:28, and Chen Lai, *Zhuzi shuxin biannian kaozheng*, 130.
34. By "myth" I mean a sacred story symbolizing some fundamental value or belief of a particular social group. A myth may or may not have a historical basis.
35. These parenthetical remarks are all by Zhu Xi.
36. *Xici* B.2 tells how the ancient Sages—Fuxi, Shennong, the Yellow Emperor, Yao, and Shun—invented various cultural implements and customs on the basis of thirteen hexagrams.
37. *Zhuzi quanshu* (Zhu Xi's "complete works"), 27:12a. "Self-cultivation" (*xiushen* 修身) and "ordering the state" (*zhiguo* 治國) are two of the eight stages of the *Great Learning* (*Daxue* 大學). See Wing-tsit Chan, *A Source Book in Chinese Philosophy*, 86-87.
38. Wang and Han, *Zhouyi Wang-Han zhu*, 2:4b.
39. These are the first two of the Four Virtues of Qian (1), as interpreted by Cheng Yi. Zhu Xi's interpretation is somewhat different.
40. *Xunjie* 訓戒, in this case "[Be] correct" and "[be a] strong man."
41. *Er Cheng ji*, 768.
42. *Zhouyi benyi* 1:33a (*Zhuzi quanshu* [2002], 1:44).
43. See the last paragraph of "Preliminaries" in chap. 1.
44. *Zhuzi yulei* 66:1625. On the contrast with Cheng Yi regarding this point see Tze-ki Hon, "Classical Exegesis and Social Change," 5.
45. These sections are later additions to the *Xici* text.
46. For a full exposition of the place of the *Yi* in Zhu Xi's thought, see Kidder Smith et al., *Sung Dynasty Uses of the I Ching*, chaps. 6-7. Regarding terminology, it should be mentioned that the locus classicus of the term *taiji* 太極 (Supreme Polarity)—the linchpin of Zhu Xi's cosmology and metaphysics—was the *Xici*, although Zhu Xi adopted it more directly from Zhou Dunyi. See Adler, *Reconstructing*.
47. See T'ang Yung-t'ung, "Wang Pi's New Interpretation of the *I-ching* and *Lun-yü*," 135. Wang may not have been the first to collate the Wings with the hexagrams (135-37).
48. Chan, *Source Book*, 321.
49. Quoting *Zhuangzi*, chap. 26 (Victor H. Mair, *Wandering on the Way*, 266-67). *Zhouyi lueli* 周易略例 (General remarks on the *Zhouyi*), in *Zhouyi Wang-Han zhu*, 10:3a, 9a; trans. Lynn, *Classic of Changes*, 26, 31.

50. *Zhouyi lueli*, 10:9b (my trans.). Horse and cow are images of Qian and Kun in *Shuogua* 8. "Artificial theories" alludes to the Han *xiangshu* experts.
51. See A. A. Petrov, *Wang Pi (226–249): His Place in the History of Chinese Philosophy*, reviewed by Arthur F. Wright in *Harvard Journal of Asiatic Studies* 10 (1947): 75–88.
52. See Tze-ki Hon, *The Yijing and Chinese Politics*, 121–23. Cheng Yi and his brother, Cheng Hao, were primarily responsible for establishing *li* as the key concept in Song Confucianism. See A. C. Graham, *Two Chinese Philosophers*.
53. Smith et al., *Sung Dynasty Uses of the I Ching*, 159.
54. In this he was following the example of his friend Lü Zuqian 呂祖謙 (1137-1181), who had gone back to the original order in his *Gu Zhouyi* 古周易 (The ancient *Zhouyi*). According to Shao Yong's second son, Shao Bo 邵博, Shao Yong had also used this "ancient *Yi*" order (Chu Ping-tzu, "The Transmission of Shao Yong's *Yi* Learning before Zhu Xi," 244).
55. Wang Mouhong, *Zhuzi nianpu*, 280n3.
56. For some reason all the collated editions I have seen arrange hexagram 1 (Qian) differently from every other hexagram. Their arrangement of Qian is as follows: hexagram statement, line statements, *Tuan*, *Daxiang*, *Xiaoxiang*, *Wenyan*—the same as Zhu Xi's original arrangement. I have retained this exception here.
57. Legge, *Yi King*; Wilhelm, *I Ching*; Lynn, *Classic of Changes*; Rutt, *Book of Changes*; Shaughnessy, *I Ching*; Redmond, *I Ching*.
58. This is an example of what Roger Ames and David Hall have called aesthetic order—the idea that meaning in Chinese thought emerges from the shifting patterns of exigent circumstances; meaning is not imposed on those circumstances by correspondence with a transcendent principle, which they call rational order. See Hall and Ames, *Thinking Through Confucius*, 11–25, 131–38. For references to discussions of modern literary theory on the issues of intentionality, meaning, etc., see Smith et al., *Sung Dynasty Uses of the I Ching*, chap. 6, nn. 32, 46.
59. Redmond, *I Ching*, 6. A few pages later Redmond adds the qualification, "I suspect that a few phrases were not understandable even 3,000 years ago" (12). For a good example of Zhu Xi's willingness to let the text speak for itself even when it is unclear or corrupt, see, in chap. 1, hexagram 19 (Lin), the Smaller Image commentary on line 2 (p. 129) and n. 219.
60. Curie Virág, "Self-Cultivation as *Praxis* in Song Neo-Confucianism," 1221. See also Daniel Gardner's "Transmitting the Way" and "Confucian Commentary and Chinese Intellectual History" (esp. 406); Peng Guoxiang, "Spiritual and Bodily Exercise"; Zhu Xi, "Dushu fa" 讀書法 (Methodology of reading), in *Zhuzi yulei*, chaps. 10–11; Zhu Xi, "Dushuzhi yao" 讀書之要 (Essentials of reading), in *Hui'an xiansheng Zhu wengong wenji*, 74:3582–84.
61. Richard Rutt identifies four elements in hexagram statements, not all of which appear in every hexagram. They are an "oracle," which may include a literary image or something like a proverb; an "indication," or injunction; the prognostication; and an "observation," which may be a verification (*Book of Changes*, 132–34). Stephen Field reduces these to three: "omen," "counsel," and "fortune" (*The Duke of Zhou Changes*, 60).
62. Lianbin Dai, "From Philology to Philosophy," 159.
63. These are the conclusions of Shu Jingnan, in *Zhu Xi nianpu changbian* (Chronological record of Zhu Xi, extended edition), 1:594, 2:911. In earlier writings I have used the prior consensus view of 1177 as the date of the *Zhouyi benyi*. See Adler, "Divination and Philosophy," appendix A.

64. Nielsen, *Companion*, 342. A Song-dynasty edition, containing the 1265 preface by Wu Ge, has been reprinted as Song Yiming, ed., *Songkan Zhouyi benyi*.
65. Ames, "*Great Commentary*," 1.
66. E.g., on Wikipedia it is part of the "Taoism Portal" (https://en.wikipedia.org/wiki/I_Ching). Various works and diagrams based on the *Yijing* are, however, found in the Daoist Canon, making it the only book found in both the Confucian and Daoist canons.
67. On these three "competing visions of the Dao" see Adler, *Reconstructing*, 17-27. For further elaboration of Fuxi's significance to Zhu Xi, see 45-48.
68. See Gerald Swanson, "The Great Treatise," 63-79; Rutt, *Book of Changes*, 406-7.
69. "With fluctuation there is continuity" (*Xici* B.2.5). Cf. Roger Ames, *Confucian Role Ethics*, 24, 51, 53-54, and Roger Ames, "The *Great Commentary* (*Dazhuan* 大傳) and Chinese Natural Cosmology," 5. See also Zhu Xi's comments on *Xici* A.1.1, A.2.1, and A.5.5. Occasionally I translate *bian* simply as "change."
70. *Er Cheng ji*, 819; also 366.
71. *Er Cheng ji*, 148, 149.
72. See Adler, "The Great Virtue of Heaven and Earth."
73. Three of the many articles on time in the *Yijing* are Hellmut Wilhelm, "The Concept of Time in the Book of Changes"; Li-chen Lin, "The Concepts of Time and Position in the *Book of Change* and Their Development"; and Zheng Wangeng, "Tracing the Source of the Idea of Time in *Yizhuan*."
74. *Zhuangzi*, chap. 19 (Mair, *Wandering on the Way*, 182). In general the idea is to swim with the current, not against it, and not "doing nothing." See also Edward G. Slingerland, *Effortless Action*, which discusses both Confucian and Daoist thought.
75. The idea of changing lines may have originated in the Han dynasty or later (see Richard J. Smith, *Fathoming the Cosmos and Ordering the World*, 27-28, and references to Shaughnessy, Rutt, and Kidder Smith there; see also Nielsen, *Companion*, 20-22). Zhu Xi, however, definitely used the method of changing lines. In his *Yixue qimeng*, chap. 4 (Adler, trans., *Introduction to the Study of the Classic of Change*, 50-52), he explains how the number of changing lines determines which part of the text of the original and derived hexagram is read for the prognostication.
76. For discussions of *xiang*, see Hellmut Wilhelm, *Heaven, Earth, and Man in the Book of Changes*, 32-35, 190-221; Swanson, "Great Treatise," 148-63, 313-15; and Smith, *Fathoming the Cosmos*, 39-40. See also Zhu Xi's essay "Yixiang shuo" (Discussion of the images of the Yi), in *Hui'an xiansheng Zhu wengong wenji*, 67:3255-56.
77. See Nielsen, "Notes on the Origins;" Rutt, *Book of Changes*, 98-100; and Zhang Zhenglang, "Interpretation of the Divinatory Inscriptions." For Zhu's comments on number, both in general and in the *Yi*, see *Zhuzi yulei* 65:1608-10.
78. On one level this is really equivalent to the Huayan Buddhist use of the word, except that for the Confucians the ordering principle is not emptiness (or interdependence), it is *yin-yang* bipolarity, or *taiji* 太極 (Supreme Polarity). See Adler, *Reconstructing*, chap. 4.
79. For the Cheng brothers' views of *li* and *qi*, see Graham, *Two Chinese Philosophers*, chaps. 1 and 3.
80. Roger Ames goes a bit further in saying that human nature, according to Mencius, is the process itself of becoming good ("Mencius and a Process Notion of Human Nature").
81. Zhang Zai, *Zhangzi quanshu*, 12:3a.

INTRODUCTION 329

82. "Coherence" was suggested by Willard Peterson in "Another Look at Li." For other discussions of translating li, see A. C. Graham, "What Was New in the Ch'eng-Chu Theory of Human Nature?" and Kirill O. Thompson, "Li and Yi as Immanent." For a stimulating proposal regarding the translation of the closely related word tian 天, for which I use "Heaven," see Stephen C. Angle, "Tian as Cosmos in Zhu Xi's Neo-Confucianism."
83. Zhu Xi quotes it in his comment on Mencius 1B.7.
84. See my discussion of ming in Adler, "Chance and Necessity in Zhu Xi's Conceptions of Heaven and Tradition."
85. See Wenyan 3, and Zhu Xi's comment on the hexagram statement of Sui (17). For the dating of the Zuozhuan see Nylan, The Five "Confucian" Classics, 259.
86. Rutt, Book of Changes, 126-28, 224; Kunst, "Original Yijing," 183, 201-2, 241; Edward L. Shaughnessy, "The Composition of 'Qian' and 'Kun' Hexagrams of the Zhouyi," 198; Redmond, I Ching, 73; Legge, Yi King, 57; Shchutskii, Researches on the I Ching, 202; Lynn, Classic of Changes, 129; Wilhelm, I Ching, 4. For a compilation of various correlations with the Four Virtues, see Nielsen, Companion, 39.
87. For a short discussion of its use on Shang oracle bones, see Keightley, Sources of Shang History, 29n7 (Keightley uses the alternative pronunciation zheng). In Zhu Xi's divination instructions (see appendix) he uses the equivalent term ming 命 (command) for the charge.
88. See Nielsen, Companion, 295.
89. Occasionally I translate zhong as "the Mean."
90. Chan, Source Book, 98, substituting "centrality" for "equilibrium" and "expressed" for "aroused." For a full discussion, see Adler, Reconstructing, chap. 3.
91. Nielsen, Companion, 85-92; Wilhelm, I Ching, 364-65; Li Guangdi, comp., Zhouyi zhezhong, 107-21 (reproduced in Nielsen, Companion, along with that of Wu Deng 吳澄 [1249-1333]).
92. Zhu Xi, Yixue qimeng, 1224; Adler, Introduction, 16. See also Georges Rey, "The Analytic/Synthetic Distinction."
93. Fabrizio Pregadio, trans., Cultivating the Tao, 3; Anne D. Birdwhistell, Transition to Neo-Confucianism, 88; Hon, "Classical Exegesis," 6-7.
94. Quoting Cheng Yi's comment on this line (Er Cheng ji, 819).
95. Paraphrasing Zhou Dunyi's Taijitu shuo ("At the maximum of stillness it returns to activity").
96. See Adler, Reconstructing, chap. 3.
97. Adler, Chinese Religious Traditions, 107.
98. Hui'an xiansheng Zhu wengong wenji, 67:3279; Mencius 2A.6 and 6A.6. Zhu Xi also makes these correlations in his comment on Wenyan, Qian, 1.
99. Chan, Source Book, 108.
100. Quoted by Yu Yan (b. ca. 1253), a Daoist follower of Shao Yong and Zhu Xi, in his Yiwai biezhuan (Special transmission outside the Yi), source unverified (the style is definitely Shao's). Cited in Douglass Alan White, "Interpretations of the Central Concept of the I-Ching during the Han, Sung, and Ming Dynasties," 127.
101. The Mawangdui version of the Yi (see n. 13) does have a systematic sequence of hexagrams (see Shaughnessy, I Ching, 17-18; Rutt, Book of Changes, 102-18). For a theory that the received sequence of pairs is not random, see Davis, Classic of Change, chap. 4.
102. They are included in the collated editions but not in those in the original arrangement.

1. PART A: HEXAGRAMS 1-30

1. My source text is *Zhouyi benyi*, in *Zhuzi quanshu* 朱子全書 (Zhu Xi's complete works), ed. Zhu Jieren, Yan Zuozhi, and Liu Yongxiang, vol. 1. I have also consulted *Zhouyi benyi* 周易本義, ed. Tanaka Keitarō 田中慶太郎, Imperial Academy 國子監 edition; Li Guangdi, comp., *Zhouyi zhezhong* 周易折中 (The *Zhouyi* judged evenly); and the two versions contained in the *Siku quanshu* 四庫全書 collection (one in Zhu Xi's original arrangement and one rearranged). The Nine Diagrams are reproduced from the Imperial Academy edition.

2. Shu compiled this newest *nianpu* 年譜 (yearly chronicle) of Zhu Xi from primary sources, not relying on earlier chronicles, such as Wang Mouhong's 王懋竑 previously standard *Zhuzi nianpu* of 1706. Shu has also written a lengthy biography of Zhu Xi (*Zhuzi dazhuan* 朱子大传, 2003).

3. See Shu Jingnan, *Zhu Xi nianpu changbian*, 2:837, 871, 886, 911.

4. See Adler, *Reconstructing the Confucian Dao*. The "theme" of this period in Zhu Xi's life is the justification for the frequent references to *Reconstructing* in these notes.

5. Wang Tingzhen 王霆震, *Guwen jicheng* 古文集成 (*Siku quanshu* ed., 5:3a-4b); Tan Shanxin 譚善心, comp., *Er Cheng wenji* 二程文集 (*Er Cheng ji*, 667-68, 689-91). Interestingly, Wang Tingzhen's version of the preface contains twenty additional characters in the first sentence, saying that Fuxi drew only the trigrams and King Wen doubled them. This contradicts Zhu Xi's clear statement that Fuxi drew the hexagrams (in the first sentence of his comment on the first hexagram, Qian). Otherwise it is the same preface found in the Imperial Academy and other collated editions—i.e., the one identified by Shu Jingnan and translated here. The fact that the title of Zhu Xi's first commentary (*Yizhuan* 易傳) was the same as that of Cheng Yi's commentary might have contributed to the confusion. Of course the contradiction could also mean that the preface was actually written by Cheng Yi. But then why would he have written two prefaces? The internal evidence of the preface itself (see n. 18) strongly suggests that it was written by Zhu Xi. The twenty extra characters in Wang Tingzhen's edition were probably added by someone (perhaps Wang), mistakenly thinking it was written by Cheng Yi, because Cheng Yi did believe that Fuxi created only the eight trigrams (see introduction, n. 11).

6. Shu, *Zhu Xi nianpu changbian*, 1:596-97. For Xiong Jie, see Wing-tsit Chan, *Zhuzi menren*, 289. For his text, see *juan* 5, 93-95, at http://ourartnet.com/Siku/Zibu/0709/0709_015_068.htm.

7. Wang Mouhong, *Zhuzi nianpu*, 281; Zhu Jieren et al., *Zhuzi quanshu*, 1:7.

8. See Adler, trans., *Introduction to the Study of the Classic of Change*, chap. 1.

9. E.g., compare it with this statement by Zhu Xi (quoted in the introduction): "People reading the *Yi* today should divide it into three levels: Fuxi's *Yi*, King Wen's *Yi*, and Confucius's *Yi*. If one reads Fuxi's *Yi* as if there were no *Tuan*, *Xiang*, and *Wenyan* discussions, then one will be able to see that the original intention of the *Yi* was to create the practice of divination" (*Zhuzi yulei* 66:1629).

10. Here Zhu Xi uses *tuan* to mean the hexagram statements, which are also referred to as *tuanci* 彖辭 (judgment statements) and *guaci* 卦辭 (hexagram statements). This usage is to be distinguished from the Commentary on the Judgments (*Tuanzhuan* 彖傳), which is also simply referred to as *Tuan* (see Bent Nielsen, *A Companion to Yi Jing Numerology and Cosmology*, 238-39).

11. Paraphrasing *Xici* A.11.1, which asks and answers the question, "What does the *Yi* do?" By "disclosing things," Zhu Xi means that Fuxi revealed their ultimate natures or principles; "completing efforts" means that he enabled people's undertakings to be successful. For *xiantian* and *houtian*, see "Key Terms and Concepts" in the introduction.
12. For the significance of "number," see "Key Terms and Concepts" in the introduction.
13. *Xici* A.11.5.
14. Paraphrasing Zhou Dunyi's *Taijitu shuo* ("*Yin* and *yang* are the unitary Supreme Polarity; the Supreme Polarity is fundamentally nonpolar"). For Zhu Xi this is an important statement of the principle that unity and multiplicity are metaphysically interpenetrating concepts (see Adler, *Reconstructing*, 102-6).
15. Paraphrasing Zhou Dunyi's *Taijitu shuo* ("Once formed, they are born; when spirit is manifested, they have intelligence").
16. When the context calls for nouns, I translate *ji xiong* as "good fortune and bad fortune." The "Great Undertaking" (*da ye* 大業), or "Great Work," begins with the ruler's responsibility to carry out the Decree of Heaven and flows down to the individual's task of actualizing his/her innate moral potential and spreading virtue throughout the world. The word *ye* occurs only in the *Wenyan* and *Xici*.
17. Zhu Xi elsewhere discusses the subtle point between stillness and activity as "incipience" (*ji* 幾). See Smith et al., *Sung Dynasty Uses of the I Ching*, 190-99.
18. "Moments" or "times" (*shi* 時) here refers to the quality of the time symbolized by the hexagram (see "Key Terms and Concepts" in the introduction). "Situations" (*shi* 事) are the more specific characteristics symbolized by the lines. Zhu Xi's point is that times and situations have no clear beginnings and ends; they flow continuously into each other. In further explanation of the idea of a "single situation," in 1182 Zhu wrote a colophon to Lü Zuqian's *Gu Zhouyi* 古周易, in which he says,

> Confucius wrote the appendixes, "lifting one corner to show the whole outline" [paraphrasing *Analects* 7.8]. But after various scholars [e.g., Wang Bi] divided up the Scripture with the appendixes, students relied on these texts in choosing their interpretations. Eventually they could no longer grasp in their minds the whole Scripture, and hastily seized upon the "one corner" of the appendixes as the correct explanation. In this way each line of each hexagram refers merely to a single situation [*yishi* 一事], and the use of the *Yi* incorrectly becomes limited, lacking the means to "penetrate [*tong* 通] all circumstances under Heaven" [*Xici* A.10.4]. This being the case, I am uneasy with it. (*Hui'an xiansheng Zhu wengong wenji*, 82:3889-90)

The similarity between this quote and the sentence in the preface is further evidence that the preface was written by Zhu Xi. The idea is that explaining each hexagram and line in detail and in reference to specific situations (as both Wang Bi and Cheng Yi did in most cases) precludes the reader's subjective engagement with the text and the access to the "mind of the Sage" it affords (see "Interpretive Approaches to the *Yi*" in the introduction). An anonymous reader has suggested that *shi* here refers to the general notion of time (having no beginning or end, etc.), but I think it more likely that Zhu's point is the specificity and uniqueness of particular moments.

19. Quoting the *Wenyan* commentary on Qian (hexagram 1), describing the "great person" (*Zhouyi benyi*, in *Zhuzi quanshu* [2002], 1:150).

20. I think the point here is that the *Yi* can penetrate the unformed and invisible, but humans cannot do so without its assistance.
21. For the *Hetu* and *Luoshu*, see Nielsen, *Companion*, 103-5, 169-71, and 236-37. The earliest extant versions are those in the *Yixue qimeng* (1186), unless they were also contained in Zhu Xi's earlier (1177), lost commentary, the *Yizhuan*. (Most sources say that the earliest appearance was in the *Zhouyi benyi*, but they are assuming 1177 to be the date of the *Benyi*.) They also appear in a work attributed to Chen Tuan 陳摶 (tenth century), the *He Luo lishu* 河洛理數, but that survives only in an edition from the late Ming dynasty (1368-1644). The *Hetu* had been extensively discussed in the Han-dynasty "aprocrypha of the *Yi*" (*Yiwei* 易緯) (see W. Allyn Rickett, *Guanzi*, 1:154-58; Nielsen, *Companion*, 103-5, 306; Richard J. Smith, *Fathoming the Cosmos and Ordering the World*, 78-82). Rickett makes a strong but circumstantial case that the diagram as we have it goes back to the Han dynasty. Something called a *Hetu* is mentioned as a symbol of royal legitimacy in the *Shujing* 書經 (*Zhoushu* 周書, "Guming" 顧命, 4), but it is not described. Similar possible references are found in *Analects* 9.8 and *Mozi* ("Feigong 3" 非攻下, 4). For evidence that the *Hetu* and *Luoshu* were originally astral diagrams, see David W. Pankenier, *Astrology and Cosmology in Early China*, 175-83. For more of Zhu's comments on these two diagrams, see *Zhuzi yulei* 65:1610-12.
22. Yu the Great (大禹), one of China's earliest mythic sages, controlled the flooding of the Yellow River and laid out the "Nine Divisions" of the world. As recounted by Kong Anguo 孔安國 (ca. 100 BCE), a descendant of Confucius quoted in the *Yixue qimeng*:

   > The River Chart came out of the Yellow River on a dragon-horse when Fuxi ruled the world. He accordingly took its design as a model and drew the Eight Trigrams. The Luo Writing was the design arrayed on the back of a spirit tortoise in the time when Yu controlled the waters. In it are the numbers up to 9. Yu accordingly followed its classifications in completing the Nine Divisions. (Adler, *Introduction*, 3)

23. *Xici* A.9.1-2.
24. Referring to the myth of Yu the Great recounted by Kong Anguo (see n. 22).
25. Cai Yuanding 蔡元定 (1135-1198) was a friend and follower of Zhu Xi's who assisted him with the *Yixue qimeng*; either he wrote a draft that Zhu Xi finished, or he added comments to Zhu's work (see Adler, *Introduction*, 54n8). This whole comment by Zhu and Cai is a summary of its first section (3-5). Liu Xin 劉歆 (ca. 50 BCE-23 CE) and his father, Liu Xiang 劉向 (77-6 BCE), were official librarians of the Former Han dynasty. Guan Lang 關朗 (Ziming 子明, fifth century CE) wrote a commentary on the *Yi* from a *xiangshu* 象數 (image and number) perspective. Shao Yong 邵雍 (Kangjie 康節, Yaofu 堯夫, 1012-1077) was the most prominent exponent during the Northern Song of the *xiangshu* approach to the *Yi*. Liu Mu 劉牧 (1011-1064) was a *xiangshu* expert who transmitted the *Hetu* and *Luoshu* to the Song Confucians. He apparently confused the two diagrams, because according to Cai Yuanding he said the *Hetu* had nine numbers and the *Luoshu* ten (see Nielsen, *Companion*, 160-61).
26. This is also called the *xiantian* 先天 (before Heaven), or "a priori," sequence.
27. Shao Yong, "Guanwu waipian A," in *Huangji jingshi shu*, 7A:24b. Shao Yong's numerological theory of history was largely based on this passage from the *Xici*.
28. Shao Yong, "Guanwu waipian B," in *Huangji jingshi shu*, 8A:22a.

29. For a tentative explanation of "reverse calculations" (*nishu* 逆數) see chap. 4, "Preliminaries."
30. This diagram is also found in the *Yixue qimeng*, chap. 1 (Adler, *Introduction*, fig. 10).
31. Also quoted in Zhu Xi's comment on *Shuogua* 3.1, but I have not found the source.
32. See also *Yixue qimeng*, chap. 1 (Adler, *Introduction*, fig. 11).
33. Li Zhicai 李之才 (Tingzhi 挺之) (d. 1045) and Mu Xiu 穆修 (Bochang 伯長) (979-1032) were the intermediaries who passed down the *Xiantian* (Before Heaven, or A Priori) Diagram—also known as the Fuxi sequences of trigrams and hexagrams (Diagrams 3-6)—from Chen Tuan to Shao Yong. This, at least, is the claim made by Zhu Zhen 朱震 (1072-1138) in his *Jin Zhouyi biao*. Chen Tuan 陳摶 (Xiyi 希夷, Tunan 圖南) (d. 989) was a well-known Daoist master who, again according to Zhu Zhen, was also the source the *Hetu* and *Luoshu* and Zhou Dunyi's *Taijitu* (Supreme Polarity diagram), among others (see Nielsen, *Companion*, 29). Zhu Xi disputed the theory that Chen was the source of the *Taijitu*, but here he accepts Chen as the source of Shao Yong's diagrams. For more on the *Taijitu*, see Adler, *Reconstructing*, 71-72, 153-57. For more on Fuxi's diagrams, see *Zhuzi yulei* 65:1612-19. See also A. C. Graham, *Two Chinese Philosophers*, appx. 2.
34. These are four of the twelve "earthly branches" (*dizhi* 地支) of the traditional calendrical system. Each of the twelve correlates with a direction, a season, a lunar month, a double hour, and a zodiacal animal.
35. In traditional Chinese cartography, south is at the top and north is at the bottom.
36. See also *Yixue qimeng* (Adler, *Introduction*, fig. 12). The correlations with directions comes from *Shuogua* 5.2.
37. Since Diagram 7 contains more than the trigram names I translate it here. The correlations with family members come from *Shuogua* 10.

TABLE 1.1

	Kun: Mother			Qian: Father		
	Dui --			— Gen		
	Li --			— Kan		
	Sun --			— Zhen		
Dui: Youngest Daughter ⚌ Kun Upper line	**Li:** Middle Daughter ☲ Kun Middle line	**Sun:** Eldest Daughter ☴ Kun First line	**Gen:** Youngest Son ☶ Qian Upper line	**Kan:** Middle Son ☵ Qian Middle line	**Zhen:** Eldest Son ☳ Qian First line

38. For "hexagram fluctuation," see "Time" under "Key Terms and Concepts" in the introduction, and Nielsen, *Companion*, 74 ("hexagram alteration"). Zhu Xi's use of the term is limited to fluctuations *within* the groups he identifies in these diagrams.
39. E.g., the *Tuan* comment on hexagram 6, Song: "The firm [line] comes [from Dun, hexagram 33] and attains the center."

40. Zhu Xi means here that Fuxi's original intent was divination, not examining the formal relationships of hexagrams. This is where he differs from the *xiangshu* (image and number) approach to the *Yi*: the images and numbers are important more for their function in divination than for their numerological and cosmological symbolism.
41. This paragraph alludes to Zhu Xi's basic hermeneutical principle regarding the *Yi*: that each of the four authors (Fuxi, King Wen, the Duke of Zhou, and Confucius) had his own intention in contributing his layer, and that readers should interpret and use the text with those intentions in mind. E.g., one should interpret the hexagrams in terms of divination, not general moral principle (*yili* 義理), as Cheng Yi had done in his eleventh-century commentary. For a full discussion of Zhu Xi's hermeneutics of the *Yi*, see Smith et al., *Sung Dynasty Uses of the I Ching*, chap. 6.
42. Chao Yuezhi 晁說之 (1059-1129) was a disciple of Sima Guang's 司馬光 (1019-1086) and a follower of Shao Yong's. Zhu Xi quotes him briefly several times in this commentary, but Chao's commentary, *Chao Yidao guyi* 晁以道古易 (Chao Yidao's ancient *Yi*), is lost (see Nielsen, *Companion*, 28). It is briefly described by his nephew, Chao Gongwu 晁公武 (1105-1180), in his *Junzhai dushu zhi* 郡齋讀書志, 1:91-92 (see Donald Sturgeon, ed., *Chinese Text Project*, https://ctext.org/wiki.pl?if=gb&res=570208).
43. Lü Zuqian was a close friend of Zhu Xi's and collaborated with him on compiling the *Reflections on Things at Hand* (*Jinsilu* 近思錄). His edition of the *Yi*, the *Gu Zhouyi* 古周易 (Ancient *Zhouyi*), separated the Ten Wings from the scripture. Zhu Xi approved of this arrangement and followed it in this commentary (see "Arrangement of the Text" in the introduction).
44. As noted in the introduction (n. 56), the arrangement of the textual layers of this hexagram differs from all other hexagrams in the collated editions, which I am following.

    Qian is highly significant for Zhu Xi, as it symbolizes the immanent creative power and potential that sustains life and allows for human beings to fulfill the moral potential of the natural world. The *Tuanzhuan* commentary calls this "the originating [power] of Qian." Nearly two entire chapters (68 and most of 69) of Zhu's *Classified Conversations* (*Zhuzi yulei*) are devoted to Qian.
45. For these trigram identifications I use the images given in *Shuogua* 3.1, although each trigram has several other associations, also given in the *Shuogua*. In table 1 in the introduction the images are given immediately below the trigrams.
46. This is the hexagram statement traditionally believed to have been written by King Wen. It is sometimes called the *Tuan* 彖 statement or "judgment," as Zhu Xi does subsequently and in his preface. But this should not be confused with the *Tuan* commentary (*Tuanzhuan* 彖傳), which is attributed to Confucius and which Zhu Xi separates from the hexagrams. For the hexagram statement, or "Four Virtues" of Qian, see "Key Terms and Concepts" in the introduction. See also Zhu Xi's comment on the first passage of the *Wenyan*.
47. On the disagreement in the literature concerning whether Fuxi was responsible only for the Eight Trigrams or for all sixty-four hexagrams, see n. 11 in the introduction.
48. *Jian* rhymes with *Qian*, and did so in the Song dynasty according to the Northern Song rhyme dictionary *Da Song chongxiu guangyun* 大宋重修廣韻 (see 健 and 乾 in Luo Zhufeng, ed., *Hanyu da cidian*). In the Mawangdui version of the *Yi* the name of the hexagram is Jian 鍵, meaning "Key" (Edward L. Shaughnessy, trans., *I Ching*, 39).
49. Note that *duan* rhymes with *tuan*.

50. See the discussion of these terms in the introduction, "Key Terms and Concepts," "The Four Virtues."
51. *Xici* A.11.1. In this context the meaning is more like "understand things and complete affairs."
52. For another translation of this commentary on Qian, see Iulian K. Shchutskii, *Researches on the I Ching*, 202–3.
53. This is the only hexagram in which the line statements are separated from the Commentary on the Smaller Images in the collated editions of Zhu Xi's commentary (see introduction, n. 56).
54. In the original Bronze Age *Zhouyi* the "dragon sequence" in the six line statements probably referred to the seasonal rising and falling of a dragon "asterism" (constellation) in the night sky, but one not equivalent to the Western constellation Draco. See, e.g., Richard Rutt, *The Book of Changes (Zhouyi)*, 291.
55. As Zhu Xi explains in his *Yixue qimeng* (chap. 4; see Adler, *Introduction*, 50–52), the number of changing lines (6 and 9) determines which part of the text is read for the prognostication. This is why *yin* and *yang* lines are referred to as 6 or 9 here.
56. See "Key Terms and Concepts" in the introduction. I am not sure why Zhu says that 9 in the second is correct. Perhaps it is because the *Wenyan* commentary on this line says that "A dragon appearing in the field; appropriate to see the great person" refers to "one with the virtue of a dragon who is correct and central." Yet four sentences later he affirms that the line is *not* in its "correct" or proper position.
57. Seeing a dragon was considered a highly auspicious, lucky event.
58. Nine in the fifth place is both central and correct.
59. *Hui* 悔 "regret," one of the standard oracular formulas in the *Yi*, originally denoted, according to Kunst, a more external sense of "trouble" (Richard A. Kunst, "The Original Yijing," 160).
60. Only hexagrams 1 (Qian) and 2 (Kun) have an "additional line" of text referring to a divination in which all six lines are changing lines.
61. *Zuozhuan*, Duke Zhao 昭公, 29th year, 2.
62. According to Zhu Xi in his *Yixue qimeng* (chap. 4), when all six *yang* lines change into *yin*, yielding the Kun hexagram, the prognostication is the hexagram statement of Kun. See Adler, *Introduction*, 48.
63. This distinction between *jing* (scripture) and *zhuan* (commentary—i.e., the Ten Wings) is widely used in discussions of the *Yijing*.
64. Although in the hexagram statement Zhu Xi defines *yuan* as "great," here he defines it as "great and beginning." The latter meaning is more fitting from here on, so I use "originating" or "origination."
65. The text actually treats only *yuan* as a separate term, but in Zhu's commentary on the following sentences he identifies allusions to the other three. The *Wenyan* more explicitly treats the four terms as four virtues.
66. Or how the Sage was successful in his enactment of the Dao.
67. "Heaven's endowment" (*tianming* 天命) in relation to things is their given conditions of existence. In the Cheng-Zhu interpretation this includes the relative clarity or turbidity of their *qi* 氣, while their "nature" (*xing* 性) is their portion of *li* 理, the universal order. See "*Li*" and "*Ming*" in the introduction, "Key Terms and Concepts."

68. Zhang Zai, one of Zhu Xi's Northern Song predecessors, adopted "Great Harmony" (written *taihe* 太和 instead of *dahe* 大和) as one of his fundamental cosmological terms, along with "Great Vacuity" (*taixu* 太虛). The latter, for Zhang Zai, refers to *qi* in its undifferentiated state, while the former refers to its orderliness when formed into things.
69. This statement in the text is problematic because Heaven normally controls things, not vice versa.
70. This is a good example of Zhu Xi's emphasizing the difference between the *Yi*s of Fuxi, King Wen, the Duke of Zhou, and Confucius.
71. Recall that the Duke of Zhou wrote the line statements, but both commentaries (Larger and Smaller) are attributed to Confucius.
72. In the collated editions that I am following, this paragraph appears at the end of the "Smaller Images."
73. Most of the Larger Image commentaries refer to the imagery of the two component trigrams, even when they are the same, but this one comments on the hexagram as a whole. E.g., under Li (30), "Light is produced twice"; under Dui (58), "Connected lakes."
74. Here Zhu Xi (and perhaps the original text) may be alluding to the idea of the Sage "concealing" his virtue, as in the *Wenyan* text on the line, "Hidden dragon; do not use" (*Wenyan* 9.4).
75. The *Wenyan* contains comments on the first two hexagrams, Qian and Kun, and their individual lines. It is a compilation of four different commentaries, identified here as Source 1–Source 4, dating from the second and first centuries BCE (Rutt, *Book of Changes*, 433-34). Sources 1 and 4 are each divided into two sections, here labeled A and B. Zhu Xi refers to these as six sections. Section 4B continues under hexagram 2, Kun. Although it could be helpful to collate the statements of the *Wenyan* with the lines to which they apply, I am following the pattern of the collated Chinese editions and keeping the statements on each hexagram together (see "Arrangements of the Text" in the introduction). Source 1B closely resembles in form *Xici* A.8.5-11 and A.12.1.
76. In the collated editions of the *Yi* these sentences appear after the first line of text.
77. I have rendered this passage of the text and Zhu Xi's comment (minus the last sentence) in verse for two reasons. First, in the Chinese they are strikingly symmetrical: the *Wenyan* text is four lines of six characters each; Zhu's comment on each of the lines is in six groups containing six, four, four, five, five, and six characters. Second, the passage and comment are another statement of the parallelism between Mencius's four universal human virtues (*Mencius* 2A.6 and 6A.6) and the four natural or cosmic virtues of Qian in the *Yi*. On this, see the section on "Fu" in the introduction.

   This and the next passage are duplicated almost exactly in the *Zuozhuan* (Duke Xiang 襄公, 9th year, 2), in the story of Mu Jiang 穆姜 (ca. 608-591 BCE), but it is not certain which came first. Zhu Xi assumes that it originated with Mu Jiang and that Confucius quoted it here. See his comment on the hexagram statement of Sui (17).
78. In the *Classified Conversations* (*Zhuzi yulei* 68:1689) Zhu has this interesting comment about these two sets of four virtues: "Humanity, rightness, ritual, and wisdom are like a *baozi* [steamed bread dumpling]: inside everything is blended together, and it is completely filled with the unitary principle, without any before and after. *Yuan*, *heng*, *li*, and *zhen* are also like this: we do not speak about them in terms of a moment of origination or a moment of penetration."

79. Note that wisdom (*zhi* 智) appears to be missing from Mencius's Four Virtues in the text. Zhu Xi's comment "he understands [*zhi* 知] where correctness lies" might be his attempt to correct the omission, since "wisdom" is the understanding of right and wrong.
80. Cheng Yi says this refers to preserving the *dao* (*Er Cheng ji*, 700). Zhu Xi might also be referring to Mencius's injunction to preserve one's true moral mind.
81. *Mencius* 7B.33. Zhu Xi is emphasizing here that the perfection of virtue is demonstrated in "ordinary" (*yong* 庸) and "everyday" (*chang* 常) activity. This is related to the fact that in Confucianism, "the secular is sacred" (see Herbert Fingarette, *Confucius*).
82. "Participate in the incipiency" (*yu ji* 與幾) means that the morally advanced person understands and acts upon incipient changes in his environment so as to maximize the advantage of acting in accordance with the flow of events, or the *dao*. This understanding of incipient changes is central to the functioning of divination in Zhu Xi's view (see the last paragraph of "Zhu Xi and 'Neo-Confucianism'" in the introduction). See also Adler, "Response and Responsibility," 130-39.
83. "Being authentic" (*cheng* 誠), for Zhu Xi, means acting in perfect accord with one's moral nature (*xing* 性). Zhou Dunyi, in his *Tongshu* 通書 (Penetrating the *Yi*), argues that it is the essence of Sagehood.
84. In other words, one must put one's virtue into practice.
85. This is all about the relationship between the superior person's private moral cultivation (the inner trigram) and public service (the outer trigram). "Rising and falling" refers to one's relative position in society or government. "Advancing and retreating" refers to public service and retirement, depending on the moral character of the government (i.e., the traditional Confucian idea that when there is no "true king" or "humane government," the morally superior person should retire from public service). The 9 in the third occupies the border between the inner and outer, and so is poised to serve when the time is right.
86. Note how the moral authority and social prestige of the Sage is grounded in prevailing ideas of natural science.
87. This passage also appears in *Xici* A.8.9.
88. In colloquial Chinese *wenming* 文明 (literally, "light of culture") means "civilization" and *wenhua* 文化 (literally, "transformations of [or wrought by] culture") means "culture." *Wen* 文 itself implies literate culture and refinement. Its earliest meaning was "pattern," especially the patterns of lines that constitute writing. In *Xici* A.4.2 "Heavenly patterns" means the constellations.
89. I.e., acting appropriately in the present circumstances.
90. Obviously these are different from the four virtues of *yuan*, *heng*, *li*, and *zhen*.
91. "Penetrate to all sides" (*pangtong* 旁通) became a technical term for one hexagram changing to another by changing each *yang* line to *yin* and vice versa—i.e., a specific type of "hexagram fluctuation" (*guabian* 卦變), attributed to Yu Fan 虞翻 (164-233). See Nielsen, *Companion*, 185-87.
92. Cf. *Tuanzhuan*, Qian, 2.
93. Zhu Xi's claim that the third place is the human realm follows Kong Yingda's explanation, but in fact both the third and fourth places are generally considered to be the human realm between Heaven above and Earth below. Legge notes the weakness of Kong's explanation in *Yi King, or Book of Changes*, 418. See also Richard John Lynn, *The Classic of Changes*, 141n11.

94. This sentence is the locus classicus of the terms *xiantian* 先天 (preceding or prior to Heaven) and *houtian* 後天 (following or after Heaven). See "Key Terms and Concepts" in the introduction.
95. See "*Li*" in the introduction, "Key Terms and Concepts."
96. Guo Ziyi 郭子儀 (697–781) was a highly honored Tang-dynasty general who put down the An Lushan rebellion of 755–763. The quote may come from an episode in Guo's negotiations with Uighur chieftains in 765 regarding a threat from the Tibetans.
97. Although Kun is the pure *yin* hexagram, the mare (its image) is a horse, which is a strong animal; hence the mixture of *yin* and *yang*. See the first line of the *Wenyan* under Kun in the following.
98. According to Zhou Dunyi's *Taijitu shuo*.
99. The word "beginning" (*shi* 始) does not appear in this passage; Zhu Xi is referring here to its appearance in the corresponding passage under Qian (1). He is contrasting the originating power of Qian, which is the beginning of unformed *qi*, with the originating power of Kun, which is giving birth and form to the myriad things. Thus the originating power of Qian is prior to and greater than the originating power of Kun. In his *Classified Conversations* (*Zhuzi yulei* 69:1734) he says, "Relying on Qian to begin [*shi* 始] and relying on Kun to give birth [*sheng* 生] cannot conflict for even a moment.... When the myriad things rely on Qian to begin, there is *qi*. Relying on Kun to give birth, there is form [*xing* 形]. When *qi* develops and gives birth, that is the originating power of Kun."
100. *Shuogua* 8 says, "Qian is the horse; Kun is the ox."
101. Although *yin* and *yang* are complementary, the relationship is hierarchical. See Zhu's comment on 6 at the beginning.
102. See Zhu's comment on the "Greater Images" commentary under Qian (1).
103. This paragraph, an interjection more than a comment on the first line, clarifies the point that *yin* and *yang* are a nondualistic bipolarity but hierarchically ranked.
104. Yellow symbolizes earth, which in Five Phases cosmology is central and perfectly balanced. "Yellow earth" also refers to the loess-covered plains of the Yellow River valley, the "central kingdom."
105. *Zuozhuan*, Duke Zhao 昭公, 12th year (530 BCE), 2 (see Sturgeon, *Chinese Text Project*). The last two sentences of the quote are Zhu Xi's abridgement of the received version of the *Zuozhuan*.
106. In traditional Chinese cosmic symbolism, Heaven is round and Earth is square. The *Wenyan* (6 in the second) defines "square" as "being right" (*yi* 義), one of Mencius's "Four Norms" (*sichang* 四常). This line expresses the basic principle of *yin-yang* bipolarity, according to which there is always some *yin* in *yang* and vice versa.
107. See *Er Cheng ji*, 711. Cheng's comment on the line is, "The Way of *yin* is harmony without leading. Thus it achieves by staying behind, and emphasizes being appropriate [*zhu li* 主利] to complete the myriad things. This is the constancy of Kun."
108. This sentence became an extremely important dictum for the Cheng brothers and for Zhu Xi after his "spiritual crisis" of the 1160s. See Adler, *Reconstructing*, 81–98. In the *Jinsilu* 近思錄 (Reflections on things at hand), compiled by Zhu Xi and Lü Zuqian, there are three instances of Cheng Hao's quoting it: chap. 2, items 16 and 44; chap. 4, item 39.
109. The "original substance," in Zhu Xi's system of thought, is the original innately good nature (*xing* 性), which is the human instantiation of moral principle (*daoli* 道理).
110. Cheng Yi says this to be consistent with Mencius's claim that rightness is internal, not external (*Mencius* 6A.4–5).

111. Although it is much more common for the fifth line to be the "ruler" of a hexagram, in the case of Kun it is 6 in the second; hence that line corresponds to the "superior person."
112. The 6 at the top is in a superior position, which makes it forget that it is *yin*, not *yang*. The dragon is a *yang* creature that lives in a *yin* environment (clouds and water).
113. In *Zhuzi yulei* (70:1742) Zhu Xi distinguishes Zhun from two similar hexagrams: "Zhun is when *yin* and *yang* are not yet developed [*tong* 通]. Jian [hexagram 39] is when there is difficulty in their flow. Kun [hexagram 47] is being exhausted." Thus Zhun characterizes the beginning of a situation, Jian its development, and Kun its end. I follow this distinction even though he uses the same word (*nan* 難, "difficult") to define the first two.
114. "Marquis" is the conventional English translation of one of the five ranks of nobility in the Zhou dynasty: "duke" (*gong* 公), "marquis" (*hou* 侯), "earl" (*bo* 伯), "viscount" (*zi* 子), and "baron" (*nan* 男).
115. See "Hexagram Rulers" in the introduction, "Key Terms and Concepts."
116. In his pronunciation note Zhu Xi says that *nan* 難 here is pronounced in the fourth tone, meaning "trouble," not "difficult"; also in the "Smaller Images" commentary on 6 in the second.
117. *Liji* 禮記, "Qu li" 曲禮 A. "Pinned" refers to the coming-of-age ritual, at age fifteen, when girls first pin up their hair.
118. A *yin* line "riding" (*cheng* 乘) a *yang* line (immediately below it) is considered inauspicious. To be proper, a *yin* line should "support" (*cheng* 承) a *yang* line immediately above it. See Nielsen, *Companion*, 30.
119. Technically the line has no warning or prognostication, but the image serves as one.
120. In order to correctly correspond one of them would have to be *yang*.
121. The *Zagua* says, "Gen is stopping [*zhi* 止]." *Shuogua* 11.7 says, "Gen is mountain."
122. "Inner" and "outer" referring, respectively, to the lower and upper trigrams.
123. I.e., in both cases the aim is to eliminate ignorance.
124. Zhu Xi follows Wang Bi here in reading *shuo* 說 (to say) as *tuo* 脫 (to remove).
125. The words used for "good order" (*zhi* 治) and "regulated" (*qi* 齊) suggest that Zhu Xi is alluding to the *Great Learning*, which says, "Desiring to order the state, one first regulates the family." Therefore, I think the sentence in the commentary means that even a state that appears to be well ordered may not truly be so if its families are not well regulated.
126. Qiu Hu 秋胡 was a Zhou-dynasty official whose wife is the subject of a story in the *Lienü zhuan* (Biographies of exemplary women), chap. 5. Actually the wife in the story is chaste and Qiu Hu is the licentious one. See C. T. Hsia, Wai-yee Li, and George Kao, eds., *The Columbia Anthology of Yuan Drama*, 99–101.
127. *Shun mo* 順墨 occurs once in the *Xunzi* (chap. 2), where it can be read either as "follow dark" or "follow Mozi." *Shen mo* 慎墨 occurs twice (chaps. 8 and 25), where it can be read either as "fearful and dark" or "Shen Dao and Mozi." Zhu Xi chooses the first option in each. Modern translators are divided. See, e.g., Burton Watson, *Hsün Tzu*, 6–7; John Knoblock, trans., *Xunzi*, 1:155, 278n51; Eric L. Hutton, trans., *Xunzi*, 12–13, 56, 266.
128. This *yin* line is surrounded by *yin* lines and corresponds with another *yin* line in the first place.
129. Referring to the two *yang* lines.
130. The character *fu* 孚 is the original form of the homophonous *fu* 俘, meaning "to capture" or "prisoner of war [to be sacrificed]." According to modern scholars, it carries the

131. Referring to 9 in the fifth place, the hexagram ruler.
132. Although "suburb" is more concise, it has misleading connotations today. However, in Xiaochu (9) I render *xijiao* 西郊 as "western suburbs." Originally *jiao* 郊 referred to a "suburban altar," like those of Heaven and Earth in imperial times, just outside the capital. "Countryside" seems too far.
133. Sand suggests desert, a place of danger.
134. Recall that even numbers (*yin*) belong in even-numbered positions.
135. This is the first instance of "hexagram fluctuation" (*guabian* 卦變) that Zhu Xi comments upon (see "Time" in the introduction and fig. 1.9D in chapter 1, where Dun and Song are adjacent hexagrams in the group containing either four *yin* or four *yang* lines).
136. "The firm comes and attains the center" is the hexagram fluctuation Zhu is referring to, as he explains in his comment on the hexagram statement.
137. I.e., the few who have words of criticism.
138. Cf. the third line of Kun (2).
139. Kan is the inner trigram, Kun is the outer.
140. This is a canonical basis for Zhu Xi's definition of *zhen* as *zheng* in the Four Virtues of Qian (1).
141. Since it is a weak line in a weak position, retreat is appropriate.
142. Zhu Xi believed that all people, no matter their social station, should benefit by *Yijing* divination. In this he differed from Cheng Yi, who believed that the *Yi* was for the guidance of the "superior person" (*junzi* 君子) or the educated elite. See Smith et al., *Sung Dynasty Uses of the I Ching*, 183; Tze-ki Hon, "Classical Exegesis and Social Change," 5.
143. Being close in the sense of intimacy.
144. Drawing close to 9 in the fifth.
145. Not human in the sense of not being humane, as Mencius says in *Mencius* 2A.6. "Above, below, and corresponding" refers to the fourth, second, and sixth lines, respectively. "Above and below" is literally "supporting and riding on" (*cheng cheng* 承乘).
146. Which is why there is no prognostication.
147. I.e., the business at hand cannot be resolved.
148. The character 畜 has two pronunciations: *chù*, meaning "domestic animal," and *xù*, meaning "to domesticate," "to restrain," or "to rear." Zhu Xi indicates that the former pronunciation is to be used, although his definition is actually closer to the latter's meaning.
149. See *Shuogua* 7 and 11.4.
150. Qi 岐 was the original Zhou capital, on the Wei River west of present-day Xi'an. King Wen was imprisoned by King Zhou 紂 of Shang in Youli 羑里, south of Anyang, more than four hundred miles to the east; thus during that time of "restraint by the lesser" he observed his home state back in the west. It was during his imprisonment that he wrote the hexagram statements, according to the tradition dating back at least to the *Han Feizi* (third century BCE). S. J. Marshall, disagreeing with Zhu Xi, does not believe that there are any references to King Wen's imprisonment in the *Yi* (*The Mandate of Heaven*, 171n18).
151. Possibly a reference to the Zhou preparing to attack the Shang, which they would do under King Wen's son, King Wu.

152. "Civil virtue" implies the outward manifestations of virtue, as opposed to its inner "substance." Zhu Xi is alluding to *Analects* 6.18: "When substance [*zhi* 質] dominates culture [*wen* 文], one is a rustic. When culture dominates substance, one is a clerk. When culture and substance are balanced, one is a superior person." *Wen* (civil) is also, of course, the (posthumous) name of the imprisoned king.
153. Zhu reads *shuo* 說 (to say) as *tuo* 脫 (to discard, shed), as had Wang Bi and Cheng Yi. Line 2 of Daxu (26) is very similar: "The cart separates from its axle housing."
154. I.e., *yin* and *yang* are not functioning harmoniously.
155. *Er Cheng ji*, 746. Cheng says that the husband and wife look angrily at each other and the wife does not obey the husband, so the marriage is like a cart that cannot function.
156. "Nurture" is *xu* 畜, the same character as *chu* in the hexagram. The semantic connection between "nurture" and "restrain" is the idea of rearing domestic animals.
157. Lü is the first of the nine hexagrams discussed in *Xici* B.7.2-4; those three sections are called the "three presentations of the nine hexagrams" (*sanchen jiugua* 三陳九卦). The statements there are "Lü is the basis of virtue," "Lü is being harmonious and reaching one's goal," and "Lü harmonizes behavior." In his comment on the first one Zhu Xi equates Lü with *li* 禮 (ritual propriety).
158. See the note to table I.2 in the introduction.
159. "Gladly [*heyue* 和說] stepping firmly and strongly" because of the virtues of the two trigrams.
160. See "Hexagram Rulers" in the introduction, "Key Terms and Concepts." The "constituting ruler" in this case is 6 in the third (Li Guangdi, *Zhouyi zhezhong*, 110; Richard Wilhelm, trans., *The I Ching, or Book of Changes*, 435).
161. Only the collated arrangements of the *Zhouyi benyi* include Cheng's comment here.
162. Literati, farmers, artisans, and merchants were the four traditional components of Chinese society, in descending order of status according to Confucians.
163. *Er Cheng ji*, 750. Cheng Yi's reputation as a stern moralist certainly comes across in this comment.
164. Qin was the famously ruthless state that conquered the last of the other Warring States in 221 BCE, but only lasted fifteen years. Xiang Ji 項籍, better known as Xiang Yu 項羽 (233-202 BCE), was a warlord from Chu 楚 who won the battle that overthrew the Qin but was soon defeated by Liu Bang 劉邦, founder of the Han dynasty.
165. This sentence alludes to Zhu Xi's theory of "incipience" (*ji* 幾), which is central to his theory of how *Yijing* divination works. See Smith et al., *Sung Dynasty Uses of the I Ching*, chap. 6; Adler, "Divination and Sacrifice in Song Neo-Confucianism."
166. The idea of the hexagram stems from the upward movement of Qian (heaven) below harmoniously mixing with the downward movement of Kun (earth) above. Both Wilhelm and Lynn translate Tai as "peace," although neither Wang Bi nor Zhu Xi use this word in their commentaries. *Ping* 平, often translated as "peace," does appear in the text of the third line, but there it means "level" as opposed to "slope" (*po* 陂). Another possible word for peace, *an* 安, is likewise not present in either the text of Tai or the commentaries of Wang Bi or Zhu Xi. It does appear, however, in Cheng Yi's commentary (*Er Cheng ji*, 753), who quotes it from the *Xugua* (Sequence of Hexagrams) appendix's statement on the preceding hexagram, Lü (Treading): "Only after Lü and Tai is there peace [*an*]." Zhu Xi, however, at this point interjects his sole annotation to the *Xugua*, quoting a statement by Chao Yuezhi, "Zheng [Xuan's] edition lacks the two words 'and Tai'" (*Zhouyi benyi*, in Zhu Jieren et al., *Zhuzi quanshu*, 1:158). Without those two words

there is no connection in the *Xugua* between Tai and peace. Cheng Yi, however, builds on that connection, going on to say, "With Tai there is peace." But the *Xugua*, in fact, goes on to explicitly define Tai as *tong* 通, "penetrating," which of course is what Zhu Xi bases his definition on. See also Rutt, *Book of Changes*, 303.

167. According to the system of "waxing and waning hexagrams" (*xiaoxi gua* 消息卦). See "Time" in the introduction, "Key Terms and Concepts," and Nielsen, *Companion*, 275.
168. Recall that the upper and lower trigrams are called outer and inner, respectively.
169. "Hexagram fluctuation": 6 in the third position of Guimei ䷵ "departs" the inner trigram to reside in the fourth position of Tai ䷊, while 9 in the fourth position of Guimei "arrives" in the inner trigram to reside in the third position of Tai. Zhu Xi could have simply said that the third and the fourth lines exchange positions, but he needed to make use of the departing/arriving terminology of the hexagram statement.
170. "Excess" or transgression (*guo* 過) and "not going far enough" (*buji* 不及) are two ways of failing to achieve the Mean (*zhong* 中).
171. Zhu Xi interprets "forgetting one's friends" in a positive sense, meaning not joining political factions (*dang* 黨). Otherwise the line statement could read, "Not neglecting the distant or forgetting one's friends, one will gain honor in moderate actions," which is probably closer to its original intention. Factionalism in the Northern Song, from the perspective of Confucians in the Southern Song, was one of the factors that weakened the empire and made it susceptible to conquest by the Jurchen in 1127 (see James T. C. Liu, *Ou-yang Hsiu*, chap. 5).
172. According to Li Guangdi, Tai has two rulers, the second and the fifth, both of which are both constituting and governing rulers (*Zhouyi zhezhong*, 110-11).
173. I translate *shi* 食 literally as "eating," but in his *Classified Conversations* Zhu Xi says, "*Shi* is like the *shi* in 'imbibing ancient virtues'" (Song [hexagram 6], 6 in the third), thus moralizing the present line.
174. Sovereign Yi (Di Yi) was the penultimate Shang king; King Wen was the founder of the Zhou dynasty. "Younger sister" could also refer to a cousin. For the story behind this tradition (which is based on *Shijing* 詩經, ode 236) and some of the questions surrounding it, see Rutt, *Book of Changes*, 347, and Marshall, *Mandate of Heaven*, 156-58.
175. "Exalted Ancestor" (Gaozong 高宗) is the temple name of King Wuding 武丁 of the Shang (thirteenth century BCE); he appears in the third line of Jiji (63). Jizi was the virtuous uncle of the wicked last king of the Shang, Zhou Xin 紂辛; he is mentioned in the fifth line of Mingyi (36).
176. For the correlations of months and hexagrams, see "Time" in the introduction, "Key Terms and Concepts."
177. All of this explains the basic idea of the hexagram: since the lower trigram, Earth (*yin*), tends to sink, and the upper trigram, Heaven (*yang*), tends to rise, they are moving away from each other and do not fruitfully interact. As Cheng Yi puts it, "When Heaven and Earth do not interact, they do not generate the myriad things. This is not the human Way, so it is called 'criminal'" (*Er Cheng ji*, 759). From another perspective, the petty (*yin*) person is arriving inside and the superior (*yang*) person is departing outside, so the petty one is gaining influence and the superior one is losing influence.
178. "What one has preserved [*shou* 守] in oneself" is a possible allusion to Mencius's statement about preserving (*cun* 存) the innate goodness in his mind (*Mencius* 7A.1).
179. *Xici* B.5.9 quotes the second part of this line in a passage concerning danger, death, and disorder.

180. This alludes to the important Confucian distinction between public (*gong* 公) and private (*si* 私) interests. As Cheng Hao put it, "In the learning of the superior person, there is nothing better than being broadly and generally impartial [public minded] [*kuoran er dagong* 廓然而大公]" (*Er Cheng ji*, 460).
181. "Great Commonality" (*datong* 大同) is a term from the "Liyun" 禮運 chapter of the *Record of Ritual* (*Liji* 禮記), meaning a time of universal peace and harmony (the age of the most ancient Sage-kings).
182. As in the second line of Tai (11), Zhu Xi here warns against factionalism. In this case it does not require a forced reading.
183. They all correspond with it in the sense of being *yang* to its *yin*, but only 9 in the second occupies the corresponding position in the other trigram. Both conditions are normally necessary for proper correspondence, but see the Commentary on the Judgment.
184. One of the symbolic correlations of the upper trigram (Li) is military weapons, hence harm (*Shuogua* 5.11).
185. See the discussion of *heng* under "The Four Virtues" in the introduction, "Key Terms and Concepts."
186. *Er Cheng ji*, 771, where the phrase is actually "an appearance of increasing fullness."
187. According to lines 3 and 4, 6 in the fifth is the noble. But as a yielding line it has "emptied itself," still maintaining its dignity.
188. This line is quoted in *Xici* B.2.5.
189. Qian is the second of the nine hexagrams discussed in *Xici* B.7.2-4. The statements there are "Qian is the handle of virtue," "Qian is being honorable and shining," and "Qian controls ritual propriety."
190. Literally, "has ends."
191. This refers to the component trigrams. Gen, the inner trigram, means "mountain" and has the virtue of "stopping," so it conveys the idea of limiting one's strength, modestly holding it within. "Complying" is the virtue of the outer trigram, Kun.
192. Neither of the trigrams is Heaven, but Gen is mountain and therefore has Heavenly qualities. It has moved below, indicating modesty. Kun (earth) normally sinks, but here is above. According to Wilhelm, this "shows how modesty functions in lowly, simple people: they are lifted up by it" (Wilhelm, *I Ching*, 63).
193. As noted earlier, *bian* refers to *yin-yang* change, or alternation.
194. Zhu's statement that 6 at the top "lacks position" is curious, because according to the principle of "matching positions" (*dangwei* 當位) or "correct positions" (*zhengwei* 正位), an even-numbered position is most properly occupied by a 6 (see "Key Terms and Concepts" in the introduction, and Nielsen, *Companion*, 295). In fact, this *yin* line not only has proper position but also corresponds (*ying* 應) correctly with the *yang* line in the third. In the *Classified Conversations* (*Zhuzi yulei* 70:1770) there is a discussion of the apparent contradiction between the militaristic language of the fifth and sixth lines and the virtue of modesty. Interestingly, Zhu Xi quotes two passages from *Laozi* (61 and 69) that support the virtue of modesty in warfare. Elsewhere, Zhu criticizes Laozi for being expedient and deceitful in this and other contexts; see Wing-tsit Chan, "Chu Hsi's Appraisal of Lao Tzu."
195. This hexagram is referred to in *Xici* B.2.8.
196. This refers to 9 in the fourth, the only *yang* line in the hexagram. As the first line in the outer trigram, it corresponds correctly to the first line in the inner trigram, which is *yin*. These factors make it the ruler of the hexagram. "Compliantly acting" means something like "going with the flow," "obeying" or following the pattern of the *dao*.

197. This line is quoted in *Xici* B.5.11.
198. The root meaning of *zan* is "hairpin," which "gathers" the hair. Zhu Xi gives these definitions because *zan* is a fairly uncommon character.
199. The center of the outer trigram is usually a strong position, but here it is a yielding line with a firm line below it.
200. The prognostication is implicit but there is no explicit one.
201. This hexagram is referred to in *Xici* B.2.7.
202. *Chunqiu Zuozhuan* 春秋左傳, "Duke Xiang 襄公, 9th year [564 BCE], 2 (see Sturgeon, *Chinese Text Project*). For an English translation of the story, see Kidder Smith Jr., "*Zhouyi* Interpretation from Accounts in the *Zuozhuan*," 435. Mu Jiang 穆姜, wife of Duke Xuan of Lu, is under house arrest in the Eastern Palace for meddling in politics. She consults the *Yi*, receiving Gen (52, Keeping Still) changing to Sui (17, Following), and the divining official says that this means she will get out. In Mu Jiang's reply, she defines the "Four Virtues" as follows: "*Yuan* is the growth of the body; *heng* is the gathering of excellences; *li* is the harmonizing of rightness; *zhen* is the trunk of affairs." This and her next sentence are also found, with two slight differences, in *Wenyan* 1-2.

   In her statements that follow, which Zhu praises, Mu Jiang admits that she lacks these virtues and therefore will not leave the palace alive, and this turns out to be the case. For a short biography of Mu Jiang, see Lily Xiao Hong Lee and A. D. Stefanowska, eds., *Biographical Dictionary of Chinese Women*, 52-53. For her entry in the *Lienü zhuan* 列女傳 (Biographies of exemplary women) by Liu Xiang 劉向 (77-6 BCE), see Anne Behnke Kinney, ed., *Exemplary Women of Early China*, 145-46.
203. Wang Su 王肅 (195-256) was the editor or author of *Kongzi jiayu* 孔子家語 (Sayings of the Confucian school). The original sentence says, "With great success and correctness with no error, all under Heaven will follow the times."
204. The original sentence, with those two characters reversed, reads, "How great is the meaning of following the times!"
205. According to Li Guangdi, the first and the fifth are both rulers of the hexagram, as they are firm lines lying below yielding lines (*Zhouyi zhezhong*, 112).
206. Hence there is no explicit prognostication.
207. Mount Qi (Qishan 岐山) is located near the first capital of the Zhou dynasty, Zhouyuan 周原, west of Chang'an. See also line 4 of Sheng (46), where the name is given in the text. "Authentic intention" (*cheng yi* 誠意) is one of the "eight items" of the *Great Learning*, where (in Zhu Xi's interpretation) it means to make one's intentions authentic or real, truly expressing one's moral nature. "Spread one's spiritual clarity" (*tong shenming* 通神明) is a phrase found in the "Appended Remarks" appendix (*Xici* B.2.1), in the story of how Fuxi created the *Yi* by surveying Heaven and Earth, to "spread the power/virtue of his spiritual clarity." The two terms are elements of Zhu Xi's theory of spirit (*shen* 神) as the purest functional modality of *qi*, constituting both spiritual beings (gods, ghosts, ancestral spirits) and the clearest form of the human mind. See Adler, "Varieties of Spiritual Experience."
208. The virtues of the component trigrams are "entering" (Sun below) and "stopping" (Gen above).
209. These are three of the ten "heavenly stems" (*tiangan* 天干), which originally named the days in the ten-day week of the Shang dynasty. Combined with the twelve "earthly branches" (*dizhi* 地支) they comprised the numbers of the sixty-day and sixty-year

calendrical cycles used throughout imperial times. *Xin* is three days before the *jia* of the next cycle.

1	*jia*	甲	6	*ji*	己
2	*yi*	乙	7	*geng*	庚
3	*bing*	丙	8	*xin*	辛
4	*ding*	丁	9	*ren*	壬
5	*wu*	戊	10	*gui*	癸

210. This is another good example of how Zhu Xi reads moral self-cultivation (here "self-renewal," *zixin* 自新) into the text. Renewal, reiterated in the Commentary on the Larger Image, resonates with "renewing the people" in the text of the *Great Learning* (as revised by Cheng Yi), and also with the theme of "return" (hexagram 24; see "Key Terms and Concepts" in the introduction).
211. "The firm supports [*cheng* 承] the yielding" normally means a *yang* line immediately below a *yin* line—an inauspicious relationship—but that can only refer to line 3 here. See n. 118. In this case Zhu Xi is referring to the relationship of 9 in the second and 6 in the fifth, son and mother, which is the correspondence he mentions.
212. The Sun trigram is correct in that as the eldest daughter (see Diagram 7, King Wen's Sequence of the Eight Trigrams) it occupies the lower, inner position.
213. Lynn explains that one of the ancient meanings of *lin* was a siege machine (*Classic of Changes*, 258n1).
214. For the hexagram-month correlations see "Time" in the introduction, "Key Terms and Concepts."
215. Lin ䷒ to Dun ䷠ is hexagram fluctuation within the group of hexagrams containing either two *yang* or two *yin* lines (the second group in Diagram 9). The difference between Lin ䷒ and Fu ䷗ is not of this type.
216. In Zhu's *Classified Conversations* (*Zhuzi yulei* 70:1776) he says, "When King Wen wrote the hexagram statements, whether or not he used only the Zhou calendar we cannot know."
217. Referring to 9 in the second, which corresponds correctly with 6 in the fifth.
218. Zhu says that *si* 思 (ordinarily "thinking") should be read in the fourth tone, making it "concern."
219. The unclear part is "not complying with commands." Wang Bi (*Zhouyi Wang-Han zhu*, 2:10a) and Cheng Yi (*Er Cheng ji*, 795) say that *xian* 咸 (together) should be read *gan* 感 (stimulate, prompt); the *xian* character served for both words before the Han dynasty. Zhu Xi says that this reading is "somewhat forced" (*Zhuzi yulei* 70:1776), but it supports Wang Bi's interpretation that "not complying with commands" refers to the *yang* line in the second not following the commands of the *yin* line in the fifth (Lynn, *Classic of Changes*, 256). Wilhelm translates it, "One need not yield to fate" (*I Ching*, 483); Legge, "Those (to whom the advance is made) are not yet obedient to the ordinances (of Heaven)" (*Yi King*, 291).
220. In Zhu's *Classified Conversations* (*Zhuzi yulei* 70:1776) he says that this line "has absolutely reached its approach to [9 at] the beginning."
221. Specifically toward the two *yang* lines of the inner trigram (see *Zhuzi yulei* 76:1776), although one might have expected Zhu Xi to read this as a reference to self-cultivation, as Wilhelm does (*I Ching*, 485).
222. "Being observed" (passive) is the meaning of *guàn* (fourth tone); "observing" (active) is the meaning of *guān* (first tone). In his comment on the hexagram name Zhu uses the

passive sense; in his comments on the *Tuanzhuan* and the line statements he uses the active sense. In a comment in his *Zhuzi yulei* he is quite explicit about this (70: 1778).

223. The eighth month is the beginning of autumn, when *yin* is growing and *yang* is declining.
224. Referring to the upper trigram and 9 in the fifth.
225. This is a good example of Zhu Xi's principle that *Yijing* divination is relevant to any person.
226. "Resides inside and observes outside": this line in the inner trigram observes 9 in the fifth in the outer. It is "correct" because the line is both central and correct, and corresponds correctly with 9 in the fifth. Wang Bi adds that a women's perspective is properly limited, which is the *dao* of the wife (Wang Bi and Han Kangbo, *Zhouyi Wang-Han zhu* 2, 11a-b; Lynn, *Classic of Changes*, 262).
227. "Free flow or blockage" (*tong sai* 通塞) alludes to Zhu's theory that only when one's *qi* 氣 is clear, flowing freely through the body and mind, does one's thought and behavior correctly manifest one's moral nature (*xing* 性). "Blockage" of *qi* causes physical, mental, and moral deficiencies.
228. Perhaps because in a well-run state the court decorum of officials would be exemplary, as Wang Bi suggests (*Zhouyi Wang-Han zhu* 2, 11b; Lynn, *Classic of Changes*, 263).
229. Alluding to Mencius's idea that the true king is "father and mother of the people," whose own virtue influences theirs (*Mencius* 1A.4, 1B.7, 3A.3).
230. This hexagram is referred to in *Xici* B.2.4.
231. Quoting a sentence from the "Commentary on the Judgment." Zhu Xi frequently quotes from this appendix in his comments on the hexagram statements, and in subsequent cases I do not note them unless I have another point to add.
232. Because the pattern of this appendix is to name the upper trigram before the lower.
233. This and the next lines are quoted in *Xici* B.5.7.
234. See the "Smaller Images" commentary on this line. As noted earlier (under line 2 of hexagram 3), a *yin* line should "support" (*cheng* 承) a *yang* line above it, not "ride on" (*cheng* 乘) a *yang* line below it.
235. Paraphrasing *Zhouli* 周禮, "Qiuguan sikan" 秋官司寇 (Office of Autumn, Department of Justice), 57 (see Sturgeon, *Chinese Text Project*). According to Legge, this is a pledge to the court of one's rectitude.
236. This line is quoted in *Xici* B.5.8. The cangue was a Chinese punishment similar to the stocks or pillory.
237. *He* 何 is sometimes used for *he* 荷, which means "to carry."
238. I.e., the ornamentation is limited by the mountain above, so it is efficacious only in small matters.
239. See n. 88.
240. "Former scholars" includes Wang Bi (see Lynn, *Classic of Changes*, 273).
241. Cf. Zhu's comment on the hexagram statement. The idea of "limiting" as part of human elegance (*renwen* 人文) alludes to the power of ritual propriety (*li* 禮) to create a truly human or humanistic culture (also *renwen* 人文) by artfully limiting and coordinating natural desires. See, e.g., *Analects* 6.18: "Confucius said, 'If the native material [*zhi* 質] outweighs refinement [*wen* 文], you have a rustic. If refinement outweighs the native material, you have a scribe. When there is a right balance of native material and refinement, you have a gentleman [*junzi* 君子]" (Annping Chin, trans., *The Analects*, 89). See

242. also Xunzi's chapter "Discussion of Ritual." The idea of "apportionment" (*fen* 分) adds the notion that one is satisfied with one's "lot" in life, in this case satisfied with being appropriate only in small matters.
242. "A single *yang* residing between two *yin* lines" describes the Kan trigram ☵ (water), hence "moist." Kan here is one of the two "nuclear" or "interlocking" trigrams (*huti* 互體), which are the second, third, and fourth lines and the third, fourth, and fifth lines (see Nielsen, *Companion*, 111–14). This is a concept that Zhu Xi makes very little use of.
243. Another example of the pervasive concept of "return" in Zhu's commentary.
244. This hexagram is referred to in *Xici* B.2.3.
245. Following Wang Bi's interpretation, although Wang simply says, "*Bian* is what is above the feet" (辨者足之上也).
246. The fifth *yin* manages the other four like a string of fish, and is managed by the *yang* above, like a ruler managing the court ladies.
247. "Palanquin" (*yu* 輿) is elsewhere translated as "cart" or "carriage," but the "Smaller Images" commentary for the line says that it is carried by people. The word actually refers to the body of a carriage, which can either be on wheels or carried on poles.
248. "The subject would fail to return" refers to the potential for Bo to give rise to Fu (Return). By "dispositions of the Sages" Zhu Xi is referring to the original intention of the Sages who created the *Yi* to help all people, regardless of their social station—again implicitly criticizing Cheng Yi, who said that it is for the guidance of superior people only. See n. 141.
249. This is one of the nine hexagrams discussed in *Xici* B.7.2-4. The statements there are "Fu is the root of virtue," "Fu is distinguishing among things when they are small," and "Fu leads to self-knowledge." For more on the significance of Fu, see "Fu" in the introduction, "Key Terms and Concepts."
250. See table 3 in the introduction for the hexagram-month correlations.
251. Counting the fifth month (Gou) as one, the eleventh month (Fu) is seven.
252. Quoting Cheng Yi's comment on this line (*Er Cheng ji*, 819).
253. Paraphrasing Zhou Dunyi's *Taijitu shuo* ("At the maximum of stillness it returns to activity").
254. For Cheng's comments on this passage (from both his Commentary and his recorded sayings), see Li Guangdi, *Zhouyi zhezhong*, 671; translated in Adler, "Divination and Philosophy," 275.
255. "Dark Wine" (*xuan jiu* 玄酒) is a metaphor for subtlety, based on the belief that in ancient times water took the place of wine in sacrificial offerings. "Great Tone" (*tai yin* 太音) comes from *Laozi* 41 (where it is *dayin* 大音) and may allude to a Tang-dynasty poem by Yin Yaofan 殷堯藩 (780–855), which also alludes to the Fu hexagram (see http://fanti.dugushici.com/ancient_proses/25186). Both terms "evoke something mild, subtle, faint, but ever present and potent, like the generative force of the first activity of *yang*, pregnant with potential" (Chengjuan Sun, message to author).
256. "Song of the Winter Solstice" (Lengzhiyin 冷至吟), in Shao Yong, *Yichuan jirangji*, 18:136a.
257. *Liji* 禮記, "Yue ling" 月令, 46. Zhu Xi's text differs somewhat from ours.
258. This line is quoted in *Xici* B.5.12.
259. Following Cheng Yi's commentary: "Although frequent return and frequent error are dangerous, nevertheless the rightness of returning to the good involves no error" (*Er Cheng ji*, 821).

260. Dong Zhongshu 董仲舒 (179-104 BCE), *Chunqiu fanlu* 春秋繁露 (Luxuriant gems of the *Spring and Autumn Annals*), 32 (see Sturgeon, *Chinese Text Project*). The second sentence quoted by Zhu is not exactly the same as what we have today.
261. This is obviously not a literal definition. It is an elaboration of Cheng Yi's definition of *wuwang* as "authenticity" (*cheng* 誠) (*Er Cheng ji*, 822), which Zhu Xi defines as "actualized order/principle," or the condition in which the nature (*xing* 性) is fully manifested (see Adler, *Reconstructing*, 224). It is "no error" in the sense of being perfectly aligned with the fundamental order (*li* 理) of things.
262. Zhu Xi is referring to the biography of Lord Chunshen 春申君 in Sima Qian's *Shiji* 史記 (Historical records), 19 (see Sturgeon, *Chinese Text Project*), and particularly expressions like "unexpected blessing" (*Zhuzi yulei* 71:1798). Neither Cheng Yi nor Wang Bi mentions this alternative reading of *wuwang*, although earlier commentators did (see Lynn, *Classic of Changes*, 297n1). Zhu Xi's choice to foreground it seems to be suggested by the second line statement, which refers to reaping rewards without deliberately seeking them. On a deeper level, though, he is making the point that if one is free from error, one's authentic, moral nature will be expressed spontaneously and unexpectedly. This would be similar to Mencius's idea that the manifestation of moral nature is like "a fire starting up or a spring coming through" (*Mencius* 2A.6; see D. C. Lau, trans., *Mencius*, 83).
263. "Without" refers to Song (6 ䷅), from which this hexagram comes via hexagram fluctuation (as Zhu explains in the preceding).
264. "The prognostication for it" means the prognostication one would expect based on the incorrect positioning of this line: a *yang* line in a *yin* position, not corresponding correctly with the *yang* line in the first.
265. "Preserving" as in "preserving the Way of the former kings" (*Mencius* 3B.4).
266. The Gen trigram is considered *yang* because it symbolizes the youngest son (see *Shuogua* 10). Contrary to what might be expected, in the six "mixed" trigrams (those with both *yang* and *yin* lines), it is the unique line that determines the *yang* or *yin* (hence male or female) character of the trigram. See also *Xici* B.4.1-2.
267. Quoting the Commentary on the Judgment. The phrase also appears in the *Great Learning*, which says that it was written on the bathtub of King Tang 湯, founder of the Shang dynasty.
268. I.e., the powerful *yang* in the third rises all the way to the top of the hexagram. Of the three *yang* lines in the inner trigram (Qian), this is the only one that is not limited by Gen (mountain) above (see *Zhuzi yulei* 71:1802). This is explained more fully by Wang Bi (see Lynn, *Classic of Changes*, 301). A "good horse" is one of the images of Qian given in *Shuogua* 11.
269. The sentence that Zhu Xi interprets as "Defend the obstructed cart daily" actually reads, "It is said to defend the obstructed cart." Cheng Yi also reads it as "daily" (*Er Cheng ji*, 830); the *Siku quanshu* edition of his commentary (*Yichuan Yizhuan* 伊川易傳) clearly prints the character as *ri* 日 (2:84a), and the editors of *Zhuzi quanshu* (2002) say that *ri* was the original word (1:58).
270. "Bi gong" 閟宮 (Mao 300) (see Sturgeon, *Chinese Text Project*). Arthur Waley translates it as "thwart" (*The Book of Songs*, 271).
271. Sturgeon, *Chinese Text Project*.
272. It corresponds properly with 9 in the second, but as a *yin* line in a *yang* position it is not correct.

273. Cheng Yi thinks "what" is a superfluous word (*Er Cheng ji*, 832); Zhu Xi says we cannot know for sure (*Zhuzi yulei* 71:1802).
274. The correctness of the line is limited to its correct correspondence with the *yang* at the top. In terms of its position in the hexagram it is incorrect (a *yin* line in a *yang*, or odd-numbered, position).
275. Despite his comment, Zhu Xi says he doesn't really understand this line (*Zhuzi yulei* 71:1804).
276. *Guo* means "exceeding" (going too far) as well as "surpassing," hence "although."
277. This line is quoted in *Xici* A.8.7.
278. Having children is meritorious because of the obligation to continue the family line. According to Mencius, not having progeny is the most unfilial act (*Mencius* 4A.26).
279. The fact that neither 9 in the second nor 6 at the beginning occupies the proper position symbolizes the "impropriety" of an old man marrying a young woman. However, they go beyond this to share with each other (see *Zhuzi yulei* 71:1806).
280. "Having another" means ignoring the proper relationship with 6 at the beginning. Both Wilhelm and Lynn translate it as "ulterior motives."
281. I.e., the two lines are inverted mirror images of each other (see "Note on the Sequence of Hexagrams" in the introduction).
282. Mencius (6A.10) says that morality is more important than life itself.
283. This hexagram is often called simply Kan 坎, like the other seven hexagrams formed by a doubled trigram, which all have the same name as the trigram.
284. The Kan trigram ☵ resembles the character for water (*shui* 水), sideways. See the note to table 1 in the introduction.
285. *Zhouli*, "Tianguan 天官," 103; *Guanzi* 管子, "Dizi zhi 弟子職," 4. For both see Sturgeon, *Chinese Text Project*.
286. Referring to Lu Deming 陸德明 (ca. 550-630), *Jingdian shiwen* 經典釋文, 2:13 (see Sturgeon, *Chinese Text Project*).
287. This hexagram is referred to in *Xici* B.2.2.
288. The two *yin* lines are both central, and the lower one is correct.

2. PART B: HEXAGRAMS 31–64

1. According to *Shuogua* 10, Gen and Dui are the youngest son and daughter, respectively. According to *Shuogua* 3 and 6, they "penetrate [each other's] *qi*." *Ganying* can also be rendered as "stimulus and response."
2. "The youngest male is below the youngest female" refers only to the trigrams, not to their social status. Since hexagrams are read from the bottom up, "the male precedes the female."
3. Note that even though the hexagram statement mentions only success and good fortune, Zhu Xi inserts the warning that this is contingent upon one's maintaining correctness.
4. When asked about the expression "the principle of influence and penetration" (*gantong-zhi li* 感通之理) Zhu says, "Like night and day, night returning to day, endlessly circulating, and 'activity and stillness alternate; each is the basis of the other' [from Zhou Dun-yi's *Taijitu shuo* 太極圖說 (Discussion of the Supreme Polarity diagram)]; these are all the principle of influence and penetration." He also says, "Influence is when things come

and influence me; penetration is the idea of my own reception of that influence" (*Zhuzi yulei* 72:1814-15). Thus he is using "penetration" (*tong* 通) in the sense of the natural response to an influence or stimulus, and also the mental response (knowing).

5. I.e., the softness of the water pervades the mountain; likewise the superior person receives others with open receptivity.
6. "Only" is based on Zhu's comment; it is not in the text. The second sentence is quoted in *Xici* B.5.1.
7. This is one of the nine hexagrams referred to in *Xici* B.7.2-4. The statements there are, "Heng is the strength of virtue," "Heng is not being fed up with complexity," and "Heng unifies virtue."
8. "Gentle, mild" is the primary meaning of *sun* apart from its use as a trigram name. All the quotes in this paragraph, other than those from the hexagram statement, come from the Commentary on the Judgment.
9. I.e., *shang* 上 and *xia* 下 are read as verbs (rising, sinking) instead of adjectives (above, below).
10. "Stillness be emphasized" (*jing wei zhu* 靜為主) comes from Zhou Dunyi's *Taijitu shuo*: "The Sage ... emphasizes stillness [*zhu jing* 主靜]" (see Adler, *Reconstructing the Confucian Dao*, 188; the terms *yin* and *yang* in n. 78 on that page are unfortunately reversed).
11. Confucius quotes and comments on this sentence in *Analects* 13.22. For a discussion of it, see Annping Chin, trans., *The Analects*, 212-13.
12. It is not appropriate for the husband because it is a *yin* line.
13. According to the principle of *yin-yang* fluctuation, when a thing or process reaches its peak or fullness, it starts to develop in the opposite direction. This is an example of how *ji* 極 (here translated as "peak," sometimes as "extreme"), in Zhu Xi's usage, means the extreme point of a cyclical process, not the end point of a linear one. See Adler, *Reconstructing*, chap. 4.
14. Most translators (e.g., Legge, Wilhelm, Lynn) take *xiao* 小 here as something like "minor matters," but in Zhu Xi's comment he defines it as the "inferior person" (*xiaoren* 小人), the opposite of "superior person" (*junzi* 君子).
15. The sixth lunar month (July-August) comes just after the summer solstice, when the *yang* has reached its peak and begins to decrease (withdraw).
16. The similarity would appear to be in the structure of the hexagrams, which differ by only one line, rather than in the prognostication statements.
17. 9 in the fifth is central, correct, and corresponds properly with 6 in the second. According to Li Guangdi it is the governing ruler of the hexagram (*Zhouyi zhezhong*, 114).
18. I.e., attachment to the advancing *yin* (inferior) lines is bad, but attachment to loyal inferiors is good.
19. This hexagram is referred to in *Xici* B.2.11.
20. Cheng Yi had also paraphrased this statement (*Er Cheng ji*, 870), and compared it with Confucius's statement, "Conquering oneself and returning to propriety is humanity" (*Analects* 12.1). Zhu Xi alludes to the latter in the *Zhuzi yulei*: "A person's ability to conquer himself is like thunder above heaven" (72:1824).
21. I.e., although the line is strong, because of its lowly position it should not try to advance.
22. In his *Classified Conversations* (*Zhuzi yulei* 72:1825) Zhu Xi further explains why this line is not extremely firm: "Coming upon two *yin* lines ahead, the image of the hedge opening,

is how it advances. But it is not [as firm] as the third line, ahead of 9 in the second, which is between the fourth and second *yang* lines and cannot advance."

23. "Like Dui" refers to the resemblance between this hexagram ䷡ and the Dui trigram ☱, with each line doubled. This makes Dazhuang one of the "great hexagrams" (*dagua* 大卦), each of which has such a resemblance (see Bent Nielsen, *A Companion to Yi Jing Numerology and Cosmology*, 36–38). "Yielding outside and firm inside" refers to the two yielding lines in the outer (upper) trigram and three firm in the inner. *Shuogua* 8 and 11 associate the Dui trigram with the ram or sheep. The other "great hexagrams" are Lin ䷒ (19), Guan ䷓ (20), Dun ䷠ (33), Zhongfu ䷼ (61), and Xiaoguo ䷽ (62).

24. E.g., in the last line of *Han shu* 漢書, "Shihuo zhi" 食貨志, A.3 (see Donald Sturgeon, ed., *Chinese Text Project*). That would make the sentence, "Losing a ram on the boundary, no regret." Modern scholars have identified a dynastic myth here, reading *yi* (易 or 埸) as short for Youyi, a place-name. Thus the line would be "Losing a ram in Yi," referring to a story about Wang Hai 王亥, an ancestor of the Shang kings who lost his flock in Youyi and was killed there. See Richard Rutt, *The Book of Changes (Zhouyi)*, 327; S. J. Marshall, *The Mandate of Heaven*, 211n1.

25. Here, too, modern scholars identify a historical reference that Zhu Xi does not recognize: that *kang hou* 康侯 (strong marquis) was originally the Marquis (*hou*) of Kang, the ninth son of King Wen, who after the conquest of the Shang was reenfeoffed as the Marquis of Wei (微). See Rutt, *Book of Changes*, 258, 327; Marshall, *Mandate of Heaven*, 7–8, 76.

26. "The trigram fluctuation" refers to "the yielding advancing and moving upward," i.e., the fluctuation from Guan to Jin that Zhu Xi describes under the hexagram statement.

27. "Illuminates his bright virtue" (*zhao mingde* 昭明德) paraphrases the *Great Learning* (*Daxue* 大學), "The ancients who wanted to make clear their bright virtue [*ming mingde* 明明德] to all under Heaven first ordered their states."

28. In his *Classified Conversations* (*Zhuzi yulei* 72:1825–26) Zhu acknowledges that this line is difficult to understand.

29. The first "late grandmother" is *wangmu* 王母 (literally, "royal mother"), an honorific term for a departed grandmother. The second one is *xianbi* 先妣, which can indicate either a late mother or late grandmother.

30. Virtuous uncle of the evil King Zhou of the Shang. Imprisoned by the king, he later served the conquering Zhou dynasty.

31. The original meaning of *mingyi* may have been some kind of bird. See Marshall, *Mandate of Heaven*, chap. 9, where other interesting possibilities are discussed (e.g., the myth of Yi the Archer).

32. Paraphrasing the preceding Commentary on the Judgment.

33. Referring to Jizi's concealing his virtue and feigning insanity to escape execution by his nephew, the evil King Zhou 紂 of the Shang. After being freed from prison by King Wu of the Zhou 周, Jizi supposedly wrote the "Hongfan" 洪範 (Great plan) chapter of the *Shujing* 書經 (Scripture of documents). He is known as one of the "three virtuous men" of the Shang dynasty and was discussed by Confucius, Mencius, and Xunzi, among others. See Ulrich Theobald, "Jizi 箕," http://www.chinaknowledge.de/History/Myth/personsjizi.html.

34. Correctly related because in premodern China, the proper sphere of activity for the male (*yang* line in the fifth) was the outer, public world, while that of the female (*yin* line in the second) was the inner, home world.

35. Probably referring to the male or female nature of the lines and their positions. Here is a tentative diagram of this comment, which is not consistent with Zhu's comment on the hexagram statement.

  — Father
  — Husband 1 (elder brother)
  -- Wife 1
  — Husband 2 (younger brother)
  -- Wife 2
  — Son

36. The idea seems to be that excessive emotional expression, at both ends of the spectrum, is bad. But if one has regrets about it, good fortune can result nonetheless.
37. Zhu specifies this pronunciation of 假, which is usually *jia* (with different meanings); also in the hexagram statements of Cui (45), Feng (55, where it is "attains"), and Huan (59). The quote is from *Liji* 禮記 (Record of ritual), chap. 25 ("Summary of Sacrifice"), 31.
38. Cheng Yi's comment continues, "This is how they 'interact with love'" (*Er Cheng ji*, 887).
39. This hexagram is referred to in *Xici* B.2.10.
40. In his *Classified Conversations* (*Zhuzi yulei* 72:1829) Zhu says that this line conveys the same idea as Confucius's principle in *Analects* 13.23, "harmony, not sameness" (*he er butong* 和而不同).
41. Referring to *Analects* 17.1, in which Confucius agrees to meet with a minister who had usurped legitimate authority in Confucius's home state of Lu.
42. Zhu Xi follows Cheng Yi (*Er Cheng ji*, 892) in interpreting *tian* 天 (Heaven) as *kun* 髡, meaning "to have the head shaved," either as punishment or as Buddhist tonsure. "Fierce resentment" and "punishment" reflect the idea that the contrariety of the hexagram is most strongly expressed by the third and sixth lines, which are opposite, both improperly positioned, and at the top of their trigrams.
43. Since skin, being soft, is easy to bite through.
44. S. J. Marshall speculates that these "ghosts" (*gui* 鬼) may instead be captives from Guifang 鬼方 (*Mandate of Heaven*, 177n63).
45. For Zhu Xi's differentiation among hexagrams 3 (Difficult Beginning), 39 (Obstructed), and 47 (Blocked), see chap. 1, n. 113.
46. In Shao Yong's comment on *Shuogua* 3.1 (quoted by Zhu Xi in his commentary), he says that Gen is the northwest, although *Shuogua* 5.2 says that Gen is the northeast. Both the northwest and northeast were, since ancient times, generally considered dangerous directions from which horse-riding nomadic peoples (e.g., the Xiongnu and Jurchen) frequently encroached on China's sedentary, agricultural population.
47. Cf. the last line of the Commentary on the Judgment under Kui (38). Both are cases of good results potentially coming from bad situations.
48. According to Shao Yong's comment on *Shuogua* 3.1, Sun, the lower trigram, symbolizes the southwest (although *Shuogua* 5.2 says it is the southeast).
49. The trigram virtues are Kan: danger, Zhen: arousing (acting).
50. I use "barbarian" because the connotation here is definitely pejorative. *Rong* 戎 was one of the ancient Chinese names for non-Chinese peoples surrounding the Central States (*Zhongguo* 中國). The others were Yi 夷, Min 蠻, and Di 狄. The latter two are written with the signifiers for "insect" and "dog," respectively, suggesting less-than-human status.

The first two contain the elements for "sword" and "bow," respectively, suggesting violence.

51. Zhu's note on pronunciation indicates that the first word of this line, which is the same as the character for the hexagram name (解), is here pronounced differently: *jie* instead of *xie*. Accordingly, I translate it "cut off" instead of "released."

52. This is one of the nine hexagrams referred to in *Xici* B.7.2-4. The statements there are, "Sun is the cultivation of virtue," "Sun is being difficult at first and then easy," and "Sun keeps harm away."

53. Sun (41) and Yi (42), a complementary pair, come via hexagram fluctuation from Tai (11) and Pi (12), another complementary pair (Penetrating/Obstructing):

    Tai ䷊ → Sun ䷨
    Pi ䷋ → Yi ䷩

    According to Cheng Yi in his comment on Yi, "Flourishing and declining, diminishing and enhancing, are like a cycle: at the peak of diminishing there must be enhancement, according to natural principle" (*Er Cheng ji*, 912). Note again the theme of reversal.

    Sun is "diminishing" because the third (yang) line of Tai has become *yin*. Cheng Yi had said (under Yi, hexagram 42), "Yang fluctuating to become *yin* is diminishing; *yin* fluctuating to become *yang* is enhancing" (*Er Cheng ji*, 912). His explanations of Sun and Yi are more detailed than those of Zhu Xi. Both cases are conceived in reference to 6 in the fifth (the hexagram ruler), which is the superior who diminishes or enhances those below.

54. Gen ☶ is lines 3, 4, and 5 of Yi. This group and lines 2, 3, and 4 ☷ are the "nuclear" or "interlocking" trigrams (*huti* 互體) of Yi.

55. See n. 53. Qian and Kun are the component trigrams of Tai.

56. The first and fourth lines correctly correspond and are correctly positioned.

57. The first sentence is the same as line 2 of hexagram 42 (Yi).

58. This is one of the nine hexagrams referred to in *Xici* B.7.2-4. The statements there are, "Yi is the abundance of virtue," "Yi is growing abundance without artifice," and "Yi promotes benefit."

59. As in the hexagram statement of Sun (41), this presupposes that Sun comes from Tai (11) and Yi comes from Pi (12).

60. Wood is one of the primary images of Sun (*Shuogua* 11.4); for Zhen it is similar to "young bamboo, sedges, and reeds" (*Shuogua* 11.3).

61. I.e., the *yang* line in the fourth position of Pi ䷋ (12), representing the ruler, descends to the first position of Yi, representing the people.

62. The *yin* in the second and the *yang* in the fifth are both central and correct.

63. Zhen, the lower trigram, is active (*Shuogua* 4, 6, 7) and Sun represents the eldest daughter (*Shuogua* 10, 11), hence gentleness.

64. Referring again to the hexagram fluctuation from Pi ䷋ to Yi ䷩. The Qian trigram of Pi "bestows" its lower *yang* line to the Kun trigram below, which "gives birth" to the *yang* in its first line.

65. I.e., emulating the good points of others and correcting one's own faults are mutually reinforcing. See *Analects* 7.22.

66. "Gets through" is *heng* 亨 and "Lord" is *di* 帝, so the real original meaning of this line, as opposed to Zhu Xi's "original meaning," is clearly in reference to sacrifice—either the

living king sacrificing to Shangdi 上帝 (the High Lord) or a deceased king interceding in Heaven with Shangdi. See "The Four Virtues" in the introduction, "Key Terms and Concepts."

67. They are both central *yin* lines and both mention the tortoises and good fortune.
68. The "suburban divination" (*bujiao* 卜郊), according to the *Liji*, was an oracle bone divination in preparation for the great sacrifices outside the city. See *Liji*, "Jiao te sheng" 郊特牲, 24, where the term is used in reference to the sacrifice to Earth on the summer solstice.
69. The *gui* 圭, or official tablet, was a symbol of enfeoffment or service to a feudal lord.
70. *Chunqiu Zuozhuan* 春秋左傳 (*Zuo Commentary* on the *Spring and Autumn Annals*), 1.6 (Duke Yin of Lu 魯隱公, 6th year). Lu 魯, Jin 晉, and Zheng 鄭 were three of the feudal states nominally under the Zhou 周. Duke Yin of Lu reigned 722 to 712 BCE. "When Zhou moved to the east" refers to the shift of the capital eastward from Chang'an to Luoyang after Chang'an was sacked by the Quanrong 犬戎 (also known as Xianyun 猃狁), a nomadic tribe from the northwest, in 771.
71. Wilhelm says the aims are those of the duke, because the fourth line has diminished itself, changing from *yang* in Pi to *yin* here. Therefore it is in service to the duke, represented by the *yang* in the fifth (Richard Wilhelm, trans., *The I Ching, or Book of Changes*, 600-601).
72. I.e., the *yang* has almost replaced all the *yin* lines in the hexagram. Zhu Xi uses *jue* 決 for "resolving, resolution" in his commentary except when quoting lines from the text. "Resolving, resolution" in the text itself is always *guai* 夬.
73. Strength and pleasure are the virtues of the component trigrams.
74. Legge renders this sentence as "[He] dislikes allowing his gifts to accumulate (undispensed)" (*The Yi King, or Book of Changes*, 320). Wilhelm: "[He] refrains from resting on his virtue" (*I Ching*, 604). Lynn: "He dwells in virtue and so clarifies what one should be averse to" (*The Classic of Changes*, 405). There is no discussion of it in Zhu X's *Classified Conversations* (*Zhuzi yulei*).
75. Quoting the Smaller Image commentary below. For the "Way of centrality" (*zhong dao* 中道), see "Central" in the introduction, "Key Terms and Concepts."
76. I.e., the person is excessively determined to expel the inferior.
77. It is the only *yang* line that corresponds correctly with any other line.
78. Wen Jiao 溫嶠 (288-329) was a Jin 晉 dynasty general who pretended to conspire with Wang Dun 王敦 (266-324) to overthrow the Jin emperor, but was actually loyal to the emperor and caused Wang's defeat. See *Jinshu* 晉書 (History of the Jin), chap. 98 (https://zh.wikisource.org/wiki/晉書/卷098).
79. This is the bottom line of the upper trigram, Dui, one of whose symbolic associations is the sheep (*Shuogua* 8).
80. "Proceed centrally," for Zhu Xi, implies acting in line with one's moral nature, which is to be "authentic" (*cheng* 誠).
81. "Rectifying the mind" (*zheng xin* 正心) and "making the intentions authentic" (*cheng yi* 誠意) are the middle two of the "eight items" of the *Great Learning* (*Daxue*). The latter is usually translated "making the will sincere." "Fully develop his illustrious [mind]" is an allusion to the endpoint of the eight items: "to illustrate one's illustrious virtue [*ming mingde* 明明德] to the world."
82. Quoting from Cheng Yi's *Yizhuan* (*Er Cheng ji*, 923).

83. When the word is *gou* 姤 I use uppercase "Encountering." When it is *yu* 遇 I render it "encountering."
84. I.e., the top *yin* line of Guai (43) becomes *yang*, yielding Qian (1), then leading to Gou: ䷪ → ䷀ → ䷫. See the upper portion of Diagram 6, "Fuxi's Directional Positioning of the Sixty-Four Hexagrams." The fifth lunar month is late June to early July, just after the summer solstice, when *yin* begins to grow again.
85. The upper trigram, Qian ☰, is Heaven; the lower trigram, Sun ☴, is a *yin* trigram associated with the eldest daughter, hence also Earth. All six of the "mixed" trigrams are classified as *yin* or *yang* according to their unique line. See also *Xici* B.4.1-2.
86. The first sentence is the same as line 4 of hexagram 43 (Guai).
87. The 6 at the beginning represents the common people (*yin*) and 9 in the second represents the minister (*yang*) who controls them.
88. "Covering a melon" (*bao gua* 包瓜): Wang Bi reads this as *pao gua* 匏瓜, a type of gourd (Wang Bi and Han Kangbo, *Zhouyi Wang-Han zhu*, 5:3b).
89. In our version of the *Liji* this is in the "Summary of Sacrifice" (Jitong 祭統) chap., 31.
90. Note how Zhu Xi introduces self-cultivation (cultivating the spirit) into a passage that is primarily about ritual correctness.
91. I.e., it is 9 in the fifth that draws 6 in the second into gathering.
92. Based on "King Wen's Directional Positioning of the Eight Trigrams" (Diagram 8 and below, with directions added from *Shuogua* 5.2). Sun is the southeast and Kun is the southwest, so south is between them at the top of the diagram (according to Chinese cartographic convention; see *Zhuzi yulei* 72:1840). The prognostication is auspicious because of the correct correspondence between the second and fifth lines, even though neither of them is properly positioned. Also, south is generally auspicious because in the northern hemisphere the sun (Li trigram: fire) is always in the southern half of the sky.

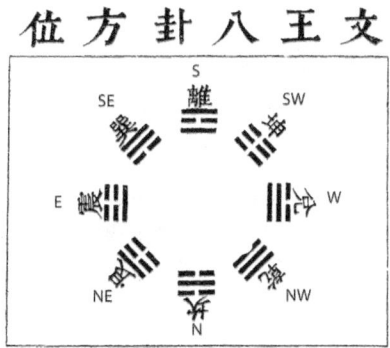

93. Wang Su 王肅 (195-256) wrote or edited the *Sayings of the Confucian School* (*Kongzi jiayu* 孔子家語).
94. This image of Kun is not mentioned in the *Shuogua*. Zhu Xi probably derives it from Kun's basic symbolism of Earth (territory).
95. In Sui (17, top line), Mount Qi, near the first Zhou capital, is referred to as the western mountain (see chap.1, n. 207).

96. In his *Classified Conversations* (*Zhuzi yulei*) Zhu Xi says that the Kun hexagram is particularly difficult to understand, and groups it with Jian 蹇 (39), Bo 剝 (23), Pi 否 (12), and Kui 睽 (38) as "bad" or inauspicious hexagrams. This is one of the nine hexagrams referred to in *Xici* B.7.2-4. The statements there are, "Kun is the discernment of virtue," "Kun is being exhausted yet persisting," and "Kun lessens resentment." See also chap.1, n.113.
97. The *yang*/firm or *yin*/yielding character of a mixed trigram is determined by the line that is unique; thus Kan is a *yang*/firm trigram and Dui is a *yin*/yielding one. See *Xici* B.4.1-2.
98. The "crimson sash" was a knee band worn by nobles in ceremonial settings.
99. This apparent contradiction is probably why Zhu Xi said that this hexagram is difficult to understand.
100. Cutting off the nose and feet was a form of punishment or torture.
101. This is one of the nine hexagrams referred to in *Xici* B.7.2-4. The statements there are, "Jing is the ground of virtue," "Jing is staying in place yet moving," and "Jing distinguishes rightness."
102. "A city can be changed" refers to the practice of changing the capital for a new dynasty.
103. "Wood" refers to the wooden beam on a hinge that lets down the clay jug on a rope into the well.
104. I.e., the well represents the constant and long-lasting basis of society, which should be respected and continued.
105. Although water is of course *yin*, the idea here is that *yin* must come from *yang*. Perhaps Zhu is thinking also of the rock underlying the well, from which water springs forth.
106. Zhu Xi's interpretation suggests that *xing ce* 行惻 might be translated as "practice suffers" instead of "causing sorrow."
107. In this section I use three variations to express the appropriate connotation of *ge*: "changing/overturning," "changing" (or "change"), and "opposing." The overall idea is the creative tension between opposites. In addition, in line 6 I use "turn," following Zhu Xi's explanation. Zhu Xi's definition, *biange*, is used in the *Liji* in reference to customs and cultural conventions that could be altered by the ruler on behalf of the people (*Liji*, "Great Treatise," 5). So *ge*, in his mind, was not limited to radical change as implied by "overturning."
108. Here Zhu is explaining how the struggle or opposition of water and fire can yield a positive prognostication—the idea of creative struggle.
109. *Geming* is the modern Chinese word for revolution. King Tang was the founder of the Shang dynasty and King Wu was the Zhou king who defeated the Shang; each of them brought about a shift of the Mandate of Heaven from one family to another. This line is consistent with Mencius's discussion of "changing the Mandate" in *Mencius* 5A.5.
110. The fire is "in" the lake because the lower trigram is "inner" and the upper is "outer." This line is the referent of the title of Frances Fitzgerald's 1972 book *Fire in the Lake: The Vietnamese and the Americans in Vietnam*. The character for Ge was on the cover of the book.
111. Its "greatness" lies in the fact that the creative tension between *yin* and *yang* brings about the transformative processes of life, symbolized by the flow of the seasons.
112. *Huang* 黃 is usually translated "yellow," but it is actually yellow-brown, the color of the loess soil in the Yellow River valley, China's traditional heartland. "Hide" is the original meaning of *ge* 革, the hexagram name.
113. "Yellow-brown" and "center" are two of the correlations with "earth" in the Five Phases system.

114. I.e., not to rush into change, but to act only after due consideration.
115. "Renewing the people" is a phrase from the *Great Learning* (*Daxue*), sect. 3, quoted there from the *Shujing*, "Kang gao" 康誥, item 4. The connection with "molting" is that the great person or Sage uses change creatively for the benefit of the people.
116. "Turns to face" is actually "alters his face" (*ge mian* 革面), but "turns to" is more consistent with Zhu Xi's explanation. The superior person here is inferior to the "great person" in line 5 (the hexagram ruler).
117. I.e., there are still details to take care of, so 6 at the top should not pursue further change.
118. A *ding* is a specific type of tripod ritual vessel, with ringed handles, used for cooked meats offered in a sacrifice or a banquet. It is lifted with a bar inserted into the ringed handles (called "ears"). Here is a bronze example from the early Zhou dynasty.

119. The text actually says, "Supreme, auspicious success," but in his comment Zhu says that "auspicious" is a superfluous word, probably because this is the only place in the *Yijing* where *yuan* 元 and *heng* 亨 are separated by one other word.
120. "Enters" is *sun* 巽, the lower trigram, one of whose virtues is "entering" (*ru* 入) (*Shuogua* 7). Wood is one of its images in *Shuogua* 11.
121. I.e., developing their most positive implications.
122. This is from an episode, in the third year of Duke Xuan of Lu 魯宣公 (r. 608–591 BCE), about the nine cauldrons that symbolized the legitimacy of a dynasty, specifically about their weight. See Stephen Durrant, Wai-yee Li, and David Schaberg, trans., *Zuo Tradition / Zuozhuan*, 602–3.
123. Taking a concubine to gain a son implies that she will become a wife, so it is "taking the humble and making it honored."
124. I.e., it can no longer be used because its ring handles are gone.
125. The text actually says, "The cauldron's feet break, getting him wet."
126. Yellow is the color associated with the center.
127. Because, as Zhu Xi points out, it is a *yang* line in a *yin* position.
128. In the following text *zhen* is translated as either "thunder" or "arousing" as appropriate. When the word for thunder is *lei* 雷, it is so identified.
129. See Cheng's commentary in *Er Cheng ji*, 963–64. The idea is that there is concern for the proper, reverential behavior of the eldest son performing the sacrifice, lest he be frightened by the thunder and drop the ladle.

130. Repeating the second line of the Commentary on the Judgment.
131. I.e., it is dangerous for a yielding (weak) line to "ride on" a firm (strong) line.
132. The word *yi* 億 actually means 100,000, or some very large amount, but in his *Classified Conversations* (*Zhuzi yulei* 73:1850) Zhu says it should be another *yi* 噫, "alas."
133. In addition to "still" and "stop" I occasionally use "come to rest" for *zhi* 止. Also, I use "stillness" for *jing* 靜, so these instances will be identified.
134. The context of this comment is Zhu Xi's theory of the relationship of activity and stillness (*dong-jing* 動靜), which is found most prominently in his discussions of Zhou Dunyi (see Adler, *Reconstructing*, chap. 3). The very last passage of Zhou Dunyi's *Tongshu* 通書 (Penetrating the *Yi*) quotes the Gen hexagram statement, "stilling the back" (Adler, *Reconstructing*, 298), and his *Taijitu shuo* says that the Sage "emphasizes stillness" (*zhu jing* 主靜, paraphrased by Zhu Xi here) (198–99). Briefly, Zhu Xi's theory of the interpenetration of activity and stillness ("stillness in activity, activity in stillness," 178), referring primarily to mental activity and stillness, linked Zhou Dunyi's *yin-yang* cosmology with his own theory of self-cultivation, which he said enabled the mind (*xin* 心) to comprehend its own moral nature (*xing* 性) or principle (*li* 理). As mentioned in the introduction, Zhu's commentaries on Zhou Dunyi's two texts and his commentary on the *Yi* were all completed within a ten-month period in 1187–1188 (Shu Jingnan, *Zhu Xi nianpu changbian*, 2:871, 886, 911), and his *Yixue qimeng* 易學啟蒙 (Introduction to the study of the *Yi*) just a year before that (837).
135. Because even in activity there should be an underlying stillness. Elsewhere Zhu Xi calls this reverent composure (*jing* 敬; see Adler, *Reconstructing*, 70, 92–98). Put differently, correct activity is always aligned with the unfolding of the moral Way or *dao*. Since that Way is a process and correct activity never departs from it, the two are "stationary" in relation to each other (stillness in activity).
136. "Hearty and substantial" is from the first sentence of the Commentary on the Judgment of Daxu: "Firm and strong, hearty and substantial, shining and luminous, daily renewing one's virtue." In his *Classified Conversations* (*Zhuzi yulei* 73:1851) Zhu Xi says that this sentence expresses the imagery of Gen, and that Gen is one of the best hexagrams.
137. This absence of contact between the second and third lines reflects the lack of "correspondence" in the hexagram as a whole. Since it is one of the eight hexagrams consisting of a doubled trigram, there is no correspondence between lines in the upper and lower trigrams.
138. I.e., there is reason for regret, but it is negated by the fact that the line is central and, with the cheeks stilled, speech is orderly.
139. I.e., someone mistakenly added it because of the rhyming appeal of *zhong* and *zheng* 中正, which are often found together in the *Yi*. In fact the line is central but not correct.
140. "The woman marries" (*nü gui* 女歸) is, literally, "the woman returns" or "returns home." The implication is that the husband's family is her true home; the word is not used for a man being married. See also the next hexagram, Guimei 歸妹 (Betrothed Sister).
141. I.e., 漸之進也 should be 漸，漸進也.
142. The third and fifth positions (odd) are both "correct" for a 9 (*yang*), while the positions they come from—the second and fourth (even), respectively—are both incorrect.
143. I.e., the original sentence was probably, "The superior person abides in virtue and improves the customs of the worthies."
144. Gen, the lower trigram, represents the youngest son (*Shuogua* 10).

145. *Shijing* 詩經, "Fa tan" 伐檀 (Mao 112), 1. Both Legge and Waley (*The Book of Songs*, 286) translate the phrase as "eat the bread of idleness" (from Proverbs 31:27).
146. The text actually says, "The wild goose gradually advances toward high ground." See Cheng Yi's comment in *Er Cheng ji*, 977, where he quotes Hu Yuan 胡瑗 (his teacher).
147. The uncollated editions of the *Zhouyi benyi*, plus the *Zhouyi zhezhong*, have the word *gai* 蓋 (now, probably) instead of *wei* 位 (position) in the next-to-last sentence.
148. Based on this sentence alone it would be appropriate to translate the hexagram name as "married sister." But lines 3 and 4 clearly imply that the marriage has not yet taken place.
149. See the family associations of the Eight Trigrams in Diagram 7 (King Wen's Sequence of the Eight Trigrams) and *Shuogua* 10.
150. The logic is that it is wrong for a woman to act independently (and to enjoy it, no less), so she should get married.
151. Because of the predominance of incorrect line positions, as Zhu explains in his comment on the hexagram statement.
152. In that case the sentence would be, "Because of the betrothed sister's lowly status she comes back as a secondary wife."
153. Sovereign Yi (Di Yi) was the penultimate king of the Shang dynasty (early eleventh century BCE). The marriage of his younger sister is also mentioned in hexagram 11 (Tai), line 5. S. J. Marshall believes that the marriage was to King Ji, father of King Wen of the Zhou (*Mandate of Heaven*, 157–58).
154. Normally it means a ten-day week, as Wilhelm takes it.
155. Seeing stars at midday obviously sounds like a total solar eclipse. S. J. Marshall has argued that this eclipse occurred on June 20, 1070 BCE, and was taken to be an omen of the conquest of the Shang dynasty by the Zhou (*Mandate of Heaven*, chaps. 4–5). He also argues that, since Feng 豐 (the hexagram name) was the name of the city from which King Wu marched on Shang, and since Fa 發 (here rendered as "developing") was King Wu's personal name, the original meaning of this sentence was, "The city of Feng was so obscured at midday the Big Dipper was seen. Though able to depart, the urgency was doubted. Having verification, Fa complied. (Prognostication:) Auspicious" (81).
156. Zhu is referring to Wang Bi (*Zhouyi Wang-Han zhu*, 6:1b; see also Lynn, *Classic of Changes*, 490).
157. Resting/stopping is a virtue of Gen (*Shuogua* 4); brightness and clinging are virtues of Li (*Shuogua* 5.2 and 7).
158. Cf. Zhu's comment to the first passage of the Commentary on the Judgment of Gen (52), and n. 135.
159. As in English, "bright" (*ming* 明) means both light and intelligent.
160. Actually Zhu Xi has added the prognostication (good fortune), which does not appear in the line.
161. For the pronunciation of Sun, see the note to table I.2 in the introduction. Zhu Xi does not specify, either here or in his *Classified Conversations* (*Zhuzi yulei*), whether it is *sun* or *xun*. Its primary meaning is "gentle, insinuating"; in the text it is sometimes translated as "gently." It is one of the nine hexagrams referred to in *Xici* B.7.2–4. The statements there are, "Sun is the controller of virtue," "Sun is assessing while being hidden," and "Sun is acting provisionally."
162. See Zhu's comment on the first line. Wu Deng 吳澄 (1249–1333) and Yu Yan 俞琰 (1258–1314), who normally follow Zhu Xi's interpretation, identify the fourth line (also *yin*) as

the ruler. Li Guangdi says both the first and fourth are "constituting rulers," while the fifth is the "governing ruler." See Nielsen, *Companion*, 87, 91, and "Hexagram Rulers" in the introduction, "Key Terms and Concepts."

163. In Zhu Xi's *Classified Conversations* (*Zhuzi yulei* 73:1861) someone asks, "Does the word *shen* 申 mean that the command is sent down two times?" Reply: "No. It is just carefully repeated, so 'the decree is reiterated.'" A more direct translation would be "the decree is issued."

164. Note how Zhu Xi omits the astrologers and shamanesses from his comment—a good example of his "rationalizing" tendency. He does the same in a comment in the *Classified Conversations* (*Zhuzi yulei* 73:1862).

165. The Heavenly Stems (*tian gan* 天干) of the calendrical system were used to number the ten days of the week in ancient times. See chap. 1, n. 209.

166. In his *Zhuzi yulei* Zhu Xi admits, "I don't understand 'three days before a change, three days after a change.' It looks like it has to do with a model for divining for a day. In [the hexagram statement of] Gu 蠱 [18], 'Three days before the first' is *xin* 辛 [the eighth day]; three days after the first is *ding* 丁 [the fourth day]. In this hexagram, 'three days before *geng*' is also *ding*, but 'three days after *geng*' is *gui*. *Ding* and *xin* were both days when people in ancient times offered sacrifice and prayer. But the *gui* day did not have this status" (73:1862).

167. Cf. 9 in the fourth of Lü (56), where possessions (provisions) and ax are found. "Deciding" (*duan* 斷) is related to the image of the ax, as in "logic chopping."

168. Another translation would be "Is this correct? Ominous." Wilhelm and Lynn interpret it this way, but I am following Zhu Xi's explanation (Wilhelm, *I Ching*, 684; Lynn, *Classic of Changes*, 505).

169. Kan 坎, which Zhu Xi defines as "doubly abysmal," is the image of water flowing downward, as in Richard Lynn's translation, "constant sinkhole." Dui is the image of water remaining on the surface, like a marsh or lake—a more positive image.

170. The firmness of each trigram is the central *yang* line; the *yin* line above is outer, just as the lower trigram is inner and the upper is outer.

171. As Wilhelm puts it, this is "a strong line in a lowly place," embodying "firmness and modesty" (*I Ching*, 687). Thus it willingly expresses its auspicious *yang* nature, without ulterior or factional motives, as Wang Bi clearly explains (see Lynn, *Classic of Changes*, 508). This is a good example of Zhu Xi's "minimalist" commentary style.

172. According to Li Guangdi, the two *yin* lines are the constituting rulers of the hexagram (*Zhouyi zhezhong*, 119).

173. "Both" referring to the wind/water imagery and the king/temple imagery.

174. The trigram Kan is associated with strong horses in *Shuogua* 11.5.

175. I.e., the power to rescue and disperse comes from 9 in the second.

176. In his *Classified Conversations* (*Zhuzi yulei* 73:1864) Zhu Xi explains that this refers to the hexagram fluctuation he describes earlier, in which 9 in the third of Jian (53) has moved (fled) into this central position, which is more comfortable.

177. "Disperse" here in the sense of breaking up one's exclusive focus on the self.

178. These statements allude to political factionalism, which Zhu Xi regarded as one of the reasons for the fall of the Northern Song dynasty to the Jurchen in 1127. Hence the value of dispersing the small group for the greater good.

179. Lu Zhi 陸贄 (754-805) was a high official under Tang emperor Dezong. I have not tracked down the quotation. The second sentence is parsed according to Zhu Xi's remarks in *Zhuzi yulei* 73:1865.

2. PART B   361

180. That line is the same as this, with the substitution that Zhu suggests here ("blood vanishes and fear departs"). Otherwise this line would be "Dispersing blood; it vanishes. Staying far away; no blame."
181. It is bounded or limited because the capacity of the lake is finite and cannot hold water in unlimited amounts.
182. I.e., the principle that taking limitation too far is wrong.
183. The gate leads from the private courtyard out to the public street. The door mentioned in the previous line leads from indoors to the private courtyard.
184. Although Zhu Xi equates the two terms here, in his *Classified Conversations* (*Zhuzi yulei* 73:1867) he quotes Cheng Yi: "'What resides inside is *fu* 孚; what is visible in affairs is *xin* 信.' This statement is very good." So *fu* is the inner quality (honesty) while *xin* is the outward manifestation (trust), resulting in people believing what one says. Zhu also says this under the hexagram statement of Xu (5).
185. What Zhu Xi means is that with "perfect trust" one can influence animals to do dangerous things, and that kind of power can be equally effective in other human affairs. The key words are "stimulate" (*gan* 感) and "responsiveness" (*ying* 應), which can have moral applications in Song Confucian thought (see Adler, "Response and Responsibility"). "Inner trust" therefore connotes the idea of moral responsiveness and sensitivity. See also Zhu Xi's last comment on the Tuan commentary under Xian (31) and n. 4.
186. I.e., being honest and correct are two ways of putting into practice the moral nature given by Heaven.
187. Being lenient in legal cases is an example of moral sensitivity or moral responsiveness—i.e., responding appropriately to the specific situation at hand rather than applying a general rule or universal principle. See my discussion of "moral responsiveness" in Adler, "Response and Responsibility."
188. This line is discussed in *Xici* A.8.5.
189. In his *Zhuzi yulei* Zhu Xi admits to some puzzlement about the meaning of this line (73:1868).
190. The first part of the sentence is the same as that of Xiaochu (9), line 5.
191. The Sun trigram is associated with fowl in *Shuogua* 8.
192. *Xiaoguo* is used in two senses, which can be expressed as "surpassing by the small" and "surpassing the small" (*Zhuzi yulei* 73:1869).
193. The hexagram structure resembles a bird, with the solid *yang* body in the center and the less substantial ("empty") *yin* wings on both sides.
194. Quoting the Greater Image Commentary. Here "passing through" is more apt than "surpassing" for *guo* 過, because in his *Classified Conversations* (*Zhuzi yulei* 73:1869) Zhu explains, "This is the sound in a high location coming down, the meaning of the 'small passing through.' 'The flying bird lets go his cry' is also a sound coming down from a high location."
195. Guo Pu 郭璞 (276-324) was a *fengshui* 風水 (geomancy) and divination expert. His *Donglin* 洞林 (Forest of grottoes) was a record of his own practice of *Yijing* divination (it is also called *Yi donglin* 易洞林). It exists today only in scattered excerpts (see Dominik Declercq, *Writing against the State*, 278-81, which includes translations of four cases).
196. The same sentence is found in the hexagram statement of Xiaoqu (9).
197. In the *Classified Conversations* (*Zhuzi yulei* 73:1870) Zhu says that "dense clouds, no rain" generally means "being unable to do something."

198. Cheng Yi explains this more fully: "When *yang* sinks and *yin* rises they combine to form rain. *Yin* is already at the top [i.e., the fifth and sixth lines], so although the clouds are dense, how can they form rain? *Yin* surpassing and being unable to make anything is the general meaning" (*Er Cheng ji*, 1017).
199. This would replicate the hexagram statement as Zhu Xi thinks it should read ("small success").
200. Or "in terms of rightness, no blame."
201. "High Ancestor" (Gaozong) was the temple name of King Wu Ding 武丁 of the Shang, whose wife was the powerful Fu Hao 婦好. "Ghost Region" (Guifang 鬼方) was somewhere northwest of the Shang territory. See Marshall, *Mandate of Heaven*, 45, 176–77n63.
202. *Er Cheng ji*, 1020–21 (Zhu Xi paraphrases Cheng). This was also Wang Bi's reading (see Lynn, *Classic of Changes*, 541). The upper trigram, of which this line is the beginning, symbolizes water. The emendation also lends itself to a clearer connection with the second sentence.
203. Referring to the Confucian theory that dynasties begin full of virtue and end in evil and chaos when their virtue dissipates. The Zhou 周, ruled by King Wen, were the western neighbors of the Shang and eventually conquered them in 1045 BCE. By the "moment" (literally, "the time") I think Zhu Xi is alluding to "their time"—i.e., the opportune moment for the Zhou to attack the Shang. So 6 in the second is the Zhou making preparations in the west (*yin*), while 9 in the fifth is the same Zhou after they have moved east (*yang*) and conquered. Before the conquest, King Wen was imprisoned by King Zhou 紂 of the Shang, and while in prison, according to the traditional account, he composed the hexagram statements of the *Yi*.
204. Being the opposite of hexagram 63, every line of this hexagram is improperly positioned, yet they all correspond correctly.
205. See the reference to the Ghost Region in Jiji (63), line 3.

3. TREATISE ON THE APPENDED REMARKS

1. Sima Qian uses *Xi*[*ci*] in chapter 47 of the *Shiji* 史記 (Historical records, ca. 100 BCE), and his father, Sima Tan, uses *Dazhuan* in chapter 130 (see Donald Sturgeon, ed., *Chinese Text Project*, http://ctext.org/shiji). Richard Rutt thinks *Xici* refers only to the sections of the text that formally comment on passages from the basic text (*The Book of Changes (Zhouyi)*, 404). I use *Xici* because that is what the Song Confucians called it.
2. See Gerald W. Swanson, "The Great Treatise," 9. "Syncretist" is A. C. Graham's term for chapters 12–15 and 33 of the *Zhuangzi* (*Chuang Tzu: The Inner Chapters*, 28), although he dates these chapters to the second century BCE. Bent Nielsen (*A Companion to Yi Jing Numerology and Cosmology*, 24) and Li Xueqin ("Basic Considerations on the Commentaries of the Silk Manuscript *Book of Changes*," 380) date the *Xici* to the third century BCE.
3. Sections A.8.5–11, A.12.1, and B.5.1. All my citations are based on Zhu Xi's redaction of the text, which differs in a few places from Wang Bi's edition.
4. For some noteworthy studies of the *Xici* in English, see Swanson, "Great Treatise"; Willard J. Peterson, "Making Connections"; Edward L. Shaughnessy, "The Writing of the *Xici Zhuan* and the Making of the *Yijing*"; and Roger Ames, "The *Great Commentary* (*Dazhuan* 大傳) and Chinese Natural Cosmology."

3. TREATISE ON THE APPENDED REMARKS   363

5. As Zhu Xi correctly states, the term "appended remarks" (*xici* 繫辭) is used in the treatise itself (A.2.1, A.8.2, A.11.9, A.12.2, A.12.5, B.1.1) in reference to the texts that King Wen and the Duke of Zhou appended to the hexagrams—i.e., the hexagram and line statements. Thus the title of this treatise implies that it is focused more on the textual levels of the *Yi* than on the symbolism of the graphic level (trigrams and hexagrams).
6. Honored and humble also connote social position. So the *Xici* begins with a statement of the parallelism between Heaven and humanity, providing a natural justification for social hierarchy.
7. *Zhuangzi* 莊子, "Tianxia" 天下 (All Under Heaven), 1 (see Sturgeon, *Chinese Text Project*).
8. This line appears in Zhou Dunyi's Diagram of Supreme Polarity (*Taijitu* 太極圖), as does one phrase from *Xici* B.5.13.
9. Note that the text of A.1.1, previously, associates "images" with Heaven and "forms" with Earth, and Zhu Xi affirms that in his comment. Elsewhere, however, Zhu uses "image" in a broader sense. E.g., the *Tuan* commentary on hexagram 4, Meng 蒙 (Dim, Ignorant), says, "Meng is danger below the mountain." Zhu Xi's comment: "This uses the trigram image [mountain] and the trigram virtue [danger] to explain the hexagram name." So "image" in this case refers to something in the earthly realm.
10. Cf. Zhou Dunyi's *Taijitu shuo* 太極圖說 (Discussion of the Supreme Polarity diagram) and Zhu Xi's commentary on it (see Adler, *Reconstructing the Confucian Dao*, 181–83).
11. For various other interpretations of *tuan* and *yao*, see Nielsen, *Companion*, 238, 289.
12. In Zhu Xi's *Zhuzi yulei* someone asks about this line of the text and gives the following explanation, with which Zhu Xi agrees: "'Regret and disgrace' are not quite auspicious or ominous: they are the first sprouts of [mental] activity, so they can become subtle [*wei* 微] instances of good fortune or misfortune. Transitions [*jie* 介] are like boundaries, such as the boundaries where good and bad are first distinguished" (74:1889). This terminology, especially "the first sprouts of activity," "subtle instances," and "the moment when good and bad have been activated but not yet taken form" alludes to Zhu's theory of "incipience" (*ji* 幾) as the key to the functional efficacy of *Yijing* divination; note in Zhu's comment here how he relates it to self-cultivation. See my discussion of incipience in Smith et al., *Sung Dynasty Uses of the I Ching*, 190–99. Incipience is mentioned in *Xici* A.10.5 (where Zhu defines it as "subtle" [*wei* 微]) and B.5.11. It is also an important term in Zhou Dunyi's *Tongshu* 通書 (Penetrating the *Yi*), sects. 3, 4, and 9 (see Adler, *Reconstructing*, chap. 7). The selection in the *Zhuzi yulei* immediately following the one quoted here is an interesting phenomenology and analysis of the feelings of regret and disgrace and their relationship to auspicious or ominous outcomes.
13. In his *Zhuzi yulei* Zhu defines "small and great" as bad and good, or ominous and auspicious, hexagrams (74:1889).
14. In *Xici* B.2.1 these activities are explicitly attributed to Fuxi in his creation of the Eight Trigrams, to whom Zhu Xi alludes in his commentary. But Zhu believed that Fuxi also created the Sixty-Four Hexagrams, as he states in the first sentence of his comment on hexagram 1.
15. For Zhu Xi's naturalistic understanding of ghosts and spirits, see Adler, "Varieties of Spiritual Experience," 122–28.
16. "Extending spirit": *shen* (spirit), *qi*, and *jing* (essence) constitute a continuum of increasing "density," so *shen* is implied even though not mentioned.

17. Zhu omits here the corresponding fate of the *hun*, which becomes the ancestral spirit. See Adler, "Varieties of Spiritual Experience." This passage and the similar one in B.2.1 describe a mythic paradigm of "investigating things and extending knowledge" (*gewu zhizhi* 格物致知), the central method of "learning to be a Sage" (*sheng xue* 聖學) by "fully understanding principle/order" (*qiong li* 窮理) in Zhu Xi's system.
18. Alluding to *Shuogua* 1.3: "[Fuxi] fully explored the order [of things], fulfilled their natures, and thereby attained [Heaven's] decree."
19. Translated thusly (instead of "what completes it") to convey the idea that human nature is the *process* of actualizing one's Heaven-endowed moral potential; it is not a fixed essence. See, by Roger Ames, "The Mencian Conception of *Ren xing* (人性)" and "Mencius and a Process Notion of Human Nature"; see also A. C. Graham, "The Background of the Mencian Theory of Human Nature."
20. Alluding to *Zhongyong* 22. The passage of text is also similar to *Zhongyong* 1 ("What is given by Heaven is the nature; according with the nature is called the Way").
21. In other words, "containing" is *yin*; what is contained is the nature received from Heaven. "Carrying out" is *yang*, and entails transforming the physical nature and nourishing the moral nature. Zhou Dunyi said, e.g., "Only humans receive the finest and most spiritually efficacious [*qi*]" (*Taijitu shuo*). The Cheng brothers discussed "transforming and nourishing" frequently.
22. *Yang* and *yin* are always defined contextually, so what is *yang* in one context may be *yin* in another. "The previous section" refers to A.4.3, which also discusses wisdom and humanity. Zhu's explanation of the difference is a bit strained, but his point is that A.4.3 is about the psychophysical constitution of the Sage, while this passage is about moral practice.
23. For a definition of the "Great Undertaking" (*da ye* 大業), see chap. 1, n. 16.
24. I.e., being humane (*ren* 仁) is creating oneself as a fully human being (*ren* 人). As Mencius said (7B.16), "Being humane is being human" (*renyezhe renye* 仁也者人也). This is how human beings share in the creativity of Heaven. In Zhu Xi's essay "Discussion of Humanity" (Renshuo 仁說) he correlates the first of the Four Virtues of Qian (hexagram 1), "origination" (*yuan* 元), with the first of Mencius's "Four Norms" (*si chang* 四常), humanity (*ren* 仁) (and likewise with the rest of each group). (See Wing-tsit Chan, *A Source Book in Chinese Philosophy*, 563). He does the same in his comment on the first passage of the *Wenyan* 文言 (Remarks on the text) appendix.
25. Zhu Xi quotes this line in his *Zhuzi yulei* (1:4). Cheng Hao had said something similar in his "Reply to Master Zhang Hengchu's Letter on Calming Human Nature": "The constant principle of Heaven and Earth is that their mind is in all things, and yet they have no mind of their own. The constant principle of the sage is that his feelings are in accord with all creation, and yet he has no feelings of his own" (*Er Cheng ji*, 460; Chan, *Source Book*, 525).
26. *Zheng meng* 正蒙, sect. 14; in Zhang Zai, *Zhangzi quanshu*, 3:15b.
27. See "Change" in the introduction, "Key Terms and Concepts."
28. I.e., daily activity performed properly demonstrates an understanding of change.
29. Zhang Zhongding 張忠定 (Zhang Yong 張詠, 946–1015) was a Northern Song official and poet. Zhu discusses him in *Zhuzi yulei* 93, where he says that this statement by Zhang is consistent with Zhou Dunyi's thought—presumably because Zhou's thought, especially as interpreted by Zhu, is based on the *yin-yang* polarity. A. C. Graham translates Zhang's

whole statement in *Two Chinese Philosophers*, 171n18. The portion relevant to Zhu's comment here is, "All judicial cases, until they are decided in writing, belong to the *yang*. What is important in the *yang* is producing; it can be adapted to changing situations. After the written decision they belong to the *yin*; what is important in the *yin* is punishment (or 'assuming form'; *xing* 刑)." Undecided cases are *yang* presumably because they are still developing; decided cases are like the previous passage, "following patterns is called Kun" (i.e., *yin*).

30. Zhang Zai, *Zheng meng*, sect. 2 (*Zhangzi quanshu*, 2:5b). See the discussion of this in Adler, "Varieties of Spiritual Experience," 136–37.

31. "Four Virtues" usually refers to the four qualities of Qian in hexagram 1 ("Great and penetrating, appropriate and correct" in Zhu Xi's interpretation). In Zhu's comment on *Wenyan*, Qian, 22, he also identifies "firm, creative, central, correct" as four virtues of Qian. Here, however, I think he is referring to the "Four Images" (*sixiang* 四象) of the *Yi*, which are the four two-line diagrams resulting from the division of the "Two Modes" (*liangyi* 兩儀), or single-line diagrams: mature *yang* ⚌, young *yin* ⚎, mature *yin* ⚏, and young *yang* ⚍. See Zhu Xi's *Yixue qimeng* 易學啟蒙 (Introduction to the study of the *Yi*, 1186), chap. 2 (Adler, trans., *Introduction to the Study of the Classic of Change*, 17 and fig. 5). The other two groups of four apply only to Qian, while this group applies to Qian and Kun, consistent with the text here. "Mature" and "young" correspond with "active" and "still."

32. By "Heaven's forms" Zhu Xi means the heavenly bodies, although "forms" (*xing* 形) are more typically associated with earth, as in A.1.1.

33. Here Zhu is emphasizing that the nature of things, or principle/order (*li*), is coeval with the universe and is complete in human beings at birth. Thus *cheng xing* cannot be "It completes the nature."

34. Referring to the Cook Ding story in *Zhuangzi*, chap. 3. "Principle can proceed" illustrates a point made frequently by Zhu Xi: that principle/pattern/order is a process that "flows forth" (*liuxing* 流行). Thus "ordering" or "patterning" might be better translations. See "*Li*" in the introduction, "Key Terms and Concepts."

35. The following seven passages are clearly an interpolation. Each consists of a quote from a line statement, which is identified by Zhu Xi in his comment, so I do not footnote them. Section A.12.1 probably goes with them, as Zhu also notes. See Zhu's comment on A.7.1 concerning the unnamed Master. In some cases it is not clear where the quote from the Master ends. These passages closely resemble source 1B of the *Wenyan* in form.

36. Cf. *Analects* 6.30: "One who is humane, desiring to establish himself, establishes others; desiring to broaden himself, broadens others."

37. Section 9 is not in the Mawangdui text of the *Yi*, and is clearly a later interpolation. It is the fragmentary source of Zhu Xi's reconstruction of the milfoil divination method (see appendix).

38. See Cheng Yi, "Remarks on the *Yi*" (*Yishuo* 易說), in *Er Cheng ji*, 1030. This short collection of statements on part A of the *Xici* is not part of Cheng's *Commentary on the Yi* (*Yizhuan* 易傳), so it may have been compiled from Cheng's oral statements. See Yung Chun Tsai, "The Philosophy of Ch'eng I," 53.

39. Diagram 1. For Zhu's full discussion of the numerology and symbolism of the *Hetu*, see his *Yixue qimeng*, chap. 1.

40. "Mature" refers to the pure *yin* and *yang* numbers (6 = 2 + 2 + 2 and 9 = 3 + 3 + 3, respectively); "young" means the numbers composed of mixtures of *yin* and *yang* (7 and 8). See

"Time" in the introduction, "Key Terms and Concepts." Note that the directions Zhu Xi mentions are based on Chinese cartographic convention, with south at the top.

41. Compare Zhu Xi's *Yixue qimeng*: "Therefore as for the positions of the River Chart: 1 and 6 are akin and reside in the north; 2 and 7 are friends and reside in the south; 3 and 8 are similar and reside in the east; 4 and 9 are cohorts and reside in the west; 5 and 10 protect each other and reside in the center. This is because as numbers they are nothing more than 'one *yin*, one *yang*,' each pair [corresponding] with one of the Five Phases.... Heaven from 1 generates water; Earth with 6 completes it. Earth from 2 generates fire, and Heaven with 7 completes it. Heaven from 3 generates wood, and Earth with 8 completes it. Earth from 4 generates metal, and Heaven with 9 completes it. Heaven from 5 generates soil, and Earth with 10 completes it. This is the meaning of 'Each has its match.'" See Adler, *Introduction*, 7.

42. For an excellent summary of the "number of the Great Expansion," see Nielsen, *Companion*, 39–43. Here it refers to the number of yarrow (milfoil) stalks used in the divination procedure.

43. See also appendix and the *Yixue qimeng*, chap. 3.

44. In his *Yixue qimeng* Zhu Xi explains this line as follows: "The 216 stalks required for Qian are obtained by adding the stalks of the 6 lines, each of which is 36. The 144 stalks required for Kun are obtained by adding the stalks of the 6 lines, each of which is 24" (Adler, *Introduction*, 44). The 36 and 24 stalks refer to those left over after the three processes of counting off and placing between the fingers—i.e., those left on the table. In the three "changes" that yield a changing (mature) *yang* line, the numbers placed between the fingers are 5 for the first and 4 for the second and third, totaling 13. Since the total stalks being used is 49, that leaves 36 on the table. For a changing (mature) *yin* line, the numbers placed between the fingers are 9 for the first and 8 for the second and third, totaling 25, and 49 − 25 = 24.

45. This is another example of Zhu Xi's naturalistic interpretation of language that clearly refers to personalized spirits (see Adler, "Varieties of Spiritual Experience," 124–28; *Zhuzi yulei* 75:1918). The idea is that through the mysterious efficacy of the numbers underlying the *Yi* and the yarrow stalks themselves (A.11.2-3), moral action can be aligned with the *dao* in ways that transcend human ability.

46. Paraphrasing the *Yili* 儀禮 (Etiquette and ritual), 1.1. The "charge" is the oral announcement of each stage of the ritual. See John Steele's translation in *The I-Li, or Book of Etiquette and Ceremonial*, 1–2 (for the Chinese text, see Sturgeon, *Chinese Text Project*). See also the *Shiyi* (Divination ritual), appendix.

47. "Maximizing these numbers" (*jiqi shu* 極其數) means developing the implications of the numbers to the utmost.

48. Three fluctuations or "changes" are required to yield a single line (see, previously, 9.6).

49. These characters (參 and 伍) are used as equivalents of the numbers 3 (*san* 三) and 5 (*wu* 五), like writing out "three" and "five" instead of using the Arabic numerals. However, in most of the classical quotes Zhu Xi gives in the following, they mean something like "to compare." In the case of 參 (pronounced *can* instead of *san*), this is the basic meaning of the word (consult, etc.). The basic meaning of 伍 (*wu*) is a group of five soldiers. According to Richard Rutt, *canwu* as an expression, based on this passage, came to mean "sorting out complications" (*Book of Changes*, 431).

50. This is for two reasons. First, as the following quotations show, the meaning of the term in earlier texts is far from clear. Second, even though Zhu Xi chooses to interpret them

as the numbers 3 and 5, those numbers are not particularly significant in the yarrow-stalk method of divination. See Wilhelm, trans., *The I Ching, or Book of Changes*, 315, and Richard Lynn, *The Classic of Changes*, 73n45. In *Hui'an xiansheng Zhu wengong wenji* Zhu Xi has a short essay on the sentence, "Threes and fives, by fluctuating, mix and combine their numbers," using the same quotations as he uses here (67:3257).

51. Eric Hutton, *Xunzi*, 152.
52. Burton Watson, *Han Fei Tzu*, 87.
53. Zhu Xi's quote differs from the version of *Han feizi* that we have today in the last word of the sentence. Burton Watson translates our version as, "Compare with concrete results; check against empty assertions" (*Han Fei Tzu*, 38).
54. Burton Watson, *Records of the Grand Historian*, 212. Watson says in a footnote, "To know 'the threes and fives' is to know the true situation" (212). Raymond Dawson translates the sentence as, "One must put them in threes and fives" (*Historical Records*, 60), adding in a note, "i.e. one must sort people out" (161). William H. Nienhauser et al. give, "One must [consider things] three times and four [sic] times" (*The Grand Scribe's Records, Volume VII*, 365).
55. Yiu-ming Fung, "The School of Names," 165. Harold Roth and Sarah Queen translate the phrase as "[the School of Names' methods of . . .] the three [tests to determine a minister's merit] and the five [tests to determine a minister's faults] do not err" (in *Sources of Chinese Tradition*, ed. Wm. Theodore de Bary and Irene Bloom, 281). The phrase is in Sima Tan's discussion of the School of Names (*mingjia* 名家) in his outline of the Six Schools of Thought, quoted by Sima Qian in his *Shiji*, chap. 30.
56. Ban Gu 班固, *Han shu* 漢書 (History of the [Former] Han), in Sturgeon, *Chinese Text Project*. The chapter where this sentence occurs (76) is not included in Homer H. Dubs, trans., *The History of the Former Han Dynasty*.
57. This passage, according to Zhu Xi, describes the ideal operation of the human mind, in which stillness and activity interpenetrate. See Adler, *Reconstructing*, 85–86, and my discussion and further comments by Zhu Xi in Smith et al., *Sung Dynasty Uses of the I Ching*, 190–94.
58. As mentioned, "incipiencies" are the crucial moments when a change has begun but has not yet become evident.
59. The true Sage does not need divination, as he has perfected his own spiritual understanding and can thereby detect subtle, incipient changes on his own. The ordinary person, although theoretically capable of this, has not reached that goal of self-cultivation. See Smith et al., *Sung Dynasty Uses of the I Ching*, 192, 202–5; Adler, "Varieties of Spiritual Experience," 136–38.
60. At least once Zhu Xi goes further than this and actually seems to identify ghosts and spirits as the effective power behind tortoise and milfoil divination:

    > The tortoise lives for a long time and so is numinous [*ling* 靈]. The milfoil grows for a hundred years, with a hundred stalks on one root; it too is a spiritual [*shen* 神] and numinous thing. Divination is actually questioning ghosts and spirits by means of the milfoil and tortoise, which are spiritual and numinous things. We thus make use of them to verify their hexagrams and omens. (quoted in *Shangshu zuanzhuan* 尚書纂傳, 22:19b–20a, by the Yuan-dynasty compiler Wang Tingyu 王天與)

    This is a comment on section 7 of the "Hongfan" 洪範 (Great plan) chapter of the *Shujing* 書經 (Scripture of documents), which deals with tortoise and milfoil divination.

Given that Zhu's understanding of ghosts and spirits was entirely naturalistic (i.e., they are manifestations of *qi*), the statement should be interpreted as metaphor. I have not found the quote in Zhu's own writings; perhaps it was ignored by those compilers because it didn't seem like what Zhu Xi "should" have said.

61. Cf. Zhou Dunyi's *Taijitu shuo*: "The Supreme Polarity in activity generates *yang*; yet at the limit of activity it is still. In stillness it generates *yin*; yet at the limit of stillness it is also active."
62. See, previously, Zhu's comment on A.5.2.
63. This passage is the earliest classical instance of the term *taiji* 太極 and was the basis of the philosophy of Shao Yong (1012–1077). The text actually reads *daji* 大極, but Zhu says *da* should be read *tai*. I have argued that if Zhu Xi's sole reason for elevating Zhou Dunyi's *Taijitu shuo* to a position of prominence was to use the concept of *taiji* in that text as a link between the metaphysical discourse of *li* and the cosmological discourse of *qi*, this passage, as he interprets it here, would have served that purpose. I propose, in *Reconstructing the Confucian Dao*, another explanation of his elevation of Zhou Dunyi.
64. The meaning here seems to be that the great Confucian task of perfecting the self and perfecting society depends in part on the ability to interpret auspicious and ominous signs or tendencies in the process of change and to act accordingly.
65. "Sages" in the last line of the text refers to both Fuxi and Yu 禹, who used the *Luoshu* as a model for the Nine Divisions of the world (see Adler, *Introduction*, chap. 1). The *Luoshu* appeared on the back of a spirit tortoise to the Sage-king Yu, although the Song court painter Ma Lin includes the tortoise in his famous painting of Fuxi (on the cover of this book). "Sage" (singular) refers specifically to Fuxi. "What the Sage followed in creating the *Yi*" alludes to Fuxi's creation of the *Yi* in *Xici* B.2.1.
66. Richard Rutt, disagreeing with Zhu Xi's interpretation, suggests that "four" here is a mistake, as the passage makes more sense just in terms of "images" (*Book of Changes*, 432).
67. Before paper was invented during the Han dynasty, the most common writing medium was thin strips of bamboo tied together.
68. Wilhelm (*I Ching*, 322) and Lynn (*Classic of Changes*, 67) both rationalize "drummed and danced" in different ways. Zhu Xi, interestingly, accepts the literal meaning: in his *Zhuzi yulei* he says of it, "Before a divination there are doubts; after a divination there are no doubts. This can naturally cause people to be light and quick of hand and foot, and to act accordingly" (75:1931). As scholars such as Richard Kunst, Edward Shaughnessy, and Richard Rutt have argued, the original *Zhouyi* came from a highly ritualistic context that had roots in early Chinese shamanism, which can involve drumming and dancing. While by the time the *Xici* was written that context was highly attenuated, its authors may well have been aware of it. Still, Zhu Xi does not go as far as saying that the drumming and dancing involved either spirit possession or spirit journeys.
69. Zhu Xi is referring to the edition of Zhou Dunyi's *Tongshu* transmitted by Hu Hong's family; see Adler, *Reconstructing*, 300.
70. The text actually says, "Are Qian and Kun the mystery [*yun* 縕] of the *Yi*?" But Zhu Xi says that this *yun* should be read as *yun* 蘊, meaning "to contain."
71. This is the locus classicus of these two terms, which in modern Chinese mean "metaphysical" and "concrete."
72. In the first part of the sentence Zhu again affirms that human nature contains the fullness of natural/moral principle. In the second part he alludes to the idea that the purest,

3. TREATISE ON THE APPENDED REMARKS 369

clearest, form of *qi* is spirit (*shen*), and with clear *qi* one can realize one's innate moral nature.

73. This is the "Fuxi 伏羲 sequence" of trigrams, also known as the *xiantian* 先天 (prior to Heaven, or a priori) sequence—Diagram 3. The sequence does not appear anywhere in the *Yijing*, although Shao Yong claims it is based on *Shuogua* 3.1. It probably originated with either Chen Tuan 陳摶 (d. 989), as Zhu claims in *Zhuzi yulei* 100:2552, or Shao Yong, who championed it. See Nielsen, *Companion*, 264-68, and "Cycles and Sequences of the Eight Trigrams," 131.
74. Firm and yielding lines "displacing each other" refers to *yang* changing to *yin* and vice versa. "Activity" refers to the inherent dynamism of a hexagram, based on its changing lines.
75. In other words, the oracular meaning of the hexagrams is based on their directional change; they are like vectors (forces with direction), not static pictures of either the present or the future.
76. "Waning and waxing" hexagrams is one of the standard methods of hexagram fluctuation (*guabian* 卦變). See "Time" in the introduction, "Key Terms and Concepts."
77. See "Change" in the introduction, "Key Terms and Concepts."
78. The original text has "people" (*ren* 人) here, but Zhu Xi says it should be "humanity" (*ren* 仁). On the first sentence, see also A.5.6 and note.
79. Quoting *Shujing*, "Da Yu mo" (Counsels of the Great Yu), 13.
80. Although this mentions only the Eight Trigrams, recall that Zhu Xi believed that Fuxi also created the sixty-four hexagrams.
81. Quoting the top line statement of Dayou (14). On the terms "change," "fluctuation," "transformation," and "continuity," see "Key Terms and Concepts" in the introduction.
82. The idea is probably that oxen and horses take pleasure in being of service.
83. I.e., the active pestle above the stationary mortar.
84. The structure of Daguo ䷛ can symbolize the firm (*yang*) coffin inside the soft (*yin*) earth.
85. Zhu Xi here is counting a broken line as two strokes and a solid line as one. Richard Rutt has the same explanation (*Book of Changes*, 432). Han Kangbo has another: "As the few are patriarchs of the many, so the One is he to whom the masses gravitate" (see Lynn, *Classic of Changes*, 80). Richard Wilhelm has yet another, referring to the numbers 6, 7, 8, and 9, which determine the type of line (*I Ching*, 337). To put his explanation more concisely, the sum of two even numbers and one odd is always odd; the sum of two odds and one even is always even. Zhu Xi's student, Chen Zhi 陳埴 (*jinshi* 1216), agrees with Han Kangbo, as does Li Guangdi (*Zhouyi zhezhong*, 1059).
86. As in A.8.5-11, in this section I don't footnote the quotes from the *Yi* because Zhu Xi identifies them. Again, see Zhu's comment on A.7.1 concerning the unnamed Master. In some cases it is not clear where the quote from the Master ends.
87. Zhang Zai, *Zheng meng*, sect. 4 (*Zhangzi quanshu*, 2:13b).
88. Note the similarity of this passage to some of the paradoxical statements in the *Laozi* (e.g., 9).
89. In his comment on the fourth line of Ding, Zhu Xi alters "its form getting wet" to "he is severely punished."
90. Ban, *Han shu*, "Biography of King Yuan of Chu" (楚元王傳), 7. The sentence there is, "Incipience is the subtle sign of activity, when the auspicious and ominous are first visible."

91. Yan Hui was the favorite disciple of Confucius. Although this passage contains the word *ji* 幾, which in the previous passage means "incipience," Zhu Xi explains in the *Zhuzi yulei* that here it means "close, almost," as it is sometimes used in the *Mencius* and the *Zuozhuan* (76:1949). Han Kangbo (Wang Bi and Han Kangbo, *Zhouyi Wang-Han zhu*, 8:5b) and Richard Rutt (*Book of Changes*, 426) read this passage as a reference to "incipience" in the previous one.
92. This phrase is also applied to Fuxi in *Xici* B.2.1.
93. "High antiquity" would be the periods of Fuxi, Shennong, and Huangdi. "Rustic simplicity" is seen, e.g., in the simplicity of the lines and hexagrams created by Fuxi, which nevertheless contained all the meanings later explicated by King Wen and the Duke of Zhou, in "middle antiquity" (eleventh century BCE). See also B.11.
94. Han Kangbo interprets *er* more straightforwardly, explaining that the "two" refers to failure and success (*Zhouyi Wang-Han zhu*, 8:6b). Cheng Yi agrees with him (*Zhouyi zhezhong*, 1075).
95. Middle antiquity refers to the late Shang and early Zhou periods, as Zhu Xi explains.
96. This and the next two passages are called the Three Presentations of the Nine Hexagrams (*sanchen jiugua* 三陳九卦). The reason for this grouping is unclear (see Nielsen, *Companion*, 194-95). In the *Zhuzi yulei* Zhu Xi describes them as "incidental" (*ouran* 偶然) oral remarks by Confucius (76:1952).
97. *Li* was an alternative pronunciation of *lü* 履 ("treading" in the sense of "proceeding correctly") in the third through tenth centuries, and was cognate with *li* 禮 (Paul W. Kroll, *A Student's Dictionary of Classical and Medieval Chinese*, 286).
98. In the *Zhuzi yulei* (76:1952) Zhu says, "'Fu is the root of virtue' is like Mencius's term 'self-reflection' [*zifan* 自反]" (in *Mencius* 2A.2 and 4B.28).
99. Quoting the Tuan commentary on Qian (15).
100. *Shujing*, "Gao Yao mo" (Counsels of Gao Yao), 2. The nine virtues, in Legge's translation, are "affability combined with dignity; mildness combined with firmness; bluntness combined with respectfulness; aptness for government combined with reverent caution; docility combined with boldness; straightforwardness combined with gentleness; an easy negligence combined with discrimination; boldness combined with sincerity; and valour combined with righteousness" (see Sturgeon, *Chinese Text Project*).
101. Here "ritual propriety" stands for Treading, as Zhu equates the two in his previous comment. The idea is that by treading carefully and properly one can achieve one's goals better than by acting forcefully. Compare *Analects* 2.3, where Confucius says that government by virtue and ritual propriety is more effective than government by law and punishment.
102. The two names "Zhou" here are unrelated. According to the Zhou dynastic doctrine of the Mandate of Heaven, the virtue of every dynasty flourishes at first and then declines, causing Heaven to award the mandate to another family. King Zhou of the Shang was the "wicked" last king of the Shang, and King Wen was the virtuous founder of the Zhou, who was imprisoned for a while by King Zhou. It was allegedly during this imprisonment that he wrote the hexagram statements of the *Yi*.
103. Zhu Xi clearly thinks the text here is overly optimistic. This is consistent with his general attitude toward the achievement of Sagehood, which he thinks is very difficult.
104. The second half of the first sentence actually reads, "[Kun] is able to examine the feudal lords' deliberations."
105. "The mind and order combining" (*xinyu lihui* 心與理會) describes Zhu Xi's concept of "being authentic" (*cheng* 誠), which is when the "human mind" (*renxin* 人心) and "moral

mind," or "mind of Dao" (*daoxin* 道心), are perfectly aligned, and one's activity perfectly reflects one's moral nature. See Adler, *Reconstructing*, 78–81, and n. 9. *Lihui* can also be a binome meaning "understanding," in which case the phrase could be rendered, "the mind's involvement with understanding."

106. They share in the *Yi*'s power by practicing divination (*Zhuzi yulei* 76:1963).
107. The hexagram drawing is only one of the meanings of "image" (*xiang* 象); that is what it means here (see "Image" in the introduction, "Key Terms and Concepts").
108. "Lost what he should preserve" might be an allusion to Mencius's statements (e.g., 4B.28, 6A.8) about preserving and nourishing the innate moral nature of the mind.

4. TREATISE DISCUSSING THE TRIGRAMS

1. See Richard Rutt, *The Book of Changes (Zhouyi)*, 434; Edward L. Shaughnessy, trans., *I Ching*, 336n34.
2. *Yixue qimeng* 2:1253 (see Adler, trans., *Introduction to the Study of the Classic of Change*, 22). Quoting from Shao Yong, *Huangji jingshi shu*, 7A:24a.
3. Bent Nielsen, "Cycles and Sequences of the Eight Trigrams," 137; Richard Lynn, *The Classic of Changes*, 124n7.
4. See Shaughnessy's translation of the Mawangdui text, with the original Chinese, in his *I Ching*, 218–19, line 15, and his comments on the relative dating of the two versions, 18.
5. See Joseph Needham, *Science and Civilisation in China, Volume 3*, 210–19. See also the explanation by Kidder Smith and Don Wyatt in Smith et al., *Song Dynasty Uses of the I Ching*, 118–20.
6. Although some translators (e.g., Legge, Wilhelm, Rutt) think this passage refers to the plural Sages who created the *Yi* (including King Wen and the Duke of Zhou), the fact that it discusses the invention of yarrow-stalk divination means it probably refers specifically to Fuxi. And while *shenming* 神明 sometimes means "gods and spirits," for Zhu Xi it typically means the spiritual capacity of human beings to intuit the natural/moral order (*li* 理), hence "spiritual clarity." See Adler, "Varieties of Spiritual Experience."
7. *Zhongyong* 22. The assistance works in the reverse direction here, but in the *Classified Conversations* (*Zhuzi yulei* 77:1965) Zhu makes clear that this is what he means.
8. Sima Qian 司馬遷, *Shiji* 史記 (Historical records), 128.7.
9. What is meant here is tripling a singular Heaven and doubling a singular Earth. In his *Classified Conversations* (*Zhuzi yulei* 77:1966) Zhu says, "One Heaven tripled makes three; one Earth doubled makes two."
10. The last sentence became a Cheng-Zhu slogan summarizing the meaning and import of the whole Confucian project of becoming a Sage. See Zhu's comment on *Xici* A.4.3.
11. I.e., as a verb in this sentence and as a noun in the next.
12. Since Zhu Xi believed that Fuxi created the sixty-four hexagrams, I am using singular "Sage," but the passage could just as well be referring to Fuxi as the creator of the eight trigrams and King Wen as the one who doubled them.
13. "Water and Fire do not combat each other" may be an error, as in the Mawangdui manuscript *Yizhi yi* 易之義 (Meanings of the *Yi*), which contains the first three sections of *Shuogua*, the text reads, "Water and Fire combat each other," which of course makes conventional sense. See Shaughnessy, *I Ching*, 218–19. Also, *Shuogua* 5.2 says that "*yin* and *yang* push against each other." In the *Classified Conversations* (*Zhuzi yulei* 77:1971–72) Zhu Xi goes to some lengths to explain the text as received, which may seem surprising as in

other cases he doesn't hesitate to say that some words are extraneous or errors—e.g., in *Xici* A.12.2 and B.6.3. One possible reason for his acceptance of "water and fire do not combat each other" is that "combat" (*she* 射, literally, "to shoot an arrow") is too dualistic a concept for a relationship that Zhu conceives as nondualistic polarity and *interpenetration*. E.g., section 16 of Zhou Dunyi's *Tongshu* 通書 (Penetrating the *Yi*) contains the line, "The *yin* of water is based in *yang*; the *yang* of fire is based in *yin*." Zhu Xi's comment on the line is, "Water is *yin*, yet it is generated from [the number] one, so it is based in *yang*. Fire is *yang*, and yet it is generated from two, so it is based in *yin*." See my discussion of this in *Reconstructing the Confucian Dao*, 260–61n151, and chap. 3. In the *Zhuzi yulei* he compares "water and fire do not combat each other" to "mountain and lake penetrate [each other's] *qi*," supporting the idea that he wants to leave conceptual space for interpenetration between water and fire.

14. This trigram arrangement is depicted in Diagram 4 (chapter 1), "Fuxi's Directional Positioning of the Eight Trigrams." For *xiantian*, see "Key Terms and Concepts" in the introduction.
15. For the first four the text uses the primary image of the trigram: thunder for Zhen 震, wind for Sun 巽, rain (water) for Kan 坎, sun (fire) for Li 離. The last four are given using the trigram names: Gen 艮, Dui 兌, Qian 乾, Kun 坤. Zhu Xi says that there is no particular significance to this (*Zhuzi yulei* 77:1972).
16. It is the same in the sense that they both describe the Fuxi sequence of trigrams: section 3 as in Fuxi's Sequence of the Eight Trigrams (Diagram 3) and section 4 as in Fuxi's Directional Positioning of the Eight Trigrams (Diagram 4).
17. Diagram 8. This sentence is found verbatim in Ma Guohan's (1794–1857) compilation of fragments from the *Lianshan*, the pre-Zhou predecessor of the *Zhouyi* (see Stephen L. Field, *Ancient Chinese Divination*, 32–33). (The *Lianshan* fragments comprise the first chapter of Ma's massive *Yuhan shanfang ji yishu* 玉函山房輯佚書.) "The Lord" is a good translation of *di* 帝 because both words can refer to either a deity (as here) or a human: the latter in *huangdi* 皇帝, "emperor." Di was originally the high god of the Shang 商 dynasty, also called Shangdi 上帝 (High Lord), who evolved into the Lord of Heaven (Tiandi 天帝) and the Jade Emperor (Yuhuang Shangdi 玉皇上帝 or Yuhuang Dadi 玉皇大帝).
18. "Six children" refers to the family correlations of the eight trigrams; see Diagram 7.
19. Referring to *Xici* B.2.1, describing how Fuxi surveyed all under Heaven to devise the hexagrams.
20. Referring to a collection of writings on the *Yi* by Xun Shuang 荀爽 (128–190) and nine unnamed affiliates. See Chen Ch'i-yün, "A Confucian Magnate's Idea of Political Violence," 73n2, 75.
21. "Luxuriant and fresh" may refer to Qian, and the sentence may allude to the *xiantian* (a priori) or Fuxi trigram sequence. See Zhu Xi's comment on section 3.2: "Starting from Zhen and passing through Li and Dui reaches Qian."

APPENDIX

1. Some also include shorter pieces in four-character verse, called "Five Appreciations of the *Zhouyi*" (*Zhouyi wuzan* 周易五贊); e.g., *Zhuzi quanshu* 朱子全書 [Zhu Xi's complete works], ed. Zhu Jieren, Yan Zuozhi, and Liu Yongxiang, 1:163–72). The Five Appreciations are "The Origin of the Images" (*Yuan xiang* 原象), "Conveying the Purpose" (*Shu zhi* 述旨), "Clarifying Divination" (*Ming shi* 明筮), "Comparing Categories" (*Ji lei* 稽類), and "Advice on Learning" (*Jing xue* 警學).

2. See Adler, trans., *Introduction to the Study of the Classic of Change*. The chapter titles are (1) "The Original [River] Chart and [Luo] Text" (Ben tushu 本圖書), (2) "The Origin of the Hexagrams" (Yuan guashu 原卦書), (3) "Explaining the Milfoil Stalks" (Ming shice 明蓍策), and (4) "Examining the Prognostications of the Changes" (Kao bianzhan 考變占).
3. *Shigua kaowu* 蓍卦考誤 (Examining errors in milfoil divination), in *Hui'an xiansheng Zhu wengong wenji* 66: 3219-39.
4. It is well summarized by Richard Wilhelm, trans., *The I Ching, or Book of Changes*, 721-23, and most other translations of the *Yi*.
5. The coin method assigns the number 2 to one side and 3 to the other, yielding 6, 7, 8, or 9 with three coins, thrown six times, building a hexagram one line at a time from the bottom. Just as in the milfoil stalk method, 6 and 8 are *yin* (broken line), 7 and 9 are *yang* (solid), 6 and 9 are "mature" (changing), and 7 and 8 are "young." However, the probabilities of yielding each type of line are different from those of the milfoil method—a fatal flaw in the eyes of some users. Others, however, point out that Zhu Xi's reconstructed milfoil method is not necessarily the one that was actually used in the Zhou dynasty, which may (speculatively) have had the same probabilities as the coin method. See, e.g., Joel Biroco's discussion at https://www.biroco.com/yijing/prob.htm (one of the better user-oriented websites; Biroco is also known as S. J. Marshall, author of *The Mandate of Heaven*), and Richard Rutt, *The Book of Changes (Zhouyi)*, 166-69. The use of three coins was called the Fire Pearl Forest (*huozhulin* 火珠林) method and was attributed to Jing Fang of the Han dynasty, but first appears in the literature in the early Tang dynasty (seventh century). See Bent Nielsen, *A Companion to Yi Jing Numerology and Cosmology*, 121-22; Richard J. Smith, *Fathoming the Cosmos and Ordering the World*, 232.
6. E.g., in the "Shisangli" 士喪禮 (Funeral ritual for an official) chapter, 37 (on divining for the day) (see Donald Sturgeon, ed., *Chinese Text Project*).
7. This random division, a chance event, is the point at which the "spiritual" (*shen* 神) power of the milfoil, in theory, exerts its influence.
8. In the *Qimeng* Zhu calls this the fourth finger (see Adler, *Introduction*, 34).
9. *Xici* A.9.3, quoted in *Yixue qimeng*, chap. 3. An intercalary month is a month added to the calendar at certain intervals to synchronize it with the sun, like leap-year day.
10. By "already counted off" Zhu means the stalks remaining in the left hand after removing some by counting off.
11. The third and fourth operations are separated like this because counting off is the third and placing between the fingers is the fourth.
12. The text says, "even is 1," but this is an error. It contradicts what Zhu Xi and his collaborator, Cai Yuanding, say in the *Yixue qimeng*: "[Zhu:] The single possible arrangement of 9 is called even. [Cai:] 9 minus the 1 placed between the fingers are 8; taking the 4s in 2 groups results in an even number. This is the *yin* number [2] of the Two Modes" (see Adler, *Introduction*, 35). In other words, a remainder of 9 in the first "change" reduces to 2.
13. In the *Yixue qimeng* Zhu Xi points out, almost parenthetically, that by taking 36, 32, 28, and 24—i.e., the numbers counted off instead of the numbers remaining in the left hand—and dividing them by 4 yields the same results: 9, 8, 7, and 6. This is a simpler, more direct way of deriving the four types of lines than that given in the preceding, which requires the rather arbitrary reduction of 9 and 8 to 2 and 5 and 4 to 3, then summing them to yield 9, 8, 7, and 6. Therefore, some people today prefer it.

BIBLIOGRAPHY

Adler, Joseph A. "Chance and Necessity in Zhu Xi's Conceptions of Heaven and Tradition." *European Journal for Philosophy of Religion* 8, no. 1 (2016): 143-62.
—. *Chinese Religious Traditions*. Upper Saddle River, N.J.: Prentice Hall, 2002.
—. "Divination and Philosophy: Chu Hsi's Understanding of the I-ching." Ph.D. diss., University of California, Santa Barbara, 1984.
—. "Divination and Sacrifice in Song Neo-Confucianism." In *Teaching Confucianism*, ed. Jeffrey L. Richey, 55-82. New York: Oxford University Press, 2008.
—. "The Great Virtue of Heaven and Earth: Deep Ecology in the *Yijing*." In *Religion and Ecological Sustainability in China*, ed. James Miller, Dan Smyer Yu, and Peter van der Veer, 48-70. London: Routledge, 2014.
—, trans. *Introduction to the Study of the Classic of Change (I-hsüeh ch'i-meng), by Chu Hsi*. Provo, Utah: Global Scholarly Publications, 2002.
—. *Reconstructing the Confucian Dao: Zhu Xi's Appropriation of Zhou Dunyi*. Albany: State University of New York Press, 2014.
—. "Response and Responsibility: Chou Tun-i and Confucian Resources for Environmental Ethics." In *Confucianism and Ecology: The Interrelation of Heaven, Earth, and Humans*, ed. Mary Evelyn Tucker and John Berthrong, 123-49. Cambridge, Mass.: Harvard University Center for the Study of World Religions, 1998.
—. "Varieties of Spiritual Experience: *Shen* in Neo-Confucian Discourse." In *Confucian Spirituality*, vol. 2, ed. Tu Weiming and Mary Evelyn Tucker, 120-48. New York: Crossroad, 2004.
Ames, Roger T. *Confucian Role Ethics: A Vocabulary*. Honolulu: University of Hawai'i Press, 2011.
—. "The *Great Commentary* (*Dazhuan* 大傳) and Chinese Natural Cosmology." *International Communication of Chinese Culture* 2, no. 1 (2015): 1-18.
—. "The Mencian Conception of *Ren xing* (人性): Does It Mean 'Human Nature'?" In *Chinese Texts and Philosophical Contexts: Essays Dedicated to Angus C. Graham*, ed. Henry Rosemont Jr., 143-75. Chicago: Open Court, 1991.
—. "Mencius and a Process Notion of Human Nature." In *Mencius: Contexts and Interpretations*, ed. Alan K. L. Chan, 72-90. Honolulu: University of Hawai'i Press, 2002.
Angle, Stephen C. "*Tian* as Cosmos in Zhu Xi's Neo-Confucianism." *Dao: A Journal of Comparative Philosophy* 17, no. 2 (2018): 169-85.
Ban Gu 班固 [32-93]. *Han shu* 漢書 (History of the [Former] Han). In Donald Sturgeon, ed., *Chinese Text Project*. http://ctext.org/han-shu.

Birdwhistell, Anne D. *Transition to Neo-Confucianism: Shao Yung on Knowledge and Symbols of Reality*. Stanford, Calif.: Stanford University Press, 1989.
Chan, Wing-tsit. "Chu Hsi's Appraisal of Lao Tzu." *Philosophy East and West* 25, no. 2 (1975): 131–44.
———. *A Source Book in Chinese Philosophy*. Princeton, N.J.: Princeton University Press, 1963.
——— [Chen Rongjie 陳榮捷]. *Zhuzi menren* 朱子門人 (Zhu Xi's disciples). Taipei: Xuesheng shuju, 1982.
Chen Ch'i-yün. "A Confucian Magnate's Idea of Political Violence: Hsün Shuang's (128–190 A.D.) Interpretation of the Book of Changes." *T'oung Pao* 54 (1968): 73–115.
Chen Lai 陈来. *Zhuzi shuxin biannian kaozheng* 朱子书信编年考证 (Investigation of the dating of Zhu Xi's letters). Shanghai: Renmin chubanshe, 1989.
Cheng Yi 程頤. *Yichuan Yizhuan* 伊川易傳 (Yichuan's commentary on the *Yi*). *Siku quanshu* 四庫全書 (Wenyuan ge 文源閣) edition. https://www.kanripo.org/text/KR1a0016/001#1a].
Cheng Yi 程頤 and Cheng Hao 程顥. *Er Cheng ji* 二程集 (Collection of the two Chengs). 4 vols. Beijing: Zhonghua shuju, 1981.
Chin, Annping, trans. *The Analects*. New York: Penguin Books, 2014.
Chu Ping-tzu 朱平次. "The Transmission of Shao Yong's *Yi* Learning before Zhu Xi." *Monumenta Serica* 61 (2013): 227–68.
Chun, Tsai Yung. "The Philosophy of Ch'eng I: A Selection of Texts from the Complete Works." Ph.D. diss., Columbia University, 1950.
Dai, Lianbin. "From Philology to Philosophy: Zhu Xi as a Reader-Annotator." In *Canonical Texts and Scholarly Practices: A Global Comparative Approach*, ed. Anthony Grafton and Glenn W. Most. 136–63. Cambridge: Cambridge University Press, 2016.
Davis, Scott. *The Classic of Changes in Cultural Context: A Textual Archaeology of the Yi jing*. Amherst, N.Y.: Cambria Press, 2012.
Dawson, Raymond, trans. *Historical Records*. Oxford: Oxford University Press, 1994.
de Bary, Wm. Theodore, and Irene Bloom, eds. *Sources of Chinese Tradition*, vol. 1. 2nd ed. New York: Columbia University Press, 1999.
Declercq, Dominik. *Writing against the State: Political Rhetorics in Third and Fourth Century China*. Leiden: Brill, 1998.
Dong Zhongshu 董仲舒. *Chun Qiu Fan Lu* 春秋繁露 (Luxuriant gems of the *Spring and Autumn Annals*). In Donald Sturgeon, ed., *Chinese Text Project*. http://ctext.org/chun-qiu-fan-lu.
Dubs, Homer H., trans. *The History of the Former Han Dynasty*. 3 vols. Baltimore: Waverly, 1938–1955.
Durrant, Stephen, Wai-yee Li, and David Schaberg, trans. *Zuo Tradition / Zuozhuan: Commentary on the "Spring and Autumn Annals."* Seattle: University of Washington Press, 2016.
Field, Stephen L. *Ancient Chinese Divination*. Honolulu: University of Hawai'i Press, 2008.
———. *The Duke of Zhou Changes: A Study and Annotated Translation of the Zhouyi* 周易. Wiesbaden: Harrassowitz, 2015.
Fingarette, Herbert. *Confucius: The Secular as Sacred*. San Francisco: Harper and Row, 1972.
Fung, Yiu-ming. "The School of Names." In *History of Chinese Philosophy*, ed. Bo Mou, 164–88. London: Routledge, 2009.
Gardner, Daniel K. "Confucian Commentary and Chinese Intellectual History." *Journal of Asian Studies* 57, no. 2 (1998): 397–422.
———. "Transmitting the Way: Chu Hsi and His Program of Learning." *Harvard Journal of Asiatic Studies* 49, no. 1 (1989): 141–72.
Graham, A. C. "The Background of the Mencian Theory of Human Nature." 1967. Reprinted in *Studies in Chinese Philosophy and Philosophical Literature*, by A. C. Graham. Singapore: Institute of East Asian Philosophies, 1986. Also reprinted in *Essays on the Moral Philosophy of Mengzi*, ed. Xiusheng Liu and Philip J. Ivanhoe, 1–63. Indianapolis: Hackett, 2002.
———. *Chuang Tzu: The Inner Chapters*. London: Allen and Unwin, 1981.
———. *Two Chinese Philosophers: Ch'eng Ming-tao and Ch'eng Yi-ch'uan*. London: Lund Humphries, 1958.
———. "What Was New in the Ch'eng-Chu Theory of Human Nature?" In *Chu Hsi and Neo-Confucianism*, ed. Wing-tsit Chan, 138–57. Honolulu: University of Hawai'i Press, 1986.
Gregory, Peter N., and Daniel A. Getz Jr., eds. *Buddhism in the Sung*. Honolulu: University of Hawai'i Press, 1999.

Gu Jiegang 顧頡剛. *Gushibian* 古史辨 (Analysis of ancient history). Vol. 3. 1931. Reprint, Hong Kong: Taiping shuju, 1963.

Hacker, Edward A., and Steve Moore. "A Brief Note on the Two-Part Division of the Received Order of the Hexagrams of the *Zhouyi*." *Journal of Chinese Philosophy* 30, no. 2 (2003): 219-21.

Hall, David L., and Roger T. Ames. *Thinking Through Confucius*. Albany: State University of New York Press, 1987.

Hon, Tze-ki. "Classical Exegesis and Social Change: The Song School of *Yijing* Commentaries in Late Imperial China." *Sungkyun Journal of East Asian Studies* 11, no. 1 (2011): 1-15.

——. *The Yijing and Chinese Politics: Classical Commentary and Literati Activism in the Northern Song Period, 960–1127*. Albany: State University of New York Press, 2005.

Hsia, C. T., Wai-yee Li, and George Kao, eds. *The Columbia Anthology of Yuan Drama*. New York: Columbia University Press, 2014.

Huang Zongxi 黃宗羲 and Quan Zuwang 全祖望, comps. *Song-Yuan xue'an* 宋元學案 (Scholarly record of the Song and Yuan dynasties). 2 vols. 1879. Reprint, Taipei: Guangwen shuju, 1971.

Hutton, Eric L., trans. *Xunzi: The Complete Text*. Princeton, N.J.: Princeton University Press, 2014.

Keightley, David N. *Sources of Shang History: The Oracle-Bone Inscriptions of Bronze Age China*. Berkeley: University of California Press, 1978.

Kinney, Anne Behnke, trans. *Exemplary Women of Early China: The Lienü Zhuan of Liu Xiang*. New York: Columbia University Press, 2014.

Knechtges, David R., trans. *Wen Xuan, or Selections of Refined Literature*. Vol. 3. Princeton, N.J.: Princeton University Press, 1996.

Knoblock, John, trans. *Xunzi: A Translation and Study of the Complete Works*. 3 vols. Stanford, Calif.: Stanford University Press, 1988-1990.

Knoblock, John, and Jeffrey Riegel, trans. *The Annals of Lü Buwei: A Complete Translation and Study*. Stanford, Calif.: Stanford University Press, 2000.

Kong Yingda 孔穎達 [574-648]. *Zhouyi zhengyi* 周易正義 (Orthodox meaning of the *Zhouyi*). Sibu beiyao 四部備要 edition.

Kroll, Paul W. *A Student's Dictionary of Classical and Medieval Chinese*. Leiden: Brill, 2015.

Kunst, Richard A. "The Original Yijing: A Text, Phonetic Transcription, Translation, Indexes, and Sample Glosses." Ph.D. diss., University of California, Berkeley, 1985.

Lau, D. C., trans. *The Analects*. Harmondsworth, UK: Penguin, 1979.

——, trans. *Lao Tzu: Tao Te Ching*. Harmondsworth, UK: Penguin, 1963.

——, trans. *Mencius*. Harmondsworth, UK: Penguin, 1970.

Lee, Lily Xiao Hong, and A. D. Stefanowska, eds. *Biographical Dictionary of Chinese Women: Antiquity through Sui, 1600 B.C.E.–618 C.E.* Armonk, N.Y.: M. E. Sharpe, 2007.

Legge, James, trans. *The Yi King, or Book of Changes*. 1899. Reprinted as *The I Ching: Book of Changes*. New York: Dover, 1963.

Levinovitz, Alan. "'Dao with a Capital D': A Study in the Significance of Capitalization." *Journal of the American Academy of Religion* 83, no. 3 (2015): 780-807.

Li Guangdi 李光地, comp. *Zhouyi zhezhong* 周易折中 (The *Yijing* judged evenly). 1716. 2 vols. Reprint, Taipei: Zhen shan mei, 1971.

Li Xueqin 李學勤. "Basic Considerations on the *Commentaries* of the Silk Manuscript *Book of Changes*." *Early China* 20 (1995): 368-80.

Liji 禮記 (Record of ritual). In Donald Sturgeon, ed., *Chinese Text Project*. http://ctext.org/liji.

Lin, Li-chen. "The Concepts of Time and Position in the *Book of Change* and Their Development." In *Time and Space in Chinese Culture*, ed. Huang Chün-chieh and Erik Zürcher, 89–113. Leiden: Brill, 1995.

Liu, James T. C. *Ou-yang Hsiu: An Eleventh-Century Neo-Confucianist*. Stanford, Calif.: Stanford University Press, 1967.

Lü Zuqian 呂祖謙. *Yishuo* 易說 / *Gu zhouyi* 古周易 (Discussions of the *Yi* / The ancient *Yi*). Beijing: Zhonghua shuju, 1991.

Luo Zhufeng 罗竹风, ed. *Hanyu da cidian* 漢語大詞典 (Comprehensive Chinese word dictionary). Shanghai: Hanyu da cidian chubanshe, 1995.

Lynn, Richard John, trans. *The Classic of Changes: A New Translation of the I Ching as Interpreted by Wang Bi*. New York: Columbia University Press, 1994.
Mair, Victor H., trans. *Wandering on the Way: Early Taoist Tales and Parables of Chuang Tzu*. New York: Bantam, 1994.
Marshall, S. J. *The Mandate of Heaven: Hidden History in the I Ching*. New York: Columbia University Press, 2001.
Minford, John, trans. *I Ching: The Book of Change*. New York: Viking, 2014.
Minford, John, and Joseph S. M. Lau, eds. *Classical Chinese Literature: From Antiquity to the Tang Dynasty*. New York: Columbia University Press, 2002.
Needham, Joseph. *Science and Civilisation in China, Volume 3: Mathematics and the Sciences of the Heavens and the Earth*. Cambridge: Cambridge University Press, 1959.
Nielsen, Bent. *A Companion to Yi Jing Numerology and Cosmology: Chinese Studies of Images and Numbers from Han (202 BCE–220 CE) to Song (960–1279 CE)*. London: RoutledgeCurzon, 2003.
——. "Cycles and Sequences of the Eight Trigrams." *Journal of Chinese Philosophy* 41, nos. 1-2 (2014): 130-47.
——. "Notes on the Origin of the Hexagrams of the *Book of Change*." *Studies in Central and East Asian Religions* 3 (1990): 42-59.
Nienhauser, William H., Jr., ed. *The Grand Scribe's Records, Volume V.1: The Hereditary Houses of Pre-Han China, Part 1*. Bloomington: Indiana University Press, 2006.
——, ed. *The Grand Scribe's Records, Volume VII: The Memoirs of Pre-Han China*. Bloomington: Indiana University Press, 1994.
Nylan, Michael. *The Five "Confucian" Classics*. New Haven, Conn.: Yale University Press, 2001.
Pankenier, David W. *Astrology and Cosmology in Early China: Conforming Earth to Heaven*. Cambridge: Cambridge University Press, 2013.
Park, George K. "Divination." In *The New Encyclopedia Britannica*, 15th ed., 1974.
Peng Guoxiang. "Spiritual and Bodily Exercise: The Religious Significance of Zhu Xi's Reading Methods." Trans. Daniel Coyle and Yahui Anita Huang. In *Returning to Zhu Xi: Emerging Patterns with the Supreme Polarity*, ed. David Jones and Jinli He, 325-42. Albany: State University of New York Press, 2015.
Peterson, Willard. "Another Look at *Li*." *Bulletin of Sung and Yüan Studies* 18 (1986): 13-31.
——. "Making Connections: 'Commentary on the Attached Verbalizations' of the *Book of Change*." *Harvard Journal of Asiatic Studies* 42, no. 1 (1982): 67-116.
Pregadio, Fabrizio, trans. *Cultivating the Tao: Taoism and Internal Alchemy; The Xiuzhen houbian (ca. 1798), by Liu Yiming*. Mountain View, Calif.: Golden Elixir Press, 2013.
Qian Mu 錢穆. *Zhuzi xin xue'an* 朱子新學案 (New scholarly record of Zhu Xi). 5 vols. Taipei: Sanmin shuju, 1971.
Raphals, Lisa. *Divination and Prediction in Early China and Ancient Greece*. New York: Cambridge University Press, 2013.
Redmond, Geoffrey. *The I Ching (Book of Changes): A Critical Translation of the Ancient Text*. London: Bloomsbury, 2017.
Rey, Georges. "The Analytic/Synthetic Distinction." In *The Stanford Encyclopedia of Philosophy*, ed. Edward N. Zalta. Fall 2015 ed. http://plato.stanford.edu/entries/analytic-synthetic.
Rickett, W. Allyn. *Guanzi: Political, Economic, and Philosophical Essays from Early China*. 2 vols. Princeton, N.J.: Princeton University Press, 1985.
Robinet, Isabelle. *Taoism: Growth of a Religion*. Trans. Phyllis Brooks. Stanford, Calif.: Stanford University Press, 1997.
Rutt, Richard. *The Book of Changes (Zhouyi): A Bronze Age Document*. Richmond, Surrey, UK: Curzon, 1996.
Saso, Michael. "What Is the Ho-t'u?" *History of Religions* 17, no. 3/4 (1978): 399-416.
Shao Yong 邵雍. *Huangji jingshi shu* 皇極經世書 (Ordering the world by the Royal Ultimate). Sibu beiyao 四部備要 edition.
——. *Yichuan jirangji* 伊川擊壤集 (Beating time by the Yi River). Sibu congkan edition.
Shaughnessy, Edward L. "The Composition of 'Qian' and 'Kun' Hexagrams of the *Zhouyi*." In *Before Confucius: Studies in the Creation of the Chinese Classics*, 197-219. Albany: State University of New York Press, 1997.

———. "The Composition of the *Zhouyi*." Ph.D. diss., Stanford University, 1983.
———, trans. *I Ching: The Classic of Changes*. New York: Ballantine Books, 1997.
———. *Unearthing the Changes: Recently Discovered Manuscripts of the Yi Jing (I Ching) and Related Texts*. New York: Columbia University Press, 2014.
———. "The Writing of the *Xici Zhuan* and the Making of the *Yijing*." Rev. ed., n.d., unpublished. Earlier version in *Measuring Historical Heat: Event, Performance, and Impact in China and the West*. Symposium in Honour of Rudolf G. Wagner on His 60th Birthday, Heidelberg, 2001. http://www.sino.uni-heidelberg.de/conf/symposium2.pdf.
Shchutskii, Iulian K. *Researches on the I Ching*. Princeton, N.J.: Princeton University Press, 1979.
Shu Jingnan 束景南. *Zhu Xi nianpu changbian* 朱熹年普長編 (Chronological record of Zhu Xi, extended edition). 2 vols. Shanghai: Donghua shifan daxue chubanshe, 2001.
———. *Zhuzi dazhuan* 朱子大传 (Complete biography of Zhu Xi). Beijing: Commercial Press, 2003.
Sima Qian 司馬遷. *Shiji* 史記 (Historical records). In Donald Sturgeon, ed., *Chinese Text Project*. https://ctext.org/shiji.
Slingerland, Edward G. *Effortless Action: Wu-wei as Conceptual Metaphor and Spiritual Ideal in Early China*. New York: Oxford University Press, 2003.
Smith, Kidder, Jr. "*Zhouyi* Interpretation from Accounts in the *Zuozhuan*." *Harvard Journal of Asiatic Studies* 49, no. 2 (1989): 421–63.
Smith, Kidder, Jr., Peter K. Bol, Joseph A. Adler, and Don J. Wyatt. *Sung Dynasty Uses of the I Ching*. Princeton, N.J.: Princeton University Press, 1990.
Smith, Richard J. *Fathoming the Cosmos and Ordering the World: The Yijing (I-Ching, or Classic of Changes) and Its Evolution in China*. Charlottesville: University of Virginia Press, 2008.
———. *Fortune-Tellers and Philosophers: Divination in Traditional Chinese Society*. Boulder, Colo.: Westview Press, 1991.
Smith, Wilfred Cantwell. *What Is Scripture? A Comparative Approach*. Minneapolis: Fortress Press, 1993.
Song Yiming 宋一明, ed. *Songkan Zhouyi benyi* 宋刊周易本義 (Song edition of *Zhouyi benyi*). 3 vols. Fuzhou: Fujian renmin chubanshe, 2008.
Steele, John. *The I-Li, or Book of Etiquette and Ceremonial*. 1917. Reprint, Taipei: Ch'eng-wen Publishing, 1966.
Strickmann, Michel. *Chinese Poetry and Prophecy: The Written Oracle in East Asia*. Ed. Bernard Faure. Stanford, Calif.: Stanford University Press, 2005.
Sturgeon, Donald, ed. *Chinese Text Project*. https://ctext.org. 2006–2018.
Swanson, Gerald William. "The Great Treatise: Commentary Tradition to the 'Book of Changes.'" Ph.D. diss., University of Washington, 1974.
T'ang Yung-t'ung. "Wang Pi's New Interpretation of the *I-ching* and *Lun-yü*." Trans. Walter Liebenthal. *Harvard Journal of Asiatic Studies* 10, no. 2 (1947): 124–61.
Theobald, Ulrich. *ChinaKnowledge.de*. http://www.chinaknowledge.de/index.html. 2000ff.
Thompson, Kirill O. "*Li* and *Yi* as Immanent: Chu Hsi's Thought in Practical Perspective." *Philosophy East and West* 38, no. 1 (1988): 30–46.
Tsai, Yung Chun. "The Philosophy of Ch'eng I: A Selection of Texts from the Complete Works." Ph.D. diss., Columbia University, 1950.
Virág, Curie. "Self-Cultivation as *Praxis* in Song Neo-Confucianism." In *Modern Chinese Religion I: Song-Liao-Jin-Yuan (960–1368 A.D.)*, ed. John Lagerwey and Pierre Marsone, 1187–1232. Leiden: Brill, 2015.
Waley, Arthur. "The Book of Changes." *Bulletin of the Museum of Far Eastern Antiquities* 5 (1933): 121–42.
———. *The Book of Songs*. New York: Grove Press, 1937.
Wang Bi 王弼 and Han Kangbo 韓康伯. *Zhouyi Wang-Han zhu* 周易王韓注 (Commentary on the *Yi* by Wang and Han). Sibu beiyao 四部備要 edition.
Wang Mouhong 王懋竑. *Zhuzi nianpu* 朱子年溥 (Chronological record of Master Zhu). Taipei: Shijie shuju, 1984.
Wang Tianyu 王天與, comp. *Shangshu zuanzhuan* 尚書纂傳 (Compiled commentaries on the *Shujing*). Siku quanshu 四庫全書 (Wenyuan ge 文源閣) edition.
Watson, Burton. *Han Fei Tzu: Basic Writings*. New York: Columbia University Press, 1964.
———, trans. *Hsün Tzu: Basic Writings*. New York: Columbia University Press, 1963.

——. *Records of the Grand Historian: Qin Dynasty*. Hong Kong: Renditions; New York: Columbia University Press, 1993.

White, Douglass Alan. "Interpretations of the Central Concept of the I-Ching during the Han, Sung, and Ming Dynasties." Ph.D. diss., Harvard University, 1976.

Wilhelm, Hellmut. *Change: Eight Lectures on the I Ching*. Trans. Cary F. Baynes. Princeton, N.J.: Princeton University Press, 1960.

——. "The Concept of Time in the Book of Changes." In *Man and Time: Papers from the Eranos Yearbooks*, ed. Joseph Campbell. Princeton, N.J.: Princeton University Press, 1957.

——. *Heaven, Earth, and Man in the Book of Changes*. Seattle: University of Washington Press, 1977.

Wilhelm, Richard, trans. *The I Ching, or Book of Changes*. Eng. trans. Cary F. Baynes. 3rd ed. Princeton, N.J.: Princeton University Press, 1967.

Yan Lingfeng 嚴靈峰, comp. *Yijing jicheng* 易經集成 (Collectanea of the *Yijing*). Taipei: Chengwen chubanshe, 1976.

Yan Pingqiu, trans. "Ceremonies of Milfoil Divination, by Zhu Xi." *Zhouyi Network* 4 (1989): 5–11.

Zhang Yachu and Liu Yu. "Some Observations about Milfoil Divination Based on Shang and Zhou *bagua* Numerical Symbols." Trans. Edward L. Shaughnessy. *Early China* 7 (1981–1982): 46–55.

Zhang Zai 張載. *Zhangzi quanshu* 張子全書 (Master Zhang's complete writings). Ed. Zhu Xi. Sibu beiyao 四部備要 edition.

Zhang Zhenglang [Chang Cheng-lang]. "An Interpretation of the Divinatory Inscriptions on Early Chou Bronzes." Trans. Jeffrey R. Ching, Scott Davis, Susan R. Weld, Robin D. S. Yates, and Horst Wolfram Huber. *Early China* 6 (1980–1981): 80–96.

Zheng Wangeng. "Tracing the Source of the Idea of Time in *Yizhuan*." Trans. Huang Deyuan. *Frontiers of Philosophy in China* 5, no. 1 (2010): 51–67.

Zhou Dunyi 周敦頤. *Zhou Lianxi xiansheng quanji* 周濂溪先生全集 (Complete collection of Zhou Dunyi's works). Compiled by Zhang Boxing 張伯行. In *Zhengyi tang quanshu* 正誼堂全書 [1708]. Baibu congshu jicheng edition, vols. 218–19.

Zhu Jieren 朱傑人, Yan Zuozhi 嚴佐之, and Liu Yongxiang 劉永翔, eds. *Zhuzi quanshu* 朱子全書 (Zhu Xi's complete works). 27 vols. Shanghai: Shanghai guji chubanshe / Anhui jiaoyu chubanshe, 2002.

Zhu Xi 朱熹. *Hui'an xiansheng Zhu wengong wenji* 晦庵先生朱文公文集 (Zhu Xi's collected papers) [1532]. In Zhu Jieren et. al., *Zhuzi quanshu*, vols. 20–25.

——. *Sishu jizhu* 四書集注 (Collected comments on the Four Books). Sibu beiyao 四部備要 edition.

——. *Songkan Zhouyi benyi* 宋刊周易本義 (The original meaning of the *Zhouyi*, Song edition). 3 vols. Ed. Song Yiming 宋一明. Fuzhou: Fujian renmin chubanshe, 2008.

——. *Yixue qimeng* 易學啟蒙 (Introduction to the study of the *Yi*). In *Zhouyi zhezhong* 周易折中 (The *Zhouyi* judged evenly) [1716], compiled by Li Guangdi 李光地, vol. 2. Taipei: Zhen shan mei, 1971.

——. *Yuanben Zhouyi benyi* 原本周易本義 (The original meaning of the *Zhouyi*, original version). *Siku quanshu* 四庫全書 (Wenyuan ge 文源閣) edition.

——. *Zhouyi benyi* 周易本義 (The original meaning of the *Zhouyi*). Ed. Tanaka Keitarō 田中慶太郎. Imperial Academy 國子監 edition. Taipei: Hualian, 1978.

——. *Zhouyi benyi* 周易本義 (The original meaning of the *Zhouyi*). Ed. Tu Yunqing 涂雲清. Taipei: Da'an, 1999.

——. *Zhouyi benyi* 周易本義 (The original meaning of the *Zhouyi*). *Siku quanshu* 四庫全書 (Wenyuan ge 文源閣) edition.

——. *Zhuzi quanshu* 朱子全書 (Zhu Xi's "complete works") [1713]. Compiled by Li Guangdi 李光地. Taipei: Guangxue, 1977.

——. *Zhuzi yulei* 朱子語類 (Master Zhu's classified conversations) [1270]. Compiled by Li Jingde 黎靖德. Beijing: Zhonghua shuju, 1986.

Zhu Xi 朱熹 and Lü Zuqian 呂祖謙, comps. 1175. *Reflections on Things at Hand: The Neo-Confucian Anthology*. Trans. Wing-tsit Chan. New York: Columbia University Press, 1967.

Zhu Zhen 朱震. *Jin Zhouyi biao* 進周易表 (Memorial presenting the *Zhouyi*). In *Hanshang yizhuan* 漢上易傳 (Zhu Zhen's commentary on the *Yi*), Tongzhitang jingjie edition [1680], vol. 1. Taipei: Taiwan datong shuju, 1969.

INDEX

Note: Individual trigrams are not indexed; nor are citations or the contents of tables.

Ames, Roger, 21, 327n59, 328n80
Analects (*Lunyu* 論語), 11, 332n21, 341n152, 350n11, 352nn40-41

Bi 比 Being Close (hexagram 8), 14, 92ff, 313
Bi 賁 Adorning (hexagram 22), 123, 135, 314
Bible, 2, 323n1
Birdwhistell, Anne, 34
Bo 剝 Declining/Breaking Down (hexagram 23), 26, 50, 138ff, 141, 144, 314
Buddhism, 10-11, 21-22, 28, 332n1, 326n29, 328n78, 352n42

Cai Yuanding 蔡元定, 45, 332n25, 373n12
Chao Yuezhi 晁說之, 52, 91, 157, 213, 219, 224, 334n42, 353n166
Chen Tuan 陳摶, 48, 332n21, 333n33, 369n73
Cheng Hao 程顥, 10, 327n52, 338n108, 343n180, 364n25
Cheng Tang 成湯 (first king of Shang), 177, 214, 348n267, 356n109
Cheng Yi 程頤, 10-11, 13-17, 19-21, 23, 33, 35, 42, 72-73, 98, 100, 113, 142, 181, 198, 221, 228, 256, 269, 324n11, 325n22, 326n31, 326n39, 326n44, 327n52, 329n94, 330n5, 331n18, 334n41, 337n80, 338n110, 340n142, 341n153, 341n163, 341n166, 342n177, 345n210, 345n219, 347n248, 347nn252-53, 347n259, 348nn261-62, 348n269, 349n273, 350n20, 352n38, 352n42, 353n53, 354n82, 359n146, 361n184, 362n198, 365n38, 370n94
Cheng-Zhu 程朱 school, 10, 23, 29, 34, 335n67, 371n10
Chunqiu 春秋 (Spring and Autumn Annals), 6, 9, 71
Confucius (Kongzi 孔子), 1, 6, 20, 52, 56-57, 61, 182, 199, 262, 271, 277, 325n14, 325n16, 330n9, 331n18, 332n22, 334n41, 334n46, 336nn70-71, 336n77, 346n241, 350n11, 350n20, 351n33, 352nn40-41, 370n91, 370n96, 370n101
Cui 萃 Gathering (hexagram 45), 202ff, 206, 314, 352n37

Daguo 大過 Surpassing by the Great (hexagram 28), 24, 153ff, 273, 289, 315, 369n84
dao 道, 6, 15-17, 22, 43, 263, 328n67, 335n66, 337n80, 337n82, 343n196, 358n135, 366n45
Daoism, 10-11, 21-22, 24, 261, 326nn28-29, 328n66, 328n74, 329n100, 333n33
daotong 道統 (succession of the Way), 6, 41
Daxu 大畜 Restrained by the Great (hexagram 26), 147ff, 223, 314, 341n153, 358n136
Daxue 大學 (Great Learning), 11, 38, 119, 326n37, 351n27, 354n81, 357n115
Dayou 大有 Great Possession (hexagram 14), 13, 111ff, 283, 315, 369n81
Dazhuan 大傳, 7, 261, 362n1; *see also Xici* (*zhuan*)
Dazhuang 大壯 Flourishing of the Great (hexagram 34), 26, 51, 170ff, 289, 315, 351n23

derived hexagram (*zhigua* 之卦), 25, 328n75
Diagrams of Hexagram Fluctuation (Diagram 9), 25, 50, 345n215, 364n24
Ding 鼎 Cauldron (hexagram 50), 217ff, 292, 315
ding 鼎 (cauldron), 357n116
"Discussion of Humanity" (*renshuo* 仁說), 23, 32, 35
divination, 2–3, 8, 11–15, 19–22, 24–25, 29, 31–32, 37, 44, 53–55, 67, 70–72, 75, 77–257 *passim*, 263, 265, 270, 278, 280–81, 285, 300, 305, 317ff, 323nn4–5, 324n7, 329n85, 330n9, 334nn40–41, 335n60, 337n82, 340n142, 341n165, 344n202, 346n225, 354n68, 360n166, 361n195, 363n12, 365n37, 366n42, 367n50, 367nn59–60, 368n68, 371n106, 371n6, 372n1, 373n3, 373n6
Doubting Antiquity School (*Yigupai* 疑古派), 8
Dui 兌 Pleasing (hexagram 58), 6, 240ff, 314
Duke of Zhou 周公, 3, 12–13, 20, 52, 54, 58, 262, 266, 323n2, 327n61, 334n41, 336nn70–71, 363n5, 370n93, 371n6
Dun 遯 Withdrawing (hexagram 33), 26, 50, 86, 127, 167, 315

Eight Trigrams (*bagua* 八卦), 3, 6–7, 12, 46–47, 49, 53, 263, 277, 281–82, 285, 287, 300, 303, 306, 308, 310, 312, 324n11, 330n5, 332n22, 334n47, 345n212, 355n92, 359n149, 363n14, 369n73, 369n80, 371n12, 372n18
Exalted Ancestor (Gaozong 高宗), 105

Fei Zhi 費直, 9
Feng 豐 Abundant (hexagram 55), 165, 231ff, 315, 352n37, 359n155
Five (Confucian) Classics, 1, 6, 9–11, 22, 323n1
Five Phases, 22, 338n104, 356n113, 366n41
Four Books, 11, 20, 38
Four Constant (Universal) Virtues (Mencius), 32–33, 35, 337n79
Four Images (*sixiang* 四象), 46, 274, 276, 281–83, 365n31
Four Seasons, 44, 46, 66, 117, 130, 165, 214, 246, 271, 275, 282, 304, 320
Four Virtues (of Qian), 8, 30–32, 35, 56–57, 60, 120, 270, 326n39, 329n86, 334n46, 335n50, 335n65, 336n78, 337n90, 340n140, 343n185, 344n202, 354n66, 364n24, 365n31
Fu 復 Returning (hexagram 24), 23, 25, 34–36, 50, 127, 140ff, 293, 295–96, 314, 336n77, 345n215, 347nn248–49, 347n251, 347n255, 370n98
fu 孚 (captive, honesty), 8, 83, 189, 248, 339n130, 361n184
Fuxi 伏羲, 3, 12–13, 15, 20–22, 28, 35, 42, 45, 50, 52–53, 57, 142, 263, 267, 282, 287, 293, 295–96, 305, 317, 324nn10–11, 326n36, 328n67, 330n5, 330n9, 331n11, 332n22, 334nn40–41, 334n47, 336n70, 344n207, 363n14, 364n18, 368n65, 369n80, 370nn92–93, 371n6, 371n12, 372n14, 372n16, 372n19
Fuxi's Directional Positioning of the Eight Trigrams (Diagram 4), 34, 46, 303–4, 308, 333n33, 372n14, 372n16
Fuxi's Directional Positioning of the Sixty-Four Hexagrams (Diagram 6), 26–27, 47, 333n33, 355n84
Fuxi's Sequence of the Eight Trigrams (Diagram 3), 26–27, 46, 303, 333n33, 369n73, 372n21
Fuxi's Sequence of the Sixty-Four Hexagrams (Diagram 5), 26, 46–47, 333n33

Ge 革 Changing/Overturning (hexagram 49), 213ff, 315, 356n107, 356n110, 356n112
Gen 艮 Stilling/Stopping (hexagram 52), 26, 34, 36, 223ff, 313, 344n202, 358n134, 358n136, 359n158
ghosts and spirits, 44–45, 66–67, 114, 232, 267–68, 275, 281, 363n15, 367–68n60
Ghost Region (Guifang 鬼方), 255, 258, 362n201
God, 36
Gou 姤 Encountering (hexagram 44), 26, 50, 141, 198, 199ff, 315–16, 347n251, 355nn83–84
Graham, A. C., 362n2, 364n29
Great Commonality (*datong* 大同), 109–10, 343n181
Great Undertaking, 43, 269–71, 282, 331n16, 364n23
Gu 蠱 Working on What Is Ruined (hexagram 18), 123ff, 314, 360n166
Gu Jiegang 顧頡剛, 8
gua 卦 (hexagram, trigram), 2–3, 42
Guai 夬 Resolving (hexagram 43), 26, 50, 196ff, 289, 316, 354n72, 355nn84–85
Guan 觀 Observed/Observing (hexagram 20), 26, 51, 127, 129ff, 173, 313, 351n23, 351n26
Guan Lang 關朗, 45, 332n25
Guanzi 管子, 157
Guicang 歸藏, 3, 324n8
Guimei 歸妹 Betrothed Sister (hexagram 54), 103, 228ff, 315, 342n169, 358n140
Guo Pu 郭璞, 252

Han 漢 dynasty, 1, 6–10, 25, 30–31, 45, 261, 325n25, 326n28, 327n50, 328n75, 332n21, 332n25, 340n130, 341n164, 345n219, 368n67, 373n5
Han Kangbo 韓康伯, 326n27, 369n85, 370n91, 370n94

INDEX 383

Han shu (History of the [Former] Han), 172, 279, 293, 351n24, 367n56, 369n90

Heaven and Earth, 23, 33–37, 42, 44–45, 47, 52, 59, 65–67, 70, 74–75, 102–4, 106, 117, 142, 150, 162, 165, 171, 179, 182, 188, 200, 203, 214, 229, 232, 246, 262, 264, 267–72, 274–75, 277–78, 282, 286–87, 293–94, 300, 304–5, 308, 328n72, 340n132, 342n177, 344n207, 364n25

Heng 恆 Everlasting (hexagram 32), 164ff, 295–96, 314, 350n7

Hetu 河圖 (River Chart), 44–45, 274, 325n25, 332n21, 332n25, 333n33, 365n39

hexagrams correlated with months, 26, 105, 126–27, 129, 138, 141, 168, 170, 196, 199, 346n223, 347n251, 350n15, 355n84

hexagram fluctuation (*guabian* 卦變), 24–25, 50, 86–87, 105, 120–21, 123, 127, 133, 136, 145, 147–48, 162, 165, 173, 181–82, 185, 205, 217, 226, 243, 317, 322, 333n38, 337n91, 340nn135–36, 342n169, 345n215, 348n263, 353n53, 353n64, 360n176, 369n76

High/Exalted Ancestor (Gaozong 高宗), 255, 342n175, 362n201

Hon, Tze-ki, 34

houtian 後天 (after Heaven), 33–34, 43, 49, 331n11, 338n94

Huan 渙 Dispersing (hexagram 59), 226, 242ff, 288, 314, 352n37

Hu Yuan 胡瑗, 228, 359n146

humane/humanity (*ren* 仁), 23, 32, 35, 59–60, 66, 70, 143–44, 155, 240, 268–69, 286, 291–92, 308, 336n78, 337n85, 340n145, 350n20, 364n22, 364n24, 365n36, 369n78; *see also* "Discussion of Humanity"

hun 魂 (yang soul), 267–68, 364n17

image. *See xiang*
intercalary month, 275–76, 320–21, 373n9

Jian 漸 Gradually Advancing (hexagram 53), 105, 225ff, 243, 315

Jian 蹇 Obstructed (hexagram 39), 184ff, 315

Jiao Yanshou 焦延壽, 9

Jiaren 家人 Family Members (hexagram 37), 178ff, 181, 314

Jie 節 Limiting (hexagram 60), 245ff, 314

Jiji 既濟 Already Complete (hexagram 63), 36, 124, 135, 254ff, 315

Jin 晉 Advancing (hexagram 35), 173ff, 314

Jin 晉 (state), 195

Jing 井 The Well (hexagram 48), 124, 210ff, 295–96, 314

Jing Fang 京房, 9, 373n5

Jizi 箕子 (Viscout of Ji), 105, 176, 178

junzi 君子 (superior person), 7–8, 12–13, 54–55, 58, 60–62, 66–69, 73–74, 76–78, 80, 83, 87, 90, 92, 97, 99–100, 103–9, 112, 114–16, 121, 124, 127, 130–32, 136–41, 148, 151, 154, 156, 162, 166, 168–72, 174, 176–79, 182, 185, 188–89, 191, 194, 197–200, 203, 205, 208, 211, 214, 216–17, 221, 224, 226, 229, 232, 235, 238, 241, 246, 248, 251, 254, 257–58, 266–69, 272–74, 278, 290–93, 316, 337n85, 339n11, 340n142, 341n152, 343n180, 350n5, 350n14, 357n116, 358n143

Kan 坎 (hexagram 48). *See* (Xi)Kan

King Wen 文王, 3, 12–13, 20, 32, 52–53, 55–57, 76, 96, 104, 176–77, 256, 262, 266, 294–95, 299, 309, 323n2, 324n11, 325n13, 330n5, 330n9, 334n41, 334n46, 336n70, 340nn150–51, 342n174, 345n216, 351n25, 359n153, 362n203, 363n5, 370n93, 370n102, 371n6, 371n12

King Wen's Directional Positioning of the Eight Trigrams (Diagram 8), 34, 49, 355n92, 372n17

King Wen's Sequence of the Eight Trigrams (Diagram 7), 49, 345n212, 359n149

King Wu 武王, 214, 340n151, 351n33, 356n109, 359n155

Kong Anguo 孔安國, 45, 332n22, 332n24

Kong Yingda 孔穎達, 10, 324n11, 337n93

Kui 睽 Contrary (hexagram 38), 181ff, 214, 288, 315, 352n47, 356n96

Kun 困 Blocked (hexagram 47), 120, 147, 207ff, 291, 295–96, 314, 339n113, 356n96

Kun 坤 Complying (hexagram 2), 17, 23, 26, 28, 34, 36, 65, 67ff, 141, 262–64, 270, 288, 294, 299, 313, 327n50, 335n60, 335n62, 336n75, 338n97, 338n99, 338n107, 339n111, 340nn138–39, 341n166, 343n191–92, 353n55, 353n64, 355n92, 355n94, 365n29, 365n31, 366n44, 368n70, 370n104, 372n15

Kunst, Richard, 8, 31, 335n59, 368n68

Laozi 老子, 16, 38, 43, 171, 326n28, 343n194, 347n255, 369n88

Legge, James, 19, 31, 304, 325n22, 327n57, 329n86, 337n93, 345n219, 346n235, 350n14, 354n74, 359n145, 370n100, 371n6

Li 離 Clinging (hexagram 30), 158ff, 181, 315, 336n73

li 理 (principle, order), 11, 17, 28, 136, 267, 289–90, 305, 308, 327n52, 328n79, 329n82, 331n11, 335n67, 338n95, 348n261, 358n134, 364n17, 365nn33–34, 368n63, 371n6

Lianshan 連山, 2, 372n17

Li Guangdi 李光地, 33, 342n172, 344n205, 350n17, 360n162, 360n172, 369n85

Liji 禮記 (Record of ritual), 9, 11, 77, 143, 149, 202, 325n23, 343n181, 352n36, 354n68, 355n89, 356n107

Li Zhicai 李之才, 48, 333n33

Lin 臨 Approaching (hexagram 19), 26, 50, 126ff, 313, 327n59, 345n213, 345n215, 351n23

line statements (*yaoci* 爻辭), 3, 7, 9, 12-13, 17, 54, 58, 67, 118, 130, 233, 266, 272, 278, 284, 290, 300, 327n56, 335nn53-54, 336n71, 342n171, 346n222, 348n262, 363n5, 365n35, 369n81

Lord (Di 帝), 217, 243, 309; 372n17; *see also* Shangdi

Liu Mu 劉牧, 45, 332n25

Liu Xin 劉歆, 45, 332n25

Liu Xiang 劉向, 332n25

Lu Deming 陸德明, 157, 349n286

Lu Jiuyuan 陸九淵, 11

Lu-Wang 陸王 school, 11

Luoshu 洛書 (Luo Writing), 45, 325n25, 332n21, 332n25, 333n33, 368n65

Lu Zhi 陸贄, 245, 360n179

Lü 履 Treading (hexagram 10), 99ff, 295-96, 315, 341n157, 341n166, 370n97

Lü 旅 The Wanderer (hexagram 56), 162, 226, 234ff, 315, 360n167

Lü Zuqian 呂祖謙, 52, 286, 327n54, 334n43, 338n108

Lynn, Richard John, 6, 19, 31, 304, 324n11, 325n22, 326n27, 327n57, 341n166, 345n213, 349n280, 350n14, 354n74, 360nn168-69, 368n68

matching positions (*dangwei* 當位), 33, 113, 298, 343n194

Mawangdui, 19, 303-4, 325n13, 329n101, 334n48, 365n37, 371n4, 371n13

Mencius (Mengzi 孟子), 1, 11, 29, 32-33, 35, 38, 41, 146, 328n80, 329n83, 336n77, 336nn79-80, 338n110, 340n145, 342n178, 346n229, 348n262, 348n265, 349n278, 349n282, 351n33, 356n109, 364n24, 370n98, 371n108

Meng 蒙 Dim (hexagram 4), 79ff, 206, 313, 363n9

Meng Xi 孟喜, 9, 25

milfoil (yarrow), 2, 25, 265, 270, 275-76, 278-82, 304, 311, 317ff, 324n10, 365n37, 366n42, 366n45, 367n50, 367n60, 371n6, 373n5, 373n7

Minford, John, 8, 325n21

ming 命 (decree, mandate, charge), 30, 43, 57, 88, 105, 107, 112, 145, 174, 202-3, 214, 216-218, 237, 259, 268, 278, 285, 305, 308, 320, 329nn84-85, 331n16, 335n67, 360n163, 364n18

Ming 明 (dynasty), 11, 332n21

Mingyi 明夷 Wounding the Light (hexagram 36), 175ff, 314, 342n175, 351n31

Mu Jiang 穆姜, 31, 60-61, 120, 336n77, 344n202

Mu Xiu 穆修, 48, 333n33

Nan Kuai 南蒯, 71

Neo-Confucianism, 10-11

Newton, Isaac, 23

Nielsen, Bent, 6, 21, 304, 362n2

Nine Diagrams, 15, 42, 44, 52, 325n25, 330n1

[Northern] Dipper, 233, 359n155

numbers. See *shu* 數

original hexagram (*bengua* 本卦), 25

Ouyang Xiu 歐陽修, 6, 325n16

Pi 否 Obstructing (hexagram 12), 26, 36, 51, 104ff, 168, 193, 292, 315, 353n53, 353n59, 353n61, 353n64, 354n71, 356n96

Plato, 34

po 魄 (*yin* soul), 268

Pregadio, Fabrizio, 34

Proverbs, 359n145

qi 氣 (psychophysical stuff), 22, 24, 29-30, 35-36, 47, 57, 62, 64-65, 68-69, 75, 97, 102, 141, 143, 162, 198, 214, 262, 267, 269, 271, 291, 308, 310, 328n79, 335n67, 336n68, 338n99, 344n207, 346n227, 349n1, 363n16, 364n21, 368n60, 368n63, 369n72, 372n13

Qi 岐 (Zhou capital), 96, 123, 206-7, 340n150, 344n207, 355n95

Qian 乾 Creating (hexagram 1), 17, 23, 26, 28, 30, 32, 34, 36, 53ff, 68-69, 72, 262-64, 270, 288, 294, 299, 308, 313, 324n11, 326n39, 327n56, 329n98, 330n5, 331n19, 334n44, 334n46, 334n48, 335n52, 335n60, 336n75, 336n77, 338nn99-100, 340n140, 341n166, 343n189, 355n84, 364n24, 365n31, 366n44, 368n70

Qian 謙 Being Modest (hexagram 15), 14, 114ff, 295-96, 314

Qin 秦 (dynasty), 101, 261, 341n164

Qing 清 dynasty, 19, 21, 33, 42

Qiu Hu 秋胡 of Lu, 81, 339n126

Redmond, Geoffrey, 8, 19, 31, 325n21, 327n59

ritual propriety (*li* 禮), 32, 60, 271, 273, 295-96, 341n157, 343n189, 346n241, 370n101

ruler (of hexagram), 16, 20, 33, 75, 77, 79, 81, 87, 89, 100, 102, 104-5, 119, 121, 130, 138, 143-45, 163, 166, 176, 190, 206, 215, 221, 230, 232-33, 236-38, 241-42, 250, 258, 298, 340n131, 341n160, 342n172, 343n196, 344n205, 350n17,

INDEX   385

353n53, 357n116, 360n162, 360n172, 370n91, 371n6
Rutt, Richard, 6–8, 19, 31, 327n57, 327n61, 328n75, 362n1, 366n49, 368n66, 368n68, 369n85

Santeria, 2
Shang 商 (dynasty), 2, 96, 104, 176–77, 256, 294–95, 299, 324n7, 324nn10–11, 329n87, 340nn150–51, 342nn174–75, 344n209, 348n267, 351nn24–25, 351n30, 351n33, 356n109, 359n153, 359n155, 362n201, 362n203, 370n95, 370n102, 372n17
Shangdi 上帝 (High Lord), 217, 354n66, 372n17
Shao Yong 邵雍, 9–11, 21, 33–36, 45–49, 142, 303–4, 308–9, 327n54, 329n100, 332n25, 332n27, 333n33, 334n42, 352n46, 352n48, 368n63, 369n73
Shaughnessy, Edward, 8, 19, 31, 324n8, 325n13, 325n21, 327n57, 328n75, 362n4, 368n68, 371n4
Shchutskii, Iulian, 31
Sheng 升 Advancing Upward (hexagram 46), 187, 205ff, 314
Shennong 神農 (Divine Farmer), 287–88, 324n11, 326n36, 370n93
Shi 師 Army (hexagram 7), 14, 89ff, 255, 313
Shihe 噬嗑 Biting Together (hexagram 21), 120, 132ff, 292, 314
Shiji 史記 (Historical records), 6, 144, 261, 305
Shijing 詩經 (Scripture of Odes), 9, 149, 227
shu 數 (number), 28, 305
Shuogua 說卦 (zhuan 傳), 6–7, 15, 28, 46–47, 49, 272, 303ff, 327n50, 333n31, 333n36–37, 334n45, 338n100, 339n121, 340n149, 348n268, 349n1, 351n23, 352n46, 352n48, 355n92, 355n94, 359n149, 360n174, 361n191, 364n18, 369n73, 371n13
Shujing 書經 (Scripture of Documents), 9
Shu Jingnan 束景南, 41–42
Shun 舜, 288, 326n36
Sima Guang 司馬光, 334n42
Sima Qian 司馬遷, 6, 261, 324n11, 348n262, 362n1, 367n55, 371n8
Sima Tan 司馬談, 261, 362n1, 367n55
sixty-four hexagrams, 1–5, 7, 26, 43, 46–48, 53, 263, 277, 285, 303, 308, 324n11, 334n47, 355n84, 363n14, 369n80, 371n12
Son of Heaven, 35, 95, 113
Song 宋 dynasty, 6–7, 9–11, 15, 22–23, 28–29, 36, 45, 261, 325n22, 326n29, 327n52, 328n64, 332n25, 334n48, 336n68, 342n171, 360n178, 361n185, 362n1, 364n29, 368n6
Song 訟 Disputing (hexagram 6), 86ff, 144, 315, 333n39, 340n135, 342n173, 348n263

sovereign hexagrams (bigua 辟卦), 26
Sovereign (Di) Yi 帝乙 (of Shang), 104–5, 231, 342n174, 359n153
spirit/spiritual (shen 神), 2, 12, 29, 31, 43–44, 123, 130, 202, 220, 243, 262, 268, 270, 277–84, 287–88, 290–92, 294, 297, 305, 310, 320, 331n15, 332n22, 344n207, 355n90, 363n16, 364n17, 364n21, 366n45, 367nn59–60, 368n65, 368n68, 369n72, 371n6, 373n7; see also ghosts and spirits
Sui 隨 Following (hexagram 17), 120ff, 206, 288, 314, 336n77, 344n202, 355n95
Sun 巽 Entering (hexagram 57), 26, 217, 237ff, 295–96, 314, 359n161
Sun 損 Diminishing (hexagram 41), 135, 190ff, 194, 293, 295–96, 313, 353nn52–53, 353n59

Tai 泰 Penetrating (hexagram 11), 26, 36, 51, 102ff, 190, 192, 315, 341n166, 342n169, 342n172, 343n182, 353n53, 353n55, 353n59, 359n153
taiji 太極 (Supreme Polarity), 30, 34, 43, 46, 265, 281
Taijitu (shuo) 太極圖(說) ([Discussion of the] Diagram of the Supreme Polarity), 41, 326n31, 326n46, 328n78, 329n95, 331nn14–15, 333n33, 338n98, 347n253, 349n4, 350n10, 358n134, 363n8, 363n10, 364n21, 368n61, 368n63
Tan Shanxin 譚善心, 42, 330n5
Tang 唐 dynasty, 9–10, 28, 317, 324n11, 338n96, 347n255, 360n179, 373n5
Ten Wings, 1, 6–9, 13, 16, 261, 271, 334n43, 335n63
Three Powers (san cai 三才), 265. 275, 281, 298, 308
Three Ultimates (san ji 三極), 265
time, 23-24, 43
Tongren 同人 Fellowship (hexagram 13), 14, 108ff, 273, 315
tortoise, 45, 151, 192, 194, 281–82, 305, 312, 332n22, 354n67, 367n60, 368n65
tuan 彖 (judgment), 42, 53, 56, 266, 289, 295, 297, 330n10, 334n46, 363n11
Tuan (zhuan) 彖傳, 6–7, 13–14, 16–17, 31–32, 50, 59, 256, 327n56, 330n9, 333n39, 334n44, 334n46, 337n92, 346n222, 361n185, 363n9, 370n99
Two Modes, 43, 46, 281, 291, 365n31, 373n12

Waley, Arthur, 8, 348n270, 359n145
Wang Bi 王弼, 9–10, 13–17, 19–20, 28, 36, 304, 324n11, 325n13, 325n22, 326n27, 331n18, 339n124, 340n130, 341n153, 341n166, 345n219, 346n226, 346n228, 346n240, 347n245, 348n262, 348n268, 355n88, 359n156, 360n171, 362n202, 362n3

Wang Mouhong 王懋竑, 42, 330n2
Wang Su 王肅, 121, 206, 344n203, 335n93
Wang Tie 王鐵, 42
Wang Tingzhen 王霆震, 42, 330n5
Wang Yangming 王陽明, 11
Warring States period, 1, 341n164
waxing and waning hexagrams (*xiaoxi gua* 消息卦), 25, 342n167
Way of Heaven, 21, 56–57, 103–4, 114, 127, 130, 165, 267–68, 271, 281, 286, 298, 308
Way of the Mean/Centrality, 125, 188, 197–99, 236, 268, 354n75
Way of the Sages, 12, 278, 280, 324n11
Weiji 未濟 Not Yet Complete (hexagram 64), 36, 120, 256ff, 316
Wenyan (zhuan) 文言傳, 6–7, 13, 16, 28, 31–32, 34, 59, 61, 274, 327n56, 330n9, 331n16, 331n19, 334n46, 335n56, 335n65, 336nn74–75, 336n77, 338n97, 338n106, 344n202, 364n24, 365n31, 365n35
Wilhelm, Richard, 6, 19, 31–32, 325n22, 341n166, 343n192, 345n219, 345n221, 349n280, 350n14, 354n71, 354n74, 359n154, 360n168, 360n171, 368n68, 369n85, 371n6, 373n4
Wudi, Han 漢武帝, 9
Wu Ge 吳革, 42, 328n64
Wujing zhengyi 五經正義 (Correct Meaning of the Five Classics), 10
Wu Xian 巫咸, 324n10
Wuwang 無妄 No Error (hexagram 25), 32, 144ff, 314, 348nn261–62

Xia 夏 (dynasty), 127, 295, 324n11
Xia Tower 夏臺, 177
Xian 咸 Mutually Influencing (hexagram 31), 34, 161ff, 172, 290–91, 314, 361n185
xiang 象 (image), 3, 12, 26, 42–43, 53, 262, 287, 328n76, 371n107, 372n1
xiangshu 象數 (image and number), 9, 15, 21, 24–25, 327n56, 332n25, 334n40
Xiang (zhuan) 象傳, 6–7, 13, 16–17, 59, 63, 198, 327n50, 330n9
Xiang Ji 項籍 (Xiang Yu 項羽), 101, 341n164
xiantian 先天 (before Heaven), 33–34, 43, 308, 331n11, 332n26, 333n33, 338n94, 369n73, 372n14, 372n21
Xiaochu 小畜 Restrained/Limited by the Lesser (hexagram 9), 24, 96ff, 245, 315, 340n132, 361n190
Xiaoguo 小過 Small Surpassing (hexagram 62), 184, 250ff, 288, 315, 351n23, 361n192
Xici (zhuan) 繫辭傳, 6–7, 11–13, 15–16, 21, 23, 26, 28, 34, 47, 107, 189, 209, 261ff, 303, 317,
325n16, 326n27, 326n36, 326n45–46, 331n11, 331n16, 332n27, 336n75, 337nn87–88, 341n157, 342n179, 343nn188–89, 343n195, 344n197, 344n201, 344n207, 346n230, 346n233, 346n236, 347n244, 347n249, 347n258, 348n266, 349n277, 349n287, 350nn6–7, 350n19, 352n39, 353n52, 353n58, 355n85, 356n96–97, 356n101, 359n161, 361n188, 362–63nn1–6, 363n8, 363n12, 363n14, 365n38, 368n65, 368n68, 370n92, 371n10, 372n13, 372n19, 373n9
Xie 解 Released (hexagram 40), 187ff, 205, 274, 292, 314, 353n51
(Xi)kan 習坎 (Doubly) Abysmal (hexagram 29), 155ff, 315, 349n283, 360n169
xing 性 (nature of something), 29–30, 41, 43, 53, 55, 57, 65, 68, 81, 109, 138, 145, 166, 181–82, 237, 253, 268–69, 271, 287, 305, 308, 310, 328n80, 331n11, 335n67, 337n83, 338n109, 344n207, 346n227, 348nn261–62, 354n80, 358n134, 361n186, 364nn18–21, 365n33, 368n72, 371n105, 371n108
xing'er shang 形而上 (above form, metaphysical), 284
xing'er xia 形而下 (within form, concrete), 284
xing ming 性命 (nature and endowment), 30, 57, 145
Xiong Jie 熊節, 42, 330n6
Xu 需 Waiting (hexagram 5), 83ff, 147, 315, 361n184
Xugua (zhuan) 序卦傳, 7, 17, 37
Xun Shuang 荀爽, 311, 372n20
Xunzi, 81, 279, 339n127, 347n241, 351n33, 367n51

Yang Huo 陽貨, 182
Yan Hui 顏回, 293, 370n91
Yao 堯, 288, 326n36
yao 爻. *See* lines
yarrow stalks. *See* milfoil
Yellow Emperor (Huangdi 黃帝), 288, 326n36, 370n93
Yi 頤 Jaws, Nourishing (hexagram 27), 36, 150ff, 315
Yi 益 Enhancing (hexagram 42), 36, 132, 142, 190, 193ff, 287, 293, 295–96, 313, 353n53, 353n57
yili 義理 (meaning and principle), 9–10, 13, 15, 110, 334n41
Yili 儀禮 (Etiquette and ritual), 319, 325n23, 366n46
yin-yang 陰/陽, 2, 13–14, 20, 22–25, 28, 35, 48, 267, 269–71, 274–77, 279, 281, 283–84, 287, 289–91, 294, 296, 305, 308–9, 311, 322, 328n78, 331n14, 335n55, 335n62, 337n91, 338n96, 338n101,

338n103, 338n103, 339nn112-13, 339n118, 341n154, 342n177, 343n183, 343nn193-94, 343n196, 345n211, 345n219, 346n223, 346n234, 347n242, 347n246, 348n264, 348n266 348n272, 349n274, 350n13, 351n34, 353n53, 353n62, 354nn71-72, 355nn84-85, 355n87, 356n97, 356n105, 356n110, 357n127, 358n134, 360n170, 361n193, 362n198, 362n203, 364nn21-22, 364n29, 365n31, 365n40, 366n41, 366n44, 368n61, 369n74, 369n84, 371n13, 373n5

Yixue qimeng 易學啟蒙 (Introduction to the study of the *Yi*), 15, 21, 25, 33, 41-42, 278, 282, 303, 317, 320, 322, 328n75, 332nn21-22, 332n25, 333n30, 335n55, 335n62, 358n134, 365n39, 366n41, 366n44, 373nn8-9, 373nn12-13

Yizhi yi 易之義 (Meanings of the *Yi*), 303, 371n13

Youli 羑里 (Shang city), 96, 177, 295, 340n150

Yu 豫 Being Happy (hexagram 16), 32, 117ff, 288, 293, 314

Yu Fan 虞翻, 9, 337n91, 359n162

Yu the Great 大禹, 45, 324n11, 332n22, 332n24, 368n65, 369n79

Yu Yan 俞琰, 329n100, 359n162

Zagua (*zhuan*) 雜卦傳, 7, 313-16, 339n121
Zhang Shi 張栻, 12
Zhang Zai 張載, 10, 29, 291, 336n68
Zhen 震 Thunder/Arousing (hexagram 51), 220ff, 313

Zheng 鄭 (state), 195
Zheng Xuan 鄭玄, 9, 324n11
Zhongfu 中孚 Inwardly Honest (hexagram 61), 181, 247ff, 272, 315, 351n23
Zhongyong 中庸 (Centrality and Commonality), 11, 33, 36, 38, 218, 264, 364n20, 371n7
Zhou 周 dynasty, 1, 3, 8, 19, 30-31, 52, 96, 104, 123, 177, 195, 261, 299, 317, 339n114, 339n126, 340nn150-51, 342n174, 344n207, 345n216, 351n33, 354n70, 355n95, 356n109, 357n118, 359n153, 359n155, 362n203, 370n95, 370n102, 372n17, 373n5
Zhou 紂 (Shang king), 176, 256, 294, 299, 340n150, 342n175, 351n30, 351n33, 362n203, 370n102
Zhou Dunyi 周敦頤, 10-11, 41, 326n46, 331nn14-15, 333n33, 337n83, 338n98, 347n253, 349n4, 350n10, 358n134, 363n8, 363n10, 363n12, 364n21, 364n29, 368n61, 368n63, 368n69, 372n13
Zhouli 周禮 (Rituals of Zhou), 134, 325n23
Zhouyuan 周原. *See* Qi 岐
Zhu Zhen 朱震, 333n33
Zhuangzi 莊子 (Zhuang Zhou 莊周), 24, 38, 261, 263, 326n28, 362n2, 365n34
Zhun 屯 Difficult Beginning (hexagram 3), 33, 75ff, 313, 339n113
Zifu Huibo 子服惠伯, 71
Zuozhuan 左傳, 6, 31, 56, 60, 71, 113, 120, 195, 218, 354n70, 357n122

TRANSLATIONS FROM THE ASIAN CLASSICS

Major Plays of Chikamatsu, tr. Donald Keene 1961

Four Major Plays of Chikamatsu, tr. Donald Keene. Paperback ed. only. 1961; rev. ed. 1997

Records of the Grand Historian of China, translated from the Shih chi of Ssu-ma Ch'ien, tr. Burton Watson, 2 vols. 1961

Instructions for Practical Living and Other Neo-Confucian Writings by Wang Yang-ming, tr. Wing-tsit Chan 1963

Hsün Tzu: Basic Writings, tr. Burton Watson, paperback ed. only. 1963; rev. ed. 1996

Chuang Tzu: Basic Writings, tr. Burton Watson, paperback ed. only. 1964; rev. ed. 1996

The Mahābhārata, tr. Chakravarthi V. Narasimhan. Also in paperback ed. 1965; rev. ed. 1997

The Manyōshū, Nippon Gakujutsu Shinkōkai edition 1965

Su Tung-p'o: Selections from a Sung Dynasty Poet, tr. Burton Watson. Also in paperback ed. 1965

Bhartrihari: Poems, tr. Barbara Stoler Miller. Also in paperback ed. 1967

Basic Writings of Mo Tzu, Hsün Tzu, and Han Fei Tzu, tr. Burton Watson. Also in separate paperback eds. 1967

The Awakening of Faith, Attributed to Aśvaghosha, tr. Yoshito S. Hakeda. Also in paperback ed. 1967

Reflections on Things at Hand: The Neo-Confucian Anthology, comp. Chu Hsi and Lü Tsu-ch'ien, tr. Wing-tsit Chan 1967

The Platform Sutra of the Sixth Patriarch, tr. Philip B. Yampolsky. Also in paperback ed. 1967

Essays in Idleness: The Tsurezuregusa of Kenkō, tr. Donald Keene. Also in paperback ed. 1967

The Pillow Book of Sei Shōnagon, tr. Ivan Morris, 2 vols. 1967

Two Plays of Ancient India: The Little Clay Cart and the Minister's Seal, tr. J. A. B. van Buitenen 1968

The Complete Works of Chuang Tzu, tr. Burton Watson 1968

The Romance of the Western Chamber (Hsi Hsiang Chi), tr. S. I. Hsiung. Also in paperback ed. 1968

The Manyōshū, Nippon Gakujutsu Shinkōkai edition. Paperback ed. only. 1969

Records of the Historian: Chapters from the Shih chi of Ssu-ma Ch'ien, tr. Burton Watson. Paperback ed. only. 1969

Cold Mountain: 100 Poems by the T'ang Poet Han-shan, tr. Burton Watson. Also in paperback ed. 1970

Twenty Plays of the Nō Theatre, ed. Donald Keene. Also in paperback ed. 1970

Chūshingura: The Treasury of Loyal Retainers, tr. Donald Keene. Also in paperback ed. 1971; rev. ed. 1997

The Zen Master Hakuin: Selected Writings, tr. Philip B. Yampolsky 1971

Chinese Rhyme-Prose: Poems in the Fu Form from the Han and Six Dynasties Periods, tr. Burton Watson. Also in paperback ed. 1971

Kūkai: Major Works, tr. Yoshito S. Hakeda. Also in paperback ed. 1972

The Old Man Who Does as He Pleases: Selections from the Poetry and Prose of Lu Yu, tr. Burton Watson 1973

The Lion's Roar of Queen Śrīmālā, tr. Alex and Hideko Wayman 1974

Courtier and Commoner in Ancient China: Selections from the History of the Former Han by Pan Ku, tr. Burton Watson. Also in paperback ed. 1974

Japanese Literature in Chinese, vol. 1: *Poetry and Prose in Chinese by Japanese Writers of the Early Period*, tr. Burton Watson 1975

Japanese Literature in Chinese, vol. 2: *Poetry and Prose in Chinese by Japanese Writers of the Later Period*, tr. Burton Watson 1976

Love Song of the Dark Lord: Jayadeva's Gītagovinda, tr. Barbara Stoler Miller. Also in paperback ed. Cloth ed. includes critical text of the Sanskrit. 1977; rev. ed. 1997

Ryōkan: Zen Monk-Poet of Japan, tr. Burton Watson 1977

Calming the Mind and Discerning the Real: From the Lam rim chen mo of Tson-kha-pa, tr. Alex Wayman 1978

The Hermit and the Love-Thief: Sanskrit Poems of Bhartrihari and Bilhaṇa, tr. Barbara Stoler Miller 1978

The Lute: Kao Ming's P'i-p'a chi, tr. Jean Mulligan. Also in paperback ed. 1980

A Chronicle of Gods and Sovereigns: Jinnō Shōtōki of Kitabatake Chikafusa, tr. H. Paul Varley 1980

Among the Flowers: The Hua-chien chi, tr. Lois Fusek 1982

Grass Hill: Poems and Prose by the Japanese Monk Gensei, tr. Burton Watson 1983

Doctors, Diviners, and Magicians of Ancient China: Biographies of Fang-shih, tr. Kenneth J. DeWoskin. Also in paperback ed. 1983

Theater of Memory: The Plays of Kālidāsa, ed. Barbara Stoler Miller. Also in paperback ed. 1984

The Columbia Book of Chinese Poetry: From Early Times to the Thirteenth Century, ed. and tr. Burton Watson. Also in paperback ed. 1984

Poems of Love and War: From the Eight Anthologies and the Ten Long Poems of Classical Tamil, tr. A. K. Ramanujan. Also in paperback ed. 1985

The Bhagavad Gita: Krishna's Counsel in Time of War, tr. Barbara Stoler Miller 1986

The Columbia Book of Later Chinese Poetry, ed. and tr. Jonathan Chaves. Also in paperback ed. 1986

The Tso Chuan: Selections from China's Oldest Narrative History, tr. Burton Watson 1989

Waiting for the Wind: Thirty-Six Poets of Japan's Late Medieval Age, tr. Steven Carter 1989

Selected Writings of Nichiren, ed. Philip B. Yampolsky 1990

Saigyō, Poems of a Mountain Home, tr. Burton Watson 1990

The Book of Lieh Tzu: A Classic of the Tao, tr. A. C. Graham. Morningside ed. 1990

The Tale of an Anklet: An Epic of South India—The Cilappatikāram of Iḷaṅkō Aṭikaḷ, tr. R. Parthasarathy 1993

Waiting for the Dawn: A Plan for the Prince, tr. with introduction by Wm. Theodore de Bary 1993

Yoshitsune and the Thousand Cherry Trees: A Masterpiece of the Eighteenth-Century Japanese Puppet Theater, tr., annotated, and with introduction by Stanleigh H. Jones Jr. 1993

The Lotus Sutra, tr. Burton Watson. Also in paperback ed. 1993

The Classic of Changes: A New Translation of the I Ching as Interpreted by Wang Bi, tr. Richard John Lynn 1994

Beyond Spring: Tz'u Poems of the Sung Dynasty, tr. Julie Landau 1994

The Columbia Anthology of Traditional Chinese Literature, ed. Victor H. Mair 1994

Scenes for Mandarins: The Elite Theater of the Ming, tr. Cyril Birch 1995

Letters of Nichiren, ed. Philip B. Yampolsky; tr. Burton Watson et al. 1996

Unforgotten Dreams: Poems by the Zen Monk Shōtetsu, tr. Steven D. Carter 1997

The Vimalakirti Sutra, tr. Burton Watson 1997

Japanese and Chinese Poems to Sing: The Wakan rōei shū, tr. J. Thomas Rimer and Jonathan Chaves 1997

Breeze Through Bamboo: Kanshi of Ema Saikō, tr. Hiroaki Sato 1998

A Tower for the Summer Heat, by Li Yu, tr. Patrick Hanan 1998

Traditional Japanese Theater: An Anthology of Plays, by Karen Brazell 1998

The Original Analects: Sayings of Confucius and His Successors (0479–0249), by E. Bruce Brooks and A. Taeko Brooks 1998

The Classic of the Way and Virtue: A New Translation of the Tao-te ching of Laozi as Interpreted by Wang Bi, tr. Richard John Lynn 1999

The Four Hundred Songs of War and Wisdom: An Anthology of Poems from Classical Tamil, The Puṟanāṉūṟu, ed. and tr. George L. Hart and Hank Heifetz 1999

Original Tao: Inward Training (Nei-yeh) and the Foundations of Taoist Mysticism, by Harold D. Roth 1999

Po Chü-i: Selected Poems, tr. Burton Watson 2000

Lao Tzu's Tao Te Ching: A Translation of the Startling New Documents Found at Guodian, by Robert G. Henricks 2000

The Shorter Columbia Anthology of Traditional Chinese Literature, ed. Victor H. Mair 2000

Mistress and Maid (Jiaohongji), by Meng Chengshun, tr. Cyril Birch 2001

Chikamatsu: Five Late Plays, tr. and ed. C. Andrew Gerstle 2001

The Essential Lotus: Selections from the Lotus Sutra, tr. Burton Watson 2002

Early Modern Japanese Literature: An Anthology, 1600–1900, ed. Haruo Shirane 2002; abridged 2008

The Columbia Anthology of Traditional Korean Poetry, ed. Peter H. Lee 2002

The Sound of the Kiss, or The Story That Must Never Be Told: Pingali Suranna's Kalapurnodayamu, tr. Vecheru Narayana Rao and David Shulman 2003

The Selected Poems of Du Fu, tr. Burton Watson 2003

Far Beyond the Field: Haiku by Japanese Women, tr. Makoto Ueda 2003

Just Living: Poems and Prose by the Japanese Monk Tonna, ed. and tr. Steven D. Carter 2003

Han Feizi: Basic Writings, tr. Burton Watson 2003

Mozi: Basic Writings, tr. Burton Watson 2003

Xunzi: Basic Writings, tr. Burton Watson 2003

Zhuangzi: Basic Writings, tr. Burton Watson 2003

The Awakening of Faith, Attributed to Aśvaghosha, tr. Yoshito S. Hakeda, introduction by Ryūichi Abé 2005

The Tales of the Heike, tr. Burton Watson, ed. Haruo Shirane 2006

Tales of Moonlight and Rain, by Ueda Akinari, tr. with introduction by Anthony H. Chambers 2007

Traditional Japanese Literature: An Anthology, Beginnings to 1600, ed. Haruo Shirane 2007

The Philosophy of Qi, by Kaibara Ekken, tr. Mary Evelyn Tucker 2007

The Analects of Confucius, tr. Burton Watson 2007

The Art of War: Sun Zi's Military Methods, tr. Victor Mair 2007

One Hundred Poets, One Poem Each: A Translation of the Ogura Hyakunin Isshu, tr. Peter McMillan 2008

Zeami: Performance Notes, tr. Tom Hare 2008

Zongmi on Chan, tr. Jeffrey Lyle Broughton 2009

Scripture of the Lotus Blossom of the Fine Dharma, rev. ed., tr. Leon Hurvitz, preface and introduction by Stephen R. Teiser 2009

Mencius, tr. Irene Bloom, ed. with an introduction by Philip J. Ivanhoe 2009

Clouds Thick, Whereabouts Unknown: Poems by Zen Monks of China, Charles Egan 2010

The Mozi: A Complete Translation, tr. Ian Johnston 2010

The Huainanzi: A Guide to the Theory and Practice of Government in Early Han China, by Liu An, tr. and ed. John S. Major, Sarah A. Queen, Andrew Seth Meyer, and Harold D. Roth, with Michael Puett and Judson Murray 2010

The Demon at Agi Bridge and Other Japanese Tales, tr. Burton Watson, ed. with introduction by Haruo Shirane 2011

Haiku Before Haiku: From the Renga Masters to Bashō, tr. with introduction by Steven D. Carter 2011

The Columbia Anthology of Chinese Folk and Popular Literature, ed. Victor H. Mair and Mark Bender 2011

Tamil Love Poetry: The Five Hundred Short Poems of the Aiṅkuṟunūṟu, tr. and ed. Martha Ann Selby 2011

The Teachings of Master Wuzhu: Zen and Religion of No-Religion, by Wendi L. Adamek 2011

The Essential Huainanzi, by Liu An, tr. and ed. John S. Major, Sarah A. Queen, Andrew Seth Meyer, and Harold D. Roth 2012

The Dao of the Military: Liu An's Art of War, tr. Andrew Seth Meyer 2012

Unearthing the Changes: Recently Discovered Manuscripts of the Yi Jing (I Ching) *and Related Texts*, Edward L. Shaughnessy 2013

Record of Miraculous Events in Japan: The Nihon ryōiki, tr. Burton Watson 2013

The Complete Works of Zhuangzi, tr. Burton Watson 2013

Lust, Commerce, and Corruption: An Account of What I Have Seen and Heard, *by an Edo Samurai*, tr. and ed. Mark Teeuwen and Kate Wildman Nakai with Miyazaki Fumiko, Anne Walthall, and John Breen 2014; abridged 2017

Exemplary Women of Early China: The Lienü zhuan *of Liu Xiang*, tr. Anne Behnke Kinney 2014

The Columbia Anthology of Yuan Drama, ed. C. T. Hsia, Wai-yee Li, and George Kao 2014

The Resurrected Skeleton: From Zhuangzi to Lu Xun, by Wilt L. Idema 2014

The Sarashina Diary: A Woman's Life in Eleventh-Century Japan, by Sugawara no Takasue no Musume, tr. with introduction by Sonja Arntzen and Itō Moriyuki 2014; reader's edition 2018

The Kojiki: An Account of Ancient Matters, by Ō no Yasumaro, tr. Gustav Heldt 2014

The Orphan of Zhao and Other Yuan Plays: The Earliest Known Versions, tr. and introduced by Stephen H. West and Wilt L. Idema 2014

Luxuriant Gems of the Spring and Autumn, attributed to Dong Zhongshu, ed. and tr. Sarah A. Queen and John S. Major 2016

A Book to Burn and a Book to Keep (Hidden): Selected Writings, by Li Zhi, ed. and tr. Rivi Handler-Spitz, Pauline Lee, and Haun Saussy 2016

The Shenzi Fragments: *A Philosophical Analysis and Translation*, Eirik Lang Harris 2016

Record of Daily Knowledge and Poems and Essays: Selections, by Gu Yanwu, tr. and ed. Ian Johnston 2017

The Book of Lord Shang: Apologetics of State Power in Early China, by Shang Yang, ed. and tr. Yuri Pines 2017; abridged edition 2019

The Songs of Chu: An Ancient Anthology of Works by Qu Yuan and Others, ed. and trans. Gopal Sukhu 2017

Ghalib: Selected Poems and Letters, by Mirza Asadullah Khan Ghalib, tr. Frances W. Pritchett and Owen T. A. Cornwall 2017

Quelling the Demons' Revolt: A Novel from Ming China, attributed to Luo Guanzhong, tr. Patrick Hanan 2017

Erotic Poems from the Sanskrit: A New Translation, R. Parthasarathy 2017

The Book of Swindles: Selections from a Late Ming Collection, by Zhang Yingyu, tr. Christopher G. Rea and Bruce Rusk 2017

Monsters, Animals, and Other Worlds: A Collection of Short Medieval Japanese Tales, ed. R. Keller Kimbrough and Haruo Shirane 2018

Hidden and Visible Realms: Early Medieval Chinese Tales of the Supernatural and the Fantastic, compiled by Liu Yiqing, ed. and tr. Zhenjun Zhang 2018

A Couple of Soles: A Comic Play from Seventeenth-Century China, by Li Yu, tr. Jing Shen and Robert E. Hegel 2019

GPSR Authorized Representative: Easy Access System Europe, Mustamäe tee 50, 10621 Tallinn, Estonia, gpsr.requests@easproject.com

www.ingramcontent.com/pod-product-compliance
Lightning Source LLC
Chambersburg PA
CBHW022025290426
44109CB00014B/754